The Female Body in Mind

The interface between the female body and mental health

Edited by Mervat Nasser,
Karen Baistow and Janet Treasure

Routledge
Taylor & Francis Group

LONDON AND NEW YORK

First published 2007
by Routledge
27 Church Road, Hove, East Sussex, BN3 2FA

Simultaneously published in the USA and Canada
by Routledge
270 Madison Avenue, New York, NY 10016

Routledge is an imprint of the Taylor & Francis Group, an informa business

Typeset in Times by Garfield Morgan, Swansea, West Glamorgan
Printed and bound in Great Britain by TJ International Ltd, Padstow,
Cornwall
Paperback cover design by Anú Design

This publication has been produced with paper manufactured to strict
environmental standards and with pulp derived from sustainable forests.

British Library Cataloguing in Publication Data
A catalogue record for this book is available from the British Library

Library of Congress Cataloging-in-Publication Data
The female body in mind : the interface between the female body and mental
  health / edited by Mervat Nasser, Karen Baistow, and Janet Treasure.
      p. cm.
  Includes bibliographical references.
  ISBN-13: 978-0-415-38514-5 (hbk)
  ISBN-13: 978-0-415-38515-2 (pbk)
  ISBN-10: 0-415-38514-8 (hbk)
  ISBN-10: 0-415-38515-6 (pbk)
  1. Women—Mental health. 2. Body image. 3. Body, Human—Miscellanea.
I. Nasser, Mervat. II. Baistow, Karen. III. Treasure, Janet.

RA564.85.F464 2007
362.2082–dc22

2006029031

ISBN 978-0-415-38514-5 (hbk)
ISBN 978-0-415-38515-2 (pbk)

Contents

Contributors

Karen Baistow is Director of the Mental Health Studies Programme at King's College, London. Her research interests and publications are concerned with the connections between mental health, child development and family welfare, with particular reference to national and international practice and policy.

Dinesh Bhugra is Professor of Mental Health and Cultural Diversity, Section of Cultural Psychiatry, Institute of Psychiatry. He has published extensively on the issue of culture and mental health.

Jane Bunclark is Clinical Nurse Leader of the Crisis Recovery Unit at Bethlem Royal Hospital, South London and Maudsley Trust.

Walter Busuttil is Director of The Dene Medium Secure Hospital for Women, East Sussex, where he has set up a psychological trauma service and ward-based treatment programme for the treatment of complex PTSD and borderline personality disorders. He has published extensively in the field of traumatic stress.

Vanessa Chow is a research medical student at King's College, London.

Sarah Davenport is Lead Consultant for Women's Secure Services at Guild Lodge, Preston. She has written on the use of psychodynamic therapy with people with serious mental illness and on women's mental health.

Janet Davies was formerly Policy Lead for Women's Mental Health at the Department of Health. She is currently on secondment to the CSIP London Development Centre, leading the national Risk Management Programme.

Nisha Dogra is Senior Lecturer at the University of Leicester, and Honorary Consultant Psychiatrist in Child and Adolescent Psychiatry at the Institute of Child Health.

Sandra Flynn is a Research Associate currently working for the National Confidential Inquiry into Suicide and Homicide by People with Mental Illness, Manchester.

Tirril Harris is Senior Research Fellow, Socio-medical Research Centre, Academic Department of Psychiatry, St Thomas' Hospital, London. She pioneered research into the social roots of depression.

Melanie Katzman is Clinical Associate Professor of Psychology, Weil Medical College of Cornell University, New York, and a private consultant clinical psychologist. She has written extensively on the subjects of culture, eating disorders and women's mental health issues.

Dora Kohen is Professor of Women's Mental Health and Consultant Psychiatrist at Lancashire Postgraduate School of Medicine.

Tennyson Lee is Specialist Registrar in Psychotherapy and Psychiatry, Cawley Centre and Psychotherapy Unit, Maudsley Hospital, London. His clinical and research interests lie in personality disorders and psychotherapy.

Helen Malson is Reader in Social Psychology at the University of West England, Bristol. Her publications deal with gender and health care.

Stirling Moorey is Lead Consultant of the Cognitive Behaviour Therapy Unit for Patients with Cancer at the Maudsley Hospital, London.

Joanna Murray is Senior Lecturer, Section of Mental Health and Aging, Health Service Research, Institute of Psychiatry, London.

Mervat Nasser is a Consultant Psychiatrist and Honorary Senior Lecturer at the Eating Disorders Research Unit of the Institute of Psychiatry, King's College (Guys Campus), London. She has written extensively on the interface between culture and eating disorders.

Greta Noordenbos is Assistant Professor in the Department of Clinical Psychology and the Department of Women's Studies at Leiden University. She specialises in research about preventing eating disorders, chronic eating disorders and recovery.

Ruth I. Ohlsen is a Clinical Research Nurse who runs the Maudsley Atypical Antipsychotic Service and the Southwark First Episode Psychosis Team. She is the author of the *Maudsley Antipsychotic Medication Review: Service Guidelines* and has published widely on this subject.

Veronica O'Keane is Senior Lecturer in Perinatal Psychiatry, Institute of Psychiatry, London. She has published several articles and chapters on the subject of perinatal psychiatric disorders.

Bob Palmer is a Senior Lecturer and Director of the Leicestershire Eating Disorders Service. He has written and edited numerous publications.

Kirsten Patrick is Clinical Researcher in Perinatal Psychiatry at the Institute of Psychiatry, London. Her research examines pregnancy, mood and hormonal changes.

Lyn S. Pilowsky is Professor and Head of Neurochemical Imaging, Department of Psychological Medicine, Institute of Psychiatry, London, and Senior Clinical Research Fellow on the UK Medical Research Council. She has written extensively on neuroimaging techniques, neurotransmitters and psychopharmacology.

Rosalind Ramsay is Consultant Psychiatrist at St Thomas' Hospital, and Chair of the Women in Psychiatry Special Interest Group, Royal College of Psychiatrists.

Varinia Sánchez-Ortiz is a PhD student at the Eating Disorders Research Unit, Institute of Psychiatry, London.

Ulrike Schmidt is Reader in Psychiatry at the Eating Disorders Research Unit, Institute of Psychiatry, London. She has published extensively on the subject of eating disorders, deliberate self-harm, brief psychological treatment and new technologies in treatment.

Jenny Shaw is Professor in Forensic Psychology at Manchester University, Consultant Forensic Psychiatrist at Guild Lodge, Preston, and Assistant Director of the National Confidential Inquiry into Suicide and Homicide by People with Mental Illness, Manchester.

Finn Skårderud is Professor of Psychiatry at the Faculty of Health and Social Studies, Lillehammer University College, Norway. He has published widely in both English and Norwegian.

Janet Treasure is Professor of Psychiatry and Head of the Eating Disorders Research Unit at the Institute of Psychiatry. She has edited four textbooks and authored two self-help books on eating disorders.

Sue Waterhouse is Programme Lead for Gender and Women's Mental Health, Violence and Abuse Works, CSIP South East Development Centre. She is also Head of Service at the Women's Mental Health Service in East Sussex.

Debbie Whight is a Clinical Nurse Specialist working within the Leicester Eating Disorders Team, trained in dialectical behaviour therapy under the guidance of Marsha Linehan and others. She is a trainer in both interpersonal therapies (IPT) and dialectical behaviour therapy (DBT).

Preface

This book began its life within the eating disorders world. Since 1984, I have been involved in studying and writing on the subject of culture and eating disorders. My first book *Culture and Weight Consciousness*, published in 1997, was an attempt to challenge the notion that such disorders were exclusive to one culture, race or society. The cultural meaning of such disorders was shown to be linked to the increasing significance of the female body, particularly at times when cultures are undergoing rapid changes, socially, politically and economically, which was the subject of the second book *Eating Disorders and Cultures in Transition*, an internationally collaborative work that was published in 2001.

The relationship between culture, body and morbidity was demonstrated in the case of "hysteria", the most womanly of all psychiatric troubles. The interface between hysteria and eating disorders was particularly relevant, as both were shown to be forms of communication conveying coded social messages through the language of the body. The story of hysteria was a story of the mind and body and the changing form of distress over time. This shift in our understanding of the nature of the neurotic illness, and recognition of its susceptibility to the moulding force of culture, came to the forefront with the new millennium, which witnessed other breakthroughs in understanding the biological body, particularly in the field of genetics. This meant that women's mental health issues could no longer be discussed in isolation from discussions of the female body, both the social and the physical.

On a personal level, the new millennium coincided with a transition in my own life following my decision to take early retirement from my NHS consultant post. The main reason behind this decision was to have the time to pursue more reading, writing and teaching. In the same year Janet Treasure took up the professorship of the department of psychiatry at Guys Hospital, King's College, in addition to her ongoing responsibility for the eating disorders research unit at the Institute of Psychiatry. Given my wide involvement with transcultural eating disorders research, I joined in with a view to creating a programme of teaching aiming to share expertise and knowledge in the field of eating disorders with newly established units worldwide. We wished to take advantage of the recent progress in technological education and develop new distance learning courses via e-learning approaches and virtual universities.

Karen Baistow joined the Guys campus of King's College to chair the MSc programme in mental health studies around the same time. She was full of enthusiasm and keen to introduce new approaches and innovative ideas into the educational programme. The time was ripe to found new courses and develop existing ones, and I was offered the opportunity to do just that with the course on eating disorders. I wished to broaden the concept of eating disorders to embrace issues related to bodies, gender and mental health in a wider sense. The publication of *Women into the Main Health Stream* added impetus and was certainly encouraging. The document was a national directive that gave a higher profile to the need to introduce issues about women and mental health into mainstream psychiatric education as well as into forms of service delivery.

This book is the product of this thinking exercise, and is modelled on the structure of the course in women's mental health I developed for the MSc in mental health studies for King's College (Guys Campus). This course has been running now for three years with increasing popularity.

The book is an edited volume, and includes contributions from notable academics in the field of women's mental health. Many have taught and continue to teach this course. The majority of the contributors are among the teaching faculty of the Institute of Psychiatry, King's College, but some come from other universities in the UK, Europe and the United States.

The book is geared towards multidisciplinary readership and revolves in its content around the notion of the female body, which is dealt with from various angles, not only the "social" but also the "biological", demonstrating how the body has become – in our modern times – a perfect platform for women's expression of their own distress and mental anguish.

The book consists of six sections; all have the theme of the body at their core:

1 **The body at risk**: this section of the book addresses the question "Why women in particular?" and looks at all the risk factors attributed to the female gender. It also discusses the relationship between bodies and identities within socio-political context.
2 **The hurting body**: this part of the book covers issues related to the traumatised body, including deliberate self harm, sexual trauma, self starvation and cancer.
3 **The reproductive body**: here the book deals with the natural history of the female body, biological programming and concepts of motherhood, perinatal mental illness and infanticide.

4 **The interactive body**: the focus of this section is on the interaction between women, society and culture, including aspects of caring for others as well as personality types.

5 **Body-sensitive therapies**: this section covers new therapeutic techniques aimed at body mindfulness and includes feminist/cognitive, dialectical behavioural approaches, self-help manuals and issues related to gender and drug treatment.

6 **The body on my mind**: the final part of the book takes us forward into the debate about whether specific services for women are needed or not. It also discusses the importance of introducing gender sensitivity/ competencies in higher education and training programmes.

The organisation and the style of this book may be viewed as rather unusual, particularly its attempt to combine and integrate issues that are conventionally discussed in isolation from one another. It is hoped, though, that the experiment will prove successful in exploring some of the complexities in the relationship between women's bodies and their mental health, and manage to introduce the reader to new ways of thinking about issues in women's mental health assessment and treatment.

Mervat Nasser

Acknowledgment

The editors wish to thank all the authors who contributed to this volume and made it possible.

The body in question

a doctor learns terrible lessons in the practice of medicine
how anguish and pain distort the body,
    contort the mind

    torsions that bring me to
    the body in question,
        the problem at hand

my medical school was renowned for its humanism
for its attention to the individuality,
    the particularity

    of those suffering with
    the body in question,
        the mind in doubt

in psychiatry I migrated to the peripheries of human pain
fractured families, fatherless children, *émigrés*
    and immigrants

    anguished refugees from
    the body in question,
        the homeless heart

a lover endures the endless solitude of his unappeased heart
the tick-tock tedium as his pulse slows
    and stalls

    over anxious memories of
    the body in question,
        the person in mind

only in poetry do I find the extravagant speech
the open window, the redemptive handrail,
      the open palm

   to save,
         to replenish the empty space of
         the body in question,
               the soul at stake

This poem was written by Vinzenzo Di Nicola, a prominent Canadian Professor of Psychiatry, who wished to contribute to this volume but could not. He gave us instead one of his poems – written in homage to a great physician-director, Jonathan Miller, who wrote about the body in question.

Part I

The body at risk

The question of *why women in particular* – that is, gender risk factors – is discussed in the first chapter of this volume. It begins with an evolutionary history of the female body from the religious to the medical to the social, touching on definitions of femininity within the social/feminist discourse. It moves on to discuss the assertion that women's bodies make them susceptible to mental health problems, outlining gender differences in the epidemiology of mental health problems and basic principles of research methodology.

The second chapter's authors discuss through the notion of the *open body* the constant dialogue between the body and its environment, through figurative re-construction. The newly-constructed form represents a more grounded self/identity, perhaps more able to negotiate the demands of transition and the forces of socio-cultural instability. It also touches on the struggle between the female body and the aging process, and how to reconcile perceptual frailty and infirmity with identity.

Chapter 1

At risk by reason of gender

Helen Malson and Mervat Nasser

INTRODUCTION

> While the name of the symbolic female disorder may change from one historical period to the next, the gender asymmetry of the representational tradition remains constant.
>
> (Showalter, 1985: 4)

Being a woman is, it could be argued, a risky business. Women in both Western and non-Western societies appear historically and often currently to have been systematically disadvantaged across almost every aspect of public and private life: in terms of, for example, economics (Olsen and Walby, 2004), education, political representation (Sayers, 1982), career prospects (Wager, 1998), unequal divisions of labour both inside (Dryden, 1999) and outside (Ussher, 1991) the home, subjection to domestic violence (Garimella et al., 2000) and some forms of violence outside of the home (Liebling, 2004) and, perhaps not surprisingly therefore, also in terms of health and mental health status (e.g. Stoppard, 2000; Ussher, 2000). Women, it seems, have been and still are more likely than men to experience mental health problems.

The aim of this chapter is to consider the assertion that women are more susceptible than men to mental health problems, and to consider explanations of women's seeming greater susceptibility. An examination of the facts about gender differences which emerge in the epidemiology of mental health is clearly crucial to an understanding of this issue, but it is by no means the only task entailed. In addition to examining the merits of the explanations of these statistics, it is also important that we trouble the key terms themselves – "women", "gender", "reality", "risk" and "mental health". How, for example, might contemporary cultural concerns about risk management in relation to an increasingly individualised responsibility for health (see e.g. Department of Health, 2004) shape our assumptions about the nature of "risk"? Do modern Western conceptualisations of "mental health problems" or "mental illness" refer simply to naturally existing psychopathologies which might occur in any culture, or are they part of a culturally and historically contingent modern Western perspective which perhaps should not be privileged above the perspectives of other cultures and which cannot therefore be applied unproblematically outside of modern Western and Westernised cultural contexts (Littlewood and Lipsedge, 1987; see also Nasser, 1997, 2000)?

Further, might our conceptualisations of mental health and illness be not only historically contingent and Eurocentric but also gendered? That is, what relationships pertain between culturally dominant ideas about "women" and about "mental health", and how might such relationships inform our understanding of women's seemingly increased susceptibility to mental health problems? And what, for example, do we mean by "women" (see Butler, 1993; Weedon, 1987)? The term's meaning may seem so blindingly obvious as to require no further consideration but, in fact, it has been subject to considerable debate and controversy within the social sciences; its apparent naturalness often masks a plethora of issues crucial to a thorough understanding of gender and mental health or indeed gender and any issue. How, for example, should we best understand the relationship(s) between sexed bodies and gender? Are women's identities, experiences and behaviours a natural consequence of having a female body? Is it a matter of biology or a culturally and historically variable *interpretation* of having a female body? Indeed, are sexed bodies themselves culturally constituted (Butler, 1993)? Does it make sense to talk of women as a universal, ahistorical category (Riley, 1988)? What assumptions are made and what differences and inequalities within the category of woman are occluded when women of different ages, sexualities, ethnicities and social classes, women living in different historical periods and in different societies, are considered as a single, monolithic homogeneity? How might we consider issues of gender in ways which are cognisant of these differences and inequalities which exist within that category of persons (e.g. Bordo, 1993; Wilkinson, 2002)?

Clearly we have raised more questions here than we could possibly answer within the space of a single chapter but they are, nevertheless, important as they illustrate some of the complexities entailed in questions about gendered differences in mental health problems and the implications of women's gendered embodiment. With all this in mind, however, a consideration of the statistics about women's mental health problems clearly represents a logical starting point in considering the nature of the relationship(s) between women and mental health problems.

MENTAL HEALTH AND GENDER DIFFERENCES: FACT, ARTEFACT, INTERPRETATION AND EXPERIENCE

Gender differences have long been apparent in the statistics on mental health and illness. While there is some controversy over the historical data (see Busfield, 1994), it is generally accepted that in Europe throughout the eighteenth and nineteenth centuries more women than men were diagnosed with and treated for "mental illness" (Ehrenreich and English, 1974; Showalter, 1985). And for some diagnoses this gender difference constituted a near-total monopoly: hysteria, neurasthenia and chlorosis, for example, were very rarely diagnosed in men (Brumberg, 1982; Showalter, 1985). Current epidemiological statistics demonstrate a continuation of this preponderance of women in overall diagnoses of mental health problems (Ussher, 1991, 2000) and in particular diagnostic categories. Depression, for instance, appears to be twice as common in women as men (Culbertson, 1997), while girls and women represent 95% of those diagnosed with eating disorders (the magnitude of such problems is discussed in detail within this volume).

These epidemiological data are obtained through quantitative research methodologies, depending on quantified variables to assess incidence and prevalence rates. The incidence of any particular disorder is taken as the number of episodes of such disorder within a specified period of time, usually of one year, while prevalence rate refers to the number of existing episodes of that disorder at any one time. However, while these data are produced within an empiricist framework of quantitative research, issues of cultural interpretation are nevertheless present. The reliability and validity of the instruments used, as well as the nature of the diagnostic manuals (ICD10 and DSMIV) with which caseness decisions are reached, introduce sources of error, misrepresentation and cultural bias. Further, incidence and prevalence data, being derived either from community data or hospital rates of admissions and referrals, are inevitably influenced by the ways in which both users and providers of mental health care services interpret service users' experiences. For example, women have been found to seek help from primary care services more often than men when experiencing distress, a gender difference which may be due to differences in help-seeking and expressing emotional dis/content as much as to gender differences in levels of distress.

This in turn often leads to women's subsequent referral to specialist psychiatric services, particularly when general practitioners' interpretation of the nature of their distress is medicalised (Johnson and Buszewicz, 1996). And, where "women" are interpreted as a homogeneous category, overall gender differences in referral rates obscure other issues: the tendency towards presentation to medical services by women is not uniform, as women from some minority racial/cultural groups were found to have little faith in conventional medical services and therefore tended to be under-represented in statistical data (Nasser, 1997).

Statistical data regarding gender differences in mental health problems cannot then be viewed as unproblematically reflecting the "reality" of women's mental health problems but, rather, are subject to the multiple and diverse influences of interpretation. And further controversy emerges when inferring causality from such data. Are women diagnosed with mental health problems in greater numbers than men because women's bodies render them/us "naturally" more susceptible to such problems, or is it because of gender differences in, for example, pay, career paths, family commitments or political and personal power? Is it a question of biology or of the consequences of systematic gender differences in lived experience, of society's gender ideologies and politics (Choi and Nicolson, 1994)?

Attributing causality either to "women's bodies" or "women's lives" or some combination of both (Stoppard, 2000: 406) results in very different kinds of research questions for which very different research methodologies are appropriate. Whilst epidemiological research and research investigating possible biological causes of gender differences in mental health deploy empiricist quantitative methods, studies investigating socially contextualised explanations and women's experiences of distress require a variety of quantitative and qualitative methods.

There is, therefore, a need for a range of different approaches to researching women's mental health. And, as we shall discuss below, recognition of the need to engage more thoroughly with issues of interpretation, sociocultural context and women's experiences of distress has given rise to increased popularity of qualitative research in this and other fields (for more in-depth discussion of this issue, see Murray and Chamberlain, 2000; Willig, 2000). Whilst some qualitative research takes an empiricist approach, born out of the modernist scientific tradition, issues such as small samples and uncontrolled conditions inevitably lead to concerns about the validity, reliability and generalisability of findings. The majority of qualitative research, however, as discussed below, is conducted within the non-empiricist, postmodern epistemological frameworks of social constructionism and poststructuralism and are concerned not with "objective truth" and generalisability, but with language and discourse, with a recognition of the contextual location of any perspective and with questions of interpretation, meaning and the specificities of the socio-cultural and historical context within which those experiences and meanings are located.

HISTORICISING "EMBODIMENT" AND THE CULTURAL PRODUCTION OF DISTRESS

Notwithstanding debates about different research methodologies, be they quantitative or qualitative, the issue remains that an affinity between women and mental health problems is apparent not only in the statistics but also in cultural and historical representations or discursive constructions of "women", "women's bodies" and "mental health" and "illness" (Richardson, 2000; Ussher, 1991; Walkerdine, 1988).

Since Egyptian (Strong, 1989) and Greek (Shafter, 1989) antiquity, hysteria had been defined as an authentic somatic disease of women in which the "wandering womb" moved up or down to produce a variety of "hysterical" symptoms throughout the body (Nasser, 1997; Porter and Porter, 1988; Veith, 1965). This was the rationale behind fumigating the vagina, in the hope of restoring this wandering vagrant uterus to its natural position (Nasser, 1987).

The Kahun Gynaecological Papyrus describes a variety of physical symptoms ascribed to a restless uterus that was thought to have a "life of its own" and needed to be constantly satisfied and pacified (Veiz, 1965). Women, according to Dirix (1869, quoted in Ehrenreich and English, 1974: 29–30), were "treated for diseases of the stomach, liver, kidney, heart, lung etc, yet in most instances these diseases would be found on due investigation, to be no disease at all, but merely the symptoms of one disease, namely, a disease of the womb."

The theory of "uterine irritation" continued well into the nineteenth century (de Berdt Hovell, 1873) but was progressively displaced by theories of nervous disease, disordered nerves and pathological mentalities (Rousseau, 1991). Thus, whether because she was dominated by an inherently troublesome reproductive system, because her nervous system was more delicate and sensitive than a man's or because she was "mentally weak", woman continued to be viewed as especially prone to nervous disorder in general and to hysteria in particular, and the alleged characteristics of the female body remained paramount in explanations of women's apparently nervous disposition (Malson, 1998; Showalter, 1985; Strong, 1989).

Cultural associations between women and "mental illness" have, of course, only been possible since the emergence of the scientific and medical discourses in which concepts of mental illness have been formulated (see Foucault, 1967/1985). However, cultural representations of "woman", defined primarily in terms of her body, particularly her reproductive body, have a considerably longer genealogy (Choi and Nicolson, 1994; Malson and Swann, 2003; Marshall and Woollett, 2000), as does the notion that female embodiment is risk-laden. It has recurred in some form or another across history and throughout most if not all cultures. As de Beauvoir (1953/1984) illustrated, since the Roman Empire up to the twentieth century woman was represented, at least in European cultures, as the other of man and as lesser in her otherness. And analyses of science, art, religion and popular cultures (Foucault, 1979/1990; Jordanova, 1989; Riley, 1988; Sayers, 1982; Walkerdine, 1988) demonstrate a similarly systematic "othering" of women and women's bodies up to the present day.

Analysing a panorama of cultural figurings of "woman", de Beauvoir's argument is not only that women have been systematically represented as the other of a masculine norm but that, as the other of man, woman has been associated with immanence in contrast to man's transcendence – an immanence which aligns her with the body such that binary oppositions between mind and body, nature and culture, reason and unreason and so forth map directly onto that between man and woman (see also Jordanova, 1989). "When woman is given over to man," de Beauvoir (1953/1984: 189) argued, "he demands that she represent the flesh purely for its own sake. Her body is . . . a thing sunk in its own immanence." Her analysis illustrates a cultural association between concepts of "woman" and bodily-ness and an oft-repeated representation of the female body as risk-laden, as a source of danger to others and herself, as rendering woman less able and more vulnerable than man – physically, intellectually, emotionally and morally (Choi, 1994; Sayers, 1982).

A brief perusal of a Bible illustrates the point. In the anti-sex dictums of the Christian Church the body, particularly the female body, appears as a source of moral corruption, polluted and polluting (Malson, 1998; Martin 1988). "It is good for a man not to touch a woman" (1-Corinthians 7: 9) since "the cycle of fleshly life derives finally from intimacy with women and polluted intercourse" (quoted in Martin, 1988: 56) – a theme which can also be found in a variety of historical and contemporary secular popular cultures (Bordo, 1993; de Beauvoir, 1953/1984; Ussher, 1991).

It might be argued that such negative cultural notions and particularly, perhaps, the religious imagery of the past have little to do with the science of mental health. The Renaissance and Classical ages, after all, saw the ascendancy of science, whereby theological power and knowledge was supplemented and then usurped by scientific and medical authority in an increasingly secular society (Foucault, 1979/1990). In these newly emerging scientific discourses, sex (both sexed bodies and sexual practices) was medicalised: "[F]lesh was brought down to the level of the organism" (Foucault, 1979/1990: 117). And yet this new way of understanding bodies did not entirely escape either "the thematics of sin" (Foucault, 1979/1990: 116) or the values, concerns and politics of its cultural location (see Porter and Porter, 1988) including the prevailing politics of gender (Sayers, 1982; Showalter, 1985). An affinity between medicine, culture and politics was particularly marked in the nineteenth-century cult of "female invalidism", with its hallmark diagnosis of "hysteria" frequently represented as a mani-festation of women's natural propensity to mental health problems (Showalter, 1985). Female nervousness and debility was highly fashionable (Douglas-Wood, 1973; Sayers, 1982) and, indeed, normative, at least among the bourgousie: "[T]he man who does not know sick women", Silas Weir Mitchell claimed in 1888, "does not know women" (quoted in Veith, 1965: 220). Nervous debility was thus not only feminised and made fashionable but "normal femininity" was itself profoundly pathologised. The category of "woman" was frequently understood as virtually synonymous with that of "nervous woman". Of course, not every Victorian medic subscribed to this view (Porter and Porter, 1988), but female puberty, menstruation, pregnancy, childbirth, menopause and the female nervous system were all predominantly represented as both causes of illness and pathological in themselves (Smith-Rosenberg and Rosenberg, 1973). This view had considerable consequences for the realities of women's lives. "Grant suffrage to women", one Massachusetts legislator claimed, "and you will have to build insane asylums in every county, and establish divorce courts in every town. Women are too nervous and hysterical to enter politics" (quoted in Ehrenreich and English, 1974: 22).

The establishment of the first colleges for women precipitated similarly dire warnings about their consequences for women's reproductive and mental health (Sayers, 1982). And, whilst from a contemporary scientific perspective these texts can be assessed as simply outdated, inaccurate or untrue, it is also the case that in the cultural authority they held they nevertheless "induce[d] effects of truth" (Foucault, 1980: 193), informing not only medical practice but also cultural assumptions and legislation about women and thus shaping and constraining women's lives and experiences in particular ways.

EMBODIED EXPERIENCE: INTERFACING BODIES AND LIVES

Whilst both culture and science have moved on considerably since the nineteenth century, the idea that women are more prone than men to mental health problems remains. Women are still more likely than men to be diagnosed with and treated for mental health problems (Ussher, 2000), and the female body continues to represent a culturally and scientifically prevalent explanation of this (Choi and Nicolson, 1994). Contemporary explanations of women's mental health problems are more likely to focus on endocrinal disorder than on "wandering wombs", "delicate nerves", suppressed feelings or "mental weakness" (Malson, 1998). Yet the Victorian notion of "woman" as naturally nervous persists today, albeit in rather different form. As Gannon (1998: 287) argues: "The primary difference between the 19th and 20th-century accounts is that, in the 19th century, a woman's uterus and ovaries were the essence of her psychological and physical well-being whereas, today, the focus is on hormones."

Scientifically and culturally prevalent explanations of "premenstrual syndrome", for example, rest on conceptualisations of the female body as a liability rendering an estimated 5–95% of women unreliable, intellectually debilitated, accident prone, mentally unstable and even violent (Choi and Nicolson, 1994; Richardson, 2000; Swann, 1997). Current biological theories of depression target reproductive endocrinology to explain women's greater vulnerability to depression (Stoppard, 2000), whilst psychobiological explanations of anorexia nervosa again represent the female body – in this case female pubertal developments – as a risk factor, explaining girls' and women's greater susceptibility to eating disorders (Hepworth, 1999). In short, "women continue to be defined in terms of their biological functions" (Phoenix and Woollett, 1991: 7) and their/our bodies defined as "biologically labile" (Ussher, 1991) causes of mental health problems.

In contrast, however, attention has turned increasingly to women's lives as an explanation for their/our mental health problems (Stoppard, 2000). Gender differences between men and women in pay, social status, political power, burdens of domestic care and mothering, relationship inequalities and rates of domestic violence (Ussher, 1991), as well as gender differences in social pressures such as expectations that women conform to particular "beauty ideals" (Bordo, 1993; Malson, 1998; Orbach, 1993) or gendered ideals about parenthood and care responsibilities (McBride, 1990; Murray, this volume; Ussher, 1991), for instance, have all been asserted as explanations for women's increased likelihood of experiencing mental health problems.

Brown and Harris's (1978, 1989) social theory of depression, for example, explains women's depression in terms of their experiences of adversity, particularly events or conditions, such as the stresses entailed in childcare, loss of income or the death of a close relative, which may have an ongoing negative impact on women's everyday lives (see Chapter 11 in this volume).

Similarly, researchers investigating the effects of media images on body image dissatisfaction and the prevalence and effects of a diet-promoting media (Grogan, 1999; Polivy and Herman, 1985; Silverstein et al., 1986) have provided socially-oriented explanations for the rise of diagnoses of eating disorders among girls and young women. Further analyses of such images have revealed both a multiplicity of cultural values (Bordo, 1993; Hepworth, 1999; Malson, 1998) and a white ethnocentrism (Bordo, 1993) entailed in these (Western) culturally dominant "beauty ideals". Gender differences in susceptibility to mental health problems are explained from this perspective, then – not as a consequence of female biology but as a result of culturally-specific gender differences in lived experience and women's greater likelihood of experiencing adverse life events and circumstances.

These latter, socially-oriented explanations of women's mental health problems usefully shift our focus onto the problematic and sometimes distressing contexts of women's lives and the consequences for women's well-being of culturally produced gender differences in lived experience. And following on from this focus on socio-cultural context, a growing number of researchers have more recently shifted their focus away from questions about the causes of women's mental health problems to questions about the nature and meanings of women's experiences of such problems.

To take the case of "anorexia nervosa", described as one of the most common chronic illnesses among teenage girls today (Touyz and Beaumont, 2001), we might leave aside, at least provisionally, questions of aetiology to ask: What is the nature of these experiences that are designated "anorexic"? What do women have to say about what it means to be thin, emaciated and self-starving? And what do their answers tell us about the cultural contexts in which they and we live?

Inevitably one network of prevalent meanings of "anorexic" experiences and body-management practices pivots around the culturally dominant idealisation of an ever-thinner body as the "ideal" of physical feminine perfection and the promotion of dieting and other potentially damaging body-management practices as the means of achieving this "ideal" (Bordo, 1993; Fallon et al., 1994; Hepworth, 1999; Malson, 1998). But the meanings of "anorexic" experiences and practices also extend well beyond preoccupation with physical "feminine perfection" (Katzman and Lee, 1997) to include expressions of, for example, ambivalence or rejection of femininities (Bordo, 1993; Malson, 1998; Orbach, 1993), the assertion of independence, autonomy, self-control (Bordo, 1993; Malson and Ussher, 1996), competitiveness (Brumberg, 1988; Rich et al., 2005), self-annhilation and the achievement of identity (Malson, 1999) and/or the negotiation of dilemmas inherent in late capitalist consumer culture (Brumberg, 1988; Malson, 1999; Turner, 1992). For those diagnosed as "anorexic" the experience has multiple, sometimes contradictory meanings which are expressive of a multiplicity of contemporary cultural values, concerns and dilemmas. And from this perspective the mental health risks entailed in female embodiment again reside not in the female body itself but in the cultural contexts in which that body and identity are interpreted.

This more recent qualitative research investigating women's experiences produces in-depth understandings of the complexities and diversity of meanings in how women experience mental health problems. Moreover, by focusing on the specificities of experiences it also avoids homogenising the category of "woman", enabling investigation of the differences as well as similarities between experiences of women of different cultures (Nasser, 1997, 2000), ethnicities (Bordo, 1993), sexualities (Wilkinson, 2002) and ages (Gannon, 1994). And by locating the meanings and experiences of mental health problems in their socio-cultural contexts, such research can also elucidate the problematics of distinguishing categorically between "normal" and "psychopathological" experiences and practices. To remain with the above example, as a diagnostic category defined primarily in terms of fear of gaining weight, "over-valuation" of thinness and reduced food intake (WHO, 1992), the resonances between "anorexia" and "the troubles of ordinary women" (Wooley et al., 1994: ix) around food and body weight are readily apparent (see also Stoppard, 2000, for a discussion of this issue in relation to depression). Yet, whilst the statistics revealing the extreme prevalence, indeed normativity (Polivy and Herman, 1985), of body dissatisfaction and dieting among girls and women are often viewed as reflecting a quasi-natural state of affairs (Orbach, 1986: 6), "anorexic" bodies and practices are often presented as shockingly abnormal. Research analysing the meanings of women's "anorexic" experiences illustrates, however, that the boundaries between normality and pathology are far from robust, which has led some researchers in this field to argue that "our notion of 'pathology' might be usefully abandoned" (Littlewood, 1991) in favour of theorising mental health problems as collectivities of distressed experiences and practices constituted within and by the same cultural values and ideas in which the experiences and practices of "normal" (but often not so trouble-free) girls and women are constituted and regulated (Bordo, 1993; Fallon et al., 1994; Malson, 1998, 1999; Nasser, 1997).

CONCLUSIONS

The relationship(s) between women and mental health problems have been addressed in terms of

- the biology of gendered bodies;
- gender differences and inequalities in social roles and life circumstances of women;
- cultural representations of "woman" as the other of a masculine "norm";
- the meanings of women's culturally-located experiences of mental health problems.

Neither the individualising, biologically-based explanations nor the more socially-oriented explanations of the causes of women's mental health problems are conclusively supported or disconfirmed by the mass of research findings that have accumulated to date. The answer to the question of why women appear more susceptible to mental health problems than men remains elusive (Stoppard, 2000). Yet, whilst questions about the causes of women's distress are clearly important, we need also, and perhaps firstly, to consider the ways in which we theorise and research those experiences that might be designated as mental health problems. By investigating the ways in which women experience mental health problems we can develop more in-depth understandings of the multiple and complex meanings of women, of women's bodies, of women's experiences of mental health problems and of the ways in which such experiences are expressive of a multiplicity of contemporary cultural concerns, values and dilemmas.

REFERENCES

Bordo, S. (1993) *Unbearable weight*, Berkely, CA, University of California Press.
Brown, G. W. and Harris, T. O. (1978) *Social origins of depression: A study of psychiatric disorder in women*, London, Tavistock Publications.

Brown, G. W. and Harris, T. O. (1989) Depression, in G. W. Brown and T. O. Harris (eds) *Life events and illness*, pp. 49–93, London, Unwin Hyman.

Brumberg, J. (1982) Chlorotic girls, 1870–1920: A historical perspective on female adolescence, *Child Development*, 53 (6), 1468–1477.

Brumberg, J. (1988) *Fasting girls: The emergence of anorexia nervosa as a modern disease*, Cambridge, MA, Harvard University Press.

Busfield, J. (1994) The female malady? Men, women and madness in nineteenth century Britain, *Sociology*, 28 (1), 259–277.

Butler, J. (1993) *Bodies that matter: On the discursive limits of sex*, New York, Routledge.

Choi, P. (1994) Women's raging hormones, in P. Y. L. Choi and P. Nicolson (eds) *Female sexualities: Psychology, biology and social context*, Hemel Hempstead, Harvester Wheatsheaf.

Choi, P. Y. L. and Nicolson, P. (eds) (1994) *Female sexualities: Psychology, biology and social context*, Hemel Hempstead, Harvester Wheatsheaf.

Culbertson, F. M. (1997) Depression and gender: An international view, *American Psychologist*, 52, 25–31.

De Beauvoir, S. (1984) *The second sex* (trans. J. Cape, 1953), Harmondsworth, Penguin.

de Berdt Hovell, D. (1873) Hysteria simplified and explained, *Lancet*, December 20, 872–874.

Department of Health (2004) *Choosing health: Making healthier choices easier* (Public Health White Paper), http://www.dh.gov.uk/publicationsandstatistics/publications/publicationspolicyandguidance/publicationspolicyandguidance article/fs/en?content_id=4094550&chk=an5cor

Douglas-Wood, A. (1973) "The fashionable diseases": Women's complaints and their treatment in nineteenth century America, *Journal of Interdisciplinary History*, 4 (1), 25–52.

Dryden, C. (1999) *Being married, doing gender: A critical analysis of gender relationships in marriage*, London, Routledge.

Ehrenreich, B. and English, D. (1974) *Complaints and disorders: The sexual politics of sickness* (Glass Mountain Pamphlet No. 2), London, Compendium.

Fallon, P., Katzman, M. A. and Wooley, S. C. (eds) (1994) *Feminist perspectives on eating disorders*, London, Guilford.

Foucault, M. (1967/1985) *Madness and civilization: A history of insanity in the age of reason*, London, Tavistock.

Foucault, M. (1979/1990) *The history of sexuality. Volume 1: An introduction*, Harmondsworth, Penguin.

Foucault, M. (1980) *Power/knowledge: Selected interviews and other writings 1972–1977* (ed. C. Gordon), London, Harvester Wheatsheaf.

Gannon, L. (1994) Sexuality and menopause, in P. Y. L. Choi and P. Nicolson (eds) *Female sexualities: Psychology, biology and social context*, Hemel Hempstead, Harvester Wheatsheaf.

Gannon, L. (1998) The impact of medical and sexual politics on women's health, *Feminism and Psychology*, 8 (3), 285–302.

Garimella, R., Plichta, S. B. and Houseman, C. (2000) Physicians' beliefs about victims of spouse abuse and about physician role, *Journal of Women's Health and Gender-Based Medicine*, 9 (4), 405–411.

Grogan, S. (1999) *Body image*, London, Routledge.

Hepworth, J. (1999) *The social constuction of anorexia nervosa*, London, Sage.

Johnson, S. and Buszewicz, M. (1996) Women's mental illness, in K. Abel, M. Buuszewicz, S. Davison et al. (eds) *Planning community mental health services for women: A multiprofessional handbook*, pp. 6–19, London, Routledge.

Jordanova, L. (1989) *Sexual visions: Images of gender in science and medicine between the eighteenth and twentieth centuries*, London, Harvester Wheatsheaf.

Katzman, M. A. and Lee, S. (1997) Beyond body image: The integration of feminist and transcultural theories in the understanding of self-starvation, *International Journal of Eating Disorders*, 22 (4), 385–394.

Liebling, H. (2004) Ugandan women's experiences of sexual violence and torture during civil war years in Luwero District, *POWS Review*, 6 (2), 29–37.

Littlewood, R. (1991) Against pathology, *British Journal of Psychiatry*, 159, 696–702.

Littlewood, R. and Lipsedge, M. (1987) The butterfly and the serpent: Culture, psychopathology and biomedicine, *Culture, Medicine and Psychiatry*, 11 (3), 289–335.

Malson, H. (1998) *The thin woman: Feminism, post-structuralism and the social psychology of anorexia nervosa*, London, Routledge.

Malson, H. (1999) Women under erasure: Anorexic bodies in postmodern context, *Journal of Community and Applied Social Psychology*, 9 (2), 137–153.

Malson, H. and Ussher, J. M. (1996) Body poly-texts: Discourses of the anorexic body, *Journal of Community and Applied Social Psychology*, 6 (4), 267–280.

Malson, H. and Swann, C. (2003) Re-producing 'woman's' body: Reflections on the (dis)place(ments) of 'reproduction' for (post)modern women, *Journal of Gender Studies*, 12 (3), 191–201.

Marshall, H. and Woollett, A. (2000) Fit to reproduce? The regulative role of pregnancy texts, *Feminism and Psychology*, 10 (3), 351–366.

Martin, L. H. (1988) Technologies of the self and self-knowledge in the Syrian Thomas tradition, in L. H. Martin, H. Gutman and P. H. Hutton (eds) *Technologies of the self: A seminar with Michel Foucault*, pp. 50–63, London, Tavistock.

McBride, A. (1990) Mental health effects of women's multiple roles, *American Psychologist*, 45 (3), 381–384.

Murray, M. and Chamberlain, K. (2000) Qualitative research and women's health research, in J. M. Ussher (ed.) *Women's health: Contemporary international perspectives*, pp. 40–50, London, British Psychological Society.

Nasser, M. (1987) Psychiatry in ancient Egypt, *Bulletin of the Royal College of Psychiatrists*, 11, 420–422.

Nasser, M. (1997) *Culture, weight and consciousness*, London, Routledge.

Nasser, M. (2000) Gender, culture and eating disorders, in J. M. Ussher (ed.) *Women's health: Contemporary international perspectives*, pp. 379–387, London, British Psychological Society.

Olsen, W. and Walby, S. (2004) *Modelling gender pay gaps*, Manchester, Equal Opportunities Commission.

Orbach, S. (1986) *Hunger strike: The anorectic's struggle as a metaphor for our age*, New York, Norton.

Orbach, S. (1993) *Hunger strike*, Harmondsworth, Penguin.

Phoenix, A. and Woollett, A. (1991) Motherhood: Social construction, politics and psychology, in A. Phoenix, A. Woollett and E. Lloyd (eds) *Motherhood: Meanings, practices and ideologies*, pp. 13–27, London, Sage.

Polivy, J. and Herman, C. P. (1985) Dieting and binging, *American Psychologist*, 40 (2), 193–201.

Porter, R. and Porter, D. (1988) *In sickness and in health: The British experience 1650–1850*, London, Fourth Estate.

Richardson, J. T. E. (2000) Hormones and behaviour: Cognition, menstruation and menopause, in J. M. Ussher (ed.) *Women's health: Contemporary international perspectives*, pp. 278–283, London, British Psychological Society.

Rich, E., Evans, J. and Allwood, R. (2005, April) *Healthism and schools*, Paper presented at the conference 'Representation, identity and practice in the areas of eating disorders, obesity and body management', Bristol.

Riley, D. (1988) *Am I that name? Feminism and the category of 'Women' in history*, Basingstoke, Macmillan.

Rousseau, G. (1991) Cultural history in a new key: Towards a semiotics of the nerve, in J. H. Pittock and A. Wear (eds) *Interpretation and cultural history*, pp. 25–81, Basingstoke, Macmillan.

Sayers, J. (1982) *Biological politics: Feminist and anti-feminist perspectives*, London, Tavistock.

Shafter, R. (1989) Women and madness: A social historical perpective, *Issues in Ego Psychology*, 12 (1), 77–82.

Showalter, E. (1985) *The female malady: Women, madness and English culture, 1830–1980*, London, Virago.

Silverstein, B., Peterson, B. and Perdue, L. (1986) Some correlates of the thin standard of bodily attractiveness for women, *International Journal of Eating Disorders*, 5 (5), 895–905.

Smith-Rosenberg, C. and Rosenberg, C. (1973) The female animal: Medical and biological views of woman and her role in nineteenth-century America, *Journal of American History*, 60, 332–356.

Stoppard, J. (2000) Understanding depression in women, in J. M. Ussher (ed.) *Women's health: Contemporary international perspectives*, pp. 405–415, London, British Psychological Society.

Strong, B. E. (1989) Foucault, Freud and French feminism: Theorizing hysteria as theorizing the feminine, *Literature and Psychology*, 35 (4), 10–26.

Swann, C. J. (1997) Reading the reproductive body: Women's accounts of premenstrual syndrome, in J. M. Ussher (ed.) *Body talk: Material discourses of sex, madness and reproduction*, pp. 176–198, London, Routledge.

Touyz, S. W. and Beaumont, P. (2001) Anorexia nervosa: A new approach to management, *Modern Medicine*, 42 (6), 95–99, 103–104, 107–110.

Turner, B. S. (1992) *Regulating bodies: Essays in medical sociology*, London, Routledge.

Ussher, J. (1991) *Women's madness: Misogyny or mental illness*, London, Harvester Wheatsheaf.

Ussher, J. M. (2000) Women's health contemporary concerns, in J. M. Ussher (ed.) *Women's health: Contemporary international perspectives*, pp. 1–26, London, British Psychological Society.

Veith, I. (1965) *Hysteria: The history of a disease*, Chicago, University of Chicago Press.

Wager, M. (1998) Women or researchers? The identities of academic women, *Feminism and Psychology*, 8 (2), 236–244.

Walkerdine, V. (1988) *The mastery of reason: Cognitive development and the production of rationality*, London, Routledge.

Weedon, C. (1987) *Feminist practice and post-structuralist theory*, Oxford, Blackwell.

Wilkinson, S. (2002) Lesbian health, in A. Coyle and C. Kitzinger (eds) *Lesbian and gay psychology*, pp. 117–134, Oxford, BPS Blackwell.

Willig, C. (2000) *Introducing qualitative research in psychology: Adventures in theory and method*, Milton Keynes, Open University Press.

Wooley, S. C., Fallon, P. and Katzman, M. A. (1994) Introduction, in P. Fallon, M. A. Katzman and S. C. Wooley (eds) *Feminist perspectives on eating disorders*, New York, Guilford Press.

World Health Organisation (1992) *ICD-10: Classification of mental and behavioural disorders: Clinical descriptions and diagnostic guidelines*, Geneva, WHO.

Chapter 2

(Re)figuring identities

My body is what I am

Finn Skårderud and Mervat Nasser

EMBODIMENT

Can we explain a body? We fell for the temptation to paraphrase Ludwig Wittgenstein: "Can we explain a Beethoven sonata?" (1989). The human body represents a very complex, ambiguous and fascinating phenomenon. Explaining a body implies reducing its ambiguity to language and language is never adequate. When we speak about the body, it is the spoken-about body we refer to, and not the body itself. Examples of the ambiguity of the human body can be found in the important distinctions between a living and a dead body, between a sick and a healthy body, and between the body as subject and object.

We have a physical body, of flesh and blood. It can be examined as an object by physicians, and we can know more about it via medical examinations. However, the body is inevitably also a symbolic tool, for subjectively expressing ourselves. The concrete physical body is a vehicle for communicating the non-physical, which is the aim of this chapter in an attempt to bring forth fruitful descriptions and concepts about such symbolic mediations, about the interactions between body, mind and culture.

The symbolic body is a general human phenomenon, but bodily practices like body building, piercing, tattooing and scarring and psychopathological phenomena like eating disorders and self-mutilation may help us to see the ambiguous role of the human body more clearly. In these cases the symbolic messages are literally brought to the surface. The body in its cultural context becomes a tool to communicate about culture itself, about norms, taboos, ideals and boundaries. Such practices communicate precisely about core significances and behavioural norms in the culture. The cultivated body is like a text, and it can be read (Ricoeur, 1977).

OPEN TO DEFINITION: THE BODY AS SELF

The American philosophers George Lakoff and Mark Johnson (1980, 1999) view human experiences as primarily "bodily" and see the "metaphorical process" as crucial to our understanding of both body and mind. In so doing, they extend the interpretation and the meaning of the metaphor from being a phenomenon of language or rhetoric, or an artistic figure of speech, to becoming a model for the general function of the human mind. Bodily metaphors are not meant to be simple linguistic metaphors about the body; instead they are *bodily qualities functioning metaphorically* – that is, they are direct analogies of what the bodies are trying to convey (Lakoff and Johnson, 1980).

Lakoff and Johnson describe how our sensory experience of colour, space, direction, form structure, smell, taste, sound, movement, closeness and distance constitutes the basis for primary metaphors. These in turn structure our concepts, thoughts and feelings. An example of this is our experience of gravitation, which organises our lives in terms of the up–down axis, and the sensory-based experience that "more is up" and "less is down": "I'm feeling down," "I am de-pressed," and "I feel burdened by heavy thoughts."

These primary metaphors are automatically and unconsciously appropriated through physical experiences. We may be unaware of them, but they are actually experienced as real. According to the authors, they are a part of our "cognitive unconsciousness". Bodily experiences are basically universal, and this explains the similarities of primary metaphors all over the world. These primary metaphors undergo a further development through language and become interwoven with cultural norms, popular conceptions and belief systems to evolve into complex metaphors which often render their connection to the original bodily source less distinct.

The body metaphor clearly echoes the concept of the "lived body" that was introduced in the early 1960s by the French philosopher Maurice Merleau-Ponty in his challenge of the Cartesian dualism of "body and soul" (Merleau-Ponty, 1962). The concern of the "lived body" is again not with the body *per se* but more with the "bodily being-in-the-world", namely the interplay between the subjective and the inter-subjective experience of the body. It refers to the individual's experience of his/her body and the way this experience transcends its physical nature and interacts with the lived-in world.

This means that the body is engaging in a constant dialogue with the ever-changing conditions of the "lived-in" culture and society, making it open to various definitions and redefinitions. The concept of the "open body" was thus introduced to take into account the fluid nature of the modern cultures we live in (Solheim, 1998). The fluidity of culture thus subjects the individual to an overwhelming sense of openness, with little distinction between the private and the public domains of human experiences, causing the body to act, react and formulate new ways out into the world in the face of the constant flux of life experiences (Duesund and Skårderud, 2003). The crossing of boundaries and the opening of all frontiers has been described as if life's "hardware" is currently being replaced with "light" software that is constantly widening and upgrading the circuits of human communications (Bauman, 2000), thus communicating through the bodily surfaces deep psychological messages about our cultural realities, and rendering the superficial deeply profound.

The problem of boundlessness is also a problem of loss of distinction. The question that confronts the individual is how to construct a self that is coherent and stable and also distinct from others, against a background of increased cultural fluidity and the rapid dissolution of all boundaries. This cultural experience of openness (and fluidity) forces the individual to search for solid and concrete references within the material and physical, leading to re-formulation of the self through the framework of the body and its terminology, interfacing the concrete with the symbolic: open–closed, liquid–solid, soft–hard, impure–pure, light–heavy, small–big, fit–indolent, boundless–bounded, etc.

THE REMIT OF RE-FIGURING AND THE RULES OF ENACTMENT

In our modern lives, there is a marked increase in the prevalence of a variety of bodily practices dictated by cognitions that are trying to explore the limits of the body to speak its mind. There is a revival of highly visual and sometimes shocking primitive body modification practices, giving the body a prominent position within the system of cultural symbolism (Nasser and Di Nicola, 2001). The notion of embodiment is undergoing a process of mass production and reproduction in individuals' quest to redefine bodies and therefore selves. All body practices reflect an act of "self-transformation" experienced by those who undergo such practices; the emphasis lies in the plasticity of the body, which challenges the idea of a stable identity and affirms a new identity grounded in the body. In other words, the body becomes the site where all identities are written. These bodily practices include art experiences such as piercing, tattooing, scarring and aesthetic modifications. Some of these are assigned rituals and pastiches reminiscent and representative of the culture we live in, conveying a kind of "symbolic" anthropology in which the concreteness of the anthropological bodily experiences is abstracted and identified with the analogies and meanings behind them (Lévi-Strauss, 1960).

These bodily expressions therefore need to be determined by the culture in question. New forms of bodily expression reflect the practice of "body maintenance" to enable the body to consume more and consume better. "[T]he new hedonism . . . is not oppositional, being perfectly geared into the market requirements of advanced capitalism. . . . [H]edonistic fascination with the body exists to enhance competitive performance. We jog, slim and sleep not for their intrinsic enjoyment, but to improve our chances at sex, work and longevity" (Turner, 1984: 112, quoted in MacSween, 1993).

Independent of the body's susceptibility to economic forces, consumerism, health slogans and media pressures, the body government serves another purpose as a locus of control over the environment, representing progression in an individual's identity from living in environment *through* the body to making the body the environment *in* which to live in. However, for the new "corporeal identity" to be socially concordant and serve social purposes, it needs to convey referential messages through the chosen form of body expression. This in turn generates in spectators a desire to copy and identify with this particular form of body expression, in order to achieve recognition and group membership. That is, forms of body expression can comprise a "referential identity" (Nasser and Di Nicola, 2001). Hence the scope for re-figuring is subject to media, to market forces, to the desire to remain young and healthy and above all to the desire for cultural affiliation and assimilation. These factors are going to be discussed here under the following headings:

1   the modern primitive body in search of "cultural authenticity";
2   the body as a marketable commodity;
3   the body, gender and time (the ageless self).

The modern primitive body in search of "cultural authenticity"

All forms of self-invention and self-reconstruction are attempts to reconcile the individual with the perplexing nature of modern culture, and the pursuit of referential identity paves the way to a plethora of bodily expressions grounded in history, native cultures and ethnic traditions. This has led to the evolution of small communities based on forms of decorative body work such as scarring, piercing and tattooing, inspired by traditional tribal designs that carry religious or cultural references (Nasser and Di Nicola, 2001). For a tattoo is more than a painting on skin: its meaning and reverberations cannot be comprehended without knowledge of the history and mythology of its bearer. "Bodies," said Foucault, "are historical constructs. . . . altered and tattooed by historical circumstances – and they are indistinguishable from these effects, alterations, tattoos" (quoted in Bailey, 1993). The revival of body tattooing and piercing is a phenomenon commonly referred to nowadays as "modern primitives". It is attributed to a universal feeling of being dislocated in a multicultural world that preaches diversity whilst continuing to behave according to a mono-cultural ethos. The need to belong pushes the individual to formulate a new identity informed by artefacts and pastiches of a historical nature that assume an aura of ethnic/tribal authenticity. In playing with new forms of tribalism, body artists are trying to challenge the idea of stable identity and affirm the conceptual need to ground identities in the body (Nasser, 2004). Those forms make their bearer recognisable within the cultural group with which he/she wishes to identify, and serve to achieve contextualised solidarity and the sought-after referential identity.

The same can be said of the clothed body, where the identity of the subject is constructed by the visible guise of its appearance style. Clothed identities are part and parcel of the body being in a continuous performance (Calefato, 1997). Clothing is a facet and signal of society; clothing forms are ruled by society's economic base, social structure and values in response to cultural transitional forces.

Within this remit, the new veiling adopted by young Moslem women all over the world has been discussed as an exercise in identity-making, through the body form and its dress code, that carries a clear traditional and religious connotation (Nasser and Di Nicola, 2001).

The body as a marketable commodity

Stylisation through clothing and body decoration is an ongoing reconstruction of the self as material identity managed by the forces of fashion, media and markets. The media have institutionalised the body beautiful and advances in aesthetic surgery have made the pursuit of corporeal perfection possible. The body is now remouldable, bionic and even theoretically clonable (Prest and Thompson, 2000). In an era where markets flourish, standardisation of shape and form becomes society's main ethos. Aesthetic surgery pushes individuals towards a standard ideal, including in many instances the removal of bodily racial features that deviate from the dominant Caucasian cultural ideal (Gilman, 1999; Rathner, 1999). The aim of such body/self technology is to achieve an identity based on sameness, to allow integration and acceptance within the larger superculture. Identities of sameness go hand in hand with the identities of difference informed by the creation of bodily distinguishing features such as tattooing, piercing and clothing, which enable those who are outside mainstream culture to achieve instead integration and acceptance within the smaller tribal sub-culture (Nasser, 1997).

The relationship between the economy and the media has been studied by Becker and Hamburg (1996), who pointed to the circular relationship between consumers and the media industry. The study showed how every media representation, be it a photograph, film, video or advertisement, is an act of selling a message coded as an image. In these images the body is portrayed as a product that can be re-created or even purchased. The media's role here is marketing the very possibility of re-manufacturing one's self through the medium of images.

Following the economic transformation of the former communist Eastern Europe, Rathner (2001) was able to show an emergence of dieting behaviour and a spread in the cult of thinness through the marketing of the thinness ideal. This was secondary to the adoption of a Western market economy and the promotion of the human body through the media as a sellable/malleable commodity. This economic transformation of the body was shown to be subject to the same stages as product manufacturing, passing through production to reproduction and simulation (Baudrillard, 1993).

The body, gender and time

The sexual objectification of female bodies was thought to decrease in intensity with their advancing age. Growing old potentially liberated women from the restrictions placed upon them by conventional gender roles, allowing them to develop a more authentic self (Arber and Ginn, 1995). In a critique of Beauvoir's analysis of womanhood and age, Deutscher (2001) argued that women rarely benefit from this apparent newly found freedom, as the prevailing cultural milieu does not value feminine subjectivity separate from youthfulness. Hence the potential for women to lead an authentic existence is hampered – not necessarily by old age but by societal attitudes towards aging which tend not to see older women as women. This means that women can only find freedom if they transcend – through age – their womanhood and their erotic possibilities, accepting their status as "gender neutral". According to Beauvoir, for the experience of this freedom to be true, it should remain connected with the issue of femininity, not with its transcendence. If social validation of women is only possible through youthful femininity, such freedom to achieve authentic identity is bound to be inhibited or at least becomes deeply ambivalent (Deutscher, 2001).

Helman (2005) explored the influence of time over individual identity independent of the gender variable, and found no direct link between time as measured by chronological age and an individual's self-perception. His finding resonated Kaufman's (1986) study of elderly Americans, which found that the elderly do not speak of being old as meaningful in itself, and often don't relate their inner feelings to their chronological age. When old people talk about themselves, they express a sense of self that is ageless, an identity that maintains continuity despite the physical and social changes that come with old age. A woman of 92 was quoted as saying: "Whenever I am walking downtown and see my reflection in a store window, I am shocked by how old it is. I never think of myself that way" (Kaufman, 1986: 9).

This indifference to aging was found to be primarily determined by how well-functioning the body is, with particular reference to the presence or absence of infirmity. This shows that the body in old age does not necessarily respond to chronological age as long as physical change and infirmity can be prevented or delayed for as long as possible. Song (2000) studied figures of aging, refering to Simone de Beauvoir's memoir and her views on her own agedness, and concluded that the body in old age with its ever-present threat of non-functioning is the main source of self-knowledge, and identity formation is therefore dependent on the negation of infirmity as the sole factor in maintaining this indifference to agedness or perceiving agelessness.

Based on this premise, the self could continue to be ageless for as long as the body remains young and healthy. This is now achievable through medical advances and surgical manoeuvres, conquering infirmity and pro-longing lives. Through cosmetic surgery, "young" bodies are constructed against aging to create a state of endless youth coinciding with the indi-vidual's heightened desire to deny frailty and the potential of death. The possibility of achieving timeless youthfulness will therefore continuc to make the question of age, gender and identity open and forever controversial.

THE PLASTICITY OF THE BODY BETWEEN THE ADAPTIVE AND THE PATHOLOGICAL

Regardless of the socio-cultural dynamics of the above body practices and their role in informing individual identity formation, practices such as body sculpting, tattooing, piercing and time-defying surgical procedures continue to be seen within the range of normality – although the definition of the normal and abnormal is subject to change over the course of time, secon-dary to changes in social conditions (Nasser, 1997).

However, there are other body modification phenomena that are recog-nisable as psychopathological – such as eating disorders, self-cutting and other forms of body abuse and harm practices. The metaphorical linkage between the body and self-construction has received a lot of attention in the case of the anorexic experience. The morbid concern with the body's shape and weight encountered among anorexics translates the psychological concerns that underpin the condition.

The experience of loss of cognitive/emotional control is common to all anorexics, giving rise to negative self-evaluation and self-reproach, which Vitousek and Ewald referred to as "the unworthy self" (1993). The pursuit of anorexia is therefore a struggle to live up to the aspiration to an idealised/celebrated body form that will subsequently be worthy of cultural acceptance, approval and applause. The act of food control through restriction or empting the stomach by vomiting or purging could also help psychologically to retrieve back the control that is experienced as lost. The same process is also a form of body management that succeeds in refashioning the body into one of reduced size and weight. This is a "retreat" from the "overwhelmed/worthless self" into a minimalist body form (Vitousek and Ewald, 1993). It is an act of withdrawal, a process of closing up aimed to create out of the body a shell, rendering the bodily transformation a protective exercise for the self (Serpell et al., 1998; Skårderud, 1997).

The deficit in worth characteristic of the anorexic experience is in essence an identity deficit, and the food control here is nothing but a bodily control aiming to create a self out of the collective norm that is unique with an extraordinary sense of individuality, compensating for the overwhelming lack of worth. The re-figuring of the body is an act of holding on to the certainty and solidity of the skeletal body form, serving as an embodied boundary against the diffuse fluidity of the prevailing cultural reality (Goodsitt, 1997; Nasser and Di Nicola, 2001; Vitousek and Ewald, 1993). This anorexic bodily manipulation achieves, besides certainty and worth, a feeling of purity amounting to spiritual perfection (Goss and Gilbert, 2002; Nasser and Katzman, 2003; Vitousek and Ewald, 1993).

In all these examples, the anorexic metaphor has clearly copied its reference, mimed the underlying problem, and also attempted to solve it. In re-figuring the body, it has intended to re-figure identity using the body vocabulary as its frame of reference (Bauman, 2004: 15–16).

Self-mutilation, like self-starvation, is seen to be a desire to be noticed, as a plea for self-recognition (Hewitt, 1997). The clinical literature is rich with cases of self-starvation associated with self-harming behaviours, some of which almost border on self-torture. Examples of these self-damaging behaviours include self-cutting, overdosing or substance misuse. In these situations, the act of self-harm functions as language, communicating inner pain and distress; it is a method of self-expression. "When I could not find the words to describe it, cutting had become the language to describe the pain, communicating everything I felt" (Pembroke, 1994: 35). The distress here is caused by the loss of the relationship between one's outer self and inner self, as well as the loss of the self to others. It is a reaction to a sense of confusion, disorganisation and disconnection (Nasser, 2004). The lack of a clear sense of the self from within, and the impaired sense of self-organisation, find expression on the surface/exterior of the body, treating the self as equivalent to a physical entity (Fonagy et al., 2002).

Anorexic practices and self-harming exercises are indeed processes of identity production whilst being in the meantime acts of self-destruction, literally and metaphorically. This paradoxical construction of the self as both self-producing and self-annihilating begs the question of where to draw the line between what is adaptive and what is pathological (Malson, 1998).

Amid the plethora of body modification practices and the quest of the self to produce a new and corporeal self, the boundary between what is normal and abnormal, aesthetic and ascetic, palatable and grotesque, sacred and profane, becomes increasingly blurred (Nasser, 2004).

And yet, the argument for the morbid or pathological perhaps lies in the individual's level of freedom within the body/self metaphorical processes – that is, in the absence or presence of the "as if" quality in the experience. In other words, the bodily expression of the new identity becomes less adaptive and more pathological once the "as if" quality of the symbolic transaction of body–mind is lost and replaced by "is". When the psychic reality is poorly integrated, the body takes on an excessively central role in the continuity of the sense of self. The concreteness of the metaphor is felt as superior to its psychic equivalent (Fonagy et al., 2002). This means that the sufferer is no longer the master of his or her metaphorical mediation and instead he or she is at the mercy of this metaphor, which no longer functions as a *representation* of an experience, but as an actual *presentation* of it; the individual feels "used by" and "trapped in" the concrete metaphorisation of the body. This is normally the case with eating disorders, personality disorders, self-harmers and traumatised individuals (Enckell, 2002).

CONCLUSION

This chapter revolves around the quest of the self to re-invent itself through body symbolism. The self's experience of increased cultural openness, fluidity and boundlessness forces it to resort metaphorically to the concrete and skeletal solidity of the body for new boundaries and re-definition. The human body functions as a concrete artefact mediating one's relationship to oneself and to others within the actual cultural context, hence producing identity.

Such corporeal practices include body decorative art such as sculpting, tattooing and piercing, as well as clothing – all of which are influenced by prevailing economic structures, media forces and the tyranny of the image industry. Women are also under increased pressure to preserve youthful femininity for as long as possible, through cosmetic surgery and time-delay procedures, to maintain socially valid identities.

Against a feeling of cultural diffusion and confusion, the spectrum of body modification is limitless despite the fact that its aim is to form an embodied boundary against the loss of limits. Attempts towards self-definition through re-figuring translate the individual's conflicted desire to acquire within culture a simultaneous distinctiveness and sameness. The paradoxical nature of such a position could potentially give rise to serious emotional upheavals, forcing the individual to formulate equally paradoxical bodily solutions. Such is the case in forms of self-starvation and deliberate self-harm practices, where the act of self-invention is achieved through self-injury, destruction and annihilation, increasingly blurring the boundaries between the adaptive and the pathological.

REFERENCES

Arber, S. and Ginn, J. (1995) *Connecting gender and aging: A sociological approach*, Buckingham, Open University Press.
Bailey, M. E. (1993) Foucauldian feminism: Contesting bodies, sexuality and identity, in C. Ramazanoglu (ed.) *Up against Foucault: Explorations of some tensions between Foucault and feminism*, pp. 99–122, London, Routledge.
Baudrillard, J. (1993) *Symbolic exchange and death*, London, Sage Publications.
Bauman, Z. (2000) *Liquid modernity*, Cambridge, Polity Press.
Bauman, Z. (2004) *Identity*, Cambridge, Polity Press.
Becker, A. and Hamburg, P. (1996) Culture, the media and eating disorders, *Harvard Review of Psychiatry*, 4 (4), 163–167.
Calefato, P. (1997) Fashion and worldiness: Language and imagery of the clothed body, *Fashion Theory: The Journal of Dress, Body and Culture*, 1 (1), 69–90.
Deutscher, P. (2001) Sartre and Beauvoir on desire and embodiment, in S. Ahmed and J. Stacey (eds) *Thinking through the skin*, pp. 143–160, London, Routledge.
Duesund, L. and Skårderud, F. (2003) Use the body and forget the body: Treating anorexia nervosa with adapted physical activity, *Clinical Child Psychology and Psychiatry*, 8, 53–72.
Enckell, H. (2002) *Metaphor and the psychodynamic functions of the mind*, Doctoral dissertation, Kuopion Yliopisto, Finland.
Fonagy, P., Gergely, G., Jurist, E. L. and Target, M. (2002) *Affect regulation, mentalization and the development of the self*, New York, Other Press.
Gilman, S. L. (1999) *Making the body beautiful: A cultural history of aesthetic surgery*, Princeton, Princeton University Press.
Goodsitt, A. (1997) Eating disorders: A self-psychological perspective, in D. M. Garner and P. E. Garfinkel (eds) *Handbook of treatment for eating disorders*, pp. 205–228, New York, Guilford Press.
Goss, K. and Gilbert, P. (2002) Eating disorders, shame and pride: A cognitive-behavioural functional analysis, in P. Gilbert and J. Miles (eds) *Body shame: Conceptualisation, research and treatment*, pp. 219–255, New York, Brunner-Routledge.
Helman, C. (2005) Cultural aspects of time and aging, *European Molecular Biology Organisation Reports*, 6 (special issue), 1–5.
Hewitt, K. (1997) *Mutilating the body: Identity in blood and ink*, Bowling Green, OH, Popular Press.
Kaufman, S. R. (1986) *The ageless self*, Madison, University of Wisconsin Press.
Lakoff, G. and Johnson, M. (1980) *Metaphors we live by*, Chicago, University of Chicago Press.
Lakoff, G. and Johnson, M. (1999) *Philosophy in the flesh: The embodied mind and its challenge to Western thought*, New York, Basic Books.

Lévi-Strauss, C. (1960) *The savage mind*, Chicago, University of Chicago Press.

MacSween, M. (1993) *Anorexic bodies: A feminist and sociological perspective on anorexia nervosa*, London, Routledge.

Malson, H. (1998) *The thin woman: Feminism, post-structuralism and the social pathology of anorexia nervosa*, London, Routledge.

Merleau-Ponty, M. (1962) *The phenomenology of perception*, London, Routledge and Kegan Paul.

Nasser, M. (1997) *Culture and weight consciousness*, London, Routledge.

Nasser, M. (2004) Dying to live: Eating disorders and self-harm behaviour in a cultural context, in J. Levitt, R. Sansone and L. Cohn (eds) *Self-harm behaviour and eating disorders: Dynamics, assessment and treatment*, pp. 15–31, New York and Hove, Brunner-Routledge.

Nasser, M. and Katzman, M. (1999) Eating disorders: Transcultural perspectives inform prevention, in N. Piran, M. Levine and C. Steiner-Adair (eds) *Preventing eating disorders: A handbook of interventions and special challenges*, pp. 26–44, Philadelphia, Brunner/Mazel.

Nasser, M. and Di Nicola, V. (2001) Changing bodies, changing cultures: An intercultural dialogue on the body as the final frontier, in M. Nasser, M. A. Katzman and R. A. Gordon (eds) *Eating disorders and cultures in transition*, pp. 171–187, New York, Brunner-Routledge.

Nasser, M. and Katzman, M. (2003) Sociocultural theories of eating disorders: An evolution of thought, in J. Treasure, U. Schmidt and E. van Furth (eds) *Handbook of eating disorders*, 2nd edn, pp. 139–151, Chichester, Wiley.

Pembroke, L. R. (ed.) (1994) *Self-harm: Perspectives from personal experience*, London, Survivors Speak Out.

Prest, J. and Thompson, H. (2000) The elusive body, in J. Prest and H. Thompson (eds) *Corporeal practices: Refiguring the body in French studies* (*Modern French identities*, vol. 4, series ed. Peter Collier), pp. 9–14, Oxford, Peter Lang.

Rathner, G. (1999, April) *The colonisation of the body*, Paper presented at the Fourth International Conference on Eating Disorders, London.

Ricoeur, P. (1977) *The rule of metaphor: Multi-disciplinary studies of the creation of meaning in language*, Toronto, University of Toronto Press.

Serpell, L., Treasure, J., Teasdale, J. and Sullivan, V. (1998) Anorexia nervosa: Friend or foe? *International Journal of Eating Disorders*, 25, 177–186.

Skårderud, F. (1997) Vekten av et selv: Spiseforstyrrelser og selvpsykologi, in S. Karterud and J. Monsen (eds) *Selvpsykologi: Utviklingen etter kohut*, pp. 228–265, Oslo: Gyldendal ad Notam.

Solheim, J. (1998) *Den åpne kroppen*, Oslo, Pax Forlag.

Song, R. (2000) Comparative figures of aging in the memoirs of Colette and Beauvoir: Corporeality, infirmity, identity, in J. Prest and H. Thompson (eds) *Corporeal practices: Refiguring the body in French studies* (*Modern French identities*, vol. 4, series ed. Peter Collier), pp. 79–91, Oxford, Peter Lang.

Turner, B. (1984) *The body and society*, Oxford, Oxford University Press.

Vitousek, K. B. and Ewald, L. S. (1993) Self-representation in eating disorders: A cognitive perspective, in Z. V. Segal and S. J. Blatt (eds) *The self in emotional distress: Cognitive and psychodynamic perspectives*, pp. 219–257, New York, Guilford Press.

Wittgenstein, L. (1989) *Om vished*, Århus, Philosophia.

Part II

The hurting body

This section of the book deals with the interface between body and trauma, including deliberate self harm, sexual trauma, the trauma of self starvation and cancer. In Chapter 3 the focus is on the meaning of deliberate self harm, the message being conveyed and the methods of helping individuals who inflict harm upon themselves. Chapter 4 is more concerned with exploring the impact of psychological trauma in general and the issue of post-traumatic stress disorder, particularly that arising from childhood sexual abuse. It also deals with how psychological trauma affects memory processing, affect regulation and the capacity to form and maintain meaningful attachments with other people. Chapter 5 covers the spectrum of eating psychopathology, dealing with different aetiological and phenomenological models. It discusses the core beliefs and assumptions of the eating disorder sufferers and addresses the therapeutic challenge. In Chapter 6, the focus is on the body's struggle with cancer, with particular reference to breast cancer. A range of psychological issues related to cancer and body image are covered, including health screening, psychological responses to diagnosis and therapeutic interventions including surgery, as well as women's coping styles in the face of the threat of death or disfigurement.

Chapter 3

Deliberate self harm

Jane Bunclark

INTRODUCTION

Self inflicted trauma or deliberate self harm is a complex and challenging phenomenon to understand, at both a personal and a societal level. To comprehend how someone finds relief through inflicting injury upon themselves is difficult, when for the majority of people preservation of one's body and appearance is valued. Contact with someone who self harms provokes profound and often extreme reactions in others. This chapter attempts to address the reasons underlying why somebody inflicts harm on themselves or elicits harm for themselves, and how this impacts upon relationships. Issues arising from this contact will be addressed and ethical dilemmas for clinicians will be considered.

Inflicting harm on oneself is not a recent phenomenon and has origins within most cultures and ideologies. To injure oneself is a long and universal human tradition and ceremonies involving blood and cutting appear in most cultures. Body mutilation, pain and the drawing of blood have had a range of deep and powerful symbolic meanings, both for individuals and for social group. Mutilation and bleeding have frequently been held as a form of healing; the use of the skin as a tension reliever takes many forms – scratching the head, etc. Self harm may also be therapeutic because of the symbolism associated with scarring: scar tissue indicates healing. Pain, body modification and mutilation can serve some social function at times of loss. Often at the core of religion one finds violence, blood, sacrifice and self mutilation, associated with either atonement for sin (especially sexual) or achieving spiritual advancement. Additionally, the history of punishment has been long and bloody, with mutilation and eventual death being socially endorsed. For further discussion of self harm behaviour in a cultural context, refer to Nasser (2004).

WHAT IS SELF HARM?

The definition of self harm is confusing. There is a wide range of terminology: self injury, self abuse, deliberate self harm, self mutilation and parasuicide. Self harm, therefore, seems to be the most encompassing. Definitions range from "self-poisoning or self-injury irrespective of the apparent purpose of the act" (NICE, 2004: 7) to "an individual intentionally damaging a part of his or her own body, apparently without a conscious intent to die" (Feldman, 1988: 252–268).

Self harm can also be viewed as "a deliberate act to damage oneself, without intending to die. It varies according to the situation and the individual and is a means of getting away from intolerable thoughts or feelings" (South London and Maudsley NHS Trust Crisis Resolution Unit/resident group, unpublished document). The issue of intent needs to be incorporated into any working definition of self harm, perhaps more than an emphasis on the method or the risk involved. However intent, especially in some forms of self harm, particularly overdosing, is sometimes difficult to uncover in the interplay of conscious and unconscious motivation.

It is possible to divide methods of self harm into four main categories: epithelial methods, internal methods, methods which acquire harm through others and methods which alter the mind (Table 3.1).

Rates of self harm in the UK have increased over the past decade and are reported to be among the highest in Europe (Horrocks, 2002). Whilst self harm is a significant public health problem, the full extent of it is not known. Many individuals are managed solely in primary care and others do not present to health services. One estimate, based on 1996 figures, suggests approximately 170,000 people annually present to hospitals in the UK after an incident of self harm (Kapur et al., 1999). Yet hospital attendances do not reflect the full extent of the problem (Hawton et al., 2002; Meltzer et al., 2002a). A national survey based on interviews indicated that in the UK between 4.6% and 6.6% of people have harmed themselves. Overall, women are far more susceptible to self harm than men. Women prisoners seem to be at particular risk. Deliberate self harm was generally found to be prevalent in prison populations (7.4%), with one study finding that 30% of female prisoners had harmed themselves in the preceding year (Adeniji and Teers, 2004).

Adolescence seems to be the period where self harm peaks. Girls are three times more likely to harm themselves than boys (Hawton et al., 2002). In a recent survey of some 12,529 young people (age 5–15 years), parental data indicated that 1.3% had tried to harm themselves (Meltzer et al., 2002b). This again is probably an under-representation, because in a school survey 13% of young people aged 15 or 16 reported having self harmed at some point in their lives, 7% in the previous year (Hawton et al., 2002). More than 24,000 teenagers are admitted to hospital in the UK each year after

Table 3.1 Methods of self harm

Epithelial (skin) damage	Internalised damage	Damage from others	Damaging the ability to think or remember
Cutting	Overdoses	Eliciting	Bloodletting
Burning	Insertion	– criticism	Alcohol
Scratching	– orifices	– rejection	Substance misuse
Biting	– under skin	Involvement in	Starvation
Hitting	Ingestion	fights	
Punching	– caustic	Seeking attack or	
Pulling out hair	substances	assault	
	– foreign objects	Abusive	
	– noxious	relationships	
	substances	Sex working	

Other forms which do not fit within these categories: use of ligatures, suffocation, drowning, sleeping rough, exacerbating physical illnesses.

deliberately harming themselves, the majority having taken overdoses or cut themselves (Samaritans and Centre for Suicide, 2002). The same study estimates that one in 10 teenagers inflict harm on themselves.

The issue of self harm among ethnic groups has also been the subject of a study carried out by Bhugra et al. (1999). The study was carried out on Asian women in London and showed rates of self harm among Asian women under 30 to be 2.5 times those of white women and seven times those of Asian men (refer to Chapter 14 in this volume).

It is important, though, to note that the scope of all these studies is limited, as they exclude other behaviours or acts which result in inflicting harm, stem from the same symbolic representation or address the same function. They fail for instance to include eating problems, substance or alcohol misuse, sex working, or involvement in abusive or harmful relationships. Individuals involved in these dilemmas may not necessarily be self harming, but to ignore the meaning of these behaviours and their links to deliberate self harm will undoubtedly limit our understanding and styles of intervention.

Hence it may be useful to place self harm on a continuum of harmful behaviours, with socially acceptable forms such as smoking, tattooing, body piercing or extreme sports at one end and suicide at the other. Whilst many individuals stress that self harm is an anti-suicidal act, the link between self harm and suicide is complex, and 0.5–2% of patients who present following an episode of deliberate self harm commit suicide within the following year (Owens et al., 2002). This represents an increased risk of 42–66 times that of the general population (Hawton et al., 2003; Harris and Barraclough, 1998).

Self harm is a communication that involves the body. Suicide and attempted suicide are also forms of communication, in that they offer an explanation to others, but self harm demands to be listened to in other ways. It primarily offers an expression to oneself and then after that to others.

WHY DO PEOPLE HARM THEMSELVES?

Self harm can be the result of early trauma: sexual, physical or emotional abuse. Individuals who suffer early trauma internalise their pain or do not learn to manage their distress may consequently have feelings of lack of self worth, self loathing, guilt, shame and the need for punishment.

Self harm is individual and very personal. It is frequently a private, secret act and may go unnoticed for years. The majority of individuals take action to ensure that their injuries are hidden, for example by wearing long sleeves, but it often feels that at some level they are desperate for their injuries to be noticed and for appropriate questions to be asked of them. This dilemma often appears to be transposed into their future contact with services. Are service providers sufficiently vigilant to ask the right questions and notice their distress or do they act like primary care givers and turn a "blind eye" (Steiner, 1985)?

Self harm behaviour commonly starts in adolescence at times of distress. In adolescence the desire to hide injuries often has an impact on school attendance, especially for games lessons, and a pattern of school absence might emerge, serving to reinforce the individual as "badly behaved" and becoming more detached from both authorities and peers.

The relief achieved through self harm tends, however, to diminish with the passage of time and increasingly severe damage is inflicted to gain the same level of relief. Most self harmers have their preferred method, which either responds to an internal need or matches a particular state of mind. For example, an individual might cut when feeling self critical or after an argument, but would overdose when a significant person in their life leaves them.

There are common themes which individuals who self harm express and put forward as possible explanations for their acts. These themes include:

1   Self harm as a coping/survival tactic: Many who self harm do it to conquer unbearable memories or negative feelings about the self. The act of self harm helps to overcome the distress generated by those memories/feelings. In this context, self harm acts rather paradoxically as a survival tool. It prevents them from killing themselves.
2   Self harm as testimony to self loathing/disgust: Self harm and scarification can offer a testament to self loathing, reinforcing self hatred for what has been experienced earlier in life. Individuals talk of their scars as the story lines of their own struggle. Individuals who have learnt

from early experiences not to trust their bodies use self harm (with its horrific scars) to communicate their sense of disgust at their own self/ body, rendering themselves physically or sexually unattractive and creating a distance between themselves and the world.

3   Self harm as affect regulation: When feelings become intolerable, self harm can serve a self soothing or tension-relieving function. Individuals describe themselves as being able to discharge their feelings and become calmer and relieved, at least for a while. The distracting nature of the self harm helps to numb the mind, or concentrating on the cut and the physical pain is a means of getting away from inner pain. The drops of blood from the cut here are the tears the distressed is unable to shed.

4   Self harm as body ownership and locus of control: Self harm provides a sense of control or mastery over one's self. It gives a feeling of autonomy, of being in charge of one's life. This could be in stark contrast to the loss of control experienced earlier in life, as is the case in childhood physical and sexual abuse. For some, the circumstances of the abusive experience offer a sense of control or resolution.

5   Self harm as a punishing, cleansing and purifying experience: Early abusive experiences can give rise to a sense of dirt or contamination, and the act of self harm, particularly blood letting, be seen as a purification ritual. Self harmers also speak of their bodies as being a source of evil and feel they deserve to be punished. Inflicting harm on their bodies is therefore an act of punishment or atonement.

6   Self harm as an encoded message and tool of communication: Self harm is an attempt to communicate with others the distress they are unable to verbally articulate. Through attacking their bodies, they are making a connection between the inner/immaterial world and the physical self, showing others something of their inner damage.

Many self harmers report repeated experiences of not being listened to or noticed, and for them the only thing that is noticed is their body. It is not surprising, therefore, that they have come to believe that bodily communications have greater influence on others. Some even believe that through harming themselves, they are inflicting harm on others.

HOW TO HELP THEM?

Traditional practices for managing self harm tended to focus on preventing the harm without offering instead an alternative coping strategy. Some forms of intervention were seen as intrusive and even counterproductive, recreating the critical, abusive environment that some of these individuals had experienced.

There was a need therefore to challenge these practices, and the last decade has witnessed a shift in our understanding and treatment approaches. Some services began to move away from interventions solely aimed at preventing the act of self harm, through the provision of nursing observation, removal of all potential implements of harm and physical containment. Some even sanctioned "safe cutting" and similar practices are currently being explored and seem to be on the increase. However, those using therapeutic models based on acceptance and tolerance need to understand the dynamics of the self harm and realise that self harm by definition is damaging. They need, therefore, to strike a balance between neglect, by making blades and other implements available, and replicating abuse through restrictive custodial forms of intervention.

The psychiatric literature describes various psychotherapeutic approaches to the management of self harm behaviour. They include dynamic intervention, cognitive restructuring, interpersonal restructuring, behaviour modification and dialectical behaviour therapy (DBT). Some of these therapeutic techniques are described in more detail within this volume (for an overview of psychotherapy strategies for the management of self harm behaviour refer to Sansone et al., 2004).

The therapeutic approach described here is based on a psychodynamic model adopted by the Maudsley unit for self harm, and my own experience as the clinical nurse leader of the South London and Maudsley (SLAM) NHS Trust Crisis Resolution Unit (CRU), as well as my interest in the symbolic representation of self harm. The main philosophy is to look beyond the skin level of the cut/injury and delve to the deeper cut that lies at the psychic level, where the damage is truly located. This framework tends to incorporate the complexity, dilemmas and relationship dynamics inherent in self harm behaviour. Self harm is never the problem – it is merely symptomatic of the inner distress. This means that any kind of intervention needs to provide an adequate supportive framework to help explore and address the underlying fundamental problem, not just its mere outward manifestation.

Therapists need to familiarise themselves with the client's full scope of damaging acts and not limit their enquiry to presenting behaviours only; they must also balance therapeutic risk taking with risk assessment.

It is important, however, for therapists working in self harm services to be able to understand and manage the anxiety that these behaviours provoke. Individuals who self harm tend to do so in response to overwhelming, intrusive, painful thoughts or memories. When their inner feelings are no longer contained, the individual resorts to self harm as a means of either controlling these feelings or purging them. During an intervention, the therapist comes into close contact with the harmer's negative feelings projected into them. The therapist's anxiety, generated by this projection, on top of all the other anxieties related to skill, competence or ability to help, can make the therapeutic task enormously difficult. This often leads to the involvement of multiple therapists, each sharing part of the burden. This may be at the expense of maintaining a consistent and balanced approach to treatment. Alternatively the therapist, by reason of his/her anxiety, may withdraw from involvement altogether, causing the self harmer to experience neglect and feelings of abandonment.

Unless anxieties can be identified, addressed and contained within the system it is likely that the system itself will produce defences that actively hinder rather than help therapeutic intervention. The organisation can become caught up in the same state of mind as the self harmer, who in turn experiences the organisation as unhelpful and even abusive. Hence, containment of both the therapist and the self harmer's anxiety is paramount for the success of any therapeutic process (Bion, 1967).

Self harming individuals who have had insufficient or inconsistent containment in their early lives may seek this in their contact with workers (containment, as described by Bion, 1967, is "the need for a vessel in terms of the community and the worker to be able to not only hold onto the disturbance but digest and process it"). Thus these relationships might be driven by a desperate need for reparation, with workers finding it impossible to fill this void (reparation, as described by Klein, 1945, is "the wish to put right, reinstate or repair the object that has been damaged or destroyed"). This often then gets translated into an impossible situation where whatever is offered is not good enough. Alternatively, individuals' previous experiences of abuse can be replayed within the relationship – almost as though there has to be an abuser and an abused, although these roles move between the therapist and the client. Milton (1994) describes this in depth.

The thinking process of some individuals who self harm oscillates between two extreme positions: they view themselves and the world in "all or nothing" terms. Things are either wholly good or wholly bad. The feelings associated with this cognitive structure also follow this pattern, leading to displays of extremes of emotion. They may either feel "absolutely hopeless" or "absolutely great". This polarised view of the world is extended to therapists, who may be idealised or denigrated at different times.

The drive to be helpful is a motivating force for many health professionals (Roberts, 1994). However, being too helpful is likely to foster dependency and compromise the individual's responsibility for their self attacks and actions. It is necessary, therefore, for therapists to be aware of these dynamics and their own valancies (Bion, 1961, defines valancy as "a capacity for instantaneous involuntary combination of one individual with another for sharing and acting on a basic assumption") and not get drawn into and enmeshed in unhelpful or unprofessional relationships. Professional engagement needs to be first and foremost based on the individual's psychological needs.

Menzies Lyth (1970) highlighted the need for therapist resilience and ability to understand the great array of emotions that self harmers evoke. Supervision, support and training are vital to enable workers in the field to reflect on and understand their clients' difficulties. Therapists need to maintain their distance while being sufficiently engaged; they need to act as containers for much of their clients' anxieties, pain and emotional chaos. Training is necessary to broaden knowledge, understanding and recognition of all these issues, and supervision helps to make therapists mindful of differences between engagement in relationships and re-enactments. Ongoing risk assessment with open communication is vital; clients and carers need to be actively involved in identifying risk factors and effective interventions. Therapists need to familiarise themselves with the harmer's full scope of damaging acts and not limit their enquiry to presenting behaviours only; balance needs to be maintained between behavioural and therapeutic risk assessments.

From Anzieu's (1985) seminal work on skin ego, the function of skin for those who self harm can be translated into an understanding of the therapeutic significance of the formation and maintenance of boundaries. If the skin is conceptualised as the fundamental boundary of the body, then symbolically self harm breaks or violates this very boundary. This is often replicated within the boundaries of relationships. Individuals who harm themselves have a desperate need to understand the limits within relationships, both with themselves and with others. This is, in essence, the purpose of all therapeutic work that revolves around maintaining boundaries. Boundaries need to be skin-like – sufficiently flexible so that cracks don't emerge, but with sufficient rigidity so that there is a shape offered. Thus the dialectic between the therapist and the self harmer becomes an integral part of the therapeutic work, and needs to be fully explored and addressed.

CONCLUSION

This chapter offers an overview of self harm, the spectrum of its definitions and the motives of people engaging in such damaging acts. The predilection of young women to self harm is discussed, as is the therapeutic strategy adopted by the SLAM Crisis Resolution Unit. This strategy is based on psychodynamic principles and aims to enable individuals who harm themselves to view themselves and their relationships with others differently. It emphasises, however, the need for the therapist to understand boundary issues and therapeutic engagement. It also highlights the need for collaboration and integration between different therapeutic techniques, to offer those who harm themselves alternative means of communication, healthier ways of coping with distress and the ability to experience relationships which are based on reparation rather than repetition, both at skin and psychic level.

REFERENCES

Adeniji, T. and Teers, R. (2004) *Recorded self-harm in HM prisons (England and Wales) during 2003*, London, Home Office.

Anzieu, D. (1985) *Le moi-peau [The skin ego]*, New Haven, CT, Yale University Press.

Bhugra, D., Desai, M. and Baldwin, D. (1999) Attempted suicide in west London, I: Rates across ethnic communities, *Psychological Medicine*, 29 (5), 1125–1130.

Bion, W. (1961) *Experiences in groups and other papers*, London, Tavistock.

Bion, W. (1967) *Second thoughts: Selected papers on psychoanalysis*, London, Karnac Books.

Feldman, M. D. (1988) The challenge of self-mutilation: A review, *Comprehensive Psychiatry*, 29 (3), 252–269.

Harris, E. C. and Barraclough, B. (1988) Excess mortality of mental disorder, *British Journal of Psychiatry*, 173, 11–53.

Hawton, K., Rodham, K., Evans, E. and Weatherall, R. (2002) Deliberate self harm in adolescents: Self report survey in schools in England, *British Medical Journal*, 325 (7374), 1207–1211.

Hawton, K., Zahl, D. and Weatherall, R. (2003) Suicide following deliberate self-harm: Long term follow-up study of patients who present to a general hospital, *British Journal of Psychiatry*, 182, 537–542.

Horrocks, J. (2002) Self-poisoning and self-injury in adults, *Clinical Medicine*, 2 (6), 509–512.

Kapur, N., House, A., Creed, F., Feldman, E., Friedman, T. and Guthrie, E. (1999) General hospital services for deliberate self-poisoning: An expensive road to nowhere?, *Postgraduate Medical Journal*, 75, 599–602.

Klein, M. (1945) *Love, guilt and reparation and other works*, London, Hogarth Press.

Meltzer, H., Harrington, R., Goodman, R., Singleton, N., Jenkins, R. and Brugha, T. (2002a) *Children and adolescents who try to harm, hurt or kill themselves: A report of further analysis from the national survey of the mental health of children and adolescents in Great Britain in 1999*, London, Office for National Statistics.

Meltzer, H., Lader, D., Corbin, T., Singleton, N., Jenkins, R. and Brugha, T. (2002b) *Non-fatal suicidal behaviour among adults aged 16 to 74 in Great Britain*, London, The Stationery Office.

Menzies Lyth, I. (1970) *The functioning of social systems as a defence against anxiety: Selected essays, vol. 1*, London, Free Association Books.

Milton, J. (1994) Abuser and abused: Perverse solutions following childhood abuse, *Psychoanalytic Psychotherapy*, 8 (3), 243–255.

Nasser, M. (2004) Dying to live: Eating disorders and self harm behaviour in the cultural context, in J. Levitt, R. Sasone and L. Cohn (eds) *Self-harm behaviour and eating disorders: Dynamics, assessment and treatment*, pp. 15–31, New York and Hove, Brunner-Routledge.

NICE (2004) *Self-harm: The short-term physical and psychological management and secondary prevention of self-harm in primary and secondary care*, London, British Psychological Society and the Royal College of Psychiatrists.

Owens, D., Horrocks, J. and House, A. (2002) Fatal and non-fatal repetition of self-harm: Systematic review, *British Journal of Psychiatry*, 181, 193–199.

Roberts, V. Z. (1994) The self assigned impossible task, in A. Obholzer and V. Z. Roberts (eds) *The unconscious at work: Individual and organisational stress in the human services*, pp. 110–118, London, Routledge.

Samaritans and Centre for Suicide (2002) *Youth and self-harm: Perspectives*, Oxford, University of Oxford.

Sansone, R. A., Levitt, J. and Sansone, L. (2004) An overview of psychotherapy strategies for the management of self-harm behaviour, in J. Levitt, R. Sasone and L. Cohn (eds) *Self-harm behaviour and eating disorders: Dynamics, assessment and treatment*, New York and Hove, Brunner-Routledge.

Steiner, J. (1985) Turning a blind eye: The cover up for Oedipus, *International Review of Psychoanalysis*, 12, 161–172.

Chapter 4

Psychological trauma and post-traumatic stress disorder

Walter Busuttil

INTRODUCTION

This chapter deals with the nature of psychological trauma and the psychiatric syndromes that are triggered by it, as well the vulnerability of women to such disorders. In contrast to "Acts of God" such as natural disasters, personal and "man-made" events are perceived as being more traumatising (Breslau et al., 1998; Janoff-Boulmann, 1985).

The age of the individual at the time of the trauma, the length and frequency of exposure and the nature of the traumatic event all seem to influence the clinical presentation and the severity of the symptom complex.

Psychological trauma can be responsible for a number of psychiatric disorders grouped under the broad term of "post-traumatic stress disorder (PTSD). All are characterised by a history of exposure to an extreme psychological stressor out of the range of ordinary human experience, which threatens life or physical integrity, and which is perceived with extreme horror, helplessness and fear. Following traumatic exposure, characteristic core cluster symptoms develop: hyper-arousal, re-experiencing of the traumatic event and avoidance (American Psychiatric Association, 1994).

Community studies estimate lifetime prevalence of PTSD in the general population to be between 1% and 1.3% (Davidson et al., 1991; Helzer et al., 1987), with point prevalence as high as 9.2% in some studies (Breslau et al., 1998). Women are consistently found to be more vulnerable than men to developing PTSD by a factor of 20% (Green et al., 1990; Smith and North, 1988; Steinglass and Gerrity, 1990). In some studies, the risk in women was almost twice as in men (Breslau et al., 1998, 1999).

Women's propensity to PTSD seems to be higher during their reproductive years. Women in the luteal phase of the menstrual cycle – a few days prior to menstruation – show higher heart rate and excessive responses to stress. Hormone and neurosteroid fluctuations at this time might contribute to PTSD symptom development, particularly since premenstrual symptoms and PTSD symptoms are somewhat similar – for example, irritability, anxiety and sleep difficulties (Rasmusson et al., 2004).

Childhood physical, emotional and sexual trauma is considered integral to the development of the PTSD phenomenon. Pathological relationships with caregivers and childhood sexual abuse are more common in women. In adulthood, women are also exposed to a multitude of other traumatic experiences including domestic violence and sexual assault (Breslau et al., 1999; Tjaden and Thoennes, 2000). PTSD has been reported as one of the most prevalent psychiatric disorders among female prison inmates (Islam-Zwart et al., 2005). Some studies have shown a lifetime prevalence of sexual victimisation of 68% in US female prisoners (Zlotnick and Pearlstein, 1997).

However, most of the research that initially influenced the categorisation of and diagnostic criteria for PTSD was conducted on male war veterans. Little at that time related to women subjects. In women, parallel syndromes were described to incorporate symptoms resulting from sexual assaults and domestic violence, such as the rape trauma syndrome (Burgess and Holstrom, 1974) and the battered wife syndrome (Walker, 1984). These syndromes described symptoms not captured within PTSD, including the effects of the assaults on the victim's sense of safety, ability to trust others, self esteem, self worth, frequent revictimisation and loss of coherent sense of self (van der Kolk et al., 2005).

THE SPECTRUM OF POST-TRAUMATIC STRESS DISORDERS

The *Diagnostic and Statistical Manual* (DSM-IV; APA, 1994), and the *International Classification of Diseases* (ICD-10; WHO, 1992) define the immediate syndrome following traumatic exposure as an acute stress disorder or reaction characterised by extreme anxiety features and dissociative symptoms together with features of the three post-traumatic stress (PTS) core symptom clusters.

The notion of "heterogeneity" of PTSD was suggested after it was observed that at one time or another PTSD may appear to mimic every personality disorder (Kolb, 1989). Differences and similarities with multiple personality disorder have been highlighted (Braun, 1993). It has been suggested, therefore, that the concept of a spectrum of post-traumatic disorders might be appropriate for inclusion in future DSM classifications.

The DSM-IV defines acute PTSD as being present if the duration of symptoms is less than three months following exposure to trauma. Chronic PTSD is said to be present if symptoms last for over three months. Both DSM-IV and ICD-10 do not distinguish between the effects of exposure to single versus multiple traumas, although ICD-10 alludes to this in its definition of the category "enduring personality change" following subjection to catastrophic stress (ICD Code F62.0; WHO, 1992). This is said to be more likely to be present in those subjected to multiple trauma in adulthood who go on to develop chronic PTSD, but whose PTSD then resolves, leaving a residual personality change characterised by a hostile or mistrustful attitude towards the world, social withdrawal, feelings of emptiness or hopelessness, a chronic feeling of being on edge as if constantly threatened, and estrangement.

A delayed version of PTSD has been demonstrated in certain groups of trauma victims, such as war veterans, disaster survivors and holocaust survivors (Flak et al., 1994). Delayed PTSD is present if the onset of symptoms takes place more than six months after the trauma. It commonly occurs following exposure to a further trauma or life event. This is because some people cope initially by using a rigid internal problem-solving coping structure, which shifts upon exposure to another trauma to an external and more emotion-focused coping style (Elder and Clipp, 1989; Elder et al., 1994; LaGuardia et al., 1983).

Recently, the issue of complex PTSD has emerged to overlap with borderline personality disorder (BPD), dissociative disorders, somatic symptoms, self identity problems and psychotic disorders (van der Kolk et al., 2005). Complex PTSD was found to be more prevalent in females, and develops following repeated multiple trauma in early development, particularly in those who are repeatedly traumatised before the age of 26 (Roth et al., 1997; van der Kolk et al., 1994).

Exposure to intense, chronic, repeated psychological trauma can precipitate severe forms of PTSD with symptoms reaching psychotic intensity, or precipitate psychotic symptoms and psychotic disorders (Janssen et al., 2004; Mueser et al., 2002).

Evidence for the existence of a complex form of PTSD was derived from survivors of prolonged and repeated trauma (Herman, 1992, 1993). There was a recognition that individuals subjected to repeated trauma such as victims of torture, prisoners in prisoner of war camps, victims of long-standing sexual abuse and victims of repeated (wife) battering, for example, present with psychiatric sequelae over and above the PTSD DSM-IV inclusion criteria. They suffer from multiple symptoms: somatic, cognitive, affective, behavioural, existential and relational (Eitinger, 1961; Turner and Gorst-Unsworth, 1990; Ursano et al., 1987). Judith Herman (1992) asserted therefore that a separate diagnostic PTSD category was needed to incorporate symptom patterns resulting from exposure to repeated traumatic experiences. Herman's work instigated the DSM-IV field trial for PTSD. This studied the relationship between the development of PTSD and a syndrome which also incorporated other psychological difficulties commonly associated with a history of exposure to extreme multiple psychological traumas (van der Kolk et al., 1994). The researchers termed the syndrome DESNOS (disorders of extreme stress not otherwise specified) and found that it incorporated seven main areas of disturbance, comprising dysregulation of:

1   affect and impulses: affect lability, anger/aggression, self mutilation, suicidal preoccupation
2   attention and concentration: dissociation, amnesia, depersonalisation
3   self perception: helplessness, guilt, shame
4   perception of perpetrator: idealisation of the perpetrator or feelings of vengeance
5   relationships with others: isolation, mistrust, victim role, victimisation of others
6   somatisation: gastrointestinal, cardiovascular, chronic pain, conversion
7   systems of meaning: despair, hopelessness, major changes to previously held beliefs.

In all, 328 psychiatric outpatients were interviewed for trauma history and PTSD and DESNOS symptoms. Prevalence of DESNOS symptoms was correlated with PTSD, younger age of onset of traumatisation and duration of traumatic exposure. The trial concluded that DESNOS described a syndrome of psychiatric disturbance related to early, chronic, interpersonal trauma associated with PTSD. The combination of DESNOS and PTSD was termed complex PTSD (van der Kolk et al., 1994, 2005). The DSM-IV field trials supported the notion that prolonged trauma that first occurs at an early age and is of an interpersonal nature can have significant effects on psychological functioning beyond PTSD symptomatology. These effects include problems with affect regulation, aggression against the self and others, dissociative and somatic symptoms, and character pathology (van der Kolk et al., 2005).

The overlap between the phenomenology of complex PTSD and border-line personality disorder (BPD) stems from the fact that both share similarities of symptom pattern, in addition to their propensity to trauma repetition (see Table 4.1). The symptomatology of BPD includes affective and cognitive dysregulation, identity disturbance, psychotic-like symptoms,

Table 4.1 PTSD Symptoms

1	Somatic symptoms	
	Affective symptoms	
	Dissociative symptoms	
2	Character changes:	Traumatic bonding
		Relationship difficulties: lens of extremity – attachment versus withdrawal
3	Identity changes:	Self structures:
		Internalised images of stress
		Malignant sense of self
		Fragmentation of self
4	Repetition of harm:	To self: faulty boundary setting
		By others: battery abuse
		Of others: become abusive

impulsive behaviours including self mutilation, suicidality, substance misuse and disordered eating, and interpersonal psychopathology characterised by unstable relationships that shift between idealisation and devaluation and frantic efforts to avoid real or imagined abandonment (APA, 1994; Zanarini, 2005).

While similarities exist between complex PTSD and BPD, clear distinctive phenomena have been deduced (Gunderson, 1996; Gunderson and Sabo, 1996). For example, in complex PTSD there is a propensity to self-imposed isolation, whereas BPD patients have intense relationships and fears of abandonment.

SPECIFIC KINDS OF TRAUMA: CHILDHOOD SEXUAL ABUSE AND SEXUAL ASSAULT

Between 13% and 25% of women have been found to experience sexual assault sometime in their lives compared to 0.6–7.2% of men (Kilpatrick and Seymour, 1992; Tjaden and Thoennes, 2000). Women with a history of childhood sexual abuse have been found to be more at risk of adult sexual assault than those without such a history. Intimate partner violence (IPV), as defined by Basile et al. (2004), is the use of actual or threatened physical, sexual, psychological or stalking violence by current or former partners of the same sex or the opposite sex.

Exposure to childhood physical and sexual abuse in women gives rise to pronounced guilt and shame as well as self dysfunction. All of these predict revictimisation and may cause recurrent deterioration in women's interpersonal coping and resources later in life (Messman-Moore et al., 2005). Self dysfunction manifests with affect dysregulation, disturbances in intimate and sexual relations and a disrupted sense of self, which follow exposure to repeated abuse (van der Kolk et al., 2005).

Women victims of adult abuse suffer fractures, bruises, miscarriages, knife wounds and gunshot wounds (Crowell and Burgess, 1996). They are more likely to develop chronic pain syndromes, gastrointestinal disorders and psychological problems including depression, substance abuse and low self esteem (Coker et al., 2000; Resnick et al., 1993).

Child sexual abuse and sexual assaults are also known to cause other disorders including substance abuse, borderline and antisocial personality disorders, and eating, affective and sexual disorders (van der Kolk et al., 2005).

Domestic violence and abuse of women gives rise to rates of PTSD between 33% and 84% (Astin et al., 1993; Kemp et al., 1991). The dissociation and emotional numbing characteristic of PTSD may also contribute towards future revictimisation by reducing the victim's ability to notice and process danger cues (Messman-Moore et al., 2005; Sandberg et al., 1999).

In one study, 22% of women surveyed reported physical or sexual abuse during childhood or adolescence (McCauley et al., 1997); in another, 60% of women exposed to childhood sexual abuse developed PTSD in adulthood (Albach and Everaerd, 1992). Childhood sexual abuse is also extremely common in BPD sufferers, with rates ranging between 16% and 75% (Silk et al., 2005), to the extent that some workers have linked PTSD with BPD by virtue of the consistent presence of a history of abuse (Stone, 2005).

History of abuse is a powerful predictor of suicidality – even more than a diagnosis of depression (Read et al., 2001). Childhood sexual abuse victims are also more likely to be repeaters of suicide attempts than PTSD sufferers who did not suffer sexual abuse (Taylor et al., 1994). Self harm by cutting is very common among complex PTSD sufferers (Busuttil, 2006a, 2006b; see also Chapter 3 in this volume).

MODELS FOR UNDERSTANDING TRAUMA REACTIONS

Dissociation model

Janet (1907) observed how victims of trauma became "attached" to the trauma and became unable to integrate the traumatic memory and move on with their lives. For Freud and First World War military psychiatrists (Myers, 1940), dissociation was considered to be at the core of the patho-genesis of PTSD, and working through this dissociation and subsequent reintegration were key elements in the treatment of these disorders (van der Kolk, 1996).

Dissociative processes are now thought of as the central "hub" in the causation and maintenance of complex trauma reactions. Dissociative processes are central features seen in the victims of multiple trauma (Bloom, 1997; Busuttil, 2006a, 2006b; Busuttil and Badat, 2001). Dissociation is a common coping mechanism among children exposed to childhood sexual abuse (Banyard et al., 2001; Butler et al., 1996; Gershuny and Thayer, 1999).

Adolescence may be a transition point for dissociation – the period at which normal dissociative tendencies such as identity confusion and imaginative involvement begin to diminish as adolescents move towards adulthood (Midgley, 2002). Pathological dissociation may interfere with the construction of a coherent sense of self and become fixed into adult dis-sociative disorders. The nature and frequency of adolescent and childhood dissociative disorders has yet to be researched (Armstrong et al., 1997). Traumatisation essentially involves a degree of dissociative division of the personality that occurs along lines of innate action systems of daily life and defence (van der Hart et al., 2005). This trauma-related structural dissociation of the personality is seen by van der Hart et al. (2005) as the central mechanism leading to complex PTSD; this observation is supported by the work of Janet (1907) and Myers (1940), and is related to the aetiological dual representational theory for PTSD proposed by Brewin et al. (1996), which is described below.

Attachment model

Attempts to understand complex forms of traumatic reaction and BPD were largely formulated on the basis of "attachment theory". Bowlby (1979) suggested that the infant's models of attachment of the self with caregivers dictate the patterns of all future attachments and relationships. The security of this attachment is responsible for regulating feelings and achieving emotional homeostasis late in life (Bowlby, 1979; Fonagy, 2002; Silk et al., 2005). Bowlby suggested that the infant's experiences with its caregiver(s) become organised into internalised working models of attachment of the self with others, and that these become prototypes for future attachments and relationships. Two patterns of disturbed attachment can occur: the first comprises emotional overinvolvement with a parent, and the other a role reversal with the parent (Silk et al., 2005).

Gunderson (1996) considers that the BPD patient's fear of abandonment and inability to tolerate aloneness have their roots in insecure attachments. Attachment theory has been seen as one of the models explaining some components of complex PTSD. Developmental failure in the child, resulting from deprivation and abuse, leads to internal splitting of the parent into a good, idealised and greatly needed attachment figure and a bad, rejecting and traumatising figure. This split identification is clearly seen in those suffering from BPD and complex PTSD (De Zulueta, 2002).

Memory models

Dual representation theory (Brewin et al., 1996) suggests that trauma memories are of two distinct types: verbally accessible memory (VAM), equivalent to explicit or declarative memory, and situationally accessible memory (SAM), equivalent to implicit or non-declarative memory. This model differentiates the cognitive processes occurring during the trauma exposure from the cognitive appraisals occurring afterwards.

Peri-traumatic images, appraisals and emotions are processed largely automatically and less consciously by the SAM system when something of the content of the original trauma crops up post-trauma. This accounts for the re-experiencing symptoms of PTSD, including flashbacks. They can be triggered by any perceptual modality (for example a noise or a smell) and lead to re-experiencing symptoms in any sensory modality including somatic manifestations. In contrast, the VAM system attempts to process information coherently and tries to reconstruct a detailed representation of the trauma. This theory introduces an integrative cognitive-behavioural model for treatment, attempting to address cognitions as well as automatic triggers and subsequent re-experiencing symptoms.

Elhers and Clark (2000) proposed a different cognitive model for PTSD, termed "mental defeat". Their model is also related to poorly elaborated memory formation, with an emphasis on traumatised negative affective appraisal, which operates during and after traumatisation. The disclosure of a coherent and reliable trauma narrative is usually an integral part of most psychotherapeutic approaches to the treatment of trauma victims.

More recently, further attempts to understand the memory of the traumatised used biological techniques such as neuroimaging, by exposing PTSD sufferers to visual stimuli pertaining to their original traumas. The studies showed evidence of malfunction in the non-dominant hemisphere, in the so-called "narrative centre" or Broca's area (Pitman, 2000; Shalev, 2001). Earlier studies demonstrated malfunction in the limbic system, particularly the amygdala and hippocampus, also known as the emotional centres of the brain (van der Kolk, 1996). This reflects the high emotional loading of the content of the traumatic material, as well as the difficulty the traumatised experience when trying to recall and construct an accurate trauma narrative (Hull, 2002; Pitman, 2000; Shalev, 2001). This is the basis of the biological-cognitive models of PTSD, which see trauma reaction as fundamentally a memory disorder characterised by fragmented, unprocessed, timeless and ego-alien memories, as well as an inability to lay down those traumatic memories and express them cohesively (Brewin and Holmes, 2003; van der Kolk, 1996).

In Bloom's (1997) model for the development of complex PTSD, the trauma victim is viewed as trapped in the time of the trauma. This is reinforced by continual re-experiencing of the trauma, which is integral to the trauma response. This "time-entrapment" gives rise to automatic memory formation which includes exaggerated memory responses that lead, in turn, to emotional numbing, aggression and avoidance symptoms. Maladaptive coping patterns emerge, using autohypnotic dissociation, amounting to amnesia as a defensive mechanism in response to the overwhelming traumatic event (Putnam and Carlson, 1998; van der Hart et al., 2005). When the trauma is over and the environment is normalised, such dissociative coping mechanisms are difficult to unlearn and become part of the personality. They can in turn lead to learned helplessness and depression.

TRAUMA REACTIONS: ASSESSMENT AND INTERVENTION

Multi-modal assessment of simple and complex PTSD should be standard practice for clinical, research and medico-legal purposes (Briere and

Spinazzola, 2005; Scott and Sembi, 2002). This includes taking a thorough psychiatric history, including trauma history, and a mental state examination with subjective (self report) and objective (clinician administered) psychometric evaluation (Newman and Lee, 1997). For assessment of simple PTSD, trauma exposure inventories such as the Traumatic Events Scale (Elliott, 1992) are used alongside the Clinician Administered PTSD Scale (CAPS; Blake et al., 1990). The Impact of Events Scale (IES) is another useful screening tool, as are the General Health Questionnaire-28 (GHQ-28) and the Beck Depression Inventory (BDI; Beck et al., 1979; Goldberg and Hillier, 1979; Horowitz et al., 1979).

Psychotherapeutic interventions include trauma-focused cognitive-behavioural therapy (TF-CBT). This deals with identification of the trauma and modification of the threat and belief system surrounding the victim's experience of the trauma (Harvey et al., 2003; Rothbaum et al., 2000). Eye movement desensitisation and reprocessing (EMDR) involves instructing the patient to hold in mind a disturbing image, an associated negative cognition and bodily sensations associated with a traumatic memory, while eye tracking the clinician's finger, which is waved in close proximity in his or her visual field. This is repeated until distressing aspects of the traumatic memory reduce and more adaptive cognitions emerge relating to the trauma. Alternative positive cognitions, coping strategies and adaptive behaviours are installed (Shapiro, 1995). Controversy surrounds the theoretical underpinning of EMDR, including whether the eye movements are essential, and whether EMDR is just another form of behavioural exposure (Blake and Sonnenberg, 1998). Nevertheless, randomised controlled trial evidence for EMDR's effectiveness is good (Chentomb et al., 2000). Comparison studies between CBT and EMDR demonstrate that CBT is more efficacious, both statistically and clinically post-treatment and at follow-up (Devilley and Spence, 1999).

Psychotherapy for complex PTSD presents greater challenges. De Zulueta's (2002) model of intervention at the Maudsley Trauma Therapy Unit uses individual psychodynamic psychotherapies to deal with interpersonal and attachment issues before using TF-CBT. This model of initial stabilisation, trauma-focused disclosure and rehabilitation or reintegration is well recognised within the field, and was initially suggested by Bloom (1997). Models using initial stabilisation with medications and intensive trauma psychoeducation, followed by disclosure and rehabilitation, have also been used (Busuttil, 2006a, 2006b).

Dialectic behavioural therapy (DBT; Linehan, 1993) was devised for the treatment of borderline personality disorder, but can be useful in helping patients with complex PTSD. The main objective is to help sufferers to learn boundaries, regulate emotions and help with interpersonal relationship difficulties, before they embark on trauma-focused psychotherapy (refer to Chapter 17 in this volume). It also facilitates disclosure work, as it helps the patient to confront the traumatic episode/s and process a trauma narrative. The issue of disclosure may be very disabling for the patient and may lead to impulsive self-harming behaviour. It requires therefore a particular safety strategy to reconstruct traumatic memories along the lines of Bloom's (1997) "sanctuary" treatment model, which emphasises the importance of safety and stabilisation (Busuttil, 2000, 2006a, 2006b).

Pharmacotherapy can be used to stabilise patients suffering from severe forms of PTSD, to allow psychotherapy to take place, and can then be stopped. Combinations of medications are frequently used in cases of severe chronic PTSD, complex PTSD or PTSD with psychotic presentations (Busuttil, 2006a, 2006b). Useful medications are: selective serotonergic reuptake inhibitor (SSRI) antidepressants, mood stabilisers and neuroleptics, including the newer atypicals as well as clozapine, prescribed for severe self harm as well as severe psychotic-like symptoms. Beta-blockers and the alpha agonist clonidine may be useful in reducing impulsivity (Davidson and van der Kolk, 1996; Friedman et al., 2000). The pharmacological treatment of borderline personality disorder also includes all these medications (Frankenberg, 2005).

CONCLUSIONS

This chapter offers a broad framework of the nature of trauma and subsequent trauma syndromes. The history of PTSD initially focused on male veterans, which has led to some limitations in current definitions and formal classification systems. Women are now recognised to be more vulnerable than men to trauma syndromes, particularly complex PTSD. Women tend to experience more multiple trauma in their lifetimes, particularly childhood sexual abuse, adult sexual assault and domestic violence in general.

Models for understanding PTSD revolve around issues of trauma perception, dissociation and memory processing. Attachment history and relational difficulties influence the complexity of symptom formation. PTS symptom severity and chronicity are related to the dose response effect of exposure as well as the level of peri-traumatic dissociation. Therapeutic interventions follow mainly psychotherapeutic lines and include dynamic psychotherapy, dialectical behavioural therapy and trauma-focused cognitive-behavioural therapy.

REFERENCES

Albach, F. and Everaerd, W. (1992) Post-traumatic stress symptoms in victims of childhood incest, *Psychotherapy and Psychosomatics*, 57 (4), 143–151.

American Psychiatric Association (1994) *Diagnostic and statistical manual of mental disorders* (4th edn) (DSM-IV), Washington, DC, APA.

Armstrong, J., Putnam, F., Carlson, E., Libero, D. and Smith, S. (1997) Development and validation of a measure of adolescent dissociation: The adolescent dissociative experiences scale, *Journal of Nervous and Mental Diseases*, 185 (8), 491–497.

Astin, M. C., Lawrence, K. J. and Foy, D. W. (1993) Posttraumatic stress disorder among battered women: Risk and resiliency factors, *Violence and Victims*, 8 (1), 17–28.

Banyard, V. L., Williams, L. M. and Siegel, J. A. (2001) The long-term mental health consequences of childhood sexual abuse: An exploratory study of the impact of multiple traumas in a sample of women, *Journal of Traumatic Stress*, 14 (4), 697–715.

Basile, K. C., Arias, I., Desai, S. and Thompson, M. P. (2004) The differential association of intimate partner physical, sexual, psychological and stalking violence and post traumatic stress symptoms in a nationally representative sample of women, *Journal of Traumatic Stress*, 17 (5), 413–421.

Beck, A. T., Rush, A. and Shaw, B. F. (1979) *Cognitive therapy of depression*, New York, Guilford Press.

Blake, D. D. and Sonnenberg, R. T. (1998) Outcome research on behavioral and cognitive-behavioral treatments for trauma survivors, in V. M. Follette, J. I. Ruzek and F. R. Abueg (eds) *Cognitive behavioural therapies for trauma*, pp. 15–47, New York, Guilford Press.

Blake, D. D., Weathers, F. W., Nagy, L. N., Kalopek, D. G., Kaluminser, G., Charney, D. S. and Keane, T. (1990) A clinician rating scale for assessing current and lifetime PTSD: The CAPS-1, *Behavioural Therapy*, 13, 187–188.

Bloom, S. (1997) *Creating sanctuary: Toward the evolution of sane societies*, London, Routledge.

Bowlby, R. (1979) *The making and breaking of affectional bonds*, London, Routledge.

Braun, B. G. (1993) Multiple personality disorder and post traumatic stress disorder, in J. P. Wilson and B. Raphael (eds) *International handbook of traumatic stress syndromes*, pp. 35–47, New York, Plenum Press.

Breslau, N., Chilcoat, H. D., Kessler, R. C., Peterson, E. L. and Lucia, V. C. (1999) Vulnerability to assaultive violence: Further specification of the sex difference in post-traumatic stress disorder, *Psychological Medicine*, 29, 813–821.

Breslau, N., Kessler, R. C., Chilcoat, H. D., Schultz, L. R., Davis, G. C. and Andreski, P. (1998) Trauma and posttraumatic stress disorder in the community: The 1996 Detroit area survey of trauma, *American Journal of Psychiatry*, 55 (7), 626–632.

Brewin, C. R. and Holmes, E. A. (2003) Psychological theories of post traumatic stress disorder, *Clinical Psychology Review*, 23 (3), 339–376.

Brewin, C. R., Dalgliesh, T. and Joseph, S. (1996) A dual representation theory of post traumatic stress disorder, *Psychology Review*, 103 (4), 670–686.

Briere, J. and Spinazzola, J. (2005) Phenomenology and psychological assessment of complex posttraumatic states, *Journal of Traumatic Stress*, 18 (5), 401–412.

Burgess, A. W. and Holmstrom, L. L. (1974) Rape trauma syndrome, *American Journal of Psychiatry*, 131 (9), 981–986.

Busuttil, W. (2000) *Group approaches in the treatment of simple and complex PTSD in victims of incarceration: Approaches used in recent release of Australian care workers*, Abstract 315 at the Third World International Conference of the International Society for Traumatic Stress Studies, Melbourne, Australia.

Busuttil, W. (2006a) The development of a 90-day residential program for the treatment of complex posttraumatic stress disorder, in M. B. Williams and J. Garrick (eds) *Trauma treatment techniques: Innovative trends*, pp. 29–55, New York, Haworth Press.

Busuttil, W. (2006b) The development of a 90-day residential program for the treatment of complex posttraumatic stress disorder, *Journal of Aggression, Maltreatment and Trauma*, 12 (1/2), 29–55.

Busuttil, W. and Badat, O. (2001, May) *Treating severe complex PTSD using a structured residential 90-day rehabilitation programme*, Abstract at the European Society for Traumatic Stress Studies, Seventh European Conference on Traumatic Stress, Edinburgh.

Butler, L. D., Duran, R. E., Jasiukaitis, P., Koopman, C. and Spiegal, D. (1996) Hypnotizability and traumatic experience: A diathesis-stress model of dissociative symptomatology, *American Journal of Psychiatry*, 144 (11), 1426–1430.

Chentomb, C. M., Tolin, D. F., van der Kolk, B. A. and Pitman, R. K. (2000) Eye movement desensitisation and reprocessing, in E. B. Foa, T. M. Keane and M. J. Friedman (eds) *Effective treatments for PTSD: Practice guidelines from the International Society for Traumatic Stress Studies*, pp. 139–145, New York, Guilford Press.

Coker, A. L., Smith, P. H., Bethea, L., King, M. R. and McKeown, R. E. (2000) Physical health consequences of physical and psychological intimate partner violence, *Archives of Family Medicine*, 9 (5), 451–457.

Crowell, N. A. and Burgess, A. W. (1996) *Understanding violence against women*, Washington, DC, National Academy Press.

Davidson, J. R. T. and van der Kolk, B. A. (1996) The psychopharmacological treatment of posttraumatic stress disorder, in B. A. van der Kolk, A. MacFarlane and L. Weisaeth (eds) *Traumatic stress: The effects of overwhelming experience on the mind, body and society*, pp. 510–524, New York, Guilford Press.

Davidson, J. R. T., Hughes, D., Blazer, D. and George, L. K. (1991) Post-traumatic stress disorder in the community: An epidemiological study, *Psychological Medicine*, 21 (1), 713–721.

Devilly, G. J. and Spence, S. H. (1999) The relative efficacy and treatment distress of EMDR and cognitive behavioural trauma treatment protocol in the amelioration of post traumatic stress disorder, *Journal of Anxiety Disorders*, 13 (1–2): 131–158.

de Zulueta, F. (2002) Post-traumatic stress disorder and dissociation: The traumatic stress service in the Maudsley hospital, in V. Sinason (ed.) *Attachment, trauma and multiplicity: Working with dissociative identity disorder*, pp. 52–67, Hove, Brunner-Routledge.

Eitinger, L. (1961) Pathology of the concentration camp syndrome, *Archives of General Psychiatry*, 5, 371–379.

Elder, G. H. and Clipp, E. C. (1989) Combat experience and emotional health: Impairment and resilience in later life, *Journal of Personality*, 57, 311–341.

Elder, G. H., Shanahan, M. J. and Clipp, E. C. (1994) When war comes to men's lives: Life course patterns in the family, *Psychology of Aging*, 9 (2), 5–16.

Elhers, A. and Clark, D. (2000) A cognitive model of post traumatic stress disorder, *Behavioural Research Therapy*, 38 (4), 319–345.

Elliott, D. M. (1992) *Traumatic events survey*, Unpublished manuscript, UCLA Medical Center, Los Angeles, CA.

Flak, B., Hersen, M. and van Hasselt, V. B. (1994) Assessment of post traumatic stress disorder in older adults: A critical review, *Clinical Psychology Review*, 14 (5), 383–415.

Fonagy, P. (2002) Multiple voices versus meta-cognition: An attachment theory perspective, in V. Sinason (ed.) *Attachment, trauma and multiplicity: Working with dissociative identity disorder*, pp. 71–85, Hove, Brunner-Routledge.

Frankenberg, F. R. (2005) Pharmacotherapy of borderline personality disorder, in M. C. Zanarini (ed.) *Borderline personality disorder*, pp. 243–257, London, Taylor and Francis.

Friedman, M. J., Davidson, J. R. T., Mellman, T. A. and Southwick, S. M. (2000) Pharmacotherapy, in E. B. Foa, T. M. Keane and M. J. Friedman (eds) *Effective treatments for PTSD: Practice guidelines from the International Society for Traumatic Stress Studies*, pp. 84–105, New York, Guilford Press.

Gershuny, B. S. and Thayer, J. F. (1999) Relations among psychological trauma, dissociative phenomena, and trauma-related distress: A review and integration, *Clinical Psychology Review*, 19 (5), 631–657.

Goldberg, D. P. and Hillier, V. F. (1979) A scaled version of the General Health Questionnaire, *Psychological Medicine*, 9 (1), 139–145.

Green, B. L., Lindy, J. D. and Grace, M. C. (1990) Buffalo Creek survivors in the second decade: Stability of stress symptoms, *American Journal of Orthopsychiatry*, 60 (1), 43–54.

Gunderson, J. (1996) The borderline patient's intolerance of aloneness: Insecure attachments and therapist availability, *American Journal of Psychiatry*, 153 (1), 752–758.

Gunderson, J. and Sabo, A. N. (1996) The phenomenological and conceptual interface between borderline personality disorder and PTSD, *American Journal of Psychiatry*, 150 (1), 19–27.

Harvey, A. G., Bryant, R. A. and Tarrier, N. (2003) Cognitive behaviour therapy for post traumatic stress disorder, *Clinical Psychology Review*, 23 (3), 501–522.

Helzer, J. E., Robins, L. N. and McEvoy, L. (1987) Post-traumatic stress disorder in the general population: Findings of the epidemiological catchment area survey, *New England Journal of Medicine*, 317, 1630–1634.

Herman, J. L. (1992) Complex PTSD: A syndrome in survivors of prolonged and repeated trauma, *Journal of Traumatic Stress*, 5 (3), 377–391.

Herman, J. L. (1993) Sequelae of prolonged and repeated trauma: Evidence for a complex post traumatic syndrome (DESNOS), in J. R. T. Davidson and E. B. Foa (eds) *Posttraumatic stress disorder: DSM-IV and beyond*, pp. 213–228, Washington, DC, American Psychiatric Press.

Horowitz, M. J., Wilner, N. and Alvarez, W. (1979) Impact of event scale: A measure of subjective stress, *Psychosomatic Medicine*, 41 (3), 209–218.

Hull, A. M. (2002) Neuroimaging findings in post traumatic stress disorder: Systematic review, *British Journal of Psychiatry*, 181 (2), 102–110.

Islam-Zwart, K. A., Heath, N. M. and Vik, P. W. (2005) Facial recognition performance of female inmates as a result of sexual assault history, *Journal of Traumatic Stress*, 18 (3), 263–266.

Janet, P. (1907) *The major symptoms of hysteria*, New York, Macmillan.

Janoff-Bulman, R. (1985) The aftermath of victimisation: Rebuilding shattered assumptions, in C. R. Figley (ed.) *Trauma and its wake: The study and treatment of post traumatic stress disorder*, Vol. 1, pp. 15–35, New York, Brunner Mazel.

Janssen, I., Krabbendam, L., Bak, M., Hanssen, M., Vollebergh, W., de Graaf, R. and van Os, J. (2004) Childhood abuse as a risk factor for psychotic experiences, *Acta Psychiatrica Scandinavica*, 109 (11), 38–45.

Kemp, A., Rawlings, E. I. and Green, B. L. (1991) Posttraumatic stress disorder (PTSD) in battered women: A shelter sample, *Journal of Traumatic Stress*, 4 (1), 137–148.

Kilpatrick, D. G. and Seymour, A. (1992) *Rape in America: A report to the nation*, Technical report, Arlington, VA, National Victims Center, and Charleston, SC, Treatment Center.

Kolb, L. C. (1989) Letter to the editor, *American Journal of Psychiatry*, 146 (6), 811–812.

LaGuardia, R. L., Smith, G., Francois, R. and Bachman, L. (1983) Incidence of delayed stress disorder among Vietnam era veterans: The effect of priming on response set, *American Journal of Orthopsychiatry*, 53, 18–25.

Linehan, M. M. (1993) *Cognitive behavioural treatment for borderline personality disorder*, New York, Guilford Press.

McCauley, J., Kern, D. E., Kolonder, K., Dill, L., Schroeder, A. F. and DeChant, H. K. (1997) Clinical characteristics of women with a history of childhood abuse, *Journal of the American Medical Association*, 277 (17), 1362–1368.

Messman-Moore, T. L., Brown, A. L. and Koelsch, L. E. (2005) Post traumatic symptom and self-dysfunction as consequences and predictors of sexual revictimization, *Journal of Traumatic Stress*, 18 (3), 253–261.

Meuser, K. T., Rosenberg, S. D., Goodman, L. A. and Trumbetta, S. L. (2002) Trauma, PTSD and the course of severe mental illness: An interactive model, *Schizophrenia Research*, 53 (1–2), 123–143.

Midgley, N. (2002) Child dissociation has its roots in adulthood, in V. Sinason (ed.) *Attachment, trauma and multiplicity: Working with dissociative identity disorder*, pp. 35–51, Hove, Brunner Routledge.

Myers, C. S. (1940) *Shellshock in France 1914–1918*, Cambridge, Cambridge University Press.

Newman, M. and Lee, D. (1997) Diagnosis and treatment, in D. Black, M. Newman, J. Harris-Hendricks and G. Mezey (eds) *Psychological trauma: A developmental approach*, pp. 219–229, London, Royal College of Psychiatrists Gaskell.

Pitman, R. (2000, October) *Neuroimaging findings in PTSD*, Paper presented at Trapped by trauma: Dissociation and other responses, Defence Medical Services Psychological Injuries Unit International Conference, York.

Putnam, F. W. and Carlson, E. B. (1998) Hypnosis, dissociation, and trauma: Myths, metaphors, and mechanisms, in J. D. Bremner and C. R. Marmar (eds) *Trauma memory and dissociation*, pp. 27–55, Washington, DC, American Psychiatric Press.

Rasmusson, A. M., Vasek, J., Lipschitz, D. S., Vojvoda, D., Mustone, M. E., Shi,

Q., Gudmundsen, G., Morgan, C. A., Wolfe Dennis, J. and Charney, S. (2004) An increased capacity for adrenal DHEA release is associated with decreased avoidance and negative mood symptoms in women with PTSD, *Neuropsychopharmacology*, 29 (8), 1546–1557.

Read, J., Agar, K., Barker-Collo, S., Davies, E. and Moskowitz, A. (2001) Assessing suicidality in adults: Integrating childhood trauma as a major risk factor, *Professional Psychiatry Research and Practice*, 32, 367–372.

Resnick, H., Kilpatrick, D., Dansky, B., Saunders, B. and Best, C. (1993) Prevalence of civilian trauma and posttraumatic stress disorder in a representative national sample of women, *Journal of Consulting and Clinical Psychology*, 61 (6), 984–991.

Roth, S., Newman, E., Pelcovitz, D., van der Kolk, B. A. and Mandel, F. (1997) Complex PTSD in victims exposed to sexual and physical abuse: Results from the DSM-IV field trial for posttraumatic stress disorder, *Journal of Traumatic Stress*, 10 (4), 539–556.

Rothbaum, B. O., Meadows, E. A., Resick, P. and Foy, D. W. (2000) Cognitive-behavioural therapy, in E. B. Foa, T. M. Keane and M. J. Friedman (eds) *Effective treatments for PTSD: Practice guidelines from the International Society for Traumatic Stress Studies*, pp. 60–83, New York, Guilford Press.

Sandberg, D. A., Matorin, A. I. and Lynn, S. J. (1999) Dissociation, posttraumatic symptomatology, and sexual revictimisation: A prospective examination of mediator and moderator effects, *Journal of Traumatic Stress*, 12 (1), 127–138.

Scott, M. J. and Sembi. S. (2002) Unreliable assessment in civil litigation, *The Psychologist*, 15, 80–81.

Shalev, A. (2001, May) Keynote address to the ESTSS Seventh European Conference on Traumatic Stress Studies, Edinburgh.

Shapiro, F. (1995) *Eye movement desensitisation and reprocessing: Basic principles*, New York, Guilford Press.

Silk, K. R., Wolf, T. L., Ben-Ami, D. A. and Poortinga, E. W. (2005) Environmental factors in the etiology of borderline personality disorder, in M. C. Zanarini (ed.) *Borderline personality disorder*, pp. 41–62, London, Taylor and Francis Group.

Smith, E. M. and North, C. S. (1988) *Aftermath of a disaster: Psychological response to the Indianapolis Ramda jet crash* (quick response research report 23), Boulder, CO, Natural Hazards Research and Applications Information Center.

Steinglass, P. and Gerrity, E. (1990). Natural disasters and post-traumatic stress disorder: Short-term versus long-term recovery in two disaster-affected communities, *Journal of Applied Social Psychology*, 20, 1746–1756.

Stone, M. H. (2005) Borderline personality disorder: History of a concept, in M. C. Zanarini (ed.) *Borderline personality disorder*, pp. 1–18, London, Taylor and Francis Group.

Taylor, C. J., Kent, G. C. and Huws, R. W. (1994) A comparison of the background of first time and repeated overdose patients, *Journal of Accident and Emergency Medicine*, 11, 238–242.

Tjaden, P. and Thoennes, N. (2000) *Full report of the prevalence, incidence, and consequences of violence against women* (National Institute of Justice research report NCJ no. 183781), Washington, DC, US Department of Justice.

Turner, S. and Gorst-Unsworth, C. (1990) Psychological sequelae of torture: A descriptive model, *British Journal of Psychiatry*, 157, 475–480.

Ursano, R. J., Wheatley, R. D., Carlson, E. H. and Rahe, A. J. (1987) The prisoner of war: Stress illness and resiliency, *Psychiatric Annals*, 17, 532–535.

van der Hart, O., Nijenhuis, E. R. S. and Steele, K. (2005) Dissociation: An insufficiently recognized major feature of complex posttraumatic stress disorder, *Journal of Traumatic Stress*, 18 (5), 413–423.

van der Kolk, B. A. (1996) Trauma and memory, in B. A. van der Kolk, A. C. MacFarlane and L. Weisaeth (eds) *Traumatic stress: The effects of overwhelming experience on the mind, body and society*, pp. 279–302, New York, Guilford Press.

van der Kolk, B. A., Roth, S., Pelcovitz, D. and Mandel, F. (1994) *Complex post traumatic stress disorder: Results from the DSM-IV field trial for PTSD*, Washington, DC, APA.

van der Kolk, B. A., Roth, S., Pelcovitz, D., Sunday, S. and Spinazzola, J. (2005) Disorders of extreme stress: The empirical foundation of a complex adaptation to trauma, *Journal of Traumatic Stress*, 18 (5), 389–399.

Walker, L. E. (1984) *The battered wife syndrome*, New York, Springer.

World Health Organization (1982) *Classification of mental and behavioural disorders: Clinical descriptions and diagnostic guidelines* (ICD-10) (10th edn), Geneva, World Health Organization.

Zanarini, M. C. (2005) The subsyndromal phenomenology of borderline personality disorder, in M. C. Zanarini (ed.) *Borderline personality disorder*, pp. 19–40, London, Taylor and Francis Group.

Zlotnick, C. and Pearlstein, T. (1997) Posttraumatic stress disorder (PTSD), PTSD comorbidity, and childhood abuse among incarcerated women, *Journal of Nervous and Mental Disease*, 185 (12), 761–763.

Chapter 5

The trauma of self starvation

Eating disorders and body image

Janet Treasure

INTRODUCTION

Self starvation is a form of body deprivation that is used to exercise control over the need for food, which in due course may lead to physical harm or even death. Other forms of self inflicted harm are also commonly encountered in patients with eating disorders (Favaro and Santonastaso, 1998; Lacey and Evans, 1986; Welch and Fairburn, 1996).

The relationship between eating disorders and self harm goes beyond simple statistical association. Both are typical of females and their onset often occurs during adolescence (Favazza, 1998). Both self harm and eating disorders could be interpreted as being linked to body dissatisfaction, ascetism or a pervading sense of ineffectiveness, which often implies an element of self punishment. Patients with eating disorders display various unhealthy weight-control practices that are self injurious, such as fasting, self induced vomiting, laxative abuse and diuretic abuse.

The framing of eating disorders has been a subject of debate. The various names given over time have reflected beliefs about aetiology and psychopathology. A psychological conceptualisation with a recognition of gender-related aspects was first apparent in the nineteenth century in Gull's description of "apepsia hysterica" (Gull, 1868). He changed the name later to "anorexia nervosa" to reflect his view of the central origin of the disorder (Gull, 1874).

Eating disorders expanded from the historical accounts, which were of restricting anorexia nervosa, to include a variety of disorders typified by the chaotic pattern of eating of the binge eating disorders. Gerald Russell (1979) described bulimia nervosa as a condition which included periodic overeating coupled with excessive concerns about weight and shape leading to behaviours to compensate for the effects of eating (Russell, 1979). He considered bulimia nervosa to be an "ominous variant" of anorexia nervosa. However, although there is movement across the diagnosis spectrum, this does not follow an inevitable pattern and the majority of cases of bulimia nervosa are not preceded by an episode of anorexia nervosa.

Eating disorders are one of the groups of psychiatric conditions with a marked sex bias. Both anorexia nervosa and bulimia nervosa are 10 times more common in females than in males. However, when a wider definition of eating problems is used, including binge eating disorder, this ratio falls to 3:1. Interestingly, the ratio is also less marked at 3:1 in prepubertal cases of anorexia nervosa. These gender differences have to be explained by models of causation. Biological, developmental and sociocultural factors have been implicated.

There is a degree of uncertainty about classification. However, in this chapter we use the broad anorexia nervosa and bulimia nervosa subgroups. These disorders have a major impact on both physical and psychological health. Also, they disrupt maturation as they occur during a critical developmental phase.

Guidelines for the management of these disorders have been produced in several countries; however, many of the recommendations are not firmly evidence-based.

EATING DISORDER CLASSIFICATION

The DSM-IV and ICD-10 classification systems for eating disorders are shown in Table 5.1. Binge eating disorder is not yet considered a separate category in the DSM-IV criteria. Eating disorder not otherwise specified is a large "catch-all" category. It can include people in the entry or resolving phase of the illness (especially for anorexia nervosa, where change occurs slowly). It also includes disorders which cause clinical impairment and yet do not meet the frequency, severity or duration criteria to be classified as full syndromes.

In DSM-IV, anorexia nervosa was subclassified into the restricting and binge purge subtypes. The validity of this remains uncertain but the binge purge subtype shares many aetiological elements with the bulimic disorders. Indeed, a proportion of people with binge purge anorexia nervosa have an initial phase of bulimia nervosa. A third of cases of anorexia nervosa transform into a bulimic disorder within five years. This appears to be particularly the case if there have been traits linked to bulimia nervosa, such as disinhibition of eating earlier in development, a more robust appetite, a tendency to obesity and high levels of parental criticism (Tozzi et al., 2005).

ANOREXIA NERVOSA: RISK FACTORS AND CLINICAL CONCEPTUALISATIONS

Anorexia occurs in 0.2–0.5% of women. It is rare in men, who comprise fewer than 10% of the cases. It usually begins in mid adolescence. The

Table 5.1 Classification systems for eating disorders

DSM-IV-R Anorexia nervosa 307.1	ICD-10 F50.0
Refusal to maintain body weight over a minimal norm, leading to body weight less than 85% of that expected or failure to make expected weight gain during a period of growth	Body weight is maintained at least 15% below that expected (either lost or never achieved) or Quetelets body mass index at < 17.5 kg/m^2; prepubertal patients may show failure to make the expected weight gain during the period of growth
Intense fear of gaining weight or becoming fat	Weight loss self-induced by avoid fattening foods; one or more of the following may also be present: • vomiting • purging • excessive exercise • appetite suppressants • diuretics
Disturbance in the way in which one's body weight, size or shape is experienced e.g. "feeling fat" (denial of the seriousness of being underweight, or undue influence of body weight and shape on self evaluation)	Body image distortion in the form of a specific psychopathology, whereby a dread of fatness persists as an intrusive overvalued idea and the patient imposes a low weight threshold on herself
In post menarchal females amenorrhoea, i.e. absence of at least three consecutive menstrual cycles	Widespread endocrine disorder: • amenorrhoea in women or loss of sexual interest and potency in men • raised growth hormone • raised cortisol • reduced T3 If onset is prepubertal the sequence of pubertal events is delayed or arrested

continues overleaf

incidence in primary care in the UK has been stable over the last 20 years at 20 per 100,000 in females aged 10–39.

Anorexia nervosa normally clusters with other internalising disorders. High levels of comorbidity with depression have been reported, perhaps as a secondary effect of starvation. Anorexia nervosa has also been linked to the obsessive compulsive spectrum of disorders. Obsessive compulsive personality traits manifest early in development (Anderluh et al., 2003), present after recovery (Bastiani et al., 1995; Matsunaga et al., 2000; Srinivasagam et al., 1995) and impact on outcome (Lock et al., 2005). Gillberg and colleagues suggest that there may also be a link with the autistic spectrum of disorders (Gillberg et al., 1996). The common features between the OCD and autistic

Table 5.1 Continued

DSM-IV-R Bulimia nervosa 307.51	ICD-10 F50.2
Recurrent episodes of binge eating	A persistent preoccupation with eating, and an irresistible craving for food; the patient succumbs to episodes of overeating in which large amounts of food are consumed in a short time
Recurrent inappropriate compensatory behaviour in order to prevent weight gain such as vomiting, misuse of laxatives, diuretics, enemas or other medications, fasting or excessive exercise	The patient attempts to counteract the fattening effects of food by one or more of the following: • vomiting • purging • alternating periods of starvation • use of appetite suppressants, diuretics or thyroid preparations. When bulimia occurs in diabetic patients they may choose to neglect their insulin treatment
Binge eating and inappropriate compensatory behaviours both occur on average at least twice a week for three months	The psychopathology consists of a morbid dread of fatness and the patient imposes a low weight threshold on herself well below the premorbid weight that constitutes the optimum or healthy weight
Self evaluation is unduly influenced by body shape and weight	
The disturbance does not occur exclusively during episodes of anorexia nervosa	

clusters of disorders and eating disorders are obsessive compulsive personality traits. In this case, thoughts about food and weight become entangled with anxiety and exaggerated concerns about harm to the self or some other overvalued meaning.

The quality of evidence from risk factor studies is for the most part weak; however, an excellent systematic review has collated all work in progress (Jacobi et al., 2004).

Biological models of anorexia nervosa show the female of the species in animal studies to be the one most severely affected (Connan and Treasure, 1998; Owen, 1998). This suggests that gender-related biology shapes the disorder. Of the genetic risk factors, being female is the most important. Linkage to chromosome 1 has been reported in families with restricting anorexia nervosa (Grice et al., 2002). A meta analysis of the results from candidate gene studies implicates anomalies in the 5 HT system (Gorwood et al., 2003). However, the effect size found from candidate gene studies is small.

A variety of environmental factors including adversities in pregnancy, birth-related complications and high-concern parenting (where the parents appear to have high levels of anxiety) increase the risk. Triggering factors include nutritional stress (caused by levels of exercise and/or dieting behaviour) in combination with hassles or life events occurring in the context of the developmental changes linked to puberty and early adolescence (including the biological maturation of the brain and social development) (Southgate et al., 2005). Cultural factors related to body image probably play less of a role in the causation of anorexia nervosa than in the causation of bulimia nervosa, and are therefore considered later.

Anorexia nervosa in the main has a prolonged course (the median duration of illness is six years), and so the factors that contribute to this persistence are highly relevant because they can inform treatment approaches. Schmidt and Treasure have detailed a model of maintenance of anorexia nervosa that includes four maintaining factors (Schmidt and Treasure, 2005). These include:

1   the reactions of close others exemplified by the features of high expressed emotion (overprotection and criticism);
2   compulsive traits, rigidity and perfectionism;
3   high anxiety and avoidance;
4   a prolonged period of starvation with a cascade of biological, psychological and psychosocial consequences.

A variety of clinical conceptualisations have been developed, but few are evidence-based. Bruch developed a psychodynamic hypothesis centred on insecure attachment and lack of attunement between the infant and the caretaker (Bruch, 1973), and there is evidence supporting this (Ward et al., 2000, 2001). Some feminists have argued that there may be gender differences in this interactional process between the mother and her child, where the mother has difficulty recognising her daughter's needs because she is supposedly the same. Speculative family models have thus been created (Eisler and Asen, 2003). The Maudsley model is a manualised form of family treatment (Lock et al., 2001) evolved from the evidence implicating expressed emotion as a key factor in maintenance. Cognitive behavioural formulations for anorexia nervosa have also been described (Waller and Kennerley, 2003), but as yet they have not been found to be highly efficacious or acceptable when they have been translated into treatment. Neurodevelopmental models have been developed (Connan et al., 2003; Southgate et al., 2005) and translated into treatment (Treasure et al., 2005).

ANOREXIA NERVOSA: ASSESSMENT AND MANAGEMENT

Characteristic features of anorexia nervosa are the patient's denial of her illness and her resistance to seeking help. Often a non-medical friend or relative makes a spot diagnosis and recommends treatment. The features to look out for include:

1   severely restricted food intake (interspersed with binging in the binge purge subtype);
2   overexercise;
3   self-induced vomiting;
4   misuse of laxatives or diuretics;
5   depression, anxiety, obsessionality and/or perfectionism;
6   premorbid personality: obsessive compulsive features and low self esteem.

The meaning of the food restriction is variable and has transcultural implications (Lee et al., 2001). However, common aspects related to food restriction are:

1   preoccupation with food issues;
2   fear of normal body weight;
3   lack of concern about low weight;
4   judging self solely in terms of weight and shape.

Anorexia nervosa impinges on all domains of social, emotional and cognitive development. Deficits in these areas can motivate people to seek help and include:

1   family distress;
2   disadvantage in career and education;
3   impaired social functioning/interactions;
4   difficulties in interpersonal and intimate relationships.

Every organ of the body is compromised by the starvation process and the interested reader should consult specific texts for examples (Birmingham and Beumont, 2004). It manifests as:

1   loss of stamina and strength;
2   altered sleep cycle;
3   sensitivity to cold;

4   dry skin (with altered hair distribution);
5   dizziness;
6   dental problems;
7   psychosexual problems;
8   sore throat;
9   abdominal symptoms (constipation, fullness after eating);
10   amenorrhea (if not taking an oral contraceptive);
11   circulatory problems: poor capillary flow;
12   problems with the gastrointestinal tract.

The details of the medical aspects of anorexia nervosa are clearly outside the remit of this chapter. They are, nonetheless, important in the process of differential diagnosis as well as in the assessment of medical risk and long-term irreversible problems such as osteoporosis (see http://www.iop.kcl.ac.uk/iop/departments/psychmed/edu/professionals.shtml).

If there are markers suggesting that the nutritional risk is high, then increasing the food intake is of highest priority. This is best done orally, starting with 50 kcal/kg/day and gradually increasing to about 3000 kcal per day. A normal soft diet is recommended but in some cases liquid food is better tolerated. This should be supplemented with micronutrient replacement (a standard dose of vitamins and minerals). For further information about nutritional management see the guidelines for the nutritional management of anorexia nervosa published on the website of the Royal College of Psychiatrists.

A disturbance in fluid and electrolyte balance usually occurs as a consequence of purging, but in some cases results from deliberate self-imposed fluid restriction. Again this is best managed conservatively with oral electrolyte replacement solutions or oral potassium and should be closely monitored, avoiding intravenous replacement whenever possible.

The role of medication in the treatment of anorexia needs to be weighed against possible side effects (QT prolongation, increasing the risk of heart rhythm problems) as well as poor evidence of benefit from antidepressants, antipsychotics and antihistamines in patients at low weight. Acceptance and adherence to medication is also problematic (Halmi et al., 2005). Nevertheless, medications are often used in an attempt to produce symptomatic benefit – that is, to alleviate depression or OCD symptoms.

The key issue in the treatment of anorexic patients is *engagement* in the therapeutic relationship. Hence, strategies of motivational interviewing are vital. The first phase of motivational interviewing starts with open questions meant to explore the overall quality of the patient's life (the domains outlined above are salient cues) and help the patient to hear herself talk about her problems. The clinician should have a compassionate, empathetic stance. Confrontation is unhelpful. It is good practice to include carers in the process:

1   to provide a multi-perspective conceptualisation;
2   to set the ground rules for information sharing;
3   to give them the knowledge and skills to avoid participating in any of the maintaining mechanisms.

Caring for someone with an eating disorder is difficult, and carers themselves may benefit from a needs assessment as many are distressed and overwhelmed by their role. Interventions to give family members the skills and knowledge to help are under investigation. A variety of ways of including the family in treatment, such as the use of separated family work (differential input to parents and individual) or multifamily groups, are also under investigation.

Issues of confidentiality can cause confusion. For a start, such a highly visible illness can never be kept a confidential matter between doctor and patient. Second, starvation impacts on capacity and decision making, and the high risk associated with severe starvation has legal implications. Thus it is good practice to balance the need for confidentiality with the need to practice safely, which includes information sharing with both professional and non-professional carers. General information is available from self help books, and specialist resources from specialist websites linked to services (see (http://www.iop.kcl.ac.uk/iop/departments/psychmed/edu/) or self help organisations such as the Eating Disorders Association (UK) (http://www.edauk.com) or the National Eating Disorders Association (USA) (http://www.nationaleatingdisorders.org/).

Planning treatment for someone with anorexia nervosa is not a simple affair resolved by entering the appropriate keywords and searching the literature for systematic reviews of evidence-based treatments. Guidelines are available but have to be interpreted judiciously (American Psychiatric Association, 2000; Beumont et al., 2004; National Collaborating Centre for Mental Health, 2004). The first question is: what stage and type of anorexia nervosa is it? What is the level of medical and psychiatric risk? What age is the patient? Treatment will be tailored to match patient needs and resources.

A variety of service models, in inpatient/day patient/outpatient settings and using various forms of therapies, have been used, including psychotherapy, drugs, massage, exercise and warmth. The broad conclusion is that specialist expertise with a focus on medical risk, diet and weight and linking this to interpersonal and psychological issues is most acceptable to people with anorexia nervosa. It may surprise many people to find that non-specific manualised supportive clinical management given by a specialist was found to produce a better clinical outcome than cognitive behaviour therapy or interpersonal psychotherpy in a mild subgroup (McIntosh et al., 2005). However, replication is needed in a more representative population. In another study there was little difference between family, focal dynamic and cognitive analytical therapies, although all of these were more effective than general psychiatric management (Dare et al., 2001).

The UK NICE guidelines recommend that outpatient treatment should be the preferred initial approach if medical risk allows. The guidelines also recommend the inclusion of members of the family, especially for adolescent cases. Early effective intervention can produce a good outcome for 60% in the first year, progressing to 90% recovery by five years (Currin and Schmidt, 2005; Treasure and Schmidt, 2005).

Good outcome is associated with minimal weight loss (BMI > $17kg/m^2$), absence of medical complications, strong motivation to change behaviour and supportive family and friends who do not condone the abnormal behaviour. A poor outcome is indicated by vomiting in very emaciated patients, onset in adulthood, co-existing psychiatric or personality disorder, disturbed family relationships and a long duration of illness (Steinhausen, 2002).

BULIMIA NERVOSA: RISK FACTORS AND CLINICAL CONCEPTUALISATIONS

The prevalence of the broad category of bulimic disorders can be as high as 10% of young women, whereas the prevalence of the narrower definition of bulimia nervosa is 2%. However, the prevalence of bulimic disorders varies according to time and place – that is, it is a culture-bound syndrome (Keel and Klump, 2003). It was rare in women born before the 1950s and incidence increased in the 1990s. There is a suggestion, however, that incidence in the twenty-first century is decreasing (Currin et al., 2005). Some of this variability represents changes in detection and presentation to services. The rapid increase in the last half of the twentieth century may have resulted from some degree of contagion or social transmission of the values and behaviours that underpin the disorder. Food and appearance, and weight and shape, are of importance in women's lives. The idealisation of thinness in terms of beauty and moral worth varies across time and place, but started to develop in the 1960s in the West. Dieting can trigger the erratic pattern of binge eating and, in conjunction with the behaviours that compensate for overeating, forms a key part of the maintaining mechanisms. These are the core features of the original cognitive behavioural model of bulimia nervosa (Fairburn, 1983).

There is more confidence in the risk factors for bulimia nervosa than those for anorexia nervosa, as there is better quality evidence within systematic reviews of the literature (Jacobi et al., 2004; Stice, 2002). Genetic mechanisms account for over 50% of the variance and linkage to chromosome 10 has been reported (Bulik et al., 2003). Perfectionism, anxiety and impulsivity are developmental dispositions that increase the risk of developing bulimia. A pattern of overeating, with associated obesity in childhood, is often seen, as is anxiety. Parental problems are also more marked than in anorexia nervosa and include alcoholism, depression and drug abuse. Adversity in childhood, such as experiences of sexual abuse and physical neglect, increase the risk. The proximal risk factors for bulimia nervosa include dieting, early puberty, low self esteem and stress in the context of body dissatisfaction, thin ideal internalisation and negative affect.

BULIMIA NERVOSA: ASSESSMENT AND MANAGEMENT

The boundaries between purging disorder, bulimia nervosa, non-purging subtype of bulimia nervosa, binge eating disorder, eating disorder not otherwise specified and overeating in obesity are somewhat indistinct. A time-limited binge can be difficult to separate from a protracted pattern of overeating. Compensatory methods other than vomiting and purging are more difficult to define. The duration and intensity of symptoms that are required to define a "case" have varied over time. Approximately a quarter of cases can dip into anorexia nervosa's binge purge subtype within five years of onset, especially in the group with low novelty-seeking. Depression is common among patients with bulimic disorders, as well as a variety of additional impulsive features and addictive disorders. Yet another subgroup has obsessive compulsive traits and behavioural inhibition, merging more with anorexia nervosa.

Spitzer et al. (1991) suggested that an additional category of binge eating disorder could be defined from within the eating disorder not otherwise specified category (Spitzer et al., 1991). This condition is now in the DSM-IV (Table 5.1) as a proposed category pending further research. People with binge eating disorder have episodes of bingeing as defined by bulimia nervosa, but they do not compensate for this by extreme behaviours such as vomiting, taking laxatives, fasting or exercising excessively, which occurs in bulimia, and the absence of these behaviours is the main diagnostic distinction from bulimia. Thus these people are often obese. The levels of psychopathology observed in individuals with binge eating disorder fall between the high levels seen in bulimia nervosa and the low levels seen in simple obesity. Emotional and personality difficulties are common and there may be impaired work and social functioning.

Research into the treatment of bulimia nervosa has been summarised in systematic reviews in the Cochrane library (Bacaltchuk et al., 1999, 2000a, 2000b; Hay and Bacaltchuk, 2000). The quality and quantity of research into bulimia nervosa is much greater than that into anorexia nervosa. Thus the NICE guidelines give a grade A recommendation for cognitive behavioural treatment for bulimia nervosa (National Collaborating Centre for Mental Health, 2004). A manual which describes the standard CBT adopted in treatment studies for bulimia nervosa is available (Fairburn et al., 1993). This treatment is moderately effective (Agras et al., 2000). Of those who responded, most did so in the first weeks of therapy.

There is also evidence supporting the use of interpersonal therapy, but it takes more time. The combination of medication and psychological treatment seems to be more effective than either treatment on its own, but has higher dropout rates (Bacaltchuk and Hay, 2003; Bacaltchuk et al., 2000b, 2001; National Collaborating Centre for Mental Health, 2004).

Many treatment centres now adopt a stepped care approach, starting with the least intensive, least costly and least invasive intervention. As the first step, guided treatment using CBT delivered from books (Cooper, 1993; Fairburn, 1995; Schmidt and Treasure, 1993), computers or the web have been successfully used (Bara-Carril et al., 2004; Carrard et al., 2006; refer also to Chapter 16 in this volume).

Follow-up studies of people with bulimia nervosa after treatment show that after 10 years about 10% continue to have the full syndrome (Keel et al., 1999). The natural course of cases, ascertained from a community study, was marked initial improvement, with only a minority continuing to meet full diagnostic criteria for bulimia nervosa, although up to two-thirds had some subclinical form of eating disorder. There are few consistent predictors of longer-term outcome, although several studies find that a shorter illness duration and reduced comorbidity are associated with an improved outcome.

CONCLUSION

The reasons for the wide gender divergence in eating disorders is not yet clear. There are many interesting possibilities that need further research. Gender-based biological factors are relevant for anorexia nervosa. Also, the greater meaning of food and appearance for females may interact in a pathoplastic manner with underlying aspects of information processing to shape compulsive, detail-focused thoughts and behaviours. Cultural transmission of the overvaluation of the thin ideal can interact with predispositions to low self esteem and emotional dysregulation, and lead to the development of a bulimic pattern of illness.

It is probable that answers may emerge from further work, especially with the male subgroup. Such cases may have a greater loading of the risk factors or fewer of the protective factors.

REFERENCES

Agras, W. S., Walsh, T., Fairburn, C. G., Wilson, G. T. and Kraemer, H. C. (2000) A multicenter comparison of cognitive-behavioral therapy and interpersonal psychotherapy for bulimia nervosa, *Archives of General Psychiatry*, 57 (5), 459–466.

American Psychiatric Association (2000) Practice guideline for the treatment of patients with eating disorders (revision): American Psychiatric Association Work Group on Eating Disorders, *American Journal of Psychiatry*, 157 (1), 1–39.

Anderluh, M. B., Tchanturia, K., Rabe-Hesketh, S. and Treasure, J. (2003) Childhood obsessive-compulsive personality traits in adult women with eating disorders: Defining a broader eating disorder phenotype, *American Journal of Psychiatry*, 160 (2), 242–247.

Bacaltchuk, J. and Hay, P. (2003) Antidepressants versus placebo for people with bulimia nervosa, *Cochrane Database of Systematic Reviews*, 4, CD003391.

Bacaltchuk, J., Trefiglio, R. P., de Oliveira, I. R., Lima, M. S. and Mari, J. J. (1999) Antidepressants versus psychotherapy for bulimia nervosa: A systematic review, *Journal of Clinical Pharmacy and Therapeutics*, 24, (1), 23–31.

Bacaltchuk, J., Hay, P. and Mari, J. J. (2000a) Antidepressants versus placebo for the treatment of bulimia nervosa: A systematic review, *Australian and New Zealand Journal of Psychiatry*, 34 (2), 310–317.

Bacaltchuk, J., Hay, P. and Trefiglio, R. (2001) Antidepressants versus psychological treatments and their combination for bulimia nervosa, *Cochrane Database of Systematic Reviews* 4, CD003385.

Bacaltchuk, J., Trefiglio, R. P., Oliveira, I. R., Hay, P., Lima, M. S. and Mari, J. J. (2000b) Combination of antidepressants and psychological treatments for bulimia nervosa: A systematic review, *Acta Psychiatrica Scandinavica*, 101 (4), 256–264.

Bara-Carril, N., Williams, C. J., Pombo-Carril, M. G., Reid, Y., Murray, K., Aubin, S., Harkin, P. J., Treasure, J. and Schmidt, U. (2004) A preliminary investigation into the feasibility and efficacy of a CD-ROM-based cognitive-behavioral self-help intervention for bulimia nervosa, *International Journal of Eating Disorders*, 35 (4), 538–548.

Bastiani, A. M., Rao, R., Weltzin, T. and Kaye, W. H. (1995) Perfectionism in anorexia nervosa, *International Journal of Eating Disorders*, 17 (2), 147–152.

Beumont, P., Hay, P., Beumont, D., Birmingham, L., Derham, H., Jordan, A., Kohn, M., McDermott, B., Marks, P., Mitchell, J., Paxton, S., Surgenor, L., Thornton, C., Wakefield, A. and Weigall, S. (2004) Australian and New Zealand clinical practice guidelines for the treatment of anorexia nervosa, *Australian and New Zealand Journal of Psychiatry*, 38 (9), 659–670.

Birmingham, C. L. and Beumont, P. (2004) *Medical management of eating disorders*, Cambridge, Cambridge University Press.

Bruch, H. (1973) *Eating disorders: Obesity, anorexia nervosa and the person within*, New York, Basic Books.

Bulik, C. M., Devlin, B., Bacanu, S. A., Thornton, L., Klump, K. L., Fichter, M. M., Halmi, K. A., Kaplan, A. S., Strober, M., Woodside, D. B., Bergen, A. W., Ganjei, J. K., Crow, S., Mitchell, J., Rotondo, A., Mauri, M., Cassano, G., Keel, P., Berrettini, W. H. and Kaye, W. H. (2003) Significant linkage on chromosome 10 in families with bulimia nervosa, *American Journal of Human Genetics*, 72 (1), 200–207.

Carrard, I., Rouget, P., Fernandez-Aranda, F., Volkart, A. C., Damoiseau, M. and Lam, T. (2005) Evaluation and deployment of evidence based patient self-management support program for bulimia nervosa, *International Journal of Medical Informatics*, 75 (1), 101–109.

Connan, F. and Treasure, J. L. (1998) Stress, eating and neurobiology, in H. Hoek, J. Treasure and M. Katzman (eds) *Neurobiology in the treatment of eating disorders*, pp. 211–236, London, John Wiley and Sons.

Connan, F., Campbell, I. C., Katzman, M., Lightman, S. L. and Treasure, J. (2003) A neurodevelopmental model for anorexia nervosa, *Physiology and Behaviour*, 79 (1), 13–24.

Cooper, P. (1993) *Bulimia nervosa and binge eating*, London, Robinson.

Currin, L. and Schmidt, U. (2005) A critical analysis of the utility of an early intervention approach in eating disorders, *Journal of Mental Health*, 14 (6), 611–624.

Currin, L., Schmidt, U., Treasure, J. and Jick, H. (2005) Time trends in eating disorder incidence, *British Journal of Psychiatry*, 186, 132–135.

Dare, C., Eisler, I., Russell, G., Treasure, J. and Dodge, L. (2001) Psychological therapies for adults with anorexia nervosa: Randomised controlled trial of out-patient treatments, *British Journal of Psychiatry*, 178, 216–221.

Eisler, I. and Asen, E. (2003) Family interventions, in J. Treasure, U. Schmidt and E. Van Furth (eds) *Handbook of eating disorders* (2nd edn), pp. 311–325, Chichester, Wiley.

Fairburn, C. G. (1983) Bulimia nervosa, *British Journal of Hospital Medicine*, 29 (6), 537–542.

Fairburn, C. G. (1995) *Overcoming binge eating*, New York, Guilford Press.

Fairburn, C. G., Marcus, M. D. and Wilson, G. T. (1993) Cognitive-behavioral therapy for binge eating and bulimia nervosa: A comprehensive treatment manual, in C. G. Fairburn and G. T. Wilson (eds) *Binge eating: Nature, assessment, and treatment*, pp. 361–404, New York, Guilford Press.

Favaro, A. and Santonastaso, P. (1998) Impulsive and compulsive self-injurious behavior in bulimia nervosa: Prevalence and psychological correlates, *Journal of Nervous and Mental Disease*, 186 (3), 157–165.

Favazza, A. R. (1998) The coming of age of self-mutilation, *Journal of Nervous and Mental Disease*, 186 (5), 259–268.

Gillberg, I. C., Gillberg, C., Rastam, M. and Johansson, M. (1996) The cognitive profile of anorexia nervosa: A comparative study including a community-based sample, *Comprehensive Psychiatry*, 37 (1), 23–30.

Gorwood, P., Kipman, A. and Foulon, C. (2003) The human genetics of anorexia nervosa, *European Journal of Pharmacology*, 480 (1–3), 163–170.

Grice, D. E., Halmi, K. A., Fichter, M. M., Strober, M., Woodside, D. B., Treasure, J. T., Kaplan, A. S., Magistretti, P. J., Goldman, D., Bulik, C. M., Kaye, W. H. and Berrettini, W. H. (2002) Evidence for a susceptibility gene for anorexia nervosa on chromosome 1, *American Journal of Human Genetics*, 70 (3), 787–792.

Gull, W. W. (1868) The address in medicine to the Annual Meeting of the British Medical Association at Oxford, *Lancet*, 2 (August 8), 171–176.

Gull, W. (1874) Anorexia nervosa, *Transactions of the Clinical Society of London*, 7, 22–28.

Halmi, K. A., Agras, W. S., Crow, S., Mitchell, J., Wilson, G. T., Bryson, S. W. and Kraemer, H. C. (2005) Predictors of treatment acceptance and completion in anorexia nervosa: Implications for future study designs, *Archives of General Psychiatry*, 62 (7), 776–781.

Hay, P. J. and Bacaltchuk, J. (2000) Psychotherapy for bulimia nervosa and binging, *Cochrane Database of Systematic Reviews*, 4, CD000562.

Jacobi, C., Hayward, C., de Zwaan, M., Kraemer, H. C. and Agras, W. S. (2004) Coming to terms with risk factors for eating disorders: Application of risk terminology and suggestions for a general taxonomy, *Psychological Bulletin*, 130 (1), 19–65.

Keel, P. K. and Klump, K. L. (2003) Are eating disorders culture-bound syndromes? Implications for conceptualizing their etiology, *Psychological Bulletin*, 129 (5), 747–769.

Keel, P. K., Mitchell, J. E., Miller, K. B., Davis, T. L. and Crow, S. J. (1999) Long-term outcome of bulimia nervosa, *Archives of General Psychiatry*, 56 (1), 63–69.

Lacey, J. H. and Evans, C. D. (1986) The impulsivist: A multi-impulsive personality disorder, *British Journal of Addiction*, 81 (5), 641–649.

Lee, S., Lee, A. M., Ngai, E., Lee, D. T. S. and Wing, Y. K. (2001) Rationales for food refusal in Chinese patients with anorexia nervosa, *International Journal of Eating Disorders*, 29 (2), 224–229.

Lock, J., Le Grange, D., Agras, W. S. and Dare, C. (2001) *Treatment manual for anorexia nervosa: A family-based approach*, New York, Guilford Press.

Lock, J., Agras, W. S., Bryson, S. and Kraemer, H. C. (2005) A comparison of short- and long-term family therapy for adolescent anorexia nervosa, *Journal of the American Academy of Child and Adolescent Psychiatry*, 44 (7), 632–639.

Matsunaga, H., Kaye, W. H., McConaha, C., Plotnicov, K., Pollice, C. and Rao, R. (2000) Personality disorders among subjects recovered from eating disorders, *International Journal of Eating Disorders*, 27 (3), 353–357.

McIntosh, V. V., Jordan, J., Carter, F. A., Luty, S. E., McKenzie, J. M., Bulik, C. M., Frampton, C. M. and Joyce, P. R. (2005) Three psychotherapies for anorexia nervosa: A randomized, controlled trial, *American Journal of Psychiatry*, 162 (4), 741–747.

National Collaborating Centre for Mental Health (2004) *National clinical practice guideline. Eating disorders: Core interventions in the treatment and management of anorexia nervosa, bulimia nervosa, and related eating disorders*, London, National Institute for Clinical Excellence.

Owen, J. B. (1998) Models of eating disturbances in animals, in H. W. Hoek, J. L. Treasure and M. A. Katzman (eds) *Neurobiology in the treatment of eating disorders*, pp. 169–194, Chichester, Wiley.

Russell, G. (1979) Bulimia nervosa: An ominous variant of anorexia nervosa, *Psychological Medicine*, 9 (3), 429–448.

Schmidt, U. and Treasure, J. (1993) *Getting better bit(e) by bit(e): A survival kit for sufferers of bulimia nervosa and binge eating disorder*, Hove, Brunner-Routledge.

Schmidt, U. and Treasure, J. (2005) Anorexia nervosa: Valued and visible. A cognitive-interpersonal maintenance model and its implications for research and practice, *British Journal of Clinical Psychology*, 45, 1–25.

Southgate, L., Tchanturia, K. and Treasure, J. (2005) Building a model of the aetiology of eating disorders by translating experimental neuroscience into clinical practice, *Journal of Mental Health*, 14 (6), 553–566.

Spitzer, R. L., Devlin, B., Walsh, A., Hasdin, D., Wing, R., Stunkard, A. J.,

Wadden, T., Yanovski, J. A., Agras, S. and Mitchell, J. E. (1991) Binge eating disorder: To be or not to be in DSMIV, *International Journal of Eating Disorders*, 10, 627–629.

Srinivasagam, N. M., Kaye, W. H., Plotnicov, K. H., Greeno, C., Weltzin, T. E. and Rao, R. (1995) Persistent perfectionism, symmetry, and exactness after long-term recovery from anorexia nervosa, *American Journal of Psychiatry*, 152 (11), 1630–1634.

Steinhausen, H. C. (2002) The outcome of anorexia nervosa in the 20th century, *American Journal of Psychiatry*, 159 (8), 1284–1293.

Stice, E. (2002) Risk and maintenance factors for eating pathology: A meta-analytic review, *Psychological Bulletin*, 128 (5), 825–848.

Tozzi, F., Thornton, L. M., Klump, K. L., Fichter, M. M., Halmi, K. A., Kaplan, A. S., Strober, M., Woodside, D. B., Crow, S., Mitchell, J., Rotondo, A., Mauri, M., Cassano, G., Keel, P., Plotnicov, K. H., Pollice, C., Lilenfeld, L. R., Berrettini, W. H., Bulik, C. M. and Kaye, W. H. (2005) Symptom fluctuation in eating disorders: Correlates of diagnostic crossover, *American Journal of Psychiatry*, 162 (4), 732–740.

Treasure, J. and Schmidt, U. (2005) The early phase of eating disorders, *Journal of Mental Health*, 14 (6), 535–538.

Treasure, J., Tchanturia, K. and Schmidt, U. (2005) Developing a model of the treatment for eating disorder: Using neuroscience research to examine the how rather than the what of change, *Counselling and Psychotherapy Research*, 5 (3), 187–190.

Waller, G. and Kennerley, H. (2003) Cognitive models, in J. Treasure, E. Van Furth and U. Schmidt (eds) *Handbook of eating disorders* (2nd edn), pp. 233–251, Chichester, Wiley.

Ward, A., Ramsay, R., Turnbull, S., Benedettini, M. and Treasure, J. (2000) Attachment patterns in eating disorders: Past in the present, *International Journal of Eating Disorders*, 28 (4), 370–376.

Ward, A., Ramsay, R., Turnbull, S., Steele, M., Steele, H. and Treasure, J. (2001) Attachment in anorexia nervosa: A transgenerational perspective, *British Journal of Medical Psychology*, 74 (4), 497–505.

Welch, S. L. and Fairburn, C. G. (1996) Impulsivity or comorbidity in bulimia nervosa: A controlled study of deliberate self-harm and alcohol and drug misuse in a community sample, *British Journal of Psychiatry*, 169 (4), 451–458.

Chapter 6

Breast cancer and body image

Stirling Moorey

INTRODUCTION

Women are far more likely than men to be concerned about their body image, and this preoccupation begins early. Cultural and media stereotypes of physical attractiveness place pressure on women to conform to unattainable standards of shape and size, and help to link acceptability and worth with appearance. Self objectification theory (Fredrickson and Roberts, 1997) suggests that because society treats women's bodies as objects, women grow up with an observer perspective based on how they appear to the male gaze. This perspective becomes internalised and so women are more likely to view their bodies in this objectified way, their value defined by how they appear to others. Conditions which bring a negative change in appearance are therefore likely to have a greater impact on women than on men.

Cancer and its treatment can have devastating effects on the body. In its early stages the disease itself may not present with much change in physical appearance, but the treatment the patient undergoes to reach a cure or remission may be disfiguring. Surgery is the most obvious example of this, such as the amputation of a breast or extensive excision of the skin surrounding a melanoma. But less invasive treatments also cause body changes, such as hair loss and weight loss from chemotherapy or the menopausal effects of endocrine therapy. In the later stages the disease itself may cause significant problems, perhaps with large visible tumours or ulcers or the general effects of extreme weight loss. Whether these changes are immediately visible to the outside world, as in skin and head and neck cancers, or are more hidden, they nonetheless pose a threat to body integrity.

This chapter will examine the concept of body image in women from a cognitive behavioural perspective, describing a cognitive behavioural model of adjustment to the threats cancer poses to survival and body appearance. Breast cancer is probably the most extensively investigated type of cancer, and illustrates well the ways in which the disease interacts with core aspects of femininity, so this diagnosis will be explored in some detail. Finally, some applications of cognitive behavioural techniques in the area will be discussed.

THE CONCEPT OF BODY IMAGE

Reas and Grilo (2004) summarise the historical and developmental influences that may affect body image, including:

> socio-demographic factors (e.g. age, gender and ethnicity), interpersonal experiences (teasing or sexual abuse), peer and familial influences (direct communication, modelling, "fat talk"), internalization of cultural ideals, physical characteristics (age of onset, body mass index [BMI], size and location of disfigurement, whether disfigurement is acquired or congenital), and personality attributes (perfectionism, self-esteem).

Body image is therefore a complex construct. Psychologists studying the area agree that it is multidimensional rather than unidimensional. Cash (2002), for instance, identifies two categories: self perceptions and attitudes to physical appearance. The perceptual dimension of body image refers to the processing of size, shape and weight relative to the person's objective body proportions. The attitudinal dimension includes global subjective dissatisfaction, affective distress, appearance investment and other cognitive and behavioural dimensions (Cash, 2002). This can be further subdivided into evaluative and investment elements. Satisfaction or unease with one's body appearance is part of the evaluative component. However, it is possible to be dissatisfied with your appearance, but not necessarily distressed about it. The degree of distress depends on the extent to which you place psychological importance on appearance (appearance investment). It seems to be the case that women are equally dissatisfied with their body image whether they are 20 or 80, but the relative importance of appearance decreases with age (Tiggeman, 2004).

Measurement of body image presents problems since there is no fully accepted definition of the concept. Many tools are available which have been primarily designed for people with eating disorders. These are not always applicable to people who have real disfigurements, as they often relate to general shape, size or weight. Cancer-specific body image measures include the Body Image Scale (Hopwood, 1998), the Body Image Instrument (Kopel et al., 1998) and the Measure of Body Apperception (Carver et al., 1998). The reader is referred to a recent handbook of body image theory, research and practice (Cash and Pruzinsky, 2000) for detailed discussion of these measures and their psychometric properties.

CANCER AND BODY IMAGE: A COGNITIVE
BEHAVIOURAL MODEL OF ADJUSTMENT

As with many other areas, cognitive behavioural models have become the main theoretical framework for understanding body image. These have been applied to body image in general (Cash, 2002; Reas and Grilo, 2004) and to body image in cancer (White, 2000). Central to these models is the idea of body image schemas which determine our orientation to body issues and our cognitive, emotional and behavioural reactions to them. A schema is a hypothetical cognitive structure that helps to make sense of the world. It helps us to make predictions about situations, selectively attend to and filter relevant information, sort it in relation to past experience, evaluate and encode it and finally guide behavioural responses. There are multiple schemas for all aspects of our life, but so-called "self-schemas" are the most emotionally salient.

Body image is obviously a key component of our sense of self and attitudes, beliefs and values about our bodies comprise the body schema. As with any social learning model, this assumes that the individual's experiences during key life stages will influence their beliefs about their body. "Body images schemas reflect one's core, affect laden assumptions or beliefs about the importance and influence of one's appearance in life, including the centrality of appearance to one's sense of self" (Cash, 2002: 42).

These schemas are likely to be activated in certain situations where the body is likely to be exposed to the gaze of self or others, such as trying on clothes, wearing a bathing costume or having sex. If the body image is basically positive there may be no difficulties in these settings, but when a negative body schema is present a set of negative thoughts will ensue, such as: "I look awful, I'm too fat, and I'm ugly." These will be accompanied by negative affect – shame or disgust. This self-critical attitude may then lead on to actions to reduce the sense of shame or exposure, such as avoiding situations where the body is exposed, wearing loose-fitting clothing or making love in the dark.

Moorey and Greer (2002) have suggested that cancer poses a threat to what they have termed the survival schema and the self schema. We spend much of our time assuming that life will go on in a relatively uninterrupted way, rarely thinking about the possibility of death. These implicit assumptions are challenged by a diagnosis of cancer and decisions need to be made about what the diagnosis means, what hope the future holds and how much the cancer patient can influence the outcome of the disease. For women, concerns not only about their own life but also about how their family and children will cope without them typically become prominent. Some may develop a "fighting spirit" and resolve to beat the illness no matter what. Others may see the diagnosis as a death sentence, becoming "helpless and hopeless". These beliefs about diagnosis, prognosis and the extent to which the woman can exert control constitute the survival schema. Women also have to decide what being a cancer patient means for them and how they will adjust to the changes in physical state, appearance and family and social role. Body image issues are a major component of this overarching self schema. Because of the threat to life, adjustment to cancer contains an extra component to other medical conditions causing disability and disfigurement. Limb amputation after a road traffic accident, or scarring from burns, imposes terrible changes in a person's life, but adjustment takes place in the presence of a stable future. A woman with cancer has to contend not only with disruption to her body image but also the uncertainty about whether she will survive.

One or other of these schemas may dominate. For a young mother with breast cancer, the loss of a breast may be overshadowed by fears about the consequences of her death for her pre-school children. For another young woman with the same condition, the impact of a mastectomy on her attractiveness and relationship with her partner may be the main concern. Underlying beliefs about illness, capacity to cope, importance of appearance and investment of self worth will shape the adjustment reaction. Body schemas are more likely to be activated in the presence of low mood, and there is some evidence from experimental research that when women are made to think about their own mortality their levels of body objectification increase (Grabe et al., 2005). Survival schemas and body schemas will therefore interact in a complex way during the process of adjustment (see Figure 6.1).

White (2000, 2002) has developed a cognitive behavioural model of body image disturbance in cancer which integrates some of the themes from work on self discrepancy theory, body image schemas and investment in personal attributes. He suggests that the content of the person's body image schema will determine their investment in the changed body image feature and also the discrepancy between their ideal and actual self image. In other words, if a woman has grown up in a culture and family where traditional ideals of feminine beauty prevail, she will base her value as a person on her appearance and so this investment will mean that the loss of a breast will be a devastating experience, while the discrepancy between her ideal body image and her new image of herself will be large.

Once a negative body image schema is activated, it will lead to the interpretation of relevant situations in a biased way, generating negative images, negative cognitions, negative affect and behavioural reactions that may maintain the negative view of the self and perpetuate the schema. For instance, following a mastectomy a woman may believe that she is no longer attractive. She may have thoughts such as: "I'm no longer a woman. I'm nothing. No one could ever love me." She may also have images of herself as deformed and ugly – although these distorted images of the self are important in body dysmorphic disorder and social phobia, we do not have any

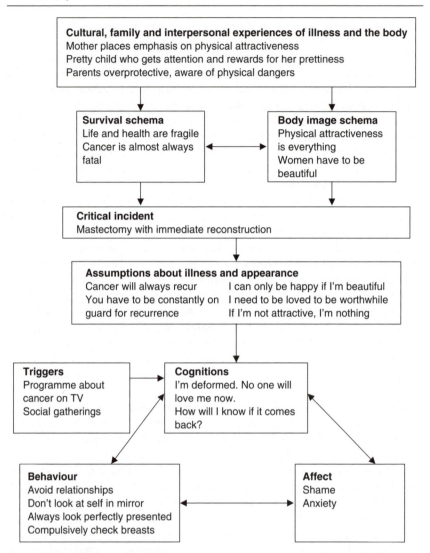

Figure 6.1 Cognitive model of adjustment to cancer – survival and body schemas.

research on the extent to which people with cancer may have distorted images of their deformities. Distressing emotions of shame may be associated with these cognitions. There may be a number of behavioural consequences:

1   avoidance of situations which might involve wearing less clothing, such as beach holidays ("They'll see I'm wearing a prosthesis");
2   avoidance of looking at self in the mirror ("The scar's disgusting");
3   avoidance of sex;

4   wearing baggy clothes;
5   sitting in a hunched posture so the breasts are less obvious.

These avoidance and safety behaviours help to prevent the feared consequence of rejection occurring, but actually serve to maintain the negative
belief because the woman can never test whether it is true. If she has a
distorted picture in her mind of how her scar looks she can never correct
this if she cannot bear to look at herself in the mirror.

BREAST CANCER, SURGICAL INTERVENTION AND BODY IMAGE

Radical mastectomy was the treatment of choice for breast cancer through
much of the twentieth century. A radical mastectomy involves removal of
all the tissue of the breast, together with the lymph nodes in the armpit
(axilla) into which lymph from the breast drains, and also removal of the
muscle on the chest wall (the pectoralis major). The argument for this
extensive and highly mutilating surgery was that it was vital to ensure that
the entire tumour was removed at operation, because breast cancer spreads
readily to other parts of the body. The problem with this operation is that
peace of mind for surgeon and patient were at the cost of considerable
disfigurement and disability. Not only is the resection of such a large part
of the chest wall unsightly, there is also a high risk of lymphoedema. When
all the lymph nodes are removed from the axilla there is no drainage
channel for the lymph and this can lead to a swelling of the arm as the fluid
builds up. Despite these side effects the conventional wisdom that extreme
action was necessary to save lives persisted well into the 1960s and 1970s.

Surgery was almost exclusively a male domain, and it has been suggested
that had there been more female surgeons the brutality of this procedure
would have been exposed long before. Some of the early psychosocial
oncology studies were influential in the shift to more conservative treatment
because they demonstrated very high levels of psychiatric morbidity in
women who had undergone this procedure – psychological distress which
persisted for years after the surgery (e.g. Maguire et al., 1980). Surgeons
began by experimenting with less radical forms of mastectomy where the
pectoralis muscle and some of the axillary lymph nodes were spared (simple
or total mastectomy), and then even more conservative surgery (lumpectomy), where the tumour and surrounding tissue are removed but the breast
spared. Indeed, 20-year follow-ups of patients treated with radical mastectomy or lumpectomy have found no advantage for the more extensive
surgery in tumours smaller than 4 cms (Fisher et al., 2002; Veronesi et al.,
2002). To reduce the chance of local recurrence, lumpectomy is usually
followed by radiotherapy to the tumour site. Mastectomy, lumpectomy

Table 6.1 Hartl et al. (2003): mean scores on quality of life subscales of 274 women with Stage I–III breast cancer on average four years after diagnosis

	Mastectomy	Breast conservation	p
Satisfaction with surgical treatment	4	11	0.01
Satisfaction with cosmetic results	57	76	<0.01
Favourable body image	17	38	<0.01
Fear of recurrence	55	64	0.04

alone and lumpectomy plus radiation therapy have equally good survival rates (Fisher et al., 2002).

Much of the early work on the psychosocial impact of surgery for breast cancer compared mastectomy and lumpectomy. The consistent but rather counterintuitive finding was that psychological morbidity was equivalent for both treatments (Bartelink et al., 1985; Fallowfield et al., 1986; Kemeny et al., 1988). Body image disturbance, however, is consistently greater in women undergoing more radical surgery. At six months 63% of women who have had a mastectomy feel comfortable when fully dressed, but only 21% feel comfortable when undressed (Harcourt et al., 2003). Yilmazer et al. (1994) compared the psychological effects of mastectomy and breast conservation. The latter was associated with a more positive body image, but there were no differences in self esteem and social support. Arora et al. (2001) investigated the immediate and delayed effects of surgery. Immediately after surgery women who had had a mastectomy described a poorer body image, and poorer functional and physical well-being. Women undergoing lumpectomy reported less disturbance of body image but worried more about the effects of stress on their illness and had lower emotional well-being. However, six months after surgery the quality of life in both groups was equal. Body image concerns are not restricted to younger women. Figueiredo (2004) and colleagues found that lumpectomy produced better body image outcomes in a study of women over 67 years of age. Concerns about appearance influenced the choice of surgery in 31%, and body image predicted mental health two years after surgery.

Hartl and colleagues (2003) discovered that although women who had a mastectomy in their sample showed a poorer body image, there was still a significant number of women in the lumpectomy group (see Table 6.1) who had a poor body image. It should be remembered that lumpectomy is not a benign procedure. If a woman has a small breast and a large tumour, the removal of the tumour may lead to a significant change in the breast shape, which may be as disfiguring as a mastectomy. In this study, women receiving a lumpectomy also had a slightly greater fear of recurrence.

Breast conservation generally gives a woman a less disfiguring outcome and consequently a more positive body image than mastectomy. However, it may not give as much assurance about recurrence as the more radical treatment. Women may know that the chances of local recurrence are lower with mastectomy, but they may also feel reassured emotionally that because a large area of tissue has been removed they are somehow "safer".

With increasing knowledge of the genetic basis of some types of breast cancer, women with a family history of the disease are opting for prophylactic mastectomy. Women who have had one breast removed may opt to have the other removed, or women at high risk of developing cancer may have bilateral prophylactic mastectomies. Hatcher et al. (2001) followed up 143 women offered bilateral mastectomy. Of these, 79 accepted the procedure. In those accepting the operation psychological morbidity dropped from 60% before the operation to 29% at 18 months. In those who declined, psychological morbidity changed less: from 57% to 41%. Frost et al. (2005) reported that whereas 83% of women were satisfied with the surgery only 33% were satisfied with their body appearance. In women undergoing prophylactic mastectomy followed by reconstruction (Metcalfe et al., 2004), perceived risk of developing cancer before surgery correlated with perceived risks after surgery ($p = -0.54$), but was also associated with less satisfaction with the surgery. Women who overestimated the risk of cancer had lower satisfaction levels.

RECONSTRUCTIVE SURGERY

In recent years psychosocial research on the effects of surgery has focused more on the possible benefits of reconstructive surgery for women who have had a mastectomy. Reconstruction does not affect the incidence of local recurrence or reduce the chances of detecting recurrence (DiMartino et al., 1993). Reconstruction is popular in the USA, being taken up by 30% of women after mastectomy, but is less common in Britain (only 5–10%; Harcourt and Rumsey, 2001). Half of British women undergoing a mastectomy, however, said they would like reconstruction if it were possible (Keith et al., 2003). There are a number of reconstructive techniques available. The least disruptive involves a breast implant. Because the skin over the chest wall needs to be stretched over a period of time, the surgeon usually inserts a balloon which can be gradually inflated as the skin accommodates. An alternative is to take a tissue flap from another part of the body and fashion this into a breast. In a trans rectus abdominis muscle (TRAM) flap reconstruction a flap of skin, fat and muscle is taken from the lower abdomen and passed up, with blood supply still intact, to be shaped into a breast. Scars are left on the abdomen and across the breast, and usually the umbilicus has to be relocated.

Alderman et al. (2000) reported a distinct superiority of TRAM flap over implants on general and aesthetic satisfaction with the reconstruction, and Wilkins et al. (2000) found greater improvements in body image in women receiving delayed TRAM flaps. Al-Ghazal et al. (1999) investigated whether the cosmetic outcome of conservation surgery was associated with better psychosocial adjustment. Using a combined measure of tape measurement and panel assessment of photographs, they found a correlation with both self esteem and feelings of sexual attractiveness. Although reconstruction gives better cosmetic results than mastectomy it still results in poorer body image than lumpectomy. In a large ($n = 1357$) sample of women with stage 0–II breast cancer in the USA, Janz et al. (2005) found that the only significant differences between a group receiving mastectomy and recon-structive surgery and a group receiving lumpectomy were in the domain of body image. Al-Ghazal et al. (2000) found that body image following lumpectomy was superior to that following mastectomy plus reconstruction, which was superior to that following mastectomy without reconstruction. Echoing the results for mastectomy and lumpectomy, Nissen et al. (2000) found that mastectomy with reconstruction and breast conservation did not differ in psychological morbidity, but the conservative treatment was associated with a more favourable body image. The interaction between survival and body image concerns also arises in this context: women considering reconstruction express a fear that reconstruction might hide recurrence (Keith et al., 2003).

In the past the loss of a breast in mastectomy was considered a major loss akin to a bereavement. It was thought that the removal of such a significant part of a woman's femininity necessitated a period of grieving. If this is the case, reconstruction is best performed after the woman has had time to process this loss; reconstructing too quickly might have a negative psycho-logical effect. One might argue, from the perspective presented so far, that worries about the life-threatening aspects of cancer could overshadow the impact on body image in the days and weeks after diagnosis, and this might also mean that the full impact of the loss is not felt until some time after a mastectomy.

Harcourt and Rumsey (2001) critically appraised the research into breast reconstruction and noted that most of these studies are limited by a retrospective or cross-sectional design. In a prospective, multicentre study Harcourt and colleagues (2003) followed 103 women over a year: 56 women had mastectomy alone, 37 had mastectomy with immediate reconstruction and 10 had chosen to have a delayed reconstruction. Subjects were assessed with questionnaires and a semi-structured interview pre-operatively (pre-mastectomy for the first two groups and pre-construction for the delayed reconstruction group) and at six and 12 months after the mastectomy. Overall body image scores improved in all groups, but about a third of women in both the mastectomy alone and the mastectomy with immediate reconstruction groups reported a deterioration in body image over the course of the study. Younger age and poorer pre-operative body image predicted poorer body image score at 12 months.

The majority of women would prefer an immediate reconstruction. If given a choice of reconstruction at three or six months after mastectomy, 74% would prefer it at three months (Keith et al., 2003). There is some evidence that women choosing immediate reconstruction at the time of mastectomy may have higher levels of psychological distress and body dissatisfaction (Roth et al., 2005); alternatively, it might be better to interpret this as the smaller number of women who opt for later surgery having less concerns about their body appearance.

IMPACT OF BREAST CANCER AND THERAPEUTIC INTERVENTIONS ON SOCIAL, MARITAL AND SEXUAL ADJUSTMENT

If a woman bases her self worth on her appearance or her sexuality, potential damage to the breast may challenge her self esteem. Indeed for some women who are preoccupied with their body shape, worries about the effect of breast feeding on their appearance may override the very function of the organ, and these women may decline to breast feed (Barnes et al., 1997). For other women, the breast may be a symbol of femininity and loss of the breast may signify a loss of reproductive function. This is compounded if adjuvant treatment such as chemotherapy causes infertility or hormone therapy induces an artificial menopause. If a woman has an unfulfilled goal to be a mother, or defines herself in relation to stereotyped maternal ideals, this may have a profound effect. One study found that in women with breast cancer, distress was more closely related to concern about appearance than concern about "body integrity" (Petronis et al., 2003).

Body image concerns correlate with general quality of life (Avis et al., 2005) and are high on women's list of fears and worries about the diagnosis. Thomas-MacLean (2005), for instance, identified three key themes in interviews with women with breast cancer: how it feels – e.g. sensation and breast loss; managing appearances – e.g. wearing prostheses; and "treatments without end" – e.g. induced menopause.

Most of the research in this area relates to the effects of treatment in the early stages of the disease. There may have been an assumption that people with advanced or terminal illness may be more concerned about their impending loss of life than their body image. Kissane and colleagues (2004), comparing women with early stage breast cancer with those with metastatic disease (i.e. cancer spread to distant sites), found the women with advanced disease were less distressed by hair loss but actually more dissatisfied with body image. They were also more likely to report lymphoedema and hot flushes than the women with early stage disease. Most patients seen by palliative care services experience decreased appetite and weight loss. In advanced disease these changes may be an external sign of the seriousness of the illness, which forces the patient and those around her to face the reality of the situation (McClement, 2005).

Body image is also an important predictor of sexual health in women with breast cancer (Ganz et al., 1999). How a woman perceives her partner's reaction to the diagnosis and treatment of her breast cancer influences marital satisfaction and psychosexual adjustment (Wimberley et al., 2005). In Wimberley's study, women were followed up for a year after surgery. Their initial perception of partner involvement predicted psychosexual adjustment, emotional distress and marital satisfaction. Adverse reaction to the scar, lack of partner initiation of sex and poor quality of the first sexual experience after treatment were associated with poorer marital adjustment and more emotional distress. However, 42% of couples reported that cancer had brought them closer together (Dorval et al., 2005).

Yurek et al. (2000) found that sexuality was more problematic for women receiving mastectomy plus reconstruction than for women undergoing mastectomy alone or breast conserving surgery. Women who had had reconstruction showed lower rates of sexual activity and less sexual responsiveness. A more negative sexual self-concept predicted greater sexual difficulties. Qualitative investigation (Wilmoth, 2001) has revealed that sexual self-concept can be affected by loss of the breast, but also loss of womanhood, loss of sexual sensations, loss of youth and loss of menstruation from a chemically induced menopause.

Some types of breast cancer are "oestrogen dependent" – their growth is influenced by oestrogen. Therefore, chemically induced artificial menopause can be beneficial. Oestrogen dependent tumours can also be treated by endocrine treatments such as Tamoxifen, which induces a reversible menopause. Menopausal symptoms will obviously have an effect on body image, with changes in body shape, weight gain, loss of breast tissue and vaginal dryness all causing psychological distress. The knowledge that one is no longer fertile may interact with changes in body image from surgery or chemotherapy to compound a feeling of loss of femininity.

Other systemic treatments to kill cancer cells are used – that is, cytotoxic chemotherapy – either before surgery to reduce the size of a large tumour so that a lumpectomy can be performed rather than a mastectomy, or after surgery as an adjuvant therapy. Reasons for giving adjuvant chemotherapy include the presence of axillary lymph nodes containing cancer, a large primary tumour or an aggressive tumour. Chemotherapy is usually given as a combination of different agents. Side effects vary but the commonest include nausea, vomiting and diarrhoea, hair loss and amenorrhoea. These potentially have a major impact on a woman's body image.

Hair loss is associated with depression, loss of confidence and shame, and for some women may be more distressing than the loss of a breast. It is the most feared side effect of chemotherapy for 56% of women, and as many as

8% may be at risk of refusing chemotherapy because of this fear. After treatment, 47% of women still rate it as the worst side effect (Freedman, 1994). McGarvey et al. (2001) identified four common reactions in a group of women experiencing hair loss after chemotherapy: feeling unprepared, feeling shocked, feeling embarrassed and feeling a loss of sense of self. When compared with cancer patients without hair loss, those with alopecia have a significantly poorer body image (Nerenz et al., 1986). Measures of self esteem and body image deteriorate over the course of chemotherapy and do not invariably recover with regrowth of hair.

It is not surprising, then, that chemotherapy is associated with higher levels of sexual dysfunction (Arora et al., 2001; Berglund et al., 2001). Endocrine therapy also has an impact, although this effect is reversible. Addition of endocrine therapy (Zoladex or Tamoxifen alone or in combination) does not increase the problems with sexual functioning (Berglund et al., 2001).

A recent study found a significant incidence of obesity in breast cancer survivors, although this seemed to be associated with premorbid obesity and decreased physical activity rather than adjuvant therapy (Herman et al., 2005).

BREAST CANCER, BODY IMAGE DISTURBANCE AND COGNITIVE BEHAVIOURAL THERAPY

Sally is a 40-year-old single teacher who has had a mastectomy with a TRAM flap reconstruction. She was very pretty when she was a girl and was a much-loved only child. Her parents were very worried about their own and her health and she grew up with her own concerns about the dangers of becoming ill. She learned that people valued her for her attractiveness and came to believe that her many boyfriends were only really interested in her because she was pretty. At the time of her diagnosis she was not in a relationship and was already feeling quite vulnerable. Breast cancer activated both her schemas related to illness and her negative body image schema. She became worried that she might have a recurrence and feared that the reconstruction would hide it. She began to ruminate about this and took to manually checking her breasts two or three times a day in response to her anxious thoughts. She also feared that no one would love her now that she was "no longer whole". She could not bring herself to look at herself undressed and worried that if she met a man now she would not be able to cope if he asked her out. She therefore avoided social situations where she might encounter eligible men. Nonetheless, she felt she had to look stunning when she did go out in order to feel OK about herself. She was caught on the horns of two dilemmas:

1   If she looked at herself undressed she felt disgusted, but if she didn't she feared she might miss a recurrence.
2   If she went out she had to look perfect, but this only seemed to draw more attention to herself.

Therapy with Sally would be based very much on developing and sharing this conceptualisation in a collaborative way, helping her to understand how this way of thinking about herself came to be. It is also important to validate her experience through this "compassionate conceptualisation" (see Figure 6.1).

Sally can begin to monitor her negative thoughts in response to situations such as coming across TV programmes about cancer or having to meet people socially. Her avoidant behaviours and her defensive over-attention to her appearance can be identified through this monitoring. Her interpretations of these situations can be explored and questioned, but one of the most important interventions will be to help her test the usefulness of her behavioural strategies. She can experiment with spending some days checking and then spending some days resisting the urge to check, to evaluate the effect on her mood.

Work on her body image schema requires her to experiment with looking at herself to test if her internal image of how she looks is actually realistic. This may need to be done in a graded way, perhaps looking at herself in her bra before looking at herself naked. She can also experiment with going out with less make up on.

Sally has a number of dysfunctional beliefs about her appearance. She believes that because she has had a breast reconstruction she is completely unattractive. She also believes that if she is not stunningly attractive she is worthless. Cognitive restructuring to challenge these beliefs might include asking her what characteristics she values in other people – usually these do not include physical attractiveness above qualities like loyalty, kindness and a sense of humour – and showing her how she operates different systems for herself and for others. She will also need to start to value herself for her own strengths and positive features unrelated to appearance. Through learning to be more gentle and compassionate in how she talks to herself, and testing whether other people will be as rejecting as she fears, she will be able to achieve a more balanced view of her attractiveness and her risk of recurrence.

This model of therapy is described in Moorey and Greer (2002), and has been evaluated in the treatment of patients with anxiety and depression (Greer et al., 1992). Although patients with body image problems formed part of the sample, this was not exclusively a treatment for body image problems.

No trials of psychological interventions specifically targeted at body image problems in breast cancer have been reported. There are, however, two of trials of interventions promoting physical activity and movement that report improvements in body image (Pinto et al., 2005; Sandel et al., 2005). Further intervention research in this area is needed.

CONCLUSIONS

Body image is central to many women's view of themselves and to their self esteem. Cultural, interpersonal and physical factors all contribute to the development of body image schemas. Cognitive behavioural models of body image emphasise how negative schemas become activated when there is a change in body appearance through illness or disfigurement. These schemas distort body image, and accompanying coping strategies of avoidance and overcompensation serve to maintain negative self image and low self esteem.

Breast cancer poses a threat to both survival and self image, and there is a complex interaction between these challenges in the adjustment process. There is evidence that the more disfiguring the surgery, the more body image is disturbed. Despite this the majority of women undergoing breast surgery are well adjusted and body image disturbance is strongly influenced by previous body image satisfaction.

Reconstructive surgery can be beneficial for women who have had mastectomies, although it is not a panacea. Other treatments such as chemotherapy and endocrine therapy can also have a negative effect on body image. Future research needs to focus on how the cognitive behavioural model can lead to more specific interventions for body image disturbance in women with cancer.

REFERENCES

Alderman, A. K., Wilkins, E. G., Lowery, J. C., Kim, M. and Davis, J. A. (2000) Determinants of patient satisfaction in postmastectomy breast reconstruction, *Plastic and Reconstructive Surgery*, 106 (4), 769–776.

Al-Ghazal, S. K., Fallowfield, L. and Blamey, R. W. (2000) Comparison of psychological aspects and patient satisfaction following breast conserving surgery, simple mastectomy and breast reconstruction, *European Journal of Cancer*, 36, 1938–1943.

Al-Ghazal, S. K., Blamey, R. W., Stewart, J. and Morgan, A. A. (1999) The cosmetic outcome in early breast cancer treated with breast conservation, *European Journal of Surgical Oncology*, 25, 566–570.

American Psychiatric Association (2000) *Diagnostic and statistical manual of mental disorders* (4th edn text revision), Washington, DC, American Psychiatric Association.

Arora, N. K., Gustafson, D. H., Hawkins, R. P., McTavish, F., Cella, D. F.,

Pingree, S., Mendenhall, J. H. and Mahvi, D. M. (2001) Impact of surgery and chemotherapy on the quality of life of younger women with breast carcinoma: A prospective study, *Cancer*, 92, 1288–1298.

Avis, N. E., Crawford, S. and Manuel, J. (2005) Quality of life among younger women with breast cancer, *Journal of Clinical Oncology*, 23, 3322–3330.

Barnes, J., Stein, A., Smith, T. and Pollock, J. I. (1997) Extreme attitudes to body shape, social and psychological factors and a reluctance to breast feed, *Journal of the Royal Society of Medicine*, 90, 551–559.

Bartelink, H., van Dam, F. and van Dongen, J. (1985) Psychological effects of breast conserving therapy in comparison with radical mastectomy, *International Journal of Radiation Oncology and Biological Physics*, 1 (1), 381–385.

Berglund, G., Nystedt, M., Boulnd, C., Sjödén, P. and Rutquist, L. (2001) Effect of endocrine treatment on sexuality in premenopausal breast cancer patients: A prospective randomised study, *Journal of Clinical Oncology*, 19, 2788–2796.

Carver, C. S., Pozo-Kaderman, C., Price, A. A., Noriega, V., Harris, S. D., Derhagopian, R. P., Robinson, D. S. and Moffatt, F. L. Jr (1998) Concern about aspects of body image and adjustment to early stage breast cancer, *Psychosomatic Medicine*, 60, 168–174.

Cash, T. F. (2002) Cognitive behavioural perspectives on body image, in T. F. Cash and T. Pruzinsky (eds) *Body image: A handbook of theory, research, and clinical practice*, pp. 269–276, New York, Guilford Press.

Cash, T. F. and Pruzinsky, T. (eds) (2000) *Body image: A handbook of theory, research, and clinical practice*, New York: Guilford Press.

Dimartino, L., Murenu, G., Demontis, B. and Licheri, S. (1993) Reconstructive surgery in operable breast cancer, *Annals of New York Academy of Sciences*, 698, 227–245.

Dorval, M., Guay, S., Mondor, M., Masse, B., Falardeau, M., Robidoux, A., Deschenes, L. and Maunsell, E. (2005) Couples who get closer after breast cancer: Frequency and predictors in a prospective investigation, *Journal of Clinical Oncology*, 23, 3588–3596.

Fallowfield, L. J., Baum, M. and Maguire, G. P. (1986) Effects of breast conservation on psychological morbidity associated with diagnosis and treatment of early breast cancer, *British Medical Journal*, 293, 1331–1334.

Figueiredo, M. I., Cullen, J., Hwang, Y.-T., Rowland, J. H. and Mandelblatt, J. S. (2004) Breast cancer treatment in older women: Does getting what you want improve your long-term body image and mental health?, *Journal of Clinical Oncology*, 22, 4002–4009.

Fisher, B., Anderson, S., Bryant, J., Margolese, R. G., Deutsch, M., Fisher, E. R., Jeong, J. H. and Wolmark, N. (2002) Twenty-year follow-up of a randomized trial comparing total mastectomy, lumpectomy, and lumpectomy plus irradiation for the treatment of invasive breast cancer, *New England Journal of Medicine*, 347, 1233–1241.

Fredrickson, B. L. and Roberts, T. (1997) Objectification theory: Toward understanding women's lived experiences and mental health risks, *Psychology of Women Quarterly*, 21, 173–206.

Freedman, T. G. (1994) Social and cultural dimensions of hair loss in women treated for breast cancer, *Cancer Nursing*, 17, 334–341.

Frost, M. H., Slezak, J. M., Tran, N. V., Williams, C. I., Johnson, J. L., Woods, J.

E., Petty, P. M., Donohue, J. H., Grant, C. S., Sloan, J. A., Sellers, T. A. and Hartmann, L. C. (2005) Satisfaction after contralateral prophylactic mastectomy: the significance of mastectomy type, reconstructive complications and body appearance, *Journal of Clinical Oncology*, 23, 7849–7856.

Ganz, P. A., Desmon, K. A., Belin, T. R., Meyerowitz, B. E. and Rowland, J. H. (1999) Predictors of sexual health in women after breast cancer, *Journal of Clinical Oncology*, 17, 2371–2380.

Grabe, S., Routledge, C., Cook, A., Andersen, C. and Arndt, J. (2005) In defense of the body: The effect of mortality salience on female body objectification, *Psychology of Women Quarterly*, 29, 33–37.

Greer, S., Moorey, S., Baruch, J. D. R., Watson, M., Robertson, B. M., Mason, A., Rowden, L., Law, M. G. and Bliss, J. M. (1992) Adjuvant psychological therapy for cancer patients: A prospective randomised trial, *British Medical Journal*, 304, 675–680.

Harcourt, D. and Rumsey, N. (2001) Psychological aspects of breast reconstruction: A review of the literature, *Journal of Advanced Nursing*, 35, 477–487.

Harcourt, D., Rumsey, N. J., Ambler, N. R., Cawthorn, S. J., Reid, C., Maddox, P., Kenealy, J., Rainsbury, R. and Umpleby, H. (2003) The psychological effect of mastectomy with or without breast reconstruction: A prospective, multicenter study, *Plastic and Reconstructive Surgery*, 111, 1060–1068.

Hartl, K., Janni, W., Kastner, R., Sommer, H., Strobl, B., Rack, B. and Stauber, M. (2003) *Annals of Oncology*, 14, 1064–1071.

Hatcher, M. B., Fallowfield, L. and A'Hern, R. (2001) The psychosocial impact of bilateral prophylactic mastectomy: Prospective study using questionnaires and semistructured interviews, *British Medical Journal*, 322, 1–7.

Herman, D. R., Ganz, P. A., Petersen, L. and Greendale, G. A. (2005) Obesity and cardiovascular risk factors in younger breast cancer survivors: The cancer and menopause study (CAMS), *Breast Cancer Research and Treatment*, 93, 13–23.

Holtzmann, J. and Timm, H. (2005) The experience of and the nursing care of breast cancer patients undergoing immediate reconstruction, *European Journal of Cancer Care*, 14, 310–318.

Hopwood, P. (1998) *Body Image Scale: CRC Psychological Medicine Group*, Manchester, University of Manchester.

Janz, N. K., Mahasin, M., Lantz, P. M., Fagerlin, A., Salem, B., Morrow, M., Deapen, D. and Katz, S. (2005) Population-based study of the relationship of treatment and sociodemographics on quality of life for early stage breast cancer, *Quality of Life Research*, 14, 1467–1479.

Keith, D. J., Walker, M. B., Walker, L. G., Heyrs, S. D., Sarkar, T. K., Hutchenon, A. W., Andrew, W., Eremia, O. and Hopwood, P. (2003) Women who wish for breast reconstruction: Characteristics, fears and hopes, *Plastic and Reconstructive Surgery*, 111, 1051–1056.

Kemeny, M. M., Wellisch, D. K. and Schain, W. S. (1988) Psychosocial outcome in a randomised surgical trial for treatment of primary breast cancer, *Cancer*, 62, 1231–1237.

Kissane, D., Grabsch, B., Love, A., Clarke, D. M., Bloch, S. and Smith, G. C. (2004) Psychiatric disorder in women with early stage and advanced breast cancer: A comparative analysis, *Australian and New Zealand Journal of Psychiatry*, 38 (5), 320–326.

Kopel, S. J., Eiser, C., Cool, P., Grimer, R. J. and Carter, S. R. (1998) Brief report: Assessment of body image in survivors of childhood cancer, *Journal of Pediatric Psychology*, 23, 141–147.

McClement, S. (2005) Cancer anorexia-cachexia syndrome: Psychological effect on the patient and family, *Journal of Wound, Ostomy and Continence Nursing*, 32, 264–268.

McGarvey, E. L., Baum, L. D., Pinkerton, R. C. and Rogers, L. M. (2001) Psychological sequelae and alopecia among women with cancer, *Cancer Practice*, 9, 283–289.

Maguire, G. P., Tait, A., Brooke, M., Thomas, C., Howatt, J. M., Sellwood, R. A. and Bush, H. (1980) Psychiatric morbidity and physical toxicity associated with adjuvant chemotherapy after mastectomy, *British Medical Journal*, 281, 1179–1180.

Metcalfe, K. A., Sempie, J. L. and Narod, S. A. (2004) Satisfaction with breast reconstruction in women with bilateral prophylactic mastectomy: A descriptive study, *Plastic and Reconstructive Surgery*, 114, 360–366.

Moorey, S. and Greer, S. (2002) *Cognitive behaviour therapy for people with cancer* Oxford, Oxford University Press.

Nerenz, D. R., Love, R. R. and Leventhal, H. (1986) Psychosocial consequences of cancer chemotherapy for elderly patients, *Health Services Research*, 20, 960–976.

Nissen, M. J., Swenson, K. K., Ritz, L. J., Farrell, J. B., Sladek, M. L. and Lally, R. M. (2001) Quality of life after breast carcinoma surgery: A comparison of three surgical procedures, *Cancer*, 91, 1238–1246.

Petronis, V. M., Carver, C. S., Antoni, M. H. and Weiss, S. (2003) Investment in body image and psychosocial well-being among women treated for early stage breast cancer: Partial replication and extension, *Psychology and Health*, 18, 1–13.

Pinto, B. M., Frierson, G. M., Rabin, C., Trunzo, J. J. and Marcus, B. H. (2005) Home based physical activity intervention for breast cancer patients, *Journal of Clinical Oncology*, 23, 3577–3587.

Pruzinsky, T. (2002) Reconstructive surgery in acquired disfigurement, in T. F. Cash and T. Pruzinsky (eds) *Body image: A handbook of theory, research, and clinical practice*, pp. 440–449, New York, Guilford Press.

Reas, D. L. and Grilo, C. M. (2004) Cognitive-behavioral assessment of body image disturbances, *Journal of Psychiatric Practice*, 10, 314–322.

Roth, R. S., Lowery, J. C., Davis, J. and Wilkins, E. G. (2005) Quality of life and affective distress in women seeking immediate versus delayed breast reconstruction after mastectomy for breast cancer, *Plastic and Reconstructive Surgery*, 116, 993–1002.

Sandel, S. L., Judge, J. O., Landry, N. et al. (2005) Dance and movement program improves quality-of-life measures in breast cancer survivors, *Cancer Nursing*, 28, 301–309.

Thomas-MacLean, R. (2005) Beyond dichotomies of health and illness: Life after breast cancer, *Nursing Inquiry*, 12, 200–209.

Tiggeman, M. (2004) Body image across the adult life span: Stability and change, *Body Image*, 1, 29–41.

Veronesi, U., Cascinelli, N., Mariani, L., Greco, M., Saccozzi, R. M. D., Luini, A., Aguilar, M. and Marubini, E. (2002) Twenty-year follow-up of a randomized study comparing breast-conserving surgery with radical mastectomy for early breast cancer, *New England Journal of Medicine*, 347, 1227–1232.

White, C. A. (2000) Body image dimensions and cancer: A heuristic cognitive-behavioural model, *Psycho-oncology*, 9, 183–192.

White, C. A. (2002) Body images in oncology, in T. F. Cash and T. Pruzinsky (eds) *Body image: A handbook of theory, research, and clinical practice*, pp. 379–386, New York, Guilford Press.

Wilkins, E. G., Cederna, P. S., Lowery, J. C., Goldfarb, S., Roth, R. S., Perkins, A., Shaheen, K. W., Izenberg, P. H. and Houin, H. (2000) Prospective analysis of psychosocial outcomes in breast reconstruction: One year postoperative results from the Michigan Breast Reconstruction Outcome Study, *Plastic and Reconstructive Surgery*, 106, 1014–1025.

Wilmoth, M. C. (2001) The aftermath of breast cancer: An altered sexual self, *Cancer Nursing*, 24, 278–286.

Wimberley, S. R., Carver, C. S., Laurenceau, J., Harris, S. D. and Antoni, M. H. (2005) Perceived partner reactions to diagnosis and treatment of breast cancer: Impact on psychosocial and psychosexual adjustment, *Journal of Consulting and Clinical Psychology*, 73, 300–311.

Yilmazer, N., Aydiner, A., Ozkan, S., Aslay, I. and Blige, N. (1994) A comparison of body image, self-esteem and social support in total mastectomy and breast-conserving therapy in Turkish women, *Supportive Care in Cancer*, 2, 238–241.

Yurek, D., Farrar, W. and Andersen, B. A. (2000) Breast cancer surgery: Comparing surgical groups and determining individual differences in postoperative sexuality and body change stress, *Journal of Consulting and Clinical Psychology*, 68, 697–709.

Part III

The reproductive body

This section covers the female body in relation to its reproductive function. Chapter 7 deals with the natural history of women's bodies, and discusses gender differences in prenatal biological programming and its effects in adult life. From there, Chapter 8 takes us onto woman's journey to become a mother, dealing with psychosocial issues related to mothering. Issues of thwarted motherhood and emerging types of motherhood are discussed. The focus of Chapter 9 is mental health problems in the perinatal period. The diathesis-stress model of disease vulnerability is discussed with reference to women's biological changes and environmental factors. Chapter 10 covers the issue of infanticide/neonaticide, including aspects related to gender, mental illness and criminal behaviour.

Chapter 7

Women's bodies

Natural history and biological programming

Dora Kohen

INTRODUCTION

Human beings are complex multifaceted organisms. There are few factors, if any, that can have effects independent of the individual as a whole. Most medical and psychiatric disorders are products of bio-psycho-social interactions and are interdependent on a series of complex and multiple biological, psychological and social factors.

The biological factors that contribute to mental health disorders, particularly genetic factors, have been the subject of extensive research, including research into the genetics, imaging and physiology of schizophrenia, affective disorders and minor psychiatric morbidity. Although there are still unanswered questions, a considerable amount of data has accumulated on the biological mechanisms of these disorders in recent years.

The interplay of human biology with lifestyle factors and their effect on pregnant women with mental health problems have received particular attention in the last decade. Today there is a large body of experimental and clinical data suggesting that environmental and lifestyle factors such as different stimuli and stresses operating *in utero* or early life affect the developing foetus, sometimes permanently and irreversibly altering structures and functions of the foetus (Andrews and Mathews, 2004; Louvart et al., 2005). This process with its persistent organizational effects has been called prenatal (foetal) programming.

The concept of biological (foetal) programming includes all the adverse effects in foetal life that permanently alter the structure and physiology of the foetus and consequently the adult offspring.

PRENATAL STRESS AND FOETAL PROGRAMMING

Maternal antenatal anxiety has a programming effect on the foetus, and this is reflected in a range of persistent behavioural abnormalities in the offspring. O'Connor et al. (2003) show that results in animal studies completed under laboratory conditions are well reflected in human off-spring. Furthermore, a direct link has been established between antenatal maternal mood and foetal behaviour. Prospective studies have shown a link between antenatal maternal stress and cognitive, behavioural and emotional problems in the child (Van den Bergh et al., 2005). High antenatal maternal stress has also been related to attention deficit and hyperactivity disorder (ADHD) symptoms (Van den Bergh and Marcoen, 2004).

Studies of prenatal stress completed on female animals show changes in behavioural responses in the offspring such as increased immobility and hypoactivity in a novel environment (Louvart et al., 2005). Prenatal programming is also known to change responses to stress, and to contribute to psychological disorders in childhood and at an adult age.

Prenatal maternal stress causes spontaneous abortion, preterm labour and low birth weight, with its association with cardio-vascular problems, metabolic disorders and neuro-endocrine dysfunction (Ward et al., 2004).

Recent studies have shown that the use of alcohol in pregnancy could disrupt maternal–foetal hormonal interactions and affect the female's ability to maintain a successful pregnancy. It may also contribute to foetal alcohol syndrome in the infant. Early environmental experiences including exposure to alcohol can re-programme the foetal hypothalamo–pituitary–adrenal axis (HPA) axis and affect immune functions (Zhang et al., 2005).

Most of the initial information on biological programming came from animal studies. Animal experiments have contributed greatly to our more recent understanding of foetal programming and have helped to elucidate issues of gender-specific programming related to energy and hormonal homeostasis (Dahlgreen et al., 2001).

PRENATAL PROGRAMMING, GENDER DIFFERENCES AND ENERGY HOMEOSTASIS

An altered nutritional milieu during pregnancy and early development has been found to set the pace for future metabolic activities. Early adaptation can change the organism's physiology and metabolism and these changes continue to be expressed even in the absence of the stimulus that initiated them. Undernutrition or malnutrition of the mother during gestation is responsible for the programming of hyperinsulinamia and hyperleptinemia in the offspring, and may lead to the later development of certain disorders such as diabetes, obesity, hypertension and their cardiovascular complications (Ward et al., 2004). Antenatal exposure to glucocorticoids (GC) has also been implicated in the process of regulating both insulin and leptin levels (O'Regan et al., 2001; Seckl, 2001).

Leptin is the hormone responsible for regulating energy balance, metabolism and reproduction. Leptin is an important regulator of adipose tissue mass and body weight. Leptin operates by inhibiting food intake and stimulating energy expenditure. The expression and secretion of leptin is correlated with body fat and is affected by the amount of food intake. Adiposity hormones such as leptin and insulin interact with food intake hormones in the brain. There is a normally robust negative feedback system that controls energy homeostasis, responding to different inputs from past changes and experiences.

Leptin is known to be elevated in obesity. The early origins of obesity and the programming of the appetite regulatory system have been studied in rodents (McMillen et al., 2005); exposure to increased or decreased levels of intra-uterine nutrition can result in increased adiposity and increased levels of leptin and other appetite regulatory peptides in rodents in adult life (McMillen et al., 2004).

Leptin is also widely implicated in the stress response. It stimulates the release of gonadotrophin hormones and corticosteroids that, in turn, contribute to the determination of sex differences in the sensitivity of the brain to adiposity hormones (Colombel and Charbonnel, 1997). Chronic stress induced in laboratory animals is followed by decreased leptin concentration in males. Hence, chronic stress results in decreased food intake in males. On the other hand, non-stressed females have lower leptin levels than males; hence, body weight in chronic stress is considered an index of behaviour adaptivity and gender differences.

Gender also influences the efficacy of adiposity hormones. The female brain is more sensitive to the catabolic actions of low doses of leptin, and the male brain is sensitive to the catabolic action of insulin (Woods et al., 2003). Levels of insulin and leptin in the blood are correlated with body fat, and high visceral fat and plasma insulin levels are known risk factors for obesity, type-2 diabetes, cardiovascular disorders and cancers.

PRENATAL PROGRAMMING, GENDER DIFFERENCES AND HORMONAL HOMEOSTASIS

Neuro-endocrine regulatory mechanisms are under the control of different factors including early life programming and environment. Prenatal stress influences behavioural and immediate response to several different kinds of stress in adulthood.

The neuro-endocrine axes are the hypothalamo–pituitary–adrenal axis (HPA), the hypothalamo–pituitary–thyroid system (HP–thyroid), the hypothalamo–pituitary–gonadal axis (HP–gonadal) and the hypothalamo–pituitary–growth hormone axis (HP–GH) (see Table 7.1).

The neuro-endocrine axes are regulated by neurohormones released from special cells in the hypothalamus, which in turn are regulated by a variety of neurotransmitters and neuropeptides (see Table 7.2).

Table 7.1 The neuro-endocrine axes

1   The hypothalamo–pituitary–adrenal axis (HPA)
2   The hypothalamo–pituitary–thyroid axis (HP–thyroid)
3   The hypothalamo–pituitary–gonadal axis (HP–gonadal)
4   The hypothalamo–pituitary–growth hormone axis (HP–GH)

Table 7.2 Neurohormones

CRH,	corticotrophin releasing hormone
ACTH,	adrenocorticotropic hormone
GHRH,	growth hormone releasing hormone
TRH,	thyrotropin releasing hormone
TSH,	thyroid stimulating hormone
GnRH,	gonadotropin releasing hormone

The hypothalamo–pituitary–adrenal axis

The HPA integrates and regulates behavioural responses to stress. The mechanism involved in the permanent programming of the HPA is complex and multifactorial (Matthews, 2000). The driving force behind the activation of the HPA axis is corticotrophin releasing hormone (CRH), released from the hypothalamus. CRH stimulates the release of ACTH. ACTH acts peripherally on the release of glucocorticoid cortisol, which has many peripheral effects on the metabolic and immune system. It inhibits immune and inflammatory activity and induces the release of several enzymes and proteins (Orth and Kovacs, 1992). The high levels of cortisol induced by stress are inhibited by a negative feedback system. Negative feedback is important in the control of adrenal steroid secretion and in the prevention of the potential harmful effects of glucocorticoid excess. Alterations in this feedback system contribute to affective changes such as depression.

The ability of the early environment to programme the developing HPA axis has been reported in several animal species. There is considerable evidence that a similar programme can occur in humans and that long-term alterations in HPA are associated with altered susceptibility and disorders in later life.

Environmental stress increases the secretion of cortisol: the programming of the HPA axis is responsible for changes in cortisol levels as a response to stress. There is also considerable interplay between the development of the HPA and the reproductive axes. There is evidence that this interaction is modified by early environmental changes. The HPA axis and glucocorticoid receptor expression are involved in the processes underlying foetal programming (O'Regan et al., 2001; Seckl, 2001). Changes in the HPA axis and GCs have been held responsible for some mental health problems.

Dysregulation of the HPA is responsible for mood and anxiety disorders. The HPA axis has involvement with the serotonergic system, which has been identified as the primary system involved in mood disorders. Adverse environmental influences affect the developing HPA, and in turn susceptibility to disease in later life, through changes in serotonin level. Understanding the mechanisms involved in this system will facilitate developmental interventions aiming to reverse or decrease the impact of adverse events (Andrews and Mathews, 2004).

The hypothalamo–pituitary–thyroid system

The HP–T system has a similar structure to that of the HPA axis. Thyroid stimulating hormone (TSH) originates in the hypothalamus and is transported to the anterior pituitary gland. It stimulates the synthesis and release of thyroid releasing hormone (TRH), which acts on the thyroid gland to stimulate the release of thyroid hormones. It is an established fact that dysfunction of the HP–T system is associated with affective disorders.

Thyroid dysfunction (TD) is more frequent in women and has unique consequences related to menstrual cycle, reproduction, generalized anxiety and mood disorders. It affects women's reproductive health. Hypothyroidism increases the rate of miscarriage and foetal death (Redmond, 2004). The incidence of post-partum thyroiditis has been noted to be as high as 5–6%.

The hypothalamo–pituitary–gonadal axis

Gonadotropin releasing factor (GnRF), produced in the hypothalamus, brings about the release of FSH and LH from the anterior pituitary. These hormones stimulate the release of gonadal steroids such as oestrogen, progesterone and testosterone.

In the luteal phase of the female's menstrual cycle, sympathetic nervous system activity is significantly greater than in the follicular phase; parasympathetic nervous activity is predominant in the follicular phase. These findings can explain fluctuations in cardiovascular reactivity to mental stress, its relationship to the menstrual cycle and the increased risk of coronary heart disease in women following menopause (Sato and Miyake, 2004).

The role of gonadal hormones extends beyond reproduction: they also have a neuroregulatory effect on mood. However, the association of the decline in pituitary gonadotropin and oestrogen with specific psychiatric disorders such as mood disorders has been controversial (Schmidt et al., 1997). In addition, the therapeutic and clinical efficacy of sex hormones in treating affective disorders has not yet been proven.

Gonadal hormones provide the biological basis for sex differences in behavioural responses to many drugs (Festa and Quinones-Jenab, 2004). Clinical and rodent studies indicate that hormonal fluctuations during the menstrual cycle modulate cocaine-induced subjective effects in women, and may form the biological basis of sex-specific differences in cocaine addiction.

Androgens play a prominent role in the organization and programming of brain circuits subsequently activated by gonadal steroids. They have a role in sexuality, aggression, cognition, emotionality and personality. Androgens also mediate gender-related differences in pharmacodynamics and pharmacokinetics, and affect the course of treatment and response to medication in several psychiatric disorders.

Androgen hormones have been associated with mood and behavioural changes (Rubinow and Schmidt, 1996). Women have low but consistent levels of androgens, and androgen levels decline further in the menopause.

However, recent epidemiological and clinical studies have not been able to show that depressive disorders significantly increase in the perimenopausal period (Soares et al., 2005). In addition, the use of synthetic oestrogen and progesterone to replace the hormones, and to treat the possible depressive symptoms associated with the changes, has shown no significant effectiveness.

THE IMPACT OF BIOLOGICAL PROGRAMMING ON MOOD AND STRESS

Prenatal biological programming occurs in every individual but in an adverse intra-uterine environment it can alter the foetal metabolic and hormonal milieu, resulting in changes to the developmental process and adaptive responses. Continuation of these changes could give rise to metabolic and cardiovascular disorders, as discussed earlier. They may also lead to the development of a number of psychiatric disorders including depression, anxiety, post-traumatic stress disorder, eating disorders and substance dependence (see Table 7.3).

Early life programming of the neuro-endocrine systems by stress underlies common psychiatric disorders (Welberg and Seckl, 2001). Early life dysregulation of HPA activity, and subsequent fluctuation of the circulating neurosteroids, is considered responsible for increasing women's propensity to such disorders (Born et al., 1995; Dinan, 2001; Nemeroff, 1996). HPA dysregulation is also associated with a range of anxiety disorders including panic and post-traumatic stress disorder.

There is evidence that maltreatment in childhood may lead to disruption of HPA axis functions. Factors such as age at maltreatment and type of

Table 7.3 Disorders associated with biological programming

Medical	Psychiatric
Obesity	Depression
Diabetes	Anxiety
Hypertension	PTSD
Hypersinsulinaemia	Sexual abuse
Metabolic syndrome	Premenstrual dysphoric disorder (PMDD)
Addiction disorders	Eating disorders
Cardiovascular and cerebrovascular problems	Alcohol dependence
Disruption in reproductive cycle	
Thyroid dysfunction	

maltreatment – physical, emotional or sexual abuse – may influence the degree and pattern of HPA disturbance (Van Voorhees and Scarpa, 2004). HPA axis hyperactivity is prominent in adults with depressive and anxiety disorders, which may constitute a link between adversity in childhood and the development of adult pathology. Dysregulation of the stress system may render victims of sex abuse more vulnerable to the development of major depression as well as eating disorders, post-traumatic stress disorder and somatization disorders. The finding of abnormal ACTH and cortisol levels in post-traumatic stress disorder supports the hypothesis (Yehuda et al., 2004).

PREMENSTRUAL SYNDROME

Population surveys show premenstrual syndrome to be quite common, especially among younger women, causing much suffering. The severe form is called premenstrual dysphoric disorder (PMDD) and is a leading cause of recurrent short-term absences from work and a common problem in women of reproductive age (APA, 1994).

Premenstrual syndrome manifests itself in fatigue, irritability, fluctuations in mood, dysregulated appetite and decreased or increased sleep.

In the case of the dysphoria associated with premenstrual syndrome, there is no evidence to show abnormalities in basal ovarian hormone secretion. FSH and LH levels in women with premenstrual syndrome have been shown to be normal (Smith et al., 2004).

In women, insomnia is influenced by hormonal cycles. HPA changes have been associated with sleep disturbances. Premenstrual insomnia and premenstrual hypersomnia have been included in the International Classification of Sleep Disorders (ICSD) as a category of sleep disorder associated with menses (Miller, 2004).

Migraine is also a common symptom of premenstrual syndrome. Migraine is frequent in women in general, especially during the reproductive years, and 60% of women affected by migraine relate the periodicity of their migraine attacks to the menstrual cycle. The menstrual migraine, which occurs immediately before, during or immediately after the menstrual flow, is an undefined condition. Hormonal changes have been implicated in the aetiology of migraine. Although the pathogenesis of menstrual migraine is not clear, oestrogen withdrawal seems to have a role as a trigger for the migraine attacks (MacGregor, 2004).

Hormonal fluctuation through the menstrual cycle is also blamed for reducing the seizure threshold, rendering women vulnerable to menstrual fits. Oestrogen is known to have a proconvulsant effect and progesterone an anticonvulsant one. The same hormonal variations also affect anti-epileptic drugs across the menstrual cycle and may contribute to increased susceptibility to seizures. It is therefore important to take a longitudinal history with a carefully-kept seizure diary to determine the seizure pattern and its association with menstrual changes (Foldvary-Schaefer et al., 2004).

CONCLUSION

The issue of prenatal biological programming and its effects in adult life has been the focus of discussion in this chapter. Laboratory tests and animal research have increased our understanding of the prenatal processes that determine our adaptive responses in adult life. Lifestyle issues such malnutrition, stress-inducing environmental situations, excessive alcohol intake and drug abuse in pregnancy may cause irreversible changes in the foetus, increasing susceptibility to both physical and psychiatric disorders later in life. It is important to note that lifestyle issues in pregnancy are all part of the well-being of the pregnant woman. It is the pregnant woman's personal, environmental and social well-being that will establish the biological programming of the unborn infant. It is also the pregnant woman's mental and biological health that will determine the well-being of the foetus and the individual in the future years.

The importance of the facts above needs to be shared with all agencies involved in supporting pregnant women and in treating the problems of the infant, child and young adult. It is important to establish a bridge between the scientists who do biological, epidemiological and social sciences research and the mental health social workers, community nurses, midwives, counsellors and voluntary organizations involved with pregnant women with vulnerabilities and lifestyle problems. It is the bridge between those two domains that will help to identify the damage sustained in pregnancy, and the outcome in the foetus and the growing adult.

Also, further research is needed, particularly longitudinal studies specifically exploring issues of adaptivity, vulnerability and the expression of illness in individuals born to mothers with specific social and biological issues. Prospective follow-up programmes beginning in pregnancy and early life will substantiate the data we already have and yield more valid information.

REFERENCES

American Psychiatric Association (1994) *Diagnostic and statistical manual of mental disorders* (4th edn), Washington, DC, American Psychiatric Association.

Andrews, M. H. and Mathews, S. G. (2004) Programming of the hypthalamo-pituitary adrenal axis and serotonergic involvement, *Stress*, 7 (10), 15–27.

Born, J., Ditschuneit, I., Schreiber, M., Dodt, C. and Fehm, H. I. (1995) Effects of age and gender on pituitary-adrenocortical responsiveness in humans, *European Journal of Endocrinology*, 132, 705–711.

Colombel, A. and Charbonnel, B. (1997) Weight gain and cardiovascular factors in the postmenopausal woman, *Human Reproduction*, 12 (1), 134–145.

Dahlgreen, J., Nilson, C., Jennische, E., Ho, H.-P., Eriksson, E., Niklasson, A. et al. (2001) Prenatal cytokine exposure results in obesity and gender specific programming, *American Journal of Physiology: Endocrinology and Metabolism*, 281, E326–E334.

Dinan, T. G. (2001) Novel approaches to the treatment of depression by modulating the hypothalamo-pituitary adrenal axis, *Human Psychopharmacology*, 16 (1), 89–93.

Festa, E. D. and Quinones-Jenab, V. (2004) Gonadal hormones provide the biological basis for sex differences in behavioural responses to cocaine, *Hormones and Behaviour*, 46 (5), 509–519.

Foldvary-Schaefer, N., Harden, C., Herzog, A. and Falcone, T. (2004) Hormones and seizures, *Cleveland Clinical Journal of Medicine*, 71 (Suppl. 2), S11–S18.

Louvart, H., Maccari, S. and Darmaudery, M. (2005) Prenatal stress affects behavioural reactivity to an intense stress in adult female rats, *Brain Research*, 1031 (1), 67–73.

MacGregor, E. A. (2004) Oestrogen and attacks of migraine with and without aura, *Lancet Neurology*, 3 (6), 354–361.

McMillen, I. C., Adam, C. L. and Muhlhausler, B. S. (2005) Early origins of obesity: Programming the appetite regulatory system, *Journal of Physiology*, 15 (565), 9–17.

McMillen, I. C., Muhlhausler, B. S., Duffield, J. A. and Yuen, B. S. (2004) Prenatal programming of postnatal obesity and the regulation of leptin synthesis and secretion before birth, *Proceedings of the Nutritional Society*, 63 (3), 405–412.

Matthews, S. G. (2000) Antenatal glucocorticoids and programming of developing CNS, *Pediatrics Research*, 47, 291–300.

Miller, E. H. (2004) Women and insomnia, *Clinical Cornerstones*, 6 (Suppl. 1B), S8–S18.

Nemeroff, C. (1996) The corticotrophin-releasing factor (CRF) hypothesis of depression: New findings and new directions, *Molecular Psychiatry*, 1, 336–342.

O'Connor, T. G., Heron, J., Golding, J. and Glover, V. (2003) Maternal antenatal anxiety and behavioural/emotional problems in children: A test of a programming hypothesis, *Journal of Child Psychology and Psychiatry*, 44 (7), 1025–1036.

O'Regan, D., Welberg, L. L., Holmes, M. C. and Seckl, J. R. (2001) Glucocorticoid programming of pituitary-adrenal function mechanism and physiological consequences, *Seminars of Neonatology*, 6 (4), 319–329.

Orth, D. N. and Kovacs, W. J. (1992) The adrenal cortex, in J. D. Wilson and D. W. Foster (eds) *William's Textbook of Endocrinology*, pp. 486–621, Philadelphia, Saunders.

Redmond, G. P. (2004) Thyroid dysfunction and women's reproductive health, *Thyroid*, 14 (Suppl. 1), S5–S15.

Rubinow, D. R. and Schmidt, P. J. (1996) Androgens, brain and behaviour, *American Journal of Psychiatry*, 153 (8), 974–984.

Sato, N. and Miyake, S. (2004) Cardiovascular reactivity to mental stress: Relationship between menstrual cycle and gender, *Journal of Physiology, Anthropology and Applied Human Sciences*, 23 (6), 215–223.

Schmidt, P. J., Roca, C., Bloch, M. and Rubinow, D. R. (1997) The perimenopause and affective disorders, *Seminars on Reproduction and Endocrinology*, 15 (1), 91–100.

Seckl, J. R. (2001) Glucocorticoid programming of the fetus: Adult phenomena and molecular mechanism, *Molecular and Cellular Endocrinology*, 185 (1–2), 61–71.

Smith, M. J., Schmidt, P. J., Su, T. P. and Rubinow, D. R. (2004) Gonadotropin-releasing hormone-stimulated gonadotropin levels in women with menstrual dysphoria, *Gynaecology and Endocrinology*, 19 (6), 335–343.

Soares, C. N., Steiner, M. and Prouty, J. (2005) Effects of reproductive hormones and selective estrogen receptor modulators on the central nervous system during menopause, in D. E. Stewart (ed.) *Menopause*, pp. 33–56, Washington, DC, American Psychiatric Publishing Inc.

Van den Bergh, B. R. and Marcoen, A. (2004) High antenatal maternal anxiety is related to ADHD symptoms, externalizing problems, and anxiety in 8- and 9-year olds, *Child Development*, 75 (4), 1085–1097.

Van den Bergh, B. R., Mulder, E. J., Mennes, M. and Glover, V. (2005) Antenatal maternal anxiety and stress and the neurobehavioural development of the fetus and child: Links and possible mechanism. A review, *Neuroscience and Biobehavioural Review*, 29 (2), 237–258.

Van Voorhees, E. and Scarpa, A. (2004) The effects of child maltreatment on the hypothalamo-pituitary-adrenal axis, *Trauma Violence Abuse*, 5 (4), 333–352.

Ward, A. M., Moore, V. M., Steptoe, A., Cockington, R. A., Robinson, J. and Phillips, D. I. (2004) Size at birth and cardiovascular responses to psychological stressors: Evidence for prenatal programming in women, *Journal of Hypertension*, 22 (12), 2295–2301.

Welberg, L. A. and Seckl, J. R. (2001) Prenatal stress, glucocorticoids and the programming of the brain, *Journal of Neuroendocrinology*, 13 (2), 113–128.

Woods, S. C., Gotoh, K. and Clegg, D. J. (2003) Gender differences in the control of energy homeostasis, *Experimental Biology and Medicine*, 228, 1175–1180.

Yehuda, R., Golier, R. A., Halligan, S. L. et al. (2004) The ACTH response to dexamethasone in PTSD, *American Journal of Psychiatry*, 161 (8), 1397–1403.

Zhang, X., Sliwowska, J. H. and Weinberg, J. (2005) Prenatal alcohol exposure and fetal programming: Effects on neuroendocrine and immune function, *Experimental and Biological Medicine*, 230 (6), 376–388.

Chapter 8

"On being a mother"
Motherhood and mental health

Karen Baistow

INTRODUCTION

Motherhood is paradoxical: on the one hand it is essential, typical and ordinary and on the other unknown, unpredictable and almost mystical. In all societies the role is laden with symbolic meaning but its fulfilment is also highly practical. The biology of becoming a mother and the psychology of being a mother entail complex processes which, even if things run smoothly in the best of all possible worlds, are marked by periods of susceptibility and fragility. In more hostile and uneasy social environments they can be subjected to a range of pressures which make motherhood very difficult and mothers themselves vulnerable to a range of problems. How we make sense of these processes of becoming and being mothers and the potential problems they give rise to forms one focus of this chapter. The other focus concerns the ways in which motherhood is connected to broader social contexts, for these not only affect the experience of motherhood but also the expectations and demands placed on the role.

Discourses on motherhood and mental health often fall into two main types, broadly categorised as medical and feminist.

"Maternal insanity", especially mental disorder associated with pregnacy and childbirth, has been the subject of medical attention for the last 200 years (Marland, 2004). The nineteenth century saw a particular rise in interest and in 1858 Louis Marcé, a French psychiatrist, wrote the first treatise entirely devoted to puerperal mental illness. Contemporary medical discourses typically present descriptions of common mental disorders associated with motherhood, aetiological analyses and discussions of treatment options (see Chapter 9 in this volume). On the whole the approach is uncritical, accepting certain underlying assumptions about women, their bodies, motherhood and mental illness. Notwithstanding these assumptions, such texts help to draw attention to a relatively neglected area of health and health care and there are many useful psychiatric texts that offer valuable, humane coverage of maternal mental illness (see Brockington, 1998; Kohen, 2000; Kornstein and Clayton, 2002).

Feminist approaches, on the other hand, start from a critical position which typically attributes maternal mental health problems to gendered power relations in the form of sexism (psychiatric or otherwise), or to the material oppression of women. These arguments, which were well rehearsed in the feminist critiques of the 1970s, 1980s and 1990s (see e.g. Miles, 1991; Nicholson, 1998; Oakley, 1979, 1984; Ussher, 1991), provoked timely re-examinations of the taken-for-granted assumptions about women that underpinned medical approaches to women's mental illness and, in particular, the ways in which women's bodies were seen (and continue to be seen) as a source of pathological, emotional vulnerability. In particular, women's reproductive processes – menstruation, pregnancy, childbirth, the period afterwards and the cessation of these in the menopause – were cited as the focuses of negative medical attention. By analysing medical attitudes and practices towards the womb, feminist discourses illuminated the unequal power relations between women and men and the social institutions that reinforce them. They also brought new attention to the socially controlling functions of medicine and psychiatry. Importantly, feminist approaches highlighted the ways in which the unequal position of women in society – economically, educationally and socially – puts them at greater risk, not only of certain forms of mental ill health, like depression, but also of a range of health problems in general (see Chapter 1 in this volume).

However, the intention here is not to follow either route, each of which in its own way is characterised by certainty. This chapter starts from the position that the relationship between motherhood and mental ill health is not clear or easily predictable, and that one way of clarifying it is to consider the kinds of problems that women, as mothers, experience in social context. Thus it concentrates on psychosocial aspects of motherhood rather than psychiatric, psychological or psychoanalytic approaches, which are already widely covered in the literature on motherhood and mental illness. The chapter is divided into three parts. The first part considers the scale of the problem of maternal mental ill health. The second discusses what motherhood means, practically and symbolically. Expectations of motherhood change over time and place, and so do the pressures put on mothers. With this in mind I examine contemporary contexts of motherhood and consider the ways in which these have contributed to new forms of motherhood and new concerns about the role. The third part focuses more closely on the mental health needs and problems most closely associated with bearing children. In conclusion I consider the implications for improving maternal mental health.

THE SCALE AND NATURE OF THE PROBLEM

When using the term "mental health problem" it is important to remember that it can include problems ranging from serious disorders to moderate and relatively minor conditions and states of being. The former have profoundly debilitating impacts on the lives of sufferers and those near to them and almost certainly require expert professional involvement; the latter may be more transient, and milder in experience and impact, but can nevertheless be distressing. These moderate to minor conditions may need professional help, but may also respond to the support of family and friends and be time limited. If we take "postnatal depression" as a widely used term to describe the most common maternal mental health problem, we can see this distinction more clearly. Epidemiological evidence indicates that the prevalence of serious maternal mental illness such as postpartum psychosis is low, affecting 1–2 mothers per 1000 births (Kumar, 1994; O'Hara and Swain, 1996), thus making it a rare condition. The extent of less serious but nevertheless distressing mental health problems after child-birth, like postnatal non-psychotic depression, is much greater, affecting 10–15% of new mothers (O'Hara and Swain, 1996). The "Baby Blues", where new mothers experience mood fluctuation, tearfulness and so forth in the first few days after birth, are reported to be experienced by between 50–80% of mothers in the Western world, with the highest prevalence in USA. These figures not only suggest that we might need to consider the Baby Blues to be a normal feature of motherhood, at least in some parts of the world, but also that the true scale of maternal mental health problems depends on how "problems" are defined and by whom.

A further difficulty lies in the under-reporting of mental health problems, especially within certain ethnic and social groups where they carry a stigma. We also know that even where problems are reported, they may not reach the threshold of a formal psychiatric diagnosis. Many mild to moderate psychiatric problems in women are treated by general practitioners, with only the most severe being referred to psychiatrists. Another complicating factor in terms of both estimating prevalence and clarifying aetiology is that, with deinstitutionalisation and accompanying shifts towards the provision of mental health care in the community, the last two decades have seen a rise in the number of seriously mentally ill women who are becoming mothers (Gopfert et al., 2004; Joseph, 1999; Nicholson et al., 1998a). In addition, since the newer antipsychotic drugs have fewer negative effects on fertility than older forms, the number of women suffering from serious mental illnesses like schizophrenia who become mothers will undoubtedly increase (Currien and Simpson, 1998, in Seeman, 2004). Aetiologically, therefore, although epidemiological data may indicate positive correlations between motherhood and certain forms of mental ill health, we cannot be sure whether being a mother is the cause of mental ill health, a precipitating risk factor or merely coincidental with it. Given the multifactorial causation of a wide range of mental health problems, it is likely that maternal mental ill health is the product of particular combinations of intrapsychic, bio-logical and social factors. The fact that the majority of adult women in the world are mothers makes it very difficult to disentangle maternal factors from others associated with women's lives and biology. Across the globe, the risk factors for women's mental ill health implicate the critical part played by social and economic disadvantage (see e.g. Patel et al., 2002; Rahman et al., 2003; WHO, 2002).

However, although causation may be unclear, what we do know is that maternal mental ill health can have a profound impact not only on the well-being of mothers themselves but also on the health and development of their children and on family life in general (Gopfert et al., 2004; Murray and Cooper, 1996; Oates, 1997; Patel et al., 2004; Rahman et al., 2004). Perinatal psychiatric disorder, for example, is the leading cause of maternal morbidity, and suicide is the leading cause of maternal mortality in the UK and probably also in northern Europe (*Confidential Enquiries into Maternal Deaths*, 2001, in Oates et al., 2004: 10). It can have serious, adverse effects on the mother–infant relationship (Martins and Gaffan, 2000), on the child's growth (Rahman et al., 2004), on emotional, social and cognitive development (Murray et al., 1999) and on future mental health (Gopfert et al., 2004; Reder et al., 2000). Severe maternal mental illness is not only associated with diminished maternal responsiveness and stimulation and increased risk of emotional and physical harm to the child – in the most acute and rare cases it can result in infanticide (Spinelli, 2004; Webb et al., 2005). Increasing awareness of the impacts of maternal mental illness on mothers and on their families, across the globe, has led to agreement that maternal mental ill health should be thought of and dealt with as a public health issue, not just a cause for private concern or psychiatric treatment (Oates et al., 2004; Patel et al., 2004; WHO, 2002).

MEANINGS OF MOTHERHOOD

There are many facets of motherhood: it is gendered; it is a social role that describes a particular relationship; it entails certain practices; it is associated with a sense of social and personal identity; it requires particular qualities, for example nurturance; and becoming a mother is typically, but not necessarily, associated with powerful bodily processes. How these features take shape depends on time and place: each society and culture has its own notions and expectations of the right constituents of good mothering and the correct recipe to combine them.

But motherhood is also highly symbolic: "the Mother" has many meanings beyond the tasks, duties and attributes that each society defines as necessary for the fulfilment of the role. What it *means* to be a mother differs from society to society, but there are also common themes. We know that cross-culturally and historically, since the earliest times, motherhood and in particular pregnancy have been powerful, embodied symbols of fertility and nurturance. The "earth mother" probably predated any earth father as the object of veneration and worship. The reproductive role of women as bearers of future generations, and the womb's fundamental part in this, have been sources of mystery and fear. It has also meant that fertile women are desirable, essential and natural to the cycle of life; this makes them, paradoxically, both powerful and vulnerable. Infertile women, on the other hand, are seen in most societies as unnatural, lacking in essential femaleness and undesirable (Morice et al., 1995). The idealised, all-nurturing potential of pregancy and motherhood commands respect and gives mothers, in theory at least, enormous social value, as families and communities depend on them for their well-being.

Of course the realities of most mothers' lives across the world have been, and for many continue to be, rather at odds with this ideal. Social and economic gender inequalities mean that women in general have more life demands made on them than men, and at the same time access to fewer of the material and non-material resources needed to deal with them (Rahman et al., 2004; WHO, 2002). Even in the USA, the richest nation in the world, approximately 75% of the poor are women and children (Stewart, 1996: 223). Mothers are particularly exposed to the pressures of poverty, which include not only lack of money and adequate housing but also lack of access to medical and preventive health services, exposure to violence (especially domestic violence) and poorer educational opportunities (WHO, 2002). Far from feeling venerated and valued, many women experience the maternal role as physically exhausting and emotionally demanding, with little real evidence of respect and few opportunities for relief.

The requirements and activities of motherhood are not fixed in any society and now, more than ever, they are in a state of flux and difficult to pin down. In addition, just as the constituents of good mothering change historically, reflecting and responding to changing social, economic and political contexts, so do the expectations and criteria by which we judge mothers and, critically, by which they judge themselves. Over the last decade or two, in the Western world especially, these shifting expectations have extended beyond mothering per se to the ways in which women combine motherhood with a range of other activities, especially paid work. Looking at its contemporary forms at the beginning of the twenty-first century it becomes clear that motherhood is much more complicated than it used to be. Now we have the possibility of controlling whether, how and when we become mothers. Just two generations ago such choices were, pun aside, inconceivable. Different phases of motherhood are no longer necessarily age-related; with new forms of IVF and advances in obstetric care, being menopausal and becoming a mother are no longer mutually exclusive. Whilst this situation does not apply to most women, the fact that it really does apply to some changes our notions about mothers and motherhood. Similarly, with changing social mores, sexual practices and economic conditions, lone motherhood, either through divorce, choice or accident, has become much more common in certain Western countries than ever before (Kiernan et al., 1998). As well as the emotional, financial and social repercussions of being a single parent for those women concerned, and their children, these changes also influence our views more widely about what is (maternally) possible, desirable and typical. These shifting views, in turn, help to create the social conditions which make new forms of lone motherhood more possible. They also, of course, have an impact on fathers and fatherhood and on the ways in which the relationship between mothers and fathers as partners and parents is negotiated and played out.

While these choices about whether, when and how to become a mother are potentially very liberating for women, they can impose physical demands and emotional and psychological pressures which require more than motivation, time management skills and financial resources. Contemporary notions of rights, needs and personal empowerment are associated with beliefs that being in control of one's life is not only desirable but possible (Baistow, 1995). However, expectations that life processes and events should be within personal control are often thwarted by unanticipated and uncontrollable contingencies and, when well-laid plans concerning conception, healthy pregnancy, pain-free labour, natural childbirth, return to work and so forth are not fulfilled or easily actualised, we may be not only shocked but unprepared. The adjustment needed to deal with circumstances that are both unexpected and physically and emotionally demanding can place such pressure on our coping abilities that our habitual methods and strategies may be neither appropriate nor sufficient. In these circumstances we are psychologically vulnerable.

Working mothers are the norm, worldwide (Chen et al., 2005; WHO, 2002). Economic necessity has meant that motherhood, for most women, has always been combined with other roles. The idea that mothers (should) only do "mothering" is bound by history, class and culture. It may perhaps be a myth, for even when women have the social and financial opportunity purely to "mother" they often employ proxies to do so for them. However, contemporary combinations of work and motherhood in the UK and other parts of the Western world make the exercise of both rather difficult. There are several features to this: the financial necessity to work often means that some mothers have to return to work sooner than they might wish; increasing emphasis on consumerism reinforces this need. Taking time to establish a career means that increasing numbers of (middle-class) women are postponing motherhood until an age when, biologically, we are less suited to bear and rear children. In spite of medical developments, it continues to be more difficult to conceive as we move towards middle age. There are also increased risks to mother and child during pregnancy, and adjusting to the demands of child rearing can be underestimated by women who have spent perhaps 20 years of their adulthood without children. Although there are more working mothers now than 50 years ago in the UK, the home–work relationship has not become "feminised". On the contrary, it can be thought of highly masculinised, with family-unfriendly policies concerning working hours and school holidays, workplace child-care facilities and maternity leave. It is so masculinised that we find ourselves referring to the need for workplaces to "make concessions" to their working mothers, as if they were a special case.

There are common features to the pressures on working mothers: they report lack of time, role conflict, work overload, worries about childcare and, above all, constant tiredness as problems that affect their physical and mental well-being (Milkie and Peltola, 1999; Noor, 2002). It is important to remember here that whether or not women are in paid employment, they also do the vast majority of unpaid work in the home (WHO, 2002). Stopping work outside the home may be one answer but we know that it can actually benefit mothers and their children (Ahmad-Nia, 2002; Brannen, 1991; Macran, 1993; McBride, 1990) and, in any case, is an unlikely option for most women for the economic reasons mentioned earlier. However, work and family life are not inevitably in opposition to one another. Indeed, family-friendly workplaces may be good for business and productivity as well as mothers and their children (Carrington and Holmstrom, 2004).

MOTHERHOOD AND MENTAL ILL HEALTH

As discussed earlier, motherhood can be conflated with womanhood, such that it is difficult to extricate any specifically maternal factors which contribute to the much higher incidence of depression generally among women than among men. However, certain aspects of motherhood are very closely associated with specific types of mental ill health. These are concerned with childbirth: having a baby involves adjusting to changes in intrapsychic, interpersonal, social and biological circumstances and this period is one of particular vulnerability for women. Child bearing is associated with a marked incidence and prevalence of psychiatric disorder (Seneviratne and Conroy, 2004) and the consequences of untreated mental illness during this period can have devastating effects on mother, child and family. In their mildest forms, and most commonly, mental health problems associated with child bearing take the form of the Baby Blues, when for a short period after childbirth many mothers report weepiness and fluctuating mood. Postnatal depression and more rarely postnatal psychosis constitute the other well-known disorders associated with child bearing.

Aetiologically, there is little evidence to support a biological basis for postnatal depression, although it is likely that the biological changes underlying postnatal blues may lead to depression when combined with genetic vulnerability, environmental stress, negative life events and a lack of social support from family and friends (Cooper and Murray, 1998). Epidemiologically, findings indicate that the main contributory factors are psychosocial in nature, especially in combination with a pre-existing vulnerability to depression (O'Hara and Swain, 1996). It appears that postnatal depression is the result of an interaction of a range of factors, some of which may be culturally specific. Studies of postnatal depression in India, for example, have found that while economic deprivation and poor marital relationships are important risk factors for the occurrence and chronicity of depression, the gender of the baby is a determinant that modifies the effect of other risk factors such as marital violence and hunger (Patel et al., 2002). Psychosocial explanations gain support from apparent transcultural differences in the prevalence of postnatal depression; however, while some studies show little evidence of postnatal depression in non-Western societies (see Stern and Kruckman, 1983; Wile and Arechiga, 1999, in Miller, 2002), others suggest that there is a consistency in incidence across different cultures (Kumas, 1994).

The findings of a recent study support the universality of a morbid state of unhappiness following childbirth, but not the interpretation of this as an illness requiring the intervention of health professionals (Oates et al., 2004). A consensus does exist, however, on the need for further systematic cross-cultural research, to study the social and cultural contributions to both maternal postnatal distress and ways of alleviating it. Some anthropological studies suggest that while childbirth is a difficult time for most new mothers, the presence of a strong social network surrounding the mother, with clear social arrangements for the ante- and postnatal periods and experienced women in attendance, serves to support the new mother, enabling rest, dependence and a "lying-in" period to recover from birth and to prepare for the demands of motherhood (Stern and Kruckman, 1983).

However, over the last 20 years or so other problems of child bearing have attracted increasing attention. In particular, the recognition of what we might call "thwarted motherhood" as a source of psychological distress has been accompanied by efforts to understand the emotional impact of miscarriage, stillbirth and abortion. Reflecting new historical shifts in relation to motherhood and mental health, in recent years the inability to conceive has been added to this list, and not only infertility but also infertility treatment has been associated with mental health problems (see Lukse and Nicholas, 1999).

The risks to the well-being of mother and baby again point to the vital importance in antenatal and postnatal care of watchfulness and support, which can only satisfactorily be brought about by training health professionals like health visitors, midwives and general practitioners to recognise the signs, symptoms and risk factors associated with serious maternal mental illness; early detection of symptoms and prompt intervention can help to reduce the adverse consequences of maternal mental illness (see Chapter 9 in this volume).

BEING A MENTALLY ILL MOTHER

As well as those who suffer mental health problems following childbirth, there is another group of mothers which warrants our attention. These are chronically mentally ill women who become mothers. Over the last 20 years a combination of social and medical factors has contributed to an increase in the number of women with mental illness who not only become pregnant but who wish to bring up their children. While motherhood can be a "normalising" experience for these women, having to cope with their ongoing mental health problems and respond to the demands of mother-hood can be very difficult. If these health problems are associated with social adversity in the form of poverty, inadequate housing, social isolation and lack of a partner, the ability to cope as a mother can become seriously compromised. Pregnancy is a time of emotional and physical change for most women, and those with mental health problems can become especially vulnerable. Being a mother requires attentiveness to the needs of the infant and the desire and capability to respond to these needs.

For mothers with chronic mental illness this can be difficult, and pro-fessional support is essential for the sake of both mother and child (see Gopfert et al., 2004: Chapter 5). However, this support depends first on the mother being in contact with or being known to health and social care services, and second on these agencies sharing information and working together effectively. This contact can be difficult to establish and maintain as some mentally ill mothers-to-be are fearful that their babies will be taken away from them because of child protection concerns; they may have already had this experience and seek to avoid contact not only with mental health workers but also with antenatal care services. This kind of situation clearly raises ethical and legal issues concerning risk to the mother and her (unborn) baby, and also poses problems for the provision of appropriate and necessary antenatal and postnatal care.

In recent years in the UK and in other countries, there has been rising concern over the lack of proper collaboration between health and social care professionals in supporting mentally ill mothers and their children, and increasing efforts are being made transnationally to exchange infor-mation on good practice and multidisciplinary training, and to improve knowledge sharing as a basis for more effective joint working (Baistow and Hetherington, 2004; Hetherington et al., 2002).

However, we have comparatively little research into women's perspectives on these situations. Some interesting qualitative research studies exploring mentally ill women's experiences of mothering and perceptions of need indicate that mothers with mental illness feel stigmatised, under pressure to prove themselves as parents and undermined by negative social attitudes. They are conscious of the competing demands of coping with their children and their own ill health, and fear losing their children if they are hospitalised (Nicholson et al., 1998a). In addition, they may experience social isolation and difficulties with establishing support networks and maintaining family relationships because of negative attitudes and ignorance about mental illness. Supportive partners were described as an asset but these mothers were also vulnerable to relationship difficulties (Nicholson et al., 1998b).

THWARTED MOTHERHOOD

While maternal health can be severely affected by bearing children, there is an increasing group of women whose mental health is affected by not bearing children. Women who experience what I earlier called "thwarted motherhood", either through infertility, miscarriage, stillbirth or abortion, are at risk of developing mental health problems. These are primarily associated with the experience of loss and tend to take the form of depression, although anxiety can also be present.

Research into clinical observations of the impact of miscarriage suggests that it can be a traumatic event which may have a profound effect on the mother (Adolfsson et al., 2004; Brier, 1999; Lee and Slade, 1996). Loss as the primary psychological experience and the grief associated with it are key themes in miscarriage and stillbirth, particularly when it is unexpected and sudden. Most women experience an intense period of emotional distress, lasting for about four to six weeks, which is characterised by grief, unhappiness, guilt and anxiety. This typically subsides within three or four months. The extent of the impact depends on a number of factors including unpredictability, whether the woman has other children, how long she had been trying to conceive, the point in pregnancy when the miscarriage occurred and the response of professionals and family (Adolfsson, 2004; Brier, 1999: 152). Surveys of parental satisfaction after miscarriage indicate a high level of dissatisfaction and anger with medical and nursing responses, which centre on professional insensitivity to the significance of the loss to parents and lack of compassion (Lee and Slade, 1996). Rarely, women go on to develop clinical depression and, although it is known that miscarriage increases the likelihood of a depressive reaction, the actual incidence of depression following miscarriage is unclear (Brier, 1999). While there has been an increase in empirical research investigating women's reactions to miscarriage it is vital that we gain more knowledge about their experiences and perspectives, by using both large-scale surveys and the kind of qualitative methodology used by Adolfsson et al. (2004), if professional responses are to become more sensitive and responsive to the needs of these women and their partners.

Even when loss is "planned", as in elective abortion, women can still experience intense emotional reactions. When abortion is chosen by a woman, studies suggest that it is associated with feelings of loss that can be difficult to adjust to, partly because the feelings themselves were unexpected, even though the abortion was not. Women may experience intense feelings of guilt, regret, sadness and self-blame post abortion (see Brockington, 1998, for a very useful overview). In general these responses tend to fade but some continue to experience emotional problems, and professional support through counselling or psychotherapy may be needed. However, these emotional responses to abortion do not necessarily equate with or result in clinical depression, and the controversy over the existence of "post-abortion syndrome" both in the USA and the UK highlights the professional and personal dilemma of being sensitive to women's needs but not overmedicalising them (Lee, 2003). Furthermore, the contentious ethical and legal implications of abortion in many countries add to the uncertainty of its status and have the potential to complicate the relationship between health professionals and women who choose abortion. It is also very likely to affect women's decisions to seek help for unresolved feelings, and it is likely that the frequency of mental health problems following abortion may therefore be underestimated.

Whilst exercising the power to end life through abortion can be associated with feelings of unhappiness and sadness, it is has been evident for a number of years that lacking the power to create life can also be the cause of substantial emotional distress (see e.g. Edelman and Connolly, 1986; Menning, 1980; Morice et al., 1995). When women have difficulty conceiving they experience a range of psychological responses including disappointment, despair, grief, anger and powerlessness (Boivin, 2003; Lukse and Nicholas, 1999). If they seek fertility treatment these feelings can be exacerbated as they also have to cope with the strain of waiting for success and the disappointment of failure. Women who have participated in an in-vitro fertilisation programme (IVF) indicate that the treatment is one of the most stressful experiences of their lives (Freeman et al., 1985, in Lukse and Nicholas, 1999: 245). In recognition of this, therapeutic counselling tailored to these specific needs has been developed with a particular focus on pre- as well as posttreatment counselling to enable these women (and their partners) to identify and develop more effective coping strategies (Boivin, 2003). Equally, studies suggest that, as with miscarriage, a more sensitive, holistic approach to fertility treatment on the part of health professionals would improve not only patient satisfaction and the quality of the patient experience but also the patient's psychological well-being (Lukse and Nicholas, 1999).

CONCLUSIONS

This chapter has considered some of the common emotional responses to motherhood, focusing in particular on child bearing as the most significant time when motherhood and mental health are compromised. The mild to moderate mental health problems associated with child bearing are widespread and socially significant; these are a function of the interaction of diverse personal, social, economic and biological factors. They cause distress and can have profound effects on the mother, her children and family life. But cross-cultural studies raise the possibility that these problems may not need medical but social "treatment" and solutions.

Unlike traditional practices surrounding childbirth, which enabled women to be dependent on others and to relinquish control temporarily, contemporary approaches allow very little time to adjust to the powerful bodily, social and psychological changes involved in becoming a mother. For many mothers, combining paid work outside the home with motherhood is economically inescapable but psychologically and practically very difficult. If motherhood was respected and the role valued, from pregnancy and childbirth onwards, and if practical and social arrangements for living were designed to reflect these, then the conditions would be created for mothering to become more straightforward.

Clearly, further research into the scale, nature, causes and effects of maternal mental health problems is always needed but equally important is the need to challenge the social, domestic and work arrangements and the received wisdom that underpins them. Raising awareness of the social value of mothers and clarifying social expectations of them is the first step; then we have to find the resources and motivation to enable ourselves and others to act on them. We need to be mindful of the powerful, increasingly global, social and economic factors underpinning women's work and maternal mental well-being, and of the profound effects on communities and families if mothers are not properly supported. As a public health issue, as well as a cause for private concern, maternal health demands understanding, resources and effort devoted to prevention and treatment.

REFERENCES

Adolfsson, A., Larsson, P. G., Wijma, B. and Bertero, C. (2004) Guilt and emptiness: Women's experiences of miscarriage, *Health Care for Women International*, 25, 543–560.

Ahmad-Nia, S. (2002) Women's work and health in Iran: A comparison of working and non-working mothers, *Social Science and Medicine*, 54, 753–765.

Baistow, K. (1995) Liberation and regulation? Some paradoxes of empowerment, *Critical Social Policy*, 14, 34–46.

Baistow, K. and Hetherington, R. (2004) Overcoming obstacles to interagency support: Learning from Europe, in M. Gopfert, J. Webster and M. Seeman (eds) *Parental psychiatric disorder: Distressed parents and their families*, Cambridge, Cambridge University Press.

Boivin, J. (2003) A review of psychosocial interventions in infertility, *Social Science and Medicine*, 57, 2325–2341.

Brannen, J. (1991) *Managing mothers: Dual earner households after maternity leave*, London, Allen Unwin.

Brier, N. (1999) Understanding and managing emotional reactions to a miscarriage, *Obstetrics and Gynecology*, 93, 151–155.

Brockington, R. (1998) *Motherhood and mental health*, Oxford, Oxford University Press.

Carrington, L. and Holmstrom, R. (2004) Signs of change, *People Management*, 10 (11), 29–32.

Chen, M., Vanek, J., Lund, F., Heintz, J., Jhabvala, R. and Bonner, C. (2005) *Progress of the world's women 2005: Women, work and poverty*, New York, United Nations Development Fund for Women.

Cooper, P. and Murray, L. (1998) Postnatal depression, *British Medical Journal*, 316, 1884–1886.

Edelman, R. J. and Connolly, K. J. (1986) Psychological aspects of infertility, *British Journal of Medical Psychology*, 59, 209–219.

Gopfert, M., Webster, J. and Seeman, M. (2004) *Parental psychiatric disorder: Distressed parents and their families*, Cambridge, Cambridge University Press.

Hetherington, R., Baistow, K., Katz, I., Mesie, J. and Trowell, J. (2002) *The welfare of children with mentally ill parents: Learning from inter-country comparison*, Chichester, John Wiley and Sons.

Joseph, J. G., Joshi, S. V., Lewin, A. B. and Abrams, M. (1999) Characteristics and perceived needs of mothers with serious mental illness, *Psychiatric Services*, 50, 1357–1359.

Kiernan, K., Land, H. and Lewis, J. (1998) *Lone motherhood in twentieth century Britain*, Oxford, Oxford University Press.

Kohen, D. (ed.) (2000) *Women and mental health*, London, Routledge.

Kornstein, S. G. and Clayton, A. H. (eds) (2002) *Women's mental health: A comprehensive textbook*, London, Guilford Press.

Kumar, R. (1994) Postnatal illness: A transcultural perspective, *Social Psychiatry and Psychiatric Epidemiology*, 29 (6), 250–264.

Lee, E. (2003) *Abortion, motherhood and mental health: Medicalising reproduction in the United States and Great Britain*, New York, Aldine de Gruyter.

Lee, C. and Slade, P. (1996) Miscarriage as a traumatic event: A review of the literature and new implcations for intervention, *Journal of Somatic Research*, 40 (3), 235–244.

Lukse, M. and Nicholas, V. (1999) Grief depression and coping in women undergoing infertility treatment, *Obstetrics and Gynecology*, 93 (2), 245–251.

Macran, S. (1993) *Role enhancement or role overload? A review of research on the health consequences of women's domestic and paid work* (Research report 93-1), London, London School of Hygiene and Tropical Medicine.

Marland, H. (2004) *Dangerous motherhood: Insanity and childbirth in Victorian England*, Basingstoke, Palgrave Macmillan.

Martins, C. and Gaffan, E. A. (2000) Effects of early maternal depression on patterns of infant–mother attachment: A meta-analytic investigation, *Journal of Child Psychology and Psychiatry and Allied Disciplines*, 41, 737–746.

McBride, B. A. (1990) Mental health effects of women's multiple roles, *American Psychologist*, 45, 381–384.

Menning, B. (1980) The emotional needs of infertile couples, *Fertility and Sterility*, 34, 313–319.

Miles, A. (1991) *Women, health and medicine*, Milton Keynes, Open University Press.

Milkie, M. A. and Peltola, P. (1999) Playing all the roles: Gender and work–family balancing act, *Journal of Marriage and Family*, 61, 476–490.

Miller, L. (2002) Postpartum depression, *Journal of the American Medical Association*, 287 (6), 762–765.

Morice, P., Josset, P., Chapron, C. and Dubuisson, J. B. (1995) History of infertility, *Human Reproduction Update*, 1 (5), 497–504.

Murray, L. and Cooper, P. (1996) Impact of postpartum depression on child development, *International Review of Psychiatry*, 8, 55–63.

Murray, L., Sinclair, D. and Cooper, P. (1999) The socioemotional development of 5 year old children of postnatally depressed mothers, *Journal of Child Psychology and Psychiatry*, 40, 1259–1271.

Nicholson, P. (1998) *Post-natal depression: Psychology, science and the transition to motherhood*, London, Routledge.

Nicholson, J., Sweeney, E. and Geller, J. (1998a) Focus on women: Mothers with mental illness: I. The competing demands of parenting and living with mental illness, *Psychiatric Services*, 49, 635–642.

Nicholson, J., Sweeney, E. and Geller, J. (1998b) Focus on women: Mothers with mental illness: II. Family relationships and the context of parenting, *Psychiatric Services*, 49, 643–649.

Noor, N. M. (2002) Work–family conflict, locus of control and women's well-being: Test of alternative pathways, *Journal of Social Psychology*, 142, 645–660.

Oakley, A. (1979) *Becoming a mother*, Oxford, Martin Robertson.

Oakley, A. (1984) *The captured womb: A history of the medical care of pregnant women*, Oxford, Basil Blackwell.

Oates, M. R. (1997) Patients as parents: The risk to children, *British Journal of Psychiatry*, 170, 22–27.

Oates, M. R., Cox, J. L., Neema, S., Asten, P., Glangeaud-Freudenthal, N., Figueiredo, B., Gorman, L., Hacking, S., Hirst, E., Kammerer, M., Klier, C., Seneviratne, G., Smith, M., Sutter-Dallay, A.-L., Valoriani, V., Wickberg, B. and Yoshida, K. (2004) Postnatal depression across countries and cultures: A qualitative study, *British Journal of Psychiatry*, 184 (Suppl. 46), 10–16.

O'Hara, M. W. and Swain, A. M. (1996) Rates and risk of postpartum depression: A meta-analysis, *International Review of Psychiatry*, 8, 37–54.

Patel, V., Rodrigues, M. and DeSouza, N. (2002) Gender, poverty and postnatal depression: A study of mothers in Goa, India, *American Journal of Psychiatry*, 159 (1), 43–47.

Patel, V., Rahman, A., Jacob, K. and Hughes, M. (2004) Effect of maternal mental health on infant growth in low income countries: New evidence from South Asia, *British Medical Journal*, 328, 8200–8223.

Rahman, A., Lovel, H., Bunn, J., Iqbal, Z. and Harrington, R. (2004) Mothers' mental health and infant growth: A case-control study from Rawalpindi, Pakistan, *Child Care Health and Development*, 30, (1), 21–27.

Reder, P., McClure, M. and Jolley, A. (2000) *Family matters: Interfaces between child and adult mental health*, London, Routledge.

Seeman, M. (2004) Schizophrenia and motherhood, in M. Gopfert, J. Webster and M. Seeman (eds) *Parental psychiatric disorder: Distressed parents and their families*, Cambridge, Cambridge University Press.

Seneviratne, G. and Conroy, S. (2004) Perinatal illness: Nature/nurture, in M. Gopfert, J. Webster and M. Seeman (eds) *Parental psychiatric disorder: Distressed parents and their families*, Cambridge, Cambridge University Press.

Spinelli, M. (2004) Maternal infanticide associated with mental illness: Prevention and the promise of saved lives, *American Journal of Psychiatry*, 161 (9), 1548–1557.

Stern, G. and Kruckman, L. (1983) Multidisciplinary perspectives on postpartum depression: An anthropological critique, *Social Science and Medicine*, 17 (15), 1027–1041.

Stewart, D. (1996) Editorial: Women's health and psychosomatic medicine, *Journal of Psychosomatic Research*, 40 (3), 221–226.

Ussher, J. (1991) *Women's madness: Misogyny or mental illness?*, Hemel Hempstead, Harvester Wheatsheaf.

Webb, R., Abel, K., Pickles, A. and Appleby, L. (2005) Mortality in offspring of parents with psychotic disorders: A critical review and meta-analysis, *American Journal of Psychiatry*, 162, 1045–1056.

World Health Organization (WHO) (2002) *Women's mental health: An evidence-based review*, Geneva, WHO.

Chapter 9

Sad motherhood

An overview of perinatal affective disorders

Kirsten Patrick and Veronica O'Keane

INTRODUCTION

Depression is at least twice as common in women as in men (Gater et al., 1998; O'Keane, 2000), and peaks during women's reproductive years. The postpartum period was thought for a long time to be the period when the risk for depression is at its highest. However, many research workers have demonstrated convincingly that rates of non-psychotic depression in the first year postpartum are not dissimilar to rates outside this period (Eberhard-Gran et al., 2002; Evans et al., 2001; Gotlib et al., 1989).

There are no biological or psychological markers for depression and, because it is a spectrum disorder in terms of symptoms and experiences, professionals rely on agreed operational definitions, or check-lists, to make a diagnosis. A diagnosis of depression according to the DSM-IV requires the presence for at least two weeks of consistent lowering of mood or inability to experience pleasure, along with a fixed number of biological (disruption of sleep, appetite, motor activity or energy levels) or cognitive (reduced concentration, guilt or suicidal thoughts) symptoms (American Psychiatric Association, 2000). Depression occurring during pregnancy is not mentioned in DSM-IV, and postpartum depression is defined as depression that has an onset within the first four weeks postpartum. The ICD-10, on the other hand, defines postpartum depression as depression occurring within six weeks of delivery; it does not allude to depression during pregnancy (WHO, 1992).

Pregnancy is traditionally thought of as a time when women are inherently contented and thus protected from mental ill health. Women are generally reluctant to admit to feelings of ambivalence or unhappiness during a pregnancy and the professional community is also not too ready to recognise it. The reality is that around half of pregnancies are unplanned, some are unwanted and many babies are conceived in and born into less than ideal circumstances. This could be due to a conflicted marital relationship, a financially insecure household or a mother who suffers from one of a spectrum of psychiatric disorders. What's more, accumulating research shows that a mother's mental state in pregnancy impacts on birth outcome and the subsequent neurological and psychological development of her child (O'Connor et al., 2002; Patton et al., 2004; Wadhwa, 1993).

PREGNANCY AND STRESS

The last three decades have witnessed growing research worldwide into the issue of stress and pregnancy, birth outcomes and long-term effects on children's mood and behaviour. What constitutes stress is difficult to define: what is normally perceived to be stressful by one woman might not be perceived so by another.

Animal research, primarily in rats, demonstrated abnormalities of size and, especially, behaviour in offspring in response to maternal prenatal stress (Welberg and Seckl, 2001). In the late 1970s, a landmark Finnish study was carried out which showed an increase in the incidence of schizophrenia and criminal behaviour in the offspring of mothers who lost their spouse during pregnancy. The study showed that maternal antenatal stress created a foetal environment that influenced the "inborn temperament" of the children involved (Huttunen and Niskanen, 1978). In another prospective investigation of women exposed to chronic or episodic stress in pregnancy, prenatal life event stress was associated with a significant decrease in gestational age at birth and low birth weight. These findings were independent of known biomedical risks such as smoking, previous preterm birth and medical complications (Wadhwa et al., 1993). These findings were confirmed in other studies (Cliver et al., 1992; Williamson et al., 1989).

Premature birth remains one of the leading causes of infant morbidity in both the developed and the developing world. Studies have shown that there are many long-term consequences for the person born early, or born "light" for gestational age. Barker et al. (1989) coined the term "foetal programming" when their research demonstrated a higher incidence of cardiovascular disease-related deaths in those who were light at birth, They also found a link between low weight gain in infancy and death due to suicide in adult life (Barker et al., 1993, 1995). Also, depression in adolescence was found to be associated with low birth weight (Patton et al., 2004).

PREGNANCY AND HORMONES

Hormonal changes in pregnancy are well recognised, with several hormones undergoing manifold increases. Oestrogen and progesterone are produced by the corpus luteum of the ovary, and subsequently by the placenta, and increase progressively during pregnancy (refer to Chapter 7 in this volume). In addition, the hormone beta human chorionic gonadotrophin (BhCG) increases exponentially in the early part of pregnancy, stimulating the ovarian corpus luteum to secrete progesterone and oestrogen during the preplacental stages of pregnancy. The raised level of BhCG allows for the detection of pregnancy in urine or blood.

The hypothalamo–pituitary–adrenal axis

Less well known, however, is that the body's "stress hormone system" is also significantly activated in pregnancy. The main stress system in the body is the hypothalamo–pituitary–adrenal (HPA) axis (see Figure 9.1). The release of corticotrophin releasing hormone (CRH) in response to stress brings about the synthesis and secretion of adrenocorticotrophic hormone (ACTH) from the pituitary gland, which in turn effects the release of cortisol from the cortex of the adrenal gland. Cortisol acts on many tissues to bring about physiological changes that prepare the body to cope with threatening stimuli. This is normally demonstrated in increased

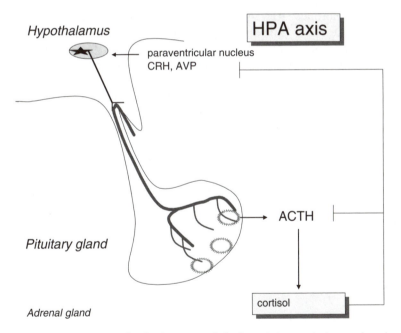

Figure 9.1 Normal negative feedback system of the hypothalamo–pituitary–adrenal (HPA) axis. This diagrammatic cross-section of the hypothalamus and pituitary schematically depicts the sequence of the hormones involved in the HPA axis. Corticotrophin releasing hormone (CRH) is released from the hypothalamus, stimulating the release of adrenocorticotrophic hormone (ACTH) from the anterior pituitary into the circulation. ACTH stimulates the release of cortisol from the adrenal cortex (not shown). Cortisol exerts a negative feedback on the central production of CRH and ACTH, thus inhibiting the axis.

alertness and awareness of the environment, diminished sleep and appetite and increased cardiovascular system drive. Cortisol also crosses the blood–brain barrier, causing a negative feedback system within the brain by inhibiting CRH secretion, thus preventing overdrive of the HPA axis (see Figure 9.1). Thus, CRH is virtually undetectable in the plasma of non-pregnant individuals.

During gestation CRH is also produced and released by the growing placenta. This placental CRH is identical to brain-derived CRH in structure and bioactivity but is not inhibited in the usual way, thus resulting in a positive, rather than a negative, feedback loop and a manifold increase in plasma CRH of placental origin as pregnancy progresses, with a consequential rise in the other stress hormones. A high level of CRH late in pregnancy is one of the key factors that stimulates the initiation of labour (Challis et al., 2001).

Clinical depression could be seen as a consequence of unremitting major psychological stress and has been shown to have a biological effect on the body through the activation of the HPA axis, leading to an elevated cortisol response to normal CRH and ACTH stimulation (O'Keane, 2000).

Recent research in animals and humans suggests that the HPA axis is a possible mediator of the effects of maternal mood on foetal development and pregnancy outcome (Welberg and Seckl, 2001). Cortisol has a vital role to play in the normal development and maturation of the foetus (Liggins and Howie, 1972), but in excess it has been shown to adversely affect growth, long-term neurological development and behavioural outcomes in animals and children (French et al., 1999; Whitelaw and Thoresen, 2000).

Neonates of antenatally depressed mothers have also been found to display "depression-like" behaviour from birth, including some soft neurological signs and greater irritability (Field et al., 2004). Maternal antenatal anxiety, as distinct from postpartum mood, also predicted children's behavioural/emotional problems including hyperactivity and attention features (O'Connor et al., 2002). This was found after controlling for key known antenatal, obstetric and socio-demographic risks such as smoking, alcohol use, maternal body mass index (BMI), birth weight for gestational age, maternal age, gender of child and socio-economic status. All of this suggests the existence of a mother–child relationship prior to birth.

PERINATAL DEPRESSION

Depression in pregnancy

Since pregnancy is a time of change, both to body and lifestyle, it is also a time of heightened risk for relapse in women with a history of depressive illness. This risk increases with discontinuation of maintenance antidepressant medication on conception. Normally, the likelihood of relapse of untreated depressive illness is high within the space of a year; hence there is a statistical probability of relapse in pregnancy, if no treatment is given, regardless of hormonal and lifestyle changes.

Depression was found in 10% of pregnant women in one study (Gotlib et al., 1989). Also, rates of depressive symptoms were found to be higher in pregnancy in the non-pregnant female population, whilst rates of post-partum depression tended to approximate to the general average in women of reproductive age (O'Hara et al., 1990).

Unplanned pregnancy was found to be a major predictive factor. Roughly half of all conceptions are unplanned. If her pregnancy is unwanted, the mental stress of coming to terms with it is more likely to destabilise a woman's mood. Also likely to do so is falling pregnant at a younger age (Gotlib et al., 1989).

Single women, who do not benefit from the support of a partner, are also at a particular disadvantage. There is evidence of increased antenatal depression in single women compared to women in a relationship. Lack of family or cultural support also predisposes to stress and low mood in pregnancy. Asylum seekers and women who are somehow separated from their families are most likely to be affected, as well as women who suffer from social isolation or are economically disadvantaged.

Research has also shown that women who are less well educated, unemployed or full-time mothers are at higher risk of experiencing depression in pregnancy than women who are employed (Gotlib et al., 1989). Depressive symptomatology also appears to be more common in women with two or more children. The demands on these women are higher than average, and practical concerns about coping with pregnancy, delivery and a new baby are, therefore, more overwhelming.

The following factors therefore predict increased risk of depression in pregnancy:

1   previous history of depression;
2   unplanned pregnancy;
3   young age, single motherhood and poor social support;
4   low level of education, unemployment and socioeconomic disadvantage;
5   multi-parity.

Depression in the postpartum period

The continuum of mood through pregnancy and the postpartum period has been examined in longitudinal studies that administered specific questionnaires at various time points during gestation and the first year of postnatal life. These studies revealed that nearly 50% of women who are depressed in pregnancy go on to suffer from postnatal depression, and 50% of women who are depressed in the postpartum period had depressive symptoms at some time during their pregnancy.

The strongest predictor of postnatal depression appears, therefore, to be antenatal depression. Interestingly, though, different epidemiological risk factors predict the occurrence of depression during these different time periods (Evans et al., 2001). Although having a previous history of depression, especially previous perinatal depression, also predisposes to postnatal depression, other factors predisposing to antenatal depression do not appear to be associated with postnatal depression, namely low socioeconomic profile and social stressors (O'Hara and Zekoski, 1988). Postpartum depression has frequently been found to be associated with having a less supportive spouse (O'Hara and Swain, 1996).

Postpartum blues

"Postpartum blues" is a time-limited mood disturbance occurring in the postpartum period. It is important because it is common and probably has prognostic implications. The frequency of the disorder varies depending on the defining criteria used. Liberal criteria yield a prevalence rate of 88%, while more stringent criteria yield a much lower prevalence rate of 26% (O'Hara, 1987). The consistent finding across studies is that mood improves immediately following the delivery of a baby but frequently deteriorates on the third or fourth day, and then improves by the eighth. Severe postpartum blues was found to be predictive of postpartum depression.

A smaller percentage of women, however, develop a transient elevation in mood, with approximately 10% showing features of elation or hypomania in the days immediately following delivery (Glover et al., 1994; Heron et al., 2005). Higher than average rates for postpartum highs were found in one Irish study (Lane et al., 1997). The presence of high mood predicted depression at six weeks postpartum.

Postpartum psychosis

Postpartum psychosis (PPP) is a severe and acute onset mood disorder occurring in the first two weeks postpartum, in roughly 1% of women. It is distinct from postpartum depression and should not be seen as a more severe form of it. It is characterised by atypical symptoms of psychosis such as confusion, mood lability, cognitive disorganisation, bizarre behaviour and frequently suicidal and infanticidal behaviour (refer to Chapter 10 in this volume).

The most plausible explanation for this unique illness is that it is an episode of bipolar disorder (BPD), precipitated by physiological changes occurring around the puerperium. There is a wealth of evidence, genetic, epidemiological and clinical, that PPP represents an atypical clinical presentation of an episode of BPD (Chaudron and Pies, 2003).

The remarkable imprint of heredity is a striking feature of PPP. The occurrence of PPP in approximately 50% of women with a history of bipolar I disorder is the most predictable precipitant known for any episode of major psychiatric illness. Jones and Craddock (2001) have shown that PPP clusters within some bipolar families. They examined rates of occurrence of PPP in two groups of women, both with a history of BPD: women with a family history of PPP, and those without such a family history. The group with both a personal history of BPD and a family history of PPP experienced occurrence rates of 74% following childbirth, whereas those without a family history of PPP only experienced rates of 30%. The rate of recurrence of postpartum psychosis in subsequent deliveries is high and has been shown to vary from 50% to 90% across studies (Kendall et al., 1987; Robertson et al., 2005). This highlights the need for a proper psychiatric history and identification of women at high risk.

MANAGEMENT OF PERINATAL DEPRESSION

Until recently, the management of affective disorders during pregnancy was largely neglected. This was mainly due to inconclusive data on the safety of antidepressant medication in pregnancy, and lack of concrete knowledge about the effects of maternal depression on the foetus. However, with mounting evidence to suggest that antenatal mood impacts on the offspring's well-being, and in the face of the finding that the leading cause of maternal death is suicide, it is an area where firm guidelines need to be in place (RCOG, 2001).

Diagnosis begins with identification. A woman who is suffering from depression in pregnancy may not present for help or volunteer information on her symptoms. She may presume her irritability, lack of energy or mood changes to be normal in the pregnant state. She may feel reluctant to admit to feelings of unhappiness whilst culturally expected to experience the opposite. It is important therefore to screen pregnant women for possible mood disturbance at routine antenatal appointments and identify the presence or absence of risk factors. The Confidential Enquiries into Maternal Deaths in the UK by RCOG, 2001 and 2004, recommended that all pregnant women should be asked about their previous psychiatric history in a sensitive and systematic way and/or administered a recognised, self-report questionnaire used for screening mood disorders. It is also important to enquire about social history, with reference to economic disadvantage, social isolation and refugee/immigrant status.

Once a woman is identified as being at potential risk for depression, this needs to be carefully managed either through primary care or specialist perinatal mental health services, depending on the woman's preference and the severity of her symptoms/risk.

Women already taking antidepressant medication need to plan their pregnancy, and discuss treatment options with their GP or psychiatrist before conceiving. This provides the opportunity to reflect on information regarding the risks and benefits of treatment, and on the possible effects of untreated depression/relapse of depression in pregnancy on both mother and unborn baby. For patients with recurrent major depression (i.e. those who have had three or more lifetime episodes) the risk of suffering another episode without maintenance treatment is high. The Confidential Enquiry into Maternal Deaths in the UK also recommended that women who have suffered from an episode of severe mental illness following birth, or at any other time, should discuss their plans for future childbearing with their psychiatrist and obstetrician with regard to diminishing the risk of recurrence following childbirth.

THE MANAGEMENT OF MODERATE TO SEVERE DEPRESSION IN PREGNANCY

Antidepressant medication and/or psychotherapy are effective treatments for depression during pregnancy. Interpersonal psychotherapy (IPT; Spinelli and Endicott, 2003) and cognitive therapy (Appelby et al., 1997) have proved to be effective in reducing depressive symptoms during pregnancy. However, the use of psychotherapy alone to prevent or manage postpartum depression has not demonstrated impressive results (see Shakespeare, 2004). Cognitive therapy, on the other hand, particularly when combined with medication, was found to be effective in those suffering with moderate depression (DeRubeis et al., 2005; Hollon et al., 2005).

The question of whether or not to treat with antidepressant medication during pregnancy remains controversial. Many primary care physicians, and indeed psychiatrists, still advise patients taking antidepressant medication at the time of conception to wean their medication, or persuade them not to take antidepressants if they develop a depressive episode in pregnancy (refer to Chapter 20 in this volume).

Four categories of risk are usually examined with respect to the potential use of psychotropic medication in pregnancy, namely: risk of miscarriage or intrauterine death, risk of organ malformation (teratogenesis), possible impairment of foetal growth and postdelivery behavioural effects on the baby. There is no evidence to suggest that exposure to the newer antidepressants (the SSRIs) during pregnancy increases the risk of pregnancy miscarriage (Chambers et al., 1996; Kulin et al., 1998) or major birth defects above the population average (Misri et al., 2000). Also, the mean birth weights among babies exposed to SSRIs were similar to controls who were medication-free (Kulin et al., 1998). There have, however, been case reports of a wide range of mild neonatal distress syndromes attributed to neonatal withdrawal from antidepressants postdelivery. These have included mild respiratory distress, excessive crying, eating and sleeping difficulties, hypotonia and irritability (Kallen, 2004; Oberlander et al., 2004; Zeskind and Stephens, 2004). In addition, some reductions in psychomotor performance have been found in SSRI-exposed babies relative to non-exposed ones whose mothers were also depressed (Casper et al., 2003). Neonates who were exposed to the older antidepressant group (tricyclics) were found to display features of withdrawal with more significant frequency. The long-term effects of *in utero* antidepressant exposure on children are yet to be established. However, untreated depression in human pregnancy is known to be positively associated with cognitive, behavioural and mood state abnormalities in the offspring, particularly in the long term.

Psychosis or suicidality are symptoms that indicate severe depression and may require a patient to be hospitalised and treated involuntarily (UK: Mental Health Act, 1983). In cases such as this, if depression is life-threatening and requires urgent treatment and time to recovery needs to be short (for example, with an imminent delivery date), ECT may be warranted.

In the case of postpartum psychosis, prophylactic treatment with lithium has been demonstrated to be effective in preventing relapse in women who have had previous episodes (Cohen et al., 1995; Stewart et al., 1991). Women with a previous history of puerperal psychosis not receiving medication during pregnancy should be commenced on a mood stabiliser either in the last trimester or on the first day postpartum. The advantage of commencing lithium, or an alternative mood stabiliser, in the last trimester is that therapeutic levels will be established when the woman enters the high-risk period, i.e. the first week postpartum (Yonkers et al., 2004).

In the management of perinatal depression, it is important, whenever possible, to discuss all aspects of the treatment with the patient herself, perhaps in consultation with her partner. All risks and benefits need to be presented in an understandable and accessible way, and ultimately all decisions about treatment should ideally be made by the patient herself.

MOTHER AND BABY UNITS

In many places, if a woman became psychiatrically unwell in the postpartum period and required admission to hospital, she would often have to be separated from her baby in order to be admitted to a general psychiatric ward. The creation of mother and baby units within mental health facilities began in the last two decades in the UK and other countries, and coincided with the establishment of perinatal psychiatry as a subspecialty. Currently, health authorities in the UK have dedicated beds for patients with postpartum depression or psychosis and their babies (and sometimes even partners), although many of them have limited resources.

An example of a highly evolved perinatal psychiatric service is that in the South London and Maudsley NHS Trust. The service consists of consultant psychiatrist-led multidisciplinary teams located in the obstetric departments of the district general hospitals. At-risk patients are usually referred to these perinatal liaison services in early pregnancy by midwives or primary care practitioners, as it is standard practice for a psychiatric screening question-naire to be administered at the antenatal booking visits. Patients developing mild to moderate depression in pregnancy or postpartum are offered appointments in the outpatient perinatal psychiatry services and can usually be treated in the community. Women who develop more severe depression, psychosis or episode of severe mental illness, either in pregnancy or post-partum, are usually referred to the trust's mother and baby inpatient unit. This state-of-the-art facility has 10 dedicated beds for mothers who develop an episode of severe mental illness in the perinatal period, and their babies. In addition to medical and nursing staff, the unit benefits from two psy-chologists, a full-time social worker, occupational therapy services and a midwife attachment.

CONCLUSION

Antenatal depression is a risk factor for postpartum depression and occurs in approximately 10% of pregnant women. It is still underdiagnosed and undermanaged. Depression in pregnancy puts both mother and child at risk. Accumulating evidence suggests that untreated antenatal depression has effects on the developing foetus, most probably through overactivation of the maternal HPA axis, that may adversely affect birth outcome and result in long-term neurological and behavioural sequelae in the offspring.

The risk of developing postpartum depression is doubled where there is a past history of depression, and the risk in subsequent pregnancies is even higher among women if the first episode of postnatal depression was their first-ever depressive episode. Screening for maternal mental illness is now universally recommended, and active management of all forms of perinatal affective illness should be prioritised.

REFERENCES

American Psychiatric Association (APA) (2000) *Diagnostic and statistical manual of mental disorders* (4th edn), Washington, DC, APA.

Appleby, L., Warner, R., Whitton, A. and Faragher, B. (1987) A controlled study of fluoxetine and cognitive-behavioural counselling in the treatment of postnatal depression, *British Medical Journal*, 314, 932–936.

Barker, D. J. P., Osmond, C., Rodin, I., Fall, C. H. D. and Winter, P. D. (1995) Low weight gain in infancy and suicide in adult life, *British Medical Journal*, 311, 1203.

Barker, D. J. P., Osmond, C., Simmonds, S. J. and Wield, G. A. (1993) The relation of small head circumference and thinness at birth to death from cardiovascular disease in adult life, *British Medical Journal*, 306, 422–426.

Barker, D. J. P., Winter, P. D., Osmond, C. et al. (1989) Weight in infancy and death from ischaemic heart disease, *Lancet*, 2, 577–580.

Casper, R. C., Fleisher, B. E., Lee-Ancajas, J. C., Gilles, A., Gaylor, E., DeBattista, A. and Hoyme, H. E. (2003) Follow-up of children of depressed mothers exposed or not exposed to antidepressant drugs during pregnancy, *Journal of Pediatrics*, 142 (4), 402–408.

Challis, J. R. G., Sloboda, D., Matthews, S. G., Holloway, A., Alfaidy, N., Patel, F. A., Whittle, W., Fraser, M., Moss, T. J. M. and Newnham, J. (2001) The fetal placental hypothalamic-pituitary-adrenal (HPA) axis, parturition and postnatal health, *Molecular and Cellular Endocrinology*, 185, 135–144.

Chambers, C. D., Johnson, K. A., Dick, L. M., Felix, R. J. and Lyons Jones, K. (1996) Birth outcomes in pregnant women taking fluoxetine, *New England Journal of Medicine*, 335 (14), 1010–1015.

Chaudron, L. H. and Pies, R. W. (2003) The relationship between postpartum psychosis and bipolar disorder: A review, *Journal of Clinical Psychiatry*, 64, 1284–1292.

Cliver, S. P., Goldenberg, R. L., Cutter, G. R., Hoffman, H. J., Copper, R. L., Gotlieb, S. J. and Davis, R. O. (1992) The relationships between psychosocial profile, maternal size and smoking in predicting fetal growth retardation, *Obstetrics and Gynecology*, 80, 262–267.

Cohen, L. S., Sichel, D. A., Robertson, L. M., Heckscher, E. and Rosenbaum, J. F. (1995) Postpartum prophylaxis for women with bipolar disorder, *American Journal of Psychiatry*, 152, 1641–1645.

DeRubeis, R. J., Hollon, S. D., Amsterdam, J. D., Shelton, R. C., Young, P. R., Salomon, R. M., O'Reardon, J. P., Lovett, M. L., Gladis, M. M., Brown, L. L. and Gallop, R. (2005) Cognitive therapy vs medications in the treatment of moderate to severe depression, *Archives of General Psychiatry*, 62, 409–416.

Eberhard-Gran, M., Eskild, A., Tambs, K., Samuelsen, S. O. and Opjordsmoen, S. (2002) Depression in postpartum and non-postpartum women: Prevalence and risk factors, *Acta Psychiatrica Scandinavica*, 106, 426–433.

Evans, J., Heron, J., Francomb, H., Oke, S. and Golding, J. (2001) Cohort study of depressed mood during pregnancy and after childbirth, *British Medical Journal*, 323, 257–260.

Field, T., Diego, M., Dieter, J., Hernandez-Reif, M., Schanberg, S., Kuhn, C., Yando, R. and Bendell, D. (2004) Prenatal effects on the fetus and the newborn, *Infant Behaviour and Development*, 27, 216–229.

French, N. P., Hagan, R., Evans, S. F., Godfrey, M. and Newnham, J. P. (1999) Repeated antenatal corticosteriods: Size at birth and subsequent development, *American Journal of Obstetrics and Gynecology*, 180, 114–121.

Gater, R., Tansella, M., Korten, A., Bea, G., Tiemens, M. A., Mavreas, V. G. and Olatawura, M. O. (1998) Sex differences in the prevalence and detection of depressive and anxiety disorders in general health care settings: Report from the

World Health Organization collaborative study on psychological problems in general health care, *Archives of General Psychiatry*, 55, 405–413.

Glover, V., Liddle, P., Taylor, A., Adams, D. and Sandler, M. (1994) Mild hypomania (the highs) can be a feature of the first postpartum week: Association with later depression, *British Journal of Psychiatry*, 164, 517–521.

Gotlib, I. H., Whiffen, V. E., Mount, J. H., Milne, K. and Cordy, N. I. (1989) Prevalence rates and demographic characteristics associated with depression in pregnancy and the postpartum, *Journal of Consulting and Clinical Psychology*, 57, 269–274.

Heron, J., Craddock, N. and Jones, I. (2005) Postnatal euphoria: Are 'the highs' an indicator of bipolarity?, *Bipolar Disorders*, 7, 103–110.

Hollon, S. D., DeRubeis, R. J., Shelton, R. C., Amsterdam, J. D., Salomon, R. M., O'Reardon, J. P., Lovett, M. L., Young, P. R., Haman, K. L., Freeman, B. B. and Gallop, R. (2005) Prevention of relapse following cognitive therapy vs medications in moderate to severe depression, *Archives of General Psychiatry*, 62, 417–422.

Huttunen, M. O. and Niskanen, P. (1978) Prenatal loss of father and psychiatric disorders, *Archives of General Psychiatry*, 35, 429–431.

Jones, I. and Craddock, N. (2001) Familiality of the puerperal trigger in bipolar disorder: Results of a family study, *American Journal of Psychiatry*, 158, 913–917.

Kallen, B. (2004) Neonate characteristics after maternal use of antidepressants in late pregnancy, *Archives of Pediatric and Adolescent Medicine*, 158, 312–316.

Kendall, R. E., Chalmers, J. C. and Platz, C. (1987) Epidemiology of puerperal psychoses, *British Journal of Psychiatry*, 150, 662–673.

Kulin, N. A., Pastuszak, A., Sage, S. R., Schick-Boschetto, B., Spivey, G., Feldkamp, M., Ormond, K., Matsui, D., Stein-Schechman, A. K., Cook, L., Brochu, J., Rieder, M. and Koren, G. (1998) Pregnancy outcome following maternal use of the new selective serotonin reuptake inhibitors: A prospective controlled multicenter study, *Journal of the American Medical Association*, 279, 609–610.

Lane, A., Keville, R., Morris, M., Kinsella, A., Turner, M. and Barry, S. (1997) Postnatal depression and elation among mothers and their partners: Prevalence and predictors, *British Journal of Psychiatry*, 171, 550–555.

Liggins, G. and Howie, R. (1972) A controlled trial of antepartum glucocorticoid treatment for prevention of respiratory distress syndrome in premature infants, *Paediatrics*, 50, 515–525.

Misri, S., Burgmann, K. and Costaras, D. (2000) Are SSRIs safe for pregnant and breastfeeding women?, *Canadian Family Physician*, 46, 626–628, 631–633.

Oberlander, T. F., Misri, S., Fitzgerald, C. E., Kostaras, X., Rurak, D. and Riggs, W. (2004) Pharmacologic factors associated with transient neonatal symptoms following prenatal psychotropic medication exposure, *Journal of Clinical Psychiatry*, 65 (2), 230–237.

O'Connor, T. G., Heron, J., Golding, J., Beveridge, M. and Glover, V. (2002) Maternal antenatal anxiety and children's behavioural/emotional problems at 4 years, *British Journal of Psychiatry*, 180, 502–508.

O'Hara, M. W. (1987) Postpartum "blues", depression, and psychosis: A review, *Journal of Psychosomatic Obstetrics and Gynecology*, 7, 205–227.

O'Hara, M. W. and Swain, A. M. (1996) Rates and risk of postpartum depression – a meta-analysis, *International Review of Psychiatry*, 8, 37–54.

O'Hara, M. W. and Zekoski, E. M. (1988) Postpartum depression: A comprehensive review, in R. Kumar and I. F. Brockington (eds) *Motherhood and mental illness 2*, pp. 17–63, London, Wright.

O'Hara, M. W., Zekoski, E. M., Philipps, L. H. and Wright, E. J. (1990) Controlled prospective study of postpartum mood disorders: Comparison of childbearing and nonchildbearing women, *Journal of Abnormal Psychology*, 99, 3–15.

O'Keane, V. (2000) Evolving model of depression as an expression of multiple interacting risk factors, *British Journal of Psychiatry*, 177, 482–483.

Patton, G. C., Coffey, C., Carlin, J. B., Olsson, C. A. and Morley, R. (2004) Prematurity at birth and adolescent depressive disorder, *British Journal of Psychiatry*, 184, 446–447.

Robertson, E., Jones, I., Haque, S., Holder, R. and Craddock, N. (2005) Risk of puerperal and non-puerperal recurrence of illness following bipolar affective puerperal (post-partum) psychosis, *British Journal of Psychiatry*, 186, 258–259.

Royal College of Obstetricians and Gynaecologists (RCOG) (2001 and 2004) Confidential enquiry into maternal deaths, London, RCOG.

Shakespeare, J. (2002) Evaluation of screening for postnatal depression against the NSC handbook criteria, Working party document, http://dev.nelh.nhs.uk/screening/adult_pps/shakespeare_final_paper.pdf

Stewart, D. E., Klompenhouwer, J. L., Kendell, R. E. and van Hulst, A. M (1991) Prophylactic lithium in puerperal psychosis: The experience of three centres, *British Journal of Psychiatry*, 158, 393–397.

Spinelli, M. G. and Endicott, J. (2003) Controlled clinical trial of interpersonal psychotherapy versus parenting education program for depressed pregnant women, *American Journal of Psychiatry*, 160, 555–562.

Wadhwa, P. D., Sandman, C. A., Porto, M., Dunkel-Schetter, C. and Garite, T. J. (1993) The association between prenatal stress and infant birth weight and gestational age at birth: A prospective investigation, *American Journal of Obstetrics and Gynecology*, 169, 858–865.

Welberg, L. A. N. and Seckl, J. R. (2001) Prenatal stress, glucocorticoids and programming of the brain, *Journal of Neuroendocrinology*, 13, 113–128.

Whitelaw, A. and Thoresen, M. (2000) Antenatal steroids and the developing brain, *Archives of the Diseases of Childhood, Fetal and Neonatal Edition*, 83, F154–F157.

Williamson, H. A., LeFevre, M. and Hector, M. (1989) Association between life stress and serious perinatal complications, *Journal of Family Practice*, 29, 489–496.

World Health Organization (WHO) (1992) *International classification of diseases* (10th revision), Geneva, WHO.

Yonkers, K. A., Wisner, K. L., Stowe, Z., Leibenluft, E., Cohen, L., Miller, L., Manber, R., Viguera, A., Suppes, T. and Altshuler, L. (2004) Management of bipolar disorder during pregnancy and the postpartum period, *American Journal of Psychiatry*, 161, 608–620.

Zeskind, P. S. and Stephens, L. E. (2004) Maternal selective serotonin reuptake inhibitor use during pregnancy and newborn neurobehaviour, *Pediatrics*, 113 (2), 368–375.

Chapter 10

Women who kill their babies

Sarah Davenport, Sandra Flynn and Jenny Shaw

INTRODUCTION

This chapter deals with a very disturbing side of motherhood: the case of women who kill their babies. It attempts to provide an explanatory framework for such a case, and explore its psychological roots, particularly how the woman unconsciously uses her own body and that of her baby to deal with unresolved conflict about her own mothering and unmet dependency, and how the act of infanticide could be seen as symbolic suicide.

The content of the chapter is based on the most recent study of infanticide, conducted by the National Confidential Inquiry in Manchester, UK, which included all infanticides (and neonaticides) committed between 1996 and 2001. The primary data of this study have been published elsewhere and are largely consistent with previous studies, but with some important differences. Psychological and social themes from the psychiatric reports were extracted and clustered together.

Fictional case studies were then created from theme clusters based on the psychiatric reports for women convicted. (These were provided by a consultant psychiatrist around the material time for the court.) The social histories and psychological conflicts present within this sample are thus illustrated (whilst all identifiable references are excluded.) This Manchester study provides a rare opportunity to advance our understanding of the psychological basis of infanticide, offer some of the predictors for British women who kill their babies and inform subsequent treatment.

RELEVANT DEFINITIONS

Neonaticide

This is the killing of a newborn child within the first 24 hours of life. The literature suggests a psychosocial aetiology, rather different to infanticide. These women kill their baby within 24 hours of birth (Resnick, 1969). They rarely suffer from psychiatric disorder, are significantly younger than other filicides, and are single or separated women who conceal their illegitimate pregnancies and kill the baby almost immediately after birth. There is usually no premeditation as they are dissociated from the pregnancy. The degree of dissociation and denial may amount to a hysterical defence mechanism (Green and Manohar, 1990).

Infanticide

This is the killing by a mother of an infant who is more than a day old and less than 12 months old. The psychological mechanisms underlying infanticide must take account of the nature of the individual mother–infant attachment relationship, which is likely to retain within it elements of the mother's attachment relationship with her own mother (Bowlby, 1988). Psychosocial factors may also be important determinants of the outcome of this dynamic relationship, including infanticide as a fatal outcome.

Legal definition of infanticide

Special legislation concerning women who kill their children originated in 1624, with the 'Act to Prevent the Murthering of Bastard Children'. If an unmarried woman concealed a pregnancy and the child was subsequently found dead, she was presumed to have killed it unless she could prove that it had been stillborn. This Act was aimed at immorality rather than child protection and the penalty was death. By the mid eighteenth century, courts had become reluctant to convict, and a further Act in 1803 changed the burden of proof so that infanticides were treated like other kinds of murder, and concealment of birth became a separate offence.

A further shift occurred in 1938 with the passing of the present Infanticide Act. This provides for women who kill their children under the age of 12 months, in circumstances which would otherwise amount to murder, but at the time: "The balance of her mind was disturbed by reason of her not having fully recovered from the effect of giving birth or by reason of the effect of lactation consequent on the birth of the child."

If these criteria are met then the woman may be convicted of infanticide, an offence punishable *as if* she had been guilty of manslaughter. In practice, this offence is usually dealt with leniently, but the frequency with which the charge is used has been reduced in favour of manslaughter on the grounds of diminished responsibility.

Homicide

This is a general term for the killing of one human being by another. Filicide is the killing of a son or a daughter by a parent. Homicide can be legally subdivided as follows:

Murder

Homicide is murder when the offender is of sound mind and discretion (over the age of 10 years) and had 'malice aforethought' (i.e. intent to cause death or grievous bodily harm). There is a mandatory sentence for murder, namely life imprisonment, and the court has no discretion where there is a conviction.

Manslaughter

Homicide is manslaughter when the circumstances do not meet the full criteria for murder (e.g. absence of intent) or where there are certain mitigating factors such as immediate and severe provocation, where the homicide was part of a suicide pact (Section 4 (1) Homicide Act 1957) or where there is "abnormality of mind" leading to diminished responsibility for the crime (Section 2 (1) Homicide Act 1957). This is sometimes referred to as "Section 2 manslaughter" and is now the more common verdict for women who kill their babies (see section on treatment).

AN OVERVIEW OF EARLIER LITERATURE ON INFANTICIDE

Resnick (1969) reviewed the world literature, and found a high frequency of depression, psychosis, previous use of psychiatric services and suicidality among mothers who committed filicide. However, mothers committing neonaticide were typically younger and unmarried, without mental illness.

The world literature review suggested that different cultural, legal or economic factors could constitute external incentives for filicide, unrelated to the mother's psychological state; these include factors such as preference for male rather than female children because of the burden of dowry provision.

In 1979, D'Orbán studied filicide by mothers admitted for psychiatric observation to the hospital ward of a prison. The findings suggested an association between maternal filicide and the presence of certain stressors in the mother's life. These stressors included being a survivor of domestic violence, early parental separation and suicidality.

In the case of neonaticide, D'Orbán also confirmed an association with unmarried status and younger mean maternal age. Lack of association with depression or psychosis was also found in this group, as in the Resnick study. Neonaticide and infanticide may therefore differ in their aetiology and psychology; in both the classic studies cited above, the neonaticide group is distinct from the infanticide group in terms of socio-demographic and clinical characteristics.

Scott (1973) studied a group of women who had killed their children and then attempted to classify the crime according to motive. He suggested the following categorisation:

1   killing an unwanted child;
2   mercy killing of a disabled or ill child;
3   killing attributable to aggression associated with severe mental pathology, such as personality disorder or mental illness;
4   stimulus arising outside the victim (displacement of anger, loss of love object, avoidance of censure, loss of status);
5   stimulus arising from within the victim (battering mother who responds to the perceived provocation of an infant who does not stop crying).

This is essentially a condensed version of the more complex classification systems suggested by Resnick (1969) and D'Orbán (1979). The case studies here will illustrate categories 3, 4 and 5.

EXPLANATORY MODELS OF INFANTICIDE

Attachment theory

Bowlby (1988) proposed a synthesis of ethology and psychoanalysis (informed by his mother–infant observations) to explain human attachment behaviour. The human infant is born entirely dependent and relies for its survival on proximity to a caregiver capable of meeting his/her basic needs for food, warmth and shelter in a reliable and responsive way. Having confirmed survival, attachment behaviour continues during childhood to underpin the psychological basis of personality development and the capacity to relate to others. The infant develops a psychological "internal working model" to predict the type of response to expect from his/her primary caregiver and this becomes an important basic model of relating.

An infant with a responsive mother "attuned" to meeting his/her needs in an appropriate and timely manner will go on to develop a sense of self and a secure attachment style predictive of the ability to sustain supportive and boundaried attachment relationships in adult life. However, an infant who lacks an appropriate response to his/her needs from an anxious, depressed, unresponsive, neglectful or abusive mother will develop a pathological attachment style, characterised by anxiety, anger, avoidance or ambivalence.

This "internal working model" endures within the developing psyche of the infant, where it becomes overlaid by subsequent experience within other attachment relationships. The model incorporates both poles of the attachment relationship, the "cared for" and the "caregiver". There are continuities between the observed attachment style of the mother and that which her own infant subsequently displays (Fonagy et al., 1995).

Attachment research has confirmed that these "internal working models" do persist into adult life and may unconsciously drive adult intimate relationships and subsequent parental relationships (Bowlby, 1988). Thus, a mother's experience of being parented herself is likely to influence strongly the development of her attachment relationship with her own infant. Neglected or abused infants may develop into abusive or neglectful mothers themselves, as they unconsciously follow their own internal working models, shifting from the neglected child to the neglectful mother.

Psychoanalytic/psychodynamic

Dinora Pines' book *A Woman's Unconscious Use of her Body* (1993) discusses the psychological conflicts that pregnancy and childbirth may awaken, and how those unconscious conflicts may then be acted out, using her body as a part object. Giving birth to a totally dependent child often reawakens the dependent child buried within the adult psyche, re-presenting the new mother with her own unresolved dependency needs embodied in her baby.

Welldon (1992) suggests that motherhood provides an excellent vehicle for some women to exercise perverse and perverting attitudes towards their offspring, and to retaliate against their own mothers. She suggests that an infant may be regarded as a narcissistic extension of the mother, and therefore subject to the rage and self-hatred expressed by many women who feel disempowered socially or through experiencing childhood abuse.

The birth of a baby presents a vulnerable mother with a helpless dependent child, likely to re-awaken unresolved dependency needs and a profound sense of helplessness, which may be intolerable. The mother may use the infant as a vehicle for projection, and then identify with it, becoming helpless and dependent herself. The identification may be intolerable, and excite violent retaliation for the perceived abandonment, which results in the killing, a symbolic suicide (Motz, 2001).

Sociological

DeMause (1990) combines psychodynamic and sociological perspectives in his explanation of infanticide. He suggests that children have been used as scapegoats to relieve personal internal conflict since the dawn of civilisation, and that they are used as "poison containers" into which disowned projections of the self can be placed, and thence controlled, tortured or killed. The "poison container" (in this case the baby) represents another body into which threatening or fearful projections can be disposed, or controlled or manipulated. DeMause (1990) suggests that infanticidal mothers have had highly inadequate mothering themselves and have harsh punitive superegos that demand punishment of their strongest wishes, i.e. to be dependent or to be a mother (to deal with their own dependency). These intolerable wishes are projected into the baby, "the poison container", where they continue to represent a threat and killing the baby becomes the primitive psychological solution.

FICTIONAL CASE STUDIES BASED ON THE FIVE-YEAR COHORT STUDY OF INFANTICIDE 1996–2001

The National Confidential Inquiry obtains national information on all homicides that occur nationally in England and Wales from the Homicide Index at the Home Office. During this five-year period, over 2500 people were convicted of homicide. Of these perpetrators, 112 were convicted of killing of an infant, which equates to 4% of all homicides. Five individuals killed more than one infant, bringing the total number of victims to 125. Consistent with previous research in England and Wales, 70% of the perpetrators were male. However, this differs from countries such as the USA, where women are more likely to kill infants than men. In all, 81% of all the victims were killed by their parent.

1   Just under a third were killed by their mother.
2   In 50% of cases the child's father was convicted.
3   Stepfathers accounted for 8% of the convictions.

In terms of criminal justice outcome, men were significantly more likely to be found guilty of murder; 58% of women when convicted received a mental health verdict, either manslaughter on the grounds of diminished responsibility or infanticide. Only 4% of men were found to have diminished responsibility, while 96% of men received a prison sentence compared to a quarter of women.

Looking at maternal filicides, the highest number of infants was killed by their mothers within their first month. A large number of these deaths can be accounted for by neonaticide. Although the number of infants killed by their mother dropped dramatically in the second month, numbers began to rise again until the infant was around six months old. Women were found to use violent methods, such as stabbing or hitting with a blunt weapon, with equal frequency to their use of non-violent methods (smothering or poisoning). Affective disorder was by far the most common mental illness diagnosed for women, with 35% having depressive symptoms at the time of the offence, which is much higher than any other diagnosis. Five of the 34 women who had psychiatric reports and were convicted of homicide had either postnatal depression or puerperal psychosis as a specified diagnosis.

Eight (26%) of the women convicted had a history of alcohol or drug misuse (a lower proportion than the men). Of the total sample of perpetrators killing infants, 14 (13%) had previous lifetime contact with psychiatric services. Eight (21%) women had been treated by mental health services and five (13%) had been seen within 12 months of committing the homicide.

Miss A (neonaticide)

Miss A was a 19-year-old single woman living with her mother. Her parents divorced in acrimonious circumstances when she was a young child. Nevertheless, she maintained a good relationship with both parents, seeing her father regularly. She had a happy childhood and was not the victim of any form of child abuse. She had a quiet disposition with a small circle of friends. She left school with a number of GSCEs and enrolled at a college of higher education, working part-time.

She had been together with her boyfriend for several months before discovering that she was pregnant. Although she had a good relationship with her boyfriend, he was immature. This was her first pregnancy and she was very frightened. She feared that if she disclosed the pregnancy to her parents they would be extremely angry, disappointed and ashamed of her. She feared abandonment by her parents and her boyfriend.

Her reaction was to deny the fact that she was pregnant, and she chose to disregard any associated symptoms and physical changes in her body shape, convincing herself that it was not real. Both her parents and boyfriend failed to notice her condition.

Having been in denial, Miss A had not attended any antenatal classes and had made no plans or preparation for the birth. Not recognising the signs, she did not associate the cramping pains as the onset of labour, believing instead that she needed to use the toilet. Alone in the house, she gave birth in the bathroom in a state of disbelief, unable to comprehend what had just happened. Her inability to respond to the newborn's needs and her attempt to stop it crying led to its death by suffocation. Having dissociated herself from the event, she placed the child in a carrier bag and disposed of the body close to her home. There were no symptoms of mental disorder prior to the pregnancy.

Commentary

Miss A was only 19 when she was convicted of neonaticide, six years below the median age of women committing infanticide. Her story is typical of the young women convicted of neonaticide, where the perceived social stigma and developmental immaturity of the mother contribute to a denial of the pregnancy and dissociation from the birth. The baby usually dies through neglect within the first few hours, rather than from an actual assault. The mother is dissociated from a part of her body, the baby, and fatally neglects it. Formal psychiatric disorder (mental illness or personality disorder) is rarely detected.

Miss A's own infancy was conducted against a background of parental disharmony resulting in a divorce during her middle childhood. She developed a rather anxious attachment style, and maintained her self-esteem (or her false self) by conforming to the social norms set by her parents. Her denial of the pregnancy was a defensive denial; the baby became a split-off part object, which had to be kept separate from the mind and body of the mother. The death of the denied baby, the ultimate separation of a split-off body part, was the only viable psychological solution for the living woman.

Miss B (domestic violence and child abuse themes)

Miss B was a 22-year-old woman who was co-habiting with her partner and children. Her parents divorced when she was a child and she had a poor relationship with her father. Her upbringing was unstable, resulting in disruptive behaviour, which often got her into trouble at school and she left with few qualifications or friends.

She had had a number of relationships. She first became pregnant at the age of 16 and terminated the pregnancy. Her next relationship was with an older man and she soon found herself to be pregnant again. Her partner was a violent man who regularly subjected her to both verbal and physical abuse. The couple both had a history of alcohol and drug use, and arguments intensified when they were both intoxicated. Following the birth of the child, the relationship broke down and they separated. Miss B and her child moved in with a new partner who was also violent towards her. The couple regularly fought, and her first child was often caught in the middle of this conflict. Her next pregnancy was with the child she killed, and he became subject to the same abuse. On the day of the offence, the child was unsettled and his demands for attention were a cause of frustration for Miss B. As she had done several times before, she lost her temper and directed her anger towards the baby. She threw the baby on the sofa. The child was put to bed as normal but later that night was found to be unconscious. An ambulance was called and the baby died later in hospital from severe head injuries. Miss B was diagnosed with personality disorder.

Commentary

Miss B had an early history of disrupted attachments and abusive relationships with her family. She grew up to expect violence and neglect within intimate relationships and was disruptive and violent at school. She dealt with her own despair and neediness by drinking to excess and attempting to find the love and care she craved with a variety of abusive partners. Her pregnancies re-awakened her own primitive desire for care but she found caring for her first infant very challenging. Her rage at her own neglect by her mother, and envy of her child's opportunity to be mothered by Miss B herself, excited intolerable feelings, which she frequently projected into the child, who acted as a "poison container". This became more pronounced in the case of her second child, who also became a "poison container". Her baby died from the injuries sustained by her retaliatory assault.

Miss C (depression, child neglect and abuse themes)

Miss C was a 26-year-old woman who was co-habiting with her partner. She had a family history of depression. She had a good relationship with her parents and her childhood, overall, was unremarkable. She was popular among her peers and had no history of alcohol or substance misuse. She developed a stable relationship with her partner and had three children by him. Following the birth of her third child, she was diagnosed with "baby blues" but was not adequately followed up. For a period before the offence, she became increasingly stressed and had regular arguments with her partner, who was unsupportive. Her inability to cope with the situation resulted in the child's needs not being met. The victim was often neglected, both being ignored and not having adequate feeds.

On the day of the offence her other children had been very demanding and when the baby started crying she became overwhelmed by the situation and began to shake the baby in her frustration. Miss C was diagnosed as suffering from depression.

Commentary

Miss C has a family history of depression and her mother had a prolonged puerperal depression, which reduced her mother's affective responsiveness to Miss C as an infant. When Miss C's mood was low, she felt that those closest to her (parents and partner) did not recognise her deepest needs and that she was left to cope alone, having failed to elicit care or additional support from her parents after the birth of her third child. Her initial diagnosis of "baby blues" had not been followed up appropriately with assessment for effective antidepressant treatment or additional support from a health visitor. The health system also behaved as a depressed and unresponsive mother, adding to Miss C's despair and frustration, which was projected into her baby. His cries provoked such identification that he came to feel much like a part of her own body and less like a separate individual. The crescendo of his cries demanded the annihilation of this needy reminder of her own neglectful mothering. She shook him to death to rid herself of an intolerable personal burden, much like a suicide attempt.

Miss D (themes from four women with serious mental illness)

Miss D was a 25-year-old woman with a family history of schizophrenia in first-degree male relatives. Hers was a strict Catholic family and her mother took solace from her religion as respite from caring for her husband and son (both of whom suffered from schizophrenia). Miss D and her mother were regular churchgoers during her childhood and adolescence; there was an emphasis for both women on pleasing and appeasing the male figures in the family, who were frequently demanding, inconsistent and sometimes unpredictably violent towards them. Miss D's role within her nuclear family was often that of the appeaser, after a violent outburst from her father. She was a shy and lonely child who found social relationships outside of the family difficult to establish. She had an unhappy school life and was often bullied because of the stigma of her father and brother's illness. She eventually left home when she got a job in a local supermarket, where she met her first boyfriend, a driver who was near in age to her father and a drinker but not a Catholic. She developed a rather dependent relationship with him, which subsequently became abusive as he beat her when he was drunk. This relationship lasted three years before he left her and she met her second partner, who drank heavily and was violent. He was interested in black magic and often frightened her with his tales of ritual child sacrifice to appease the devil. When she became pregnant, he threatened to leave her, and was only persuaded to stay by her agreement to increasingly bizarre and ritualistic sexual activity.

As her pregnancy advanced, she became increasingly preoccupied by the way in which she had neglected her religion since leaving home. Her impending role as a mother seemed threatened by her apparent loss of faith; she became increasingly religious to compensate and angered her partner. He left her when her advanced pregnancy made sexual activity impossible. The delivery was difficult, but she was discharged home after 48 hours and found the child difficult to feed and to settle. She began to believe that God was punishing her for neglecting Him. However hard she tried to make up for this by nurturing the baby, she saw that God would not forgive her as the baby never settled and repeatedly reminded her of her failure with his cries. She filled her flat with religious artefacts to appease God, the Father, and struggled to satiate and silence the baby, who came to remind her of the bad irreligious part of herself who had so angered God the Father and the father of her child. She began to hear voices telling her she was damned and would go to burn in hell. She became increasingly agitated and failed to respond to the baby who then took on a "devilish" quality and seemed to criticise her too. In a frenzy of agitation, she locked herself in, smothered the baby and tried to burn the body in the fireplace to "return the devil to the fires of hell". Miss D was diagnosed with puerperal psychosis.

Commentary

Miss D had a biological predisposition to schizophrenia and her first psychotic episode was triggered by the birth of her baby son. Her own mothering was impoverished by the added caring responsibilities that her mother was required to give to her ill father. She learnt quite early that her demands were unlikely to be met from sources other than herself; she became compulsively self reliant and rather cut off from alternative support outside of her church and her family. This rather avoidant attachment style was reinforced by her school experience of bullying. Her relationship with her partners represented her attachment relationship with her own father, with the partners remote and unresponsive to her own needs and the relationships maintained by her wish to appease their aggression through her own sexual subjugation. Her relationship with God was probably based on the same anxious attachment dynamic.

Her unborn baby, inside her own body, was perceived to have driven away her "father-partner", as she was unable to appease his sexual demands; his devil worship contravened her religious faith and woke it again as she struggled with the impending loss of him as a father figure. Re-awakened religious faith led to the fear of the "Lord my God a jealous God" and the re-instatement of the appeasement dynamic. After the baby was born, she struggled to appease God for her wrongdoing, by caring excessively for the baby, who represented the "wrongdoing" part of herself. However, she perceived herself as failing to care for the baby, who cried ceaselessly, and unconsciously reminded her of herself, as an uncared-for infant. When she began to hear voices telling her that she was damned and would burn in hell, she knew what she should do. She sacrificed the bad irreligious part of herself, her baby son. Her psychosis led her to act out her symbolic experience in a very concrete manner, and to kill her baby. This death was in fact a suicide of the bad part of herself, to appease the "good Father".

ISSUES RELATED TO THE ASSESSMENT AND MANAGEMENT OF INFANTICIDE

Maternal infanticide is a crime which bewilders and horrifies both professionals and the public. It has an impact on the perpetrator, her family and friends, and the father of the dead baby. The crime will be reported in the local and/or national press amidst what is usually a horrified public outcry. The woman will have been remanded to prison, prior to the preparation of psychiatric reports. Her fellow inmates are likely to treat her with incredulity and aggression. She may need special protection whilst in prison.

All cases require a psychiatric report for the Crown Prosecution Service before going to court. Most women will have a second psychiatric report prepared at the request of their defence solicitor. Those women who are evidently seriously psychiatrically disturbed may be transferred pre-trial to hospital and detained under the Mental Health Act 1983. Some will be treated in prison pre-trial, provided they can give informed consent to their treatment. This is usually confined to prescription of antidepressant or antipsychotic medication, and the provision of psychological support through a mental health in-reach team. The chief risk at this stage is that of a completed suicide attempt. Where the risk is high, urgent attempts should be made to transfer the woman to an appropriate hospital setting. Managing actively suicidal women in segregation for long periods is unacceptable.

Preparation of psychiatric reports for court should be the first step towards a psychiatric and psychological formulation of the offence. The woman's mental state when first seen will provide important evidence as to her mental state at the material time and her subsequent response to the killing. Depositions and witness statements will provide some collateral information to help reconstruct the circumstances in which the crime was committed. This can then be matched to the woman's own account. Any mismatch between her account and the evidence should be explored.

It is essential to establish the woman's own attachment history, initially with her mother, father and family, and subsequently with peers and intimates. Her own attachment and separation experiences will predict some continuities within the attachment relationship with her own baby. The manner in which she bonds with her infant is likely to be predicted, at least in part, by her own experience of bonding with her own mother.

Mental illness is a crucial consideration in infanticide. Is mental illness such as depression or psychosis present, and/or is the main issue disordered personality resulting from disturbed early attachments? Skilled psychiatric assessment is always required following infanticide, to inform treatment and disposal from court.

The presence or absence of others at the time of the killing may provide important clues to formulating an understanding of the offence. The method used – violent or non-violent method, or profound neglect – may also be instructive.

A detailed understanding of the context in which the killing occurred is essential, and may be gained from talking to the mother herself and from collateral or witness statements. Discrepancies between the mother's own account and collateral information may be revealing. Each circumstance (or discrepancy) may have particular explanatory power and should be incorporated into a psychological formulation for the individual mother.

Hence, the following are the main points to bear in mind in the assessment of any infanticide case:

1   the history of child care prior to the offence;
2   the mental state of the mother at the material time;
3   the specific circumstances.

To satisfy the criteria of infanticide it must be proved that a mother's mind was disturbed by reason of her not having fully recovered from the effects of giving birth, or by reason of the effects of lactation (a rather archaic concept). No such criteria are required for a verdict of manslaughter on the grounds of diminished responsibility, arguably a more appropriate outcome for mothers with abnormality of mind who have killed their infant. Women who are convicted of manslaughter on the grounds of diminished responsibility (or very rarely infanticide) receive a mental health disposal, usually a hospital order for treatment under Section 37 of the Mental Health Act 1983.

Both psychological and social treatments are central to the management of women who have killed their baby. The woman and her family are likely to have been very traumatised by the killing and will require support to address the impact of the crime on the family system. Further family work may be required to ameliorate anti-therapeutic responses to the perpetrator and to promote family inclusion and support where appropriate in the future. Psychosocial interventions should also be considered to promote the woman's recovery and social inclusion long-term.

Psychological treatments are likely to be at the centre of necessary interventions to address the antecedents, experience and consequences of infanticide. When denial of the killing is breached, or psychosis improved to the point where the reality of the killing becomes apparent to the perpetrator, the struggle for the woman to live with herself, as the murderer of her child, is usually experienced as intolerable. The risk of a completed suicide attempt at this stage is high.

CONCLUSION

The most recent crime statistics (Home Office, 2005) suggest that the courts are reluctant to charge women with infanticide. In the late 1960s an average of 19 infanticide verdicts were recorded each year, compared to only one case in the last three years.

The Manchester Infanticide Study identified that 21% of the women who had killed their babies had had previous treatment within mental health services. Only 13% of these women had been seen within 12 months of committing filicide, and not all of them during their pregnancy. The incidence of postnatal depression ranges between 8% and 14% (Cox et al., 1982; Kumar and Robson, 1984; Watson et al., 1984). One of the emergent themes from reports was poor follow-up for "baby blues". As 35% of mothers who had killed their babies had depressive symptoms at the time of the offence, all women in contact with mental health services who become pregnant should be actively followed up and screened for postpartum depression. Whilst this may occur in some mental health or obstetric services, it is not universal. This could potentially reduce the incidence of such a devastating event.

REFERENCES

Bowlby, J. (1988) *A secure base: Clinical applications of attachment theory*, London, Routledge.

Cox, J. L., Connor, W. and Kendell, R. E. (1978) Prospective study of the psychiatric disorders of childbirth by personal interview, *British Journal of Psychiatry*, 140, 111–117.

DeMause, L. (1990) The history of child assault, *The Journal of Psychohistory*, 18 (1), 1–29.

D'Orbán, P. T. (1979) Women who kill their children, *British Journal of Psychiatry*, 134, 560–571.

Fonagy, P., Steele, M., Steele, H., Leigh, T. et al. (1995) Attachment, the reflective self and borderline states: The predictive specificity of the adult attachment interview and pathological emotional development, in S. Goldberg, R. Muir and J. Kerr (eds) *Attachment theory: Social, developmental and clinical significance*, Hillsdale, NJ, Analytic Press.

Green, C. M. and Manohar, S. V. (1990) Neonaticide and hysterical denial of pregnancy, *British Journal of Psychiatry*, 156, 121–123.

Home Office (2005) *Crime in England and Wales 2003/2004: Supplementary volume 1: Homicide and gun crime* (ed. David Povey), London, Home Office.

Kumar, R. and Robson, K. (1984) A prospective study of emotional disorders in childbearing women, *British Journal of Psychiatry*, 144, 35–37.

Motz, A. (2001) *The psychology of female violence*, Hove, Brunner Routledge.

Pines, D. (1993) *A woman's unconscious use of her body*, London, Virago.

Resnick, P. J. (1969) Child murder by parents: A psychiatric review of filicide, *American Journal of Psychiatry*, 126: 325–334.

Scott, P. D. (1973) Parents who kill their children, *Medicine, Science and the Law*, 13, 120–126.

Watson, J. P., Elliot, S. A., Rugg, A. J. and Brough, D. I. (1984) Psychiatric disorder in pregnancy and the first postnatal year, *British Journal of Psychiatry*, 144, 453–462.

Welldon, E. V. (1992) *Mother, madonna, whore: The idealization and denigration of motherhood*, New York, Guilford Press.

Part IV

The interactive body

This part of the book focuses on women and society, personality issues, the burden of caring and the interface between gender and culture (as in the case of women from different ethnicities). Chapter 11 explores the multitude of social processes and the many pathways by which they influence women's mental health. The emphasis in Chapter 12 is on personality types, with a critique of the existing personality typology as applied to gender and gender role development. Chapter 13 revolves around the issue of care, the factors associated with the burden of care and the quality of the life of the carer. Chapter 14 attempts to discuss the case of the "other women" and the impact of culture and immigration on women's mental health, touching on different help-seeking behaviour among those groups and the argument for and against specific minority services.

Chapter 11

Society and women's distress

Tirril Harris

INTRODUCTION

It may seem strange to begin this chapter with Mrs Thatcher's famous remark, "There is no such thing as society." Rather than viewing it as an attack upon radical social thinkers, it can also be taken as a spur towards more complex thought on the multiplicity of social processes and the many pathways by which they influence women's health.

The main line of argument here is that society is indeed not a "thing" but covers processes in a person's outer world which need to be conceptualised at different levels, which range in distance from that person. These levels are here identified as being five in number, and the processes by which they influence mental health can co-vary considerably for each individual. However, each process tends to have an overall patterning of interactions with the other processes that remains remarkably similar between persons. In the end the influences of the more distant levels upon health are filtered through those social processes closest to the person's core identity. They exercise their impact largely via self-evaluation and the control of emotions that this engenders. However, emotional regulation is where the mind most clearly overlaps with the body and thus, ultimately, society also has its impact via physiological processes.

The focus in this chapter will be on unipolar depression and how societal processes influence its development, but a similar theoretical framework is also applicable to numerous other disorders. The data presented here are drawn from general population research that was carried out over three decades by the team of Professor George Brown and myself. Onset and remission of depression were defined in terms comparable to the DSM-IV threshold for major depression (for further details of this threshold see Finlay-Jones et al., 1980).

LEVELS OF OPERATION OF SOCIAL PROCESSES

Bronfenbrenner (1979) pioneered a model of human development from an ecological perspective, where influences upon development can profitably be distinguished according to their level of "proximity" to the developing person. By adopting a modified version of this approach it is possible to separate out not only a simple list of important influences but also whether and how they interact and how these interactions change over the individual's life span.

1   *Epidemiological categories*: the most distant level of social processes relevant to depression involves traditional epidemiological factors such as socio-economic status, urban/rural residence, historical birth cohort, ethnicity, religious affiliation and the outer world contexts into which a person is born but which s/he may often enter or leave as s/he develops. Gender is one of the most frequently used epidemiological categories. It is indeed also something into which a person is born (opportunities to change are expensive and rare), but it may be more illuminating to think of it less in terms of a context than in terms of the impact of the differing attitudes and activities required by *roles*, in this case the gender role. Of course, as will be discussed later, the category also overlaps with the physiological category of sex, with the attendant implications of hormonal influence on health and distress.

2   *Social roles*: the varying activities prescribed by the adoption of different roles and the attitudes incumbent upon a commitment to each role can all influence women's health. As just implied, there is considerable overlap between the classic categories used in epidemiological research and the categories of social roles, with marital status and employment joining gender, age and social class in the basic first table of many journal articles' results sections. Other roles which can be of similar importance but which do not routinely figure in health reports are parenthood and filial roles, and memberships of neighbourhood or leisure organisations such as political or sports clubs which, aside from their usual activities, also commit people to offer care to other members should it be necessary. Childcare and care of elderly parents are activities which can afford particularly high degrees of stress. Lone motherhood is an established risk factor for depression (e.g. Brown and Moran, 1997; Davies et al., 1997; Forgatch et al., 1988).

3   *Life events and difficulties*: severely stressful life events and ongoing difficulties arising in the outer world are established influences on health (Brown and Harris, 1978, 1989; Paykel, 1974, 2003). Certain contexts such as inner cities (Prudo et al., 1984; van Os, 2000) and certain roles such as lone motherhood (op. cit.) regularly produce more severe events than comparable localities or roles and have been found

to be associated with higher prevalence of depressive disorder. However, it is the meaning of these experiences which is crucial, rather than their mere occurrence, and this may vary according to the features of level 1, the cultural context. Thus a pregnancy out of wedlock in nineteenth-century England or twenty-first-century Saudi Arabia would have a much more negative meaning than it has in London today.

4   *Social networks, resources and social capital*: the important role of social support in promoting both physical and mental health has long been acknowledged in research circles (Cobb, 1976) but has gained much wider acceptance in recent years. Sheldon Cohen has admirably sum-marised the current evidence-based perspective (Cohen, 2004). He distinguishes between support as social integration and support as a close person buffering the effects of life stress by listening and offering an empathic response. The former involves networks of relationships at a slightly more distant level from the core self than the latter. The graded relation between social integration and good health found in many studies (Cohen et al., 2000) is the other side of a perspective which views social isolation as a cause of disease (Cacioppo et al., 2002). "Social capital" is a concept much in vogue at present as an explanation for good outcomes, not only in the health field (Kawachi et al., 1999; McKenzie et al., 2002) but also in the area of economic production. Some writers see social capital as representing the sum of an individual's resources, but others define it as belonging to whole communities so that each individual residing in that locality can benefit from such capital. Putnam uses the concept of social capital to refer to the "glue" which holds societies together. In his view it becomes a contextual property of communities rather than an individual trait: its benefits are assumed to affect everyone equally within that community, regardless of differences in individual behaviour or values (Putnam, 1995). The emphasis in his work is on networks, establishing obligations, expectations and trust-worthiness and creating channels for information, backed by efficient sanctions, to enable participants to act together more effectively to pursue shared objectives. This approach views social capital as "the collection of resources owned by the members of an individual's personal social network, which may become available to the individual as a result of the history of these relationships" (van der Gaag and Snijders, 2002: 3). Thus the expertise of other members in one's network becomes available through acquaintance: it is helpful to know a lawyer, a car mechanic, a computer buff, a doctor, a plumber, a person who might be willing to lend you money in times of need, because it may mean easier access to such services in a crisis. This shows the degree of overlap between this idea of social capital and what Cohen has identified as "social integration", in that both involve access to networks.

5   *Social support via intimate one-to-one relationships*: it is worth distinguishing the type of social support offered by a one-to-one relationship from the more practical resources involved in the networks detailed in level 4. It is perfectly possible to be integrated into a network without having any relationships intimate enough to provide a true emotional buffer against the knocks of fate which afflict us all to greater or lesser degree. Cohen follows the literature in distinguishing three subtypes which are again listed in order of gradually increasing proximity to the individual:

- *instrumental support* whereby material aid is provided, for example financial assistance or help with daily tasks;
- *informational support* whereby relevant information is provided, typically taking the form of advice or guidance;
- *emotional support* which involves the expression of empathy, reassurance, caring and trust, and offers an opportunity to express or ventilate emotion.

This is the least "social" of these levels of society, in that here it is the nature of only one other individual, specifically their sensitive responsiveness, which is the key outer world feature determining the quality of emotional support. The corollary of this idea is that some relationships are the opposite of such positive support, and that far from promoting resilience their negative interaction may actually produce depression or weaken the immune system and lead to physical illness. Thus families may be sources of rivalry and conflict as well as of comfort.

It is worth pointing out that this scheme is not offered as a system of exclusive categories – there can be overlap between these levels. For example, a violent marriage may produce severe life events (level 3) as well as a failure of intimate support (level 5). Being unemployed spans level 2 (roles) and level 3 (stressful events and difficulties). Moreover, different authors' terminology may locate factors differentially – knowing someone who has resources which might help you (more level 4) as compared with actually being offered those resources (more like level 5). Furthermore, sometimes it is a matter of degree. Thus a poor marriage with no confiding of emotional distress may not be poor enough to be producing negative life events (level 3), just an absence of positive emotional support (level 5).

Before leaving the theme of levels of societal impact on well-being/ distress it is worth visiting one last factor of importance.

6   *Self-image*: it can be argued that the self-monitoring process to which we all subject ourselves is also a level of society, in that views of the self

are modelled on other people's views about us. Certainly this level needs to be considered if the modes of impact of the other five levels are to be understood, and certainly in a listing of levels it must be the final one, the least distant from the person whose health is in focus.

SOCIAL PATHWAYS, THEIR INTERACTIONS AND DISTRESS

The often cited stress-diathesis model of distress has been supported by many studies, although some authors talk of "vulnerability" rather than diathesis and of "provoking factors" rather than stress. Early work on depression in women in London (Brown and Harris, 1978) suggested that negative life events (level 3) provoked depressive onset, and that the frequency of such events was increased according to level 1 contextual features such as low social class. A crucial insight was that features of level 2, such as employment outside the home or caring for as many as three children under 15, rendered women more or less vulnerable to the impact of these life events, even though without such events unemployed women and mothers of three were no more likely to become depressed than other women. But a distinction was made between merely fulfilling such roles and the sense of identity arising in addition given the occupation of such roles. The concept of "role-identity", originating in symbolic interactionist thought (McCall and Simmons, 1966), was invoked to explain such vulnerability, thus involving the self-monitoring level 6.

A similar role is played by the presence or absence of a confiding relationship (level 5). Women with such a relationship within the household were only one quarter as likely as women with no confidant at all to become depressed after a severe provoking factor. Rates of depressive onset in women who had a weekly confiding relationship outside the household were twice those of women with a household member confidant, and only half those for women without any confidant. Women with such a confidant contacted less than weekly were no more protected than those with no confidant at all.

The same study could not identify a parallel role as vulnerability factor for the simple existence of social networks of various types (level 4), but no conclusion could be drawn about the role of the social capital provided by different women's networks, since adequate measures of this were not obtained. Thus, although two women might have had similar sized networks one may have had acquaintances involved in occupations such as banking, medicine and the law whose advice was easily accessible in the course of social conversation, whereas the other's friends may not have had the expertise to point to reparative action in time to prevent the development of a severely stressful life event (level 3) (see Figure 11.1).

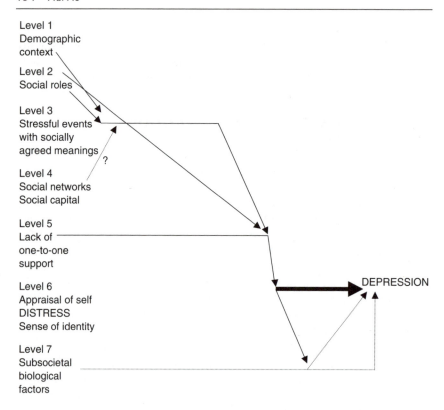

Figure 11.1 Levels of societal (and other) pathways to distress/depression.

Childhood loss of mother, either by death or by long-term separation, was another vulnerability factor in this Brown and Harris study. Later research established that it was less the loss of mother itself which was associated with greater risk of depression in adulthood and more the lesser supportiveness of the subsequent surrogate care (Bifulco et al., 1987; Harris et al., 1986). It was as if the process by which lack of current intimate support promotes depression had begun decades earlier for such women, reinforcing the old adage that a mother can be a girl's best friend. Speculations concerning this process involved level 6. It seemed self-image might be the bridge between society and emotional distress, not only where symptoms of depression such as self-depreciation and hopelessness overlapped with feelings about oneself and the ability to control and trust in the future, but also where self-appraisals might be reflecting appraisals by others. It was as if an empathic confidant acted as a mirror reflecting back an image of someone worth listening to and deserving of help. Moreover, these speculations suggested that the self was not a unitary entity but composed of many strands corresponding to the various role-identities available. Thus a woman employed outside the home would have an extra role-identity where she might feel she could show competence, and this would compensate if a severe life event threatened her self-regard, say, in her marital role. Women with several children face more difficulty in locating child care than women with only one or two and so will be less likely to be able to develop roles outside the home, imposing a restriction on the range of potentially compensating identities when something goes wrong in another role domain.

These speculations were confirmed in later research. A measure of self-esteem was developed which incorporated not just a score on a dimension of positive/negative attitude towards the self in general, but specific sub-scores on role performance in a range of role domains and sub-scores for a range of attributes such as efficiency, sympathy, personality, sociability and attractiveness. An overall negative evaluation of self, based on these scores at baseline, interacted with severe life events to predict depressive onset during 12-month follow-up, empirically establishing the relevance of level 6 for the societal model (Brown et al., 1986). What appears to be significant is the actual presence of negative evaluation rather than the mere absence of positive evaluation (Brown et al., 1990). This negative aspect of self-image was later highlighted by work focusing on shame (Andrews, 1998). Behavioural shame (shame about something done), characterological shame (shame generalised to apply to the person as a whole) and bodily shame were all associated with depressive episodes taking a chronic course (Andrews and Hunter, 1997). Experience of childhood sexual/physical abuse was particularly associated with the third kind of (bodily) shame.

The literature contains at least two other similar life-span models of depression involving social provoking and vulnerability factors (Kendler et al., 1993; Ormel and Neeleman, 2000). Moreover, attachment theory (Bowlby, 1988) has many similarities, highlighting how life events interact with an ongoing intrapsychic personal style of relating or "attachment style", resembling level 6 here, and embodied in schemata called "internal working models of relationships" derived from level 5. In fact some exponents of attachment theory have deliberately invoked concepts involving the self-image to explain Bowlby's typology of attachment styles (Bartholomew and Horowitz, 1991; Parkes, 1984). However, a more crucial concept than self-esteem in attachment theory is security, or containment through the satisfactory regulation of emotions.

SOCIETY – GENDER ROLES AND DISTRESS

It has long been recognised that depression is twice as common among women as among men (Weissman and Klerman, 1977). Explaining this variation between the sexes can benefit from these models explaining variations between different women. For example, more women than men are "trapped" in the home with restricted opportunities to develop alternative role-identities. Studies of the socialisation processes that contribute to gender role differences suggest women are discouraged from self-assertion and encouraged to affiliate to others, so that their sense of value becomes dependent on the approval of others. Such gender role differences have clear relevance within the models of depression outlined above (Bebbington, 1998). However, the differential prevalence of depression in women has not been replicated in studies of cultural groups which accord high status to the home-making role (Loewenthal et al., 1995; Mavreas et al., 1986), suggesting that when the woman's central role is valued, the need for alternative role-identities may become less important.

However, the nurturing role may itself increase the number of "provoking" experiences at level 3 in that, by caring for more people than do men, women expose themselves to a greater number of "others" whose events will also impact on themselves. This is commonly referred to as the "cost of caring" (Kessler and McLeod, 1984; see also Chapter 13 in this volume).

Another aspect of the caring role is the degree of involvement with those cared for, such that the impact of a severe event (level 3) may be stronger if involvement is greater and this involvement will vary with gender. For instance, events within the parenthood role domain probably involve mothers more than fathers. This was investigated in married couples selected because of a shared life event (Nazroo et al., 1997). A shared event was defined so that it was equally severe for the husband and the wife and vice versa; thus the death of one of their parents would not usually be considered a shared event since it would be likely to be less severe for the spouse for whom the deceased was merely a parent in law. Sometimes a husband losing his job would be rated severe only for him, particularly if the financial ramifications were only minor; however, the situation would be different if these ramifications were more serious and affected the whole household. Among couples with severe events involving work or marriage, rates of depression were much the same between the sexes, but among 47 couples with events in domains concerning children, reproduction or housing, rates were higher among the wives. It proved possible to relate this to women's higher rated rates of commitment and involvement in such domains (Nazroo et al., 1997). For 13 of these 47, women's "role salience" was rated considerably lower than for the other 34 given the relatively greater involvement of the male partner in the home domain, and for these 13 there was no gender difference in rate of depressive onset.

In the same series, gender differences in social support were also explored. A supportive marriage was found to be protective for both sexes. Women, on the other hand, expressed greater need for support within marriage, and were also more likely to seek support from close relationships outside marriage. Receiving support from outside marriage was protective for women but was associated with higher depression among men (Edwards et al., 1998). The authors argue that this may be due to men feeling negative about themselves for confiding their emotions to others and their reluctance to seek support until the emotional pressure is enormous and the depressive disorder has already begun. Again the pressures of the socialisation process to "be a man", and not to disclose emotions readily to others, may be the explanation.

It is important to remember, however, that gender prevalence differences in depression probably also have their biological roots (see level 7 in Figure 11.1). There may be direct hormonal links (Angold et al., 1999; Goodyer et al., 2000; see also Chapter 10 in this volume) or there may be indirect links via sex differences in response to stress. Thus it has been suggested that although no direct links with depressive onset have been found for oxytocin it is important because it underlies the contrasting stress responses, with males adopting the "fight or flight" reaction while women gravitate towards a "tend or befriend" response (Taylor et al., 2000). While acknowledging that there are widespread social conventions underpinning this differential acceptability of aggressive behaviour between the sexes, Taylor et al. argue convincingly that oxytocin, potentiated by oestrogen, may also be crucial. It is tempting to speculate that women's affiliative tendency could be bio-logically induced, thus providing women with support-seeking behaviour that in turn affords them with protection against depression. However, if this support is not forthcoming it can equally render them more vulnerable than men to depression (see Edwards et al., 1998).

GENDER AND DISTRESS OTHER THAN DEPRESSION

Mention of the "fight or flight" reaction of men is a reminder that what has been discussed so far (depression) is only one of many forms of distress. "Internalising" disorders of depression or anxiety in women are often con-trasted with "externalising" ones in men, such as sociopathy or substance abuse. Moreover, links have been made between the narrowing of differ-ences between gender roles in the postfeminist era and the increasing rates of conduct problems and substance abuse (the so-called externalising disorders) among young women in recent times.

However, even within the internalising category, different types of distress such as anxiety and the various eating disorders have been linked to different types of social provocation. Loss events, especially losses of cher-ished ideas – which often means loss of self-esteem or humiliation due to career failure or rejection by key close others, or shaming experiences – are particularly associated with depression (Brown et al., 1995). Events pre-ceding anxiety disorders more often involve dangers (alerting the individual to take necessary actions against them in the future) rather than tragedies which have already occurred (Finlay Jones, 1989). Work on eating disorders identified another type of provocation – "pudicity" events involving major shame around a sexual theme (Schmidt et al., 1997). Interestingly, the early life vulnerability factor for depression (loss of mother by death or separation) does not appear relevant for anxiety disorder. Interestingly too, a confiding relationship does not seem to provide protection against anxiety in the way it does against depression – both findings suggesting that specific feelings about the self might be less crucial for anxiety than for depression. But there is some indication that the childhood experiences of these clinical groups differ in ways which echo the event types identified. Thus the emotional theme of danger was echoed by the high rate of parental discord in the childhoods of those with anxiety disorder, and the theme of pudicity by high rates of childhood sexual abuse in those with eating disorder. These studies suggest, on the one hand, that somehow these different types of recent event influence the type of distress (perhaps because they have agreed different emotional meanings – agreed, that is, throughout a society) and, on the other hand, that matching childhood experiences render some people more vulnerable than others to particular types of event.

SOCIETY AND THE SELF: MIND AND BODY

Hitherto this chapter has accorded a key role to level 6, the societal self-image, in explaining how societal processes impact upon women's distress, but it now seems it might be of lesser relevance for anxiety. In the search for an alternative mediating process between society and the distress of anxiety disorder, a key concept of attachment theory seems relevant: affect regulation, the ability to regulate emotions and thus feel settled (Schore, 1994), a capacity that could promote the containment of supervigilance and thus of anxiety disorder. Affect regulation does not necessarily involve any of the cognitive self-monitoring that here characterises level 6, although that can be an influence. It is a more fundamental, precognitive capacity where communication through touch, and the pitch and rhythm of the voice, promote containment rather than communication through the conceptual meaning of the voice's words promoting self-acceptance. Affect regulation involves direct effects upon the physiological manifestations of emotion in the form of autonomic nervous system symptoms such as palpitations, trembling, sweating, giddiness and so on, thus introducing level 7 in Figure 11.1.

CONCLUSION

This chapter has outlined the various levels at which society operates in shaping distress, including demographic categories, social roles, life events, social networks and intimate relationships, and in turn how these variables interface with self-image and possibly the physiology of emotional regulation. The processes by which these levels interact over the life span to produce human distress were discussed, with particular reference to depression in women, and this model was extended to explain gender differences in the prevalence of mental health problems. Emphasis was placed on the continuity between the verbal level of the self-image and the level of non-verbal emotional experience with its attendant behavioural and physiological manifestations. Future research should therefore acknowledge that only an integrated perspective, which gives the body full weight in the societal model by combining societal, psychological and physiological factors, will ultimately give us the understanding required to lessen women's distress.

REFERENCES

Andrews, B. (1998) Shame and childhood abuse, in P. Gilbert and B. Andrews (eds) *Shame: Interpersonal behaviour, psychopathology and culture*, Oxford, Oxford University Press.

Andrews, B. and Hunter, E. (1997) Shame, early abuse and course of depression in a clinical sample: A preliminary study, *Cognition and Emotion*, 11, 373–381.

Angold, A., Costello, E. J., Erkani, A. et al. (1999) Pubertal changes in hormone levels and depression in girls, *Psychological Medicine*, 29, 1043–1053.

Bartholomew, K. and Horowitz, L. M. (1991) Attachment styles among young adults: A test of a four-category model, *Journal of Personality and Social Psychology*, 61, 226–244.

Bebbington, P. E (1998) Sex and depression (Editorial), *Psychological Medicine*, 28, 1–8.

Bifulco, A., Brown, G. W. and Harris, T. O. (1987) Childhood loss of parent, lack of adequate parental care and adult depression: A replication, *Journal of Affective Disorders*, 12, 115–128.

Bowlby, J. (1988) *A secure base: Clinical applications of attachment theory*, London, Routledge.

Bronfenbrenner, U. (1979) *The ecology of human development*, Cambridge, MA, Harvard University Press.

Brown, G. W. and Harris, T. O. (1978) *Social origins of depression: A study of psychiatric disorder in women*, London, Tavistock Publications; New York, Free Press.

Brown, G. W. and Harris, T. O. (1989) *Life events and illness*, New York, Guilford Press; London, Unwin and Hyman.

Brown, G. W. and Moran, P. (1997) Single mothers, poverty and depression, *Psychological Medicine*, 27, 21–33.

Brown, G. W., Andrews, B., Bifulco, A. and Veiel, H. (1990) Self-esteem and depression: 1. Measurement issues and prediction of onset, *Social Psychiatry and Psychiatric Epidemiology*, 25, 200–209.

Brown, G. W., Andrews, B., Harris, T. O., Adler, Z. and Bridge, L. (1986) Social support, self-esteem and depression, *Psychological Medicine*, 16, 813–831.

Brown, G. W., Harris, T. O. and Hepworth, C. (1995) Loss, humiliation and entrapment among women developing depression: A patient and non patient comparison, *Psychological Medicine*, 25, 7–21.

Cacioppo, J. T., Hawkley, L. C., Crawford, E., Ernst, J. M., Burleson, M. H., Kowalewski, R. B., Malarkey, W. B., van Cauter, E. and Berntson, G. G. (2002) Loneliness and health: Potential mechanisms, *Psychosomatic Medicine*, 64, 407–417.

Cobb, S. (1976) Social support as a moderator of life stress, *Psychosomatic Medicine*, 38, 300–314.

Cohen, S. (2004) Social relationships and health, *American Psychologist*, 59, 676–684.

Cohen, S., Gottlieb, B. and Underwood, L. (2000) Social relationships and health, in S. Cohen, L. Underwood and B. Gottlieb (eds) *Measuring and intervening in social support*, pp. 3–25, New York, Oxford University Press.

Davies, L., Avison, W. R. and McAlpine, D. D. (1997) Significant life experiences and depression among single and married mothers, *Journal of Marriage and the Family*, 59, 294–308.

Edwards, A. C., Nazroo, J. and Brown, G. W. (1998) Gender differences in marital support following a shared life event, *Social Science and Medicine*, 46, 1077–1085.

Finlay-Jones, R. (1989) Anxiety, in G. W. Brown and T. O. Harris (eds) *Life events and illness*, New York, Guilford Press; London, Unwin and Hyman.

Finlay-Jones, R., Brown, G. W., Duncan-Jones, P., Harris, T. O., Murphy, E. and Prudo, R. (1980) Depression and anxiety in the community, *Psychological Medicine*, 10, 445–454.

Forgatch, M. S., Patterson, G. R. and Skinner, M. L. (1988) A mediational model of the effect of divorce on antisocial behaviour in boys, in E. M. Hetherington and J. D. Arasteh (eds) *Impact of divorce, single parenting on children*, New York, Lawrence Erlbaum Associates.

Goodyer, I., Herbert, J., Tamplin, A. et al. (2000) Recent life events, cortisol, dihydroepiandrosterone and the onset of major depression in high-risk adolescents, *British Journal of Psychiatry*, 177, 499–504.

Harris, T. O., Brown, G. W. and Bifulco, A. (1986) Loss of parent in childhood and adult psychiatric disorder: The role of lack of adequate parental care, *Psychological Medicine*, 16, 641–659.

Kawachi, I., Kennedy, B. P. and Glass, R. (1999) Social capital and self-rated health: A contextual analysis, *American Journal of Public Health*, 89, 1187–1193.

Kendler, K. S., Kessler, R., Neale, M. et al. (1993) The prediction of major depression in women: Toward an integrated etiologic model, *American Journal of Psychiatry*, 150, 1139–1148.

Kessler, R. C. and McLeod, J. (1985) Social support and mental health in community samples, in S. Cohen and L. Syme (eds) *Social support and health*, New York, Academic Press.

Loewenthal, K., Goldblatt, V., Gorton, T. et al. (1995) Gender and depression in Anglo-Jewry, *Psychological Medicine*, 25, 1051–1063.

Mavreas, V. G., Beis, A., Mouyias, A., Rigoni, F. and Lyketsos, G. C. (1986)

Prevalence of psychiatric disorder in Athens: A community study, *Social Psychiatry*, 21, 172–181.

McCall, G. J. and Simmons, J. L. (1966) *Identities and interactions*, New York, Free Press.

McKenzie, K., Whitley, R. and Weich, S. (2002) Social capital and mental health, *British Journal of Psychiatry*, 181, 280–283.

Nazroo, J. Y., Edwards, A. C. and Brown, G. W. (1997) Gender differences in the onset of depression following a shared life event: A study of couples, *Psychological Medicine*, 27, 9–19.

Ormel, J. and Neeleman, J. (2000) Towards a dynamic stress-vulnerability model of depression, in T. Harris (ed.) *Where inner and outer worlds meet: Psychosocial research in the tradition of George W. Brown*, London, Routledge.

Parkes, C. M. (1984) *Attachment, bonding and psychiatric problems after bereavement in adult life*, Presentation at the Annual Conference of the British Psychological Society, Warwick.

Paykel, E. S. (1974) Recent life events and clinical depression, in E. K. E. Gunderson and R. H. Rahe (eds) *Life stress and illness*, Springfield, IL, C. C. Thomas.

Paykel, E. S. (2003) Life events: Effects and genesis (Editorial), *Psychological Medicine*, 33, 1145–1147.

Prudo, R., Brown, G. W. and Harris, T. O. (1984) Psychiatric disorder in a rural and an urban population: 3. Social integration and the morphology of affective disorder, *Psychological Medicine*, 14, 327–345.

Putnam, R. (1995) Bowling alone: America's declining social capital, *Journal of Democracy*, 6 (1), 65–78.

Schmidt, U. H., Tiller, J. M., Andrews, B., Blanchard, M. and Treasure, J. (1997) Is there a specific trauma precipitating onset of an eating disorder?, *Psychological Medicine*, 27, 523–530.

Schore, A. (1994) *Affect regulation and the origins of the self*, Hillsdale, NJ, Lawrence Erlbaum Associates.

Taylor, S. E., Klein, L. C., Lewis B. P. et al. (2000) Biobehavioural responses to stress in females: Tend-and-befriend, not fight-or-flight, *Psychological Review*, 107, 411–429.

van der Gaag, M. and Snijders, T. A. B. (2002, December) *An approach to the measurement of individual social capital*, Paper presented at the SCALE Conference on Social Capital, Amsterdam.

Van Os, J. (2000) Social influences on risk for disorder and natural history, *Current Opinion in Psychiatry*, 13, 209–213.

Weissman, M. M. and Klerman, G. L. (1977) Sex differences and the epidemiology of depression, *Journal of Health and Social Behaviour*, 26, 156–182.

Chapter 12

When the personal gets in the way of the (inter)personal

Tennyson Lee

INTRODUCTION

This chapter deals with the issue of personality and personality disorder types and how these concepts relate to gender and gender role development. The term "gender" will be used here to refer to aspects of masculinity and femininity that are socioculturally determined, in contrast to sex, which is biologically determined. Gender role is understood to comprise the behaviours, attitudes and values which a particular society expects from its male and female members, based on biological sex.

The concept of personality refers to consistent patterns of thinking, perceiving and feeling, and how these traits are organized to make up the person (Livesley, 2001). Personality encompasses both temperament and character. Temperament is the biological, heritable substratum of personality, whereas character consists of aspects of personality that are assumed to be the product of learning and interaction with the environment. However, not all studies in behavioural genetics support the distinction between temperament and character (e.g. Turkheimer, 1998). A model of linking both has been provided (Cloninger, 1993). Personality within this model is viewed as resulting from a mixture of temperament and character, each contributing approximately 50%. Novelty seeking, harm avoidance, reward dependence and persistence are included under temperament, while the three character variables are self-directedness, cooperativeness and self-transcendence. These character variables correspond to concepts of the self as, respectively, an autonomous individual, an integral part of humanity and an integral part of the universe as a whole. The usefulness of this conceptualization is twofold. First, it maps onto personality disorder – character variables distinguish whether someone has a personality disorder, whereas the temperament variables help determine the subtype of personality disorder and susceptibility to emotional disorders (Cloninger et al., 1993). Second, the model has therapeutic implications: symptoms such as impulsivity and affective lability may be targeted with medication while problems with self-directedness and cooperation may be approached psychotherapeutically. The issue of personality will be dealt with here from psychodynamic, psychocognitive and psychosocial perspectives.

PSYCHODYNAMIC VIEWS OF PERSONALITY

Freud thought that personality traits resulted from a fixation at one of the psychosexual stages of development. He identified several character types, for example anal characters who are precise, parsimonious and punctual (Freud, 1908/1959), and obsessional characters who are rigid and dominated by a harsh superego. He regarded character traits as the end result of the successful use of defence mechanisms (particularly those of repression and identification). His finding that some people can only give up an object by identifying with it led him to conclude that much of the child's character formation is linked to identification with the child's parents.

Reich (1933/1949) developed the concept of character by discussing the way that psychosexual conflicts lead to relatively fixed patterns which he termed character armour. The present psychoanalytic understanding of character views character traits as both a series of compromise formations between wishes and defences against these wishes, and sets of internal representations of self and others (Gabbard, 2000).

Freud pointed to the complexity of the issue of gender with reference to "the concepts of 'masculine' and 'feminine', whose meaning seems so unambiguous to ordinary people, are amongst the most confused that occur in science" (Freud, 1905: 219). While some have seen Freud's theory as ascribing an inescapable biological destiny to man and woman, others believe that Freud's view was that we are not born man or woman psychologically speaking, and instead that masculinity and femininity are constructed over a period of time and are relatively independent of biological sex (Breen, 1993).

For Freud, masculinity and femininity are formed at recognition of genital difference (Breen, 1993). However, what is critical is the meaning of the perception – not the perception per se. Freud believed that the meaning for the boy is that the penis can be lost (the "castration complex") and the meaning for the girl is that she has something missing ("penis envy"). However, boys and girls do not necessarily ascribe meaning in this way. If a girl maintains the fantasy belief that she has a penis then her development will be masculine and not feminine (Freud, 1925). Alternatively, if a boy renounces his penis in fantasy, his development will be feminine.

It can be seen then that although "anatomy is destiny" it is the meaning which is attributed to the difference which will determine object relations. The emphasis on the phallus has also been challenged by the view that girls, rather than having an overriding sense of lack, have a rich sense of what they have – they will ultimately be able to bear a child.

COGNITIVE VIEWS OF PERSONALITY

Eysenck (1987) proposed a model of personality based on a hierarchical structure, in which a large number of specific traits are organized into three higher-order factors: extraversion, neuroticism and psychoticism. The specific traits defining each factor are as follows (Eysenck and Eysenck, 1985):

1   extraversion: sociable, lively, active, assertive, sensation-seeking, carefree, dominant, venturesome;
2   neuroticism: anxious, depressed, guilt feelings, low self-esteem, tense, irrational, shy, moody, emotional;
3   psychoticism: aggressive, cold, egocentric, impersonal, impulsive, antisocial, unempathic, creative, tough-minded.

More recently, Costa and McCrae (1992) suggested a five-factor structure which retains neuroticism and extraversion but adds openness to experience, agreeableness and conscientiousness.

Meta-analysis of gender-personality studies showed that although there are gender differences, the differences are trivial, suggesting that most gender differences in personality variables are quite weak, perhaps with the exception of assertiveness (men somewhat higher) and nurturance (women considerably higher) (Feingold, 1994). One of the limitations of Feingold's study is that no consideration is given to the possible confounding effects of age, education or ethnic/racial status. When these demographic confounders have been controlled for, the gender difference in personality decreases, with evidence only for assertiveness being higher in men (Goldberg et al., 1998). Gender differences have been replicated across cultures: women reported themselves to be higher in neuroticism, agreeableness, warmth and openness to feelings, whereas men were higher in assertiveness and openness to ideas (Costa et al., 2001). However, these gender differences are small relative to individual variation within genders.

PSYCHOSOCIAL VIEWS OF PERSONALITY

This chapter does not address personality from a sociological perspective but rather from a social psychology perspective, emphasizing the impinging interpersonal environment on the individual rather than larger social structures. Caregivers, for instance, talk more to babies dressed in pink than to those in blue, and interact more physically when the same babies are dressed in blue (Rogers, 1999). Mothers of young children have been observed with stranger infants who are cross-dressed or given cross-sex names (Baby X experiments). The perceived sex of the infant influenced the mother's behaviour. Infants believed to be boys were more likely to be encouraged to physical action, and to be presented with a football, whereas infants believed to be girls were more likely to be given a doll (Sidorowicz and Lunney, 1980). Children become aware of sex role stereotypes early. At the age of two or three, boys believe that boys like to play with cars, help their father and build things, and that only boys like to play with trains. They also believe that girls like to play with dolls, help mother and cook dinner, and are more likely to say, "I need help" (Kuhn et al., 1978).

PERSONALITY AND NEUROSCIENCE

Perhaps surprisingly, it is neuroscience which has usefully broken down the divide between what is biological and what is environmental. There are anatomical differences between the brains of males and females (Solms and Turnbull, 2002). The corpus callosum (the fibre bundle connecting the left and right cerebral hemispheres) is proportionately larger in the female brain than in the male. The left and right hemispheres are thus more intimately connected in the average female brain than in her male counterpart. This difference may result in less lateral specialization in females, whereas in males there is a larger division of labour between the hemispheres. This is believed to result in women having superior language abilities and men having superior visuospatial abilities (Springer and Deutsch, 1988). Solms and Turnbull (2002) emphasize that although these differences are statistically significant they are small – suggesting that the importance attached to these differences is more due to societal than neuroscientific factors.

A second main neuroanatomical difference lies in the hypothalamus (Solms and Turnbull, 2002). One of the interstitial nuclei of the anterior hypothalamus (INAH-3) is much larger in the male than in the female. This is significant, as the activities of the hypothalamus are critical in hormonal control and therefore in reproductive function. These hypothalamic differences may also influence neurophysiological differences. The anterior cingulate gyrus may be linked with nurturant and social behaviour while the amygdala may be linked to anger and rage. The anterior cingulate gyrus in more active in women than in men, whereas the amygdyla is more active in men than in women. This may relate to the observation that boys are typically more aggressive and active than girls.

While genetic differences exist between male and female, they are tiny. The anatomical and physiological differences arising from these genetic differences are also very small when compared to their commonalities. However, the psychological effects of these small differences are multiplied during development as indicated in the examples above, where caregivers respond to children differently depending on their perceived sex. This effect is further multiplied by male and female children eliciting different types of responses due to their male-typical and female-typical behaviours. This response will in turn influence behaviour. Therefore, although the biological differences may be very small to begin with, they widen in response to the environment. Ultimately the genotype (the design according to which one is built) is very open to manipulation by the environment, which shapes the phenotype (which includes one's observable characteristics); gender therefore is not predetermined from the time of conception by our genetic make-up (Solms and Turnbull, 2002).

The interaction between genes and the environment has been demonstrated by Kandel (1983, 1998) in a series of experiments with the marine snail *Aplysia*. It was demonstrated that synaptic connections are strengthened and permanently altered through environmental learning influencing gene expression. The experiments suggest that psychotherapy may make similar neuroanatomical changes in the synapses. While the template function or gene sequence is not affected by the environment, the transcriptional function of the gene (the ability of a gene to direct the synthesis of specific proteins) is responsive to the environment.

Heritable characteristics of children shape their relationships with their parents and siblings (Reiss et al., 1991). In turn, the response of family members to the child affects gene expression. There is thus a dynamic interplay between genetic expression and the environment.

PERSONALITY DISORDER: ISSUES IN CLASSIFICATION

A similarity of personality disorder (PD) to personality theory is that traits are the major conceptual unit for describing and analyzing PD (Berrios, 1993). A major difference is that PD adopts a categorical rather than a dimensional approach to diagnosis. Current classifications incorporate diagnostic concepts from divergent theoretical systems including phenomenology, traditional psychoanalytic theory, object relations theory, self psychology and social learning theory (Livesley, 2001).

The main classification systems in modern psychiatry are the fourth edition of the American Psychiatric Association's (APA) *Diagnostic and Statistical Manual of Mental Disorders* (DSM-IV; APA, 2000) and the 10th edition of the World Health Organization's (WHO) *International Classification of Diseases* (ICD-10; WHO, 1992).

General diagnostic criteria for a PD in DSM-IV are "an enduring pattern of inner experience and behaviour that deviates markedly from the expectations of the individual's culture" (APA, 2000: 689). This pattern is manifested in two or more of the following areas: cognition, affectivity, impulse control and interpersonal functioning. DSM-IV requires that this enduring pattern is pervasive, has an onset in adolescence or early adulthood, and leads to clinically significant distress or impairment in social, occupational or other important areas of functioning.

There are several problems with the DSM-IV classification (Westen and Shedler, 1999; Widiger, 2001). These include:

1   "The diagnostic approach used [in DSM-IV and ICD-10] represents the categorical perspective that Personality Disorders represent qualitatively distinct clinical syndromes" (APA, 2000: 633). The categorical approach is more useful than a dimensional approach to clinicians, who need to formulate assessments and make decisions in the heat of busy routines. However, the empirical support for the categorical approach is minimal relative to the alternative perspective that personality disorders are on a continuum with normal personality functioning, with one another and with other mental disorders. The distinction between normal and disordered personality is hence necessarily arbitrary.

2   The categories and criteria are not empirically based and often disagree with empirical findings from cluster and factor analyses.

3   The polythetic format contributes to substantial heterogeneity among persons sharing the same diagnosis. For example, as there are nine criteria for borderline personality disorder (BPD), of which only five need to be present to make the diagnosis, 151 different combinations of criteria for a BPD diagnosis are possible (Skodal et al., 2002). It is possible for two individuals to receive the same diagnosis but only share one out of nine criteria, which is problematic (see Table 12.1).

4   Current thresholds for diagnosis are largely unexplained and perhaps weakly justified.

5   Comorbidity of axis II disorders is too high. A patient who receives one PD diagnosis is often also diagnosed with four to six axis II disorders out of a possible 10. This suggests lack of discriminant validity in the constructs, the assessment instruments or both.

6   It lacks the capacity to weight criteria that differ in diagnostic importance.

7   It has not sufficiently accounted for gender and culture. There are opposing arguments regarding gender. One view is that the inclusion of gender-related, stereotypically feminine behaviours within diagnostic criteria reflects a biased attitude towards women and results in misdiagnosis of normal women (Francis et al., 1995). This view recommends that PD diagnostic criteria should be either gender neutral or gender balanced. Thus no gender-related behaviours should be included or a sufficient number of masculine-related behaviours should be included to offset feminine-related behaviours. An alternative view is that PDs represent maladaptive variants of gender-related traits (Widiger and Spitzer, 1991). Males and females have been found to differ on average in some personality traits (Feingold, 1994). Females

Table 12.1 DSM-IV diagnostic criteria for BPD

A pervasive pattern of instability of interpersonal relationships, self-image and affects, and marked impulsivity, beginning by early adulthood and present in a variety of contexts, as indicated by five (or more) of the following:

1 Frantic efforts to avoid real or imagined abandonment
2 A pattern of unstable and intense interpersonal relationships characterized by alternating between extremes of idealization and devaluation
3 Identity disturbance: markedly and persistently unstable self-image or sense of self
4 Impulsivity in at least two areas that are potentially self-damaging (e.g. spending, sex, substance abuse, reckless driving, binge eating)
5 Recurrent suicidal behaviour, gestures or threats, or self-mutilating behaviour
6 Affective instability due to marked reactivity of mood (e.g. intense episodic dysphoria, irritability or anxiety usually lasting a few hours and only rarely more than a few days)
7 Chronic feelings of emptiness
8 Inappropriate intense anger or difficulty controlling anger (e.g. frequent displays of temper, constant anger, recurrent physical fights)
9 Transient stress-related paranoid ideation or severe dissociative symptoms

are on average higher than males in levels of anxiousness, trust, warmth, gregariousness, emotionality, tender-mindedness, compliance, modesty and altruism (Corbitt and Widiger, 1995; Feingold, 1994). Thus PDs which involve maladaptation of these traits will have different sex prevalence rates (Corbitt and Widiger, 1995).

The problem of gender-biased diagnoses exists. Clinicians tend to over-diagnose histrionic personality disorder (Garb, 1997) and BPD (Becker and Lamb, 1994) in females. While it has previously been held that BPD is more prevalent in women (e.g. Swartz et al., 1990), this may be an artifact arising from not taking into account the fact that populations from which samples were drawn had more females (de Girolamo and Dotto, 2000). There have been studies which show no predominance of BPD in women (Golomb et al., 1996; Zimmerman and Coryell, 1989).

Male and female patients with BPD present with different lifetime patterns of impulse-related disorders. Lifetime substance use disorder and antisocial, schizotypal and narcissistic PD are more common among men, and lifetime eating disorders, post-traumatic stress disorder and the BPD criterion of identity disturbance are more common among women (Johnson et al., 2003; Zanarini et al., 1998a, 1998b; Zlotnick et al., 2002).

While there are substantial and probably irremediable problems with the categorical approach adopted by the DSM and ICD systems, clinicians still find they serve as useful shorthand for communication and decision making.

In this context the case of BPD will be discussed in some detail (refer also to Chapters 4 and 17 in this volume).

PSYCHODYNAMIC, PSYCHOSOCIAL AND COGNITIVE VIEWS OF BORDERLINE PERSONALITY DISORDER

Stern (1938) used the term "borderline", placing patients on the border between psychosis and neurosis; Deutsch (1942) wrote of the "as if" personality; Schmideberg (1947) described borderline as a disorder of character which was "stable in its instability"; Zetzel (1968) wrote of the "so-called good hysteric" (who turns out in treatment to be highly disturbed and difficult); and Winnicott (1965) discussed the "false self" (for a review refer to Bateman and Holmes, 1995).

Kernberg (1967), a seminal modern thinker in BPD, systematized his view of BPD into borderline personality organization (BPO). The four intrapsychic features in BPO are: identity diffusion, primitive defences, partially intact reality testing and characteristic object relations. Primitive defences include: projection, projective identification, splitting and denial. Splitting and projection lead to part-objects relations rather than to internal integrated representations of people which can include both good and bad aspects.

Kernberg (1975) attempted to incorporate the psychodynamic theory of BPD with the psychosocial perspective, proposing that excessive early aggression in the young child leads to excessive splitting – the separate representation of positive and negative aspects of the self and other. A result of this is that borderline patients cannot establish a realistic and balanced view, and instead tend to oscillate between extremes of good or bad. The cause of this excessive splitting may be environmental (frustration) or constitutional.

A second psychosocial approach to BPD causation focuses on a failure of early mothering, leading to a failure of object constancy (Adler and Buie, 1979). The mothering of children who go on to develop BPD is viewed as insensitive and non-empathic. This leads to a failure to develop a consistent self-image or an image of a comforting caregiver. A third approach is drawn from Margaret Mahler's (1971) developmental theory, particularly focusing on the separation-individuation phase. Masterson and Rinsley (1975) proposed that fear of abandonment is the organizing conflict in borderline pathology. Mothers were felt to undermine the child's straining for autonomy, and thus attempts to establish autonomy in later life trigger fear of abandonment.

Not surprisingly, based on the role of early childhood experience in the development of BPD, attachment difficulties have been seen as a core characteristic of BPD patients. The early attachment experiences of BPD patients tend to be of the anxious-ambivalent subtype (Gunderson, 1996). The variables found to be most strongly related to BPD features are lack of expressed care and over-protection by mother and an anxious and ambivalent attachment pattern (Nickell et al., 2002). BPD patients in turn have extremely insecure attachment, characterized by alternating fear of involvement and intense neediness (Bateman and Fonagy, 2004). While there are some inconsistencies in attachment studies, there is a clear indication that BPD diagnosis is linked with insecure, pre-occupied, ambivalent and perhaps fearful attachment patterns (Bateman and Fonagy, 2004).

The main psychosocial factors that are linked to BPD, as summarized by Zanarini and Frankenburg (1997) and Zanarini (2000), include prolonged early parental separation or loss, disturbed parental involvement, childhood physical or sexual abuse and a high prevalence of affective disorder in the first degree relatives of borderline probands. A multi-factorial model for BPD was thus proposed, viewing BPD as a final common pathway from a complex mixture of innate temperament, challenging childhood experiences and neurological and biochemical dysfunctions (which themselves possibly result from early adverse experiences and innate vulnerability; Zanarini and Frankenburg, 1994).

The cognitive view of BPD emphasizes the role of childhood environmental influences on personality (Beck et al., 2004; Young, 1990). Beck takes an evolutionary perspective, believing that some of our behaviours are genetically programmed (Davidson, 2000). In personality disorder, behaviours that were initially adaptive and had survival value have become problematic in the present setting.

Information processing precedes the genetically determined strategies that have facilitated survival and reproduction. How the situation is evaluated depends in part on underlying beliefs. These beliefs lie within more or less stable structures – "schemas" – that organize incoming data. The term "schema" has been used to describe those structures that integrate and attach meaning to events The schemas on which cognitive, affective and motivational processes depend are regarded as the fundamental units of personality.

There are three main CBT conceptualizations of BPD: Linehan's (1993) dialectical behavioural therapy, Young's (1990) schema model and that of Beck et al. (2004). Pretzer (1990) hypothesized that three key assumptions are central in BPD: "The world is dangerous and malevolent," "I am powerless and vulnerable" and "I am inherently unacceptable." These three key assumptions and cognitive characteristics are assumed to be critical in maintaining the disorder and thus are specifically targeted in therapy. Zanarini et al. (1998c) suggest three further typical cognitions in patients with BPD: "I am endangered," "I am like a small child" and "I feel uncared for." Three cognitive characteristics are assumed to be central to BPD: hypervigilence, dichotomous thinking and a weak sense of identity.

CASE VIGNETTE: THE CASE OF URSULA

Ursula is a 36-year-old single unemployed woman living with her 15-year-old daughter, Kirsty. She presented with a range of issues, including a difficult relationship with her daughter, low mood, self-harm and bingeing.

Ursula's father left home when she was two. She has never met him since. Ursula's mother remarried when she was six. Ursula's stepfather, Michel, sexually abused her on a regular basis from the age of seven. Ursula ran away from home when she was 14. She was placed in several care homes but ran away repeatedly. By the age of 15 she was using street drugs and sexually promiscuous. She had two abortions before Kirsty was born.

Kirsty was born when Ursula was 21. The father was Liam, who Ursula had met at a music festival and moved in with immediately. They were together for three years. It was a relationship marked by huge instability. Liam was a roadie and Ursula found the long periods he was away unbearable. Believing that he planned to abandon her, she frequently threatened to harm herself. Liam eventually did leave, precipitating Ursula's most serious overdose, which required a fortnight's hospitalization. Ursula has since been in three shorter-term relationships, all marked by a similar instability. She also has had innumerable brief sexual encounters with both men and women.

Ursula's earliest memory of her mother is of waiting to be picked up by her from a family friend. The family friend kept on reassuring Ursula, who was four at the time, that her mother would be coming. She eventually did come – three months later. Ursula was later to discover that her mother had decamped to Belfast on a fruitless chase after a man who'd abandoned her. By the time she married Michel she was an alcoholic, unable to care for or protect her daughter. It was Michel who sexually abused Ursula.

Ursula is presently desperate not to repeat her own childhood history with her daughter. Kirsty has, however, run away a few times, unable to stand her mother's changeable moods and overprotectiveness.

Ursula was first in contact with psychiatric services as an adolescent, when she was self-harming, and has been in intermittent contact since. She has had three psychiatric admissions due to concerns about her self-harm. In one of these she was involuntarily detained. She has self-harmed by overdosing and cutting. She previously cut her wrists but has recently been cutting her upper thighs to hide this from Kirsty.

Ursula had been unemployed for eight years and previously worked sporadically in a wide range of jobs – from clerical roles to bar hostessing.

Ursula presented as an attractive woman in her mid-30s. Her attitude towards Keith, her psychiatric nurse, veered from neediness to detachment. However, she felt he was the only member of the team she could tolerate and complained that the other team members were dismissive of her. At one meeting she reported hearing the voice of her stepfather sneering "slut" at her. When pushed on this, she said she experienced this as a thought inside her head. She also was again having problems with Kirsty. Her mood changed and she became extremely angry with Keith when he discussed referring her on to a day hospital specializing in people with interpersonal difficulties. She accused him of wanting to get rid of her and stormed out of the clinic, saying he would regret this as she had tablets at home.

How would we understand

1   whether this woman has a personality disorder;
2   the development of her personality;
3   how it is presently organised?

1   From the above description, Ursula meets criteria for a PD. She meets at least six criteria for BPD according to DSM-IV guidelines; these include her efforts to avoid abandonment, unstable and intense personal relationships, identity disturbance, self-damaging impulsivity, recurrent suicidal and self-harming behaviour and affective instability.
2   A psychodynamic view (based on Kernberg's model) would consider Ursula's frustration with a mother who was absent emotionally as leading to excessive early aggression and hence splitting into only good or bad – an inability to have a more integrated and balanced view. Ursula's experience of failure of early mothering could have contributed to her inability to form either a consistent self-image or an image of a comforting caregiver. A psychosocial formulation would identify factors leading to Ursula's personality traits – including separation from her mother, loss of her father, disturbed involvement with her mother, sexual abuse and a history of depression in her mother.
3   Ursula has typical intrapsychic features commonly seen in borderline personality organization. There is, first, identity diffusion (her subjective experience of chronic emptiness, her contradictory view of herself and of others). Second, reality testing remains intact. Third, there is the use of primitive defences: splitting, projective identification, denial, omnipotence and devaluation are all present. Finally there are characteristic object relations – Ursula's internal objects are part objects – the psychiatric nurse is seen initially as all good then, when he discusses referring her, as all bad.

A cognitive formulation of Ursula's personality would identify her key cognitions regarding her own powerlessness and vulnerability, and her belief about being inherently unacceptable and of the world as being dangerous.

As a female, Ursula was more at risk of sexual abuse, and more likely to take on care for Kirsty. Her presentation of identity diffusion and eating disorder is consistent with the finding that this is more common in women than men with BPD.

Ursula was finally referred to a day hospital which specializes in patients with PD and operates along therapeutic milieu principles using psychodynamic, cognitive and systemic principles. Her engagement with this unit was tenuous in the first five months. She did, however, become much attached to the nurse therapist and through this relationship it became more possible to clarify, confront and interpret her behaviour. In the seventh month, she took her most serious overdose but she has been more settled since then. A turning point for her seems to have been the consistent approach taken by the nurse therapist and the team as a whole. She is now two months away from her planned date of discharge. On standard psychiatric measures she is showing an improvement; there is evidence of healthier personality functioning and an attenuation of her BPD traits on a standardized PD instrument (Westen and Shedler, 1999). She feels most pleased that her relationship with Kirsty has improved; they are planning to go to Paris for a weekend – the first holiday they will ever have taken together.

CONCLUSION

There is a clear need for further conceptual clarity on personality and personality disorder. Only then can their complex relations with sex, gender and gender role be better understood.

There are at least two compelling reasons for optimism. First, there is a move away from an inflexible biological determinism on different fronts: from a psychodynamic perspective that biological sex is what is made of it, to a genetic understanding that finally gene expression is dependent on the environment. Second, sufficient advances are being made in our understanding of PD that effective treatments are now possible (Bateman and Fonagy, 1999, 2001; Leichsenring and Leibing, 2003). It is a step forward to view the subjective experience of the individual as formed through an idiosyncratic narrative involving interaction between genes, intrapsychic factors and the environment. Our contribution as clinicians, health planners and researchers lies in our ability to intervene at all three levels.

REFERENCES

Adler, G. and Buie, D. (1979) Aloneness and borderline psychopathology: The possible relevance of some child developmental issues, *International Journal of Psychoanalysis*, 60, 83–96.

American Psychiatric Association (2000) *Diagnostic and statistical manual of mental disorders* (4th edn), text revision, Washington, DC, American Psychiatric Association.

Bateman, A. and Fonagy, P. (1999) The effectiveness of partial hospitalization in the treatment of borderline personality disorder: A randomised controlled trial, *American Journal of Psychiatry*, 156, 1563–1569.

Bateman, A. and Fonagy, P. (2001) Treatment of borderline personality disorder with psychoanalytically orientated partial hospitalization: An 18-month follow-up, *American Journal of Psychiatry*, 158, 36–42.

Bateman, A. and Fonagy, P. (2004) *Psychotherapy for borderline personality disorder: Mentalization based treatment*, Oxford, Oxford University Press.

Bateman, A. and Holmes, J. (1995) *Introduction to psychoanalysis: Contemporary theory and practice*, London, Routledge.

Beck, A. T., Freeman, A. and Davis, D. D. (2004) *Cognitive therapy of personality disorders*, New York, Guilford Press.

Becker, D. and Lamb, S. (1994) Sex bias in the diagnosis of borderline personality disorder and posttraumatic stress disorder, *Professional Psychology: Research and Practice*, 25, 55–61.

Berrios, G. E. (1993) European views on personality disorders: A conceptual history, *Comprehensive Psychiatry*, 34, 14–30.

Breen, D. (1993) *The gender conundrum*, London, Routledge.

Cloninger, C. R. (1993) Commentary, in M. H. Klein, D. Kupfer and M. T. Shea (eds) *Personality and depression: A current view*, pp. 61–67, New York, Guilford Press.

Cloninger, C. R., Svravik, D. M. and Pryzbeck, T. R. (1993) A psychobiological model of temperament and character, *Archives of General Psychiatry*, 50, 975–990.

Corbitt, E. M. and Widiger, T. A. (1995) Sex differences among the personality disorders: An exploration of the data, *Clinical Psychology: Science and Practice*, 2, 225–238.

Costa, P. T. and McCrae, R. R. (1992) *Revised NEO Personality Inventory (NEO-PI-R) and the NEO Five-Factor Inventory (NEO-FFI) professional manual*, Odessa, FL, Psychological Assessment Resources.

Costa, P., Terracciano, A. and McCrae, R. (2001) Gender differences in personality traits across cultures: Robust and surprising findings, *Journal of Personality and Social Psychology*, 81 (2), 322–331.

Davidson, K. (2000) *Cognitive therapy for personality disorders*, Oxford, Butterworth Heinemann.

de Girolamo, G. and Dotto, P. (2000) Epidemiology of personality disorders, in M. G. Gelder, J. J. Lopez-Ibor and N. C. Andreasen (eds) *New Oxford textbook of psychiatry*, pp. 959–964, Oxford, Oxford University Press.

Deutsch, H. (1942) Some forms of emotional disturbance and their relationship to schizophrenia, *Psychoanalytic Quarterly*, 11, 301–321.

Eysenck, H. (1987) The definition of personality disorders and the criteria appropriate to their definition, *Journal of Personality Disorders*, 1, 211–219.

Eysenck, H. J. and Eysenck, M. W. (1985) *Personality and individual differences: A natural science approach*, New York, Plenum.

Feingold, A. (1994) Gender differences in personality: A meta-analysis, *Psychological Bulletin*, 116, 429–456.

Francis, A. J., First, M. B. and Pincus, H. A. (1995) *DSM-IV guidebook*, Washington, DC, American Psychiatric Press.

Freud, S. (1905, footnote 1915) Three essays on sexuality, in J. Strachey (ed. and trans.) *The standard edition of the complete psychological works of Sigmund Freud, vol. 7*, 219, London, Hogarth Press.

Freud, S. (1925) Some psychical consequences of the anatomical distinction between the sexes, in J. Strachey (ed. and trans.) *The standard edition of the complete psychological works of Sigmund Freud, vol. 19*, pp. 248–258, London, Hogarth Press.

Freud, S. (1959) Character and anal eroticism, in J. Strachey (ed. and trans.) *The standard edition of the complete psychological works of Sigmund Freud, vol. 9*, pp. 167–175, London, Hogarth Press. (Original work published 1908)

Gabbard, G. (2000) Psychoanalysis, in H. I. Kaplan and B. J. Sadock (eds) *Comprehensive textbook of psychiatry VI, vol. 1*, pp. 431–478, Baltimore, Williams and Wilkins.

Garb, H. N. (1997) Race bias, social class bias, and gender bias in clinical judgement, *Clinical Psychology: Science and Practice*, 4, 99–120.

Goldberg, L. R., Sweeney, D., Merenda, P. F. and Hughes, J. E. (1998) Demographic variables and personality: The effects of gender, age, education, and ethnic/racial status on self-descriptions of personality attributes, *Personality and Individual Differences*, 24, 393–403.

Golomb, M., Fava, M., Abraham, M. and Rosenbaum, J. F. (1996) Gender differences in personality disorders, *American Journal of Psychiatry*, 153 (6), 846–847.

Gunderson, J. G. (1996) The borderline patient's intolerance of aloneness: Insecure attachments and therapist availability, *American Journal of Psychiatry*, 153, 752–758.

Johnson, D. M., Shea, M. T., Yen, S., Battle, C. L., Zlotnick, D. M., Sanislow, C. A., Grilo, C. M., Skodol, A. E., Bender, D. S., McGlashan, T. H., Gunderson, J. G. and Zanarini, M. C. (2003) Gender differences in borderline personality disorder: Findings from the collaborative longitudinal personality disorders study, *Comprehensive Psychiatry*, 44 (4), 284–292.

Kandel, E. R. (1983) From metapsychology to molecular biology: Explorations into the nature of anxiety, *American Journal of Psychiatry*, 140, 1277–1293.

Kandel, E. R. (1998) A new intellectual framework for psychiatry, *American Journal of Psychiatry*, 155, 457–469.

Kernberg, O. F. (1967) Borderline personality organisation, *Journal of the American Psychoanalytic Association*, 15, 641–685.

Kernberg, O. F. (1975) *Borderline conditions and pathological narcissism*, New York, Jason Aronson.

Kuhn, D., Nash, S. and Brubern, L. (1978) Sex role concept of two and three-year-olds, *Child Development*, 49, 445–451.

Leichsenring, F. and Leibing, E. (2003) The effectiveness of psychodynamic therapy and cognitive behavior therapy in the treatment of personality disorders: A meta-analysis, *American Journal of Psychiatry*, 160, 1223–1232.

Linehan, M. M. (1993) *Cognitive-behavioral treatment of borderline personality disorder*, New York, Guilford Press.

Livesley, J. W. (2001) Conceptual and taxonomic issues, in J. W. Livesley (ed.) *Handbook of personality disorders: Theory, research and treatment*, pp. 3–38, New York, Guilford Press.

Mahler, M. S. (1971) A study of separation-individuation process and its possible application to borderline phenomena in the psychoanalytic situation, *The Psychoanalytic Study of the Child*, 26, 403–424.

Masterson, J. F. and Rinsley, D. (1975) The borderline syndrome: The role of the mother in the genesis and psychic structure of the borderline personality, *International Journal of Psychoanalysis*, 56, 163–177.

Nickell, A. D., Waudby, C. J. and Trull, T. J. (2002) Attachment, parental bonding and borderline personality disorder features in young adults, *Journal of Personality Disorders*, 16, 148–159.

Pretzer, J. (1990) Borderline personality disorder, in A. T. Beck, A. Freeman and D. D. Davis (eds) *Cognitive therapy of personality disorders*, pp. 176–207, New York, Guilford Press.

Reich, W. (1949) *Character analysis* (3rd edn), New York, Farrar, Strauss, and Giroux. (Original work published 1933)

Reiss, D., Plomin, R. and Hetherinton, E. M. (1991) Genetics and psychiatry: An unheralded window on the environment, *American Journal of Psychiatry*, 148, 283–291.

Rogers, L. (1999) *Sexing the brain*, New York, Columbia University Press.

Schmideberg, M. (1947) The treatment of psychopathic and borderline patients, *American Journal of Psychotherapy*, 1, 45–71.

Sidorowicz, L. and Lunney, G. (1980) Baby X revisited, *Sex Roles*, 6, 67–73.

Skodal, A. E., Gunderson, J. G., Pfohl, B., Widiger, T. A., Livesley, W. J. and Siever, L. J. (2002) The borderline diagnosis I: Psychopathology, comorbidity and personality and personality structure, *Biological Psychiatry*, 51, 936–950.

Solms, M. and Turnbull, O. (2002) *The brain and the inner world: An introduction to the neuroscience of subjective experience*, London, Karnac.

Springer, S. P. and Deutsch, G. (1998) *Left brain, right brain: Perspectives from cognitive neuroscience*, New York, W. H. Freeman.

Stern, A. (1938) Psychoanalytic investigation and therapy in borderline group of neuroses, *Psychoanalytic Quarterly*, 7, 467–489.

Swartz, M., Blazer, D., George, L. and Winfield, I. (1990) Estimating the prevalence of borderline personality disorder in the community, *Journal of Personality Disorders*, 4, 257–272.

Turkheimer, E. (1998) Heritability and biological explanation, *Psychological Review*, 105, 782–791.

Westen, D. and Shedler, J. (1999) Revising and assessing axis II, part I: Developing a clinically and empirically valid assessment method, *American Journal of Psychiatry*, 156, 258–272.

Widiger, T. A. (2001) Official classification systems, in J. W. Livesley (ed.) *Handbook of personality disorders: Theory, research and treatment*, pp. 60–83, New York, Guilford Press.

Widiger, T. A. and Spitzer, R. L. (1991) Sex bias in the diagnosis of personality disorders: Conceptual and methodological issues, *Clinical Psychology Review*, 11, 1–22.

Winnicott, D. (1965) *The maturational process and the facilitating environment*, London, Hogarth.

World Health Organization (1992) *The ICD-10 classification of mental and behavioural disorders: Clinical descriptions and diagnostic guidelines*, Geneva, World Health Organization.

Young, J. E. (1990) *Cognitive therapy for personality disorders: A schema-focused approach*, Sarasota, FL, Professional Resource Press.

Zanarini, M. C. (2000) Childhood experiences associated with the development of borderline personality disorder, *The Psychiatric Clinics of North America*, 23, 89–101.

Zanarini, M. C. and Frankenburg, F. R. (1994) Emotional hypochondriasis, hyperbole and the borderline patient, *Journal of Psychotherapy Practice and Research*, 3, 25–36.

Zanarini, M. C. and Frankenburg, F. R. (1997) Pathways to the development of borderline personality disorder, *Journal of Personality Disorders*, 11, 93–104.

Zanarini, M. C., Frankenburg, F. R., DeLuca, C. J., Hennen, J., Khera, G. S. and Gunderson, J. G. (1998c) The pain of being borderline: Dysphoric states specific to borderline personality disorder, *American Journal of Psychiatry*, 147, 57–63.

Zanarini, M. C., Frankenburg, F. R., Dubo, E. D., Sickel, A. E., Trikha, A., Levin, A. and Reynolds, V. (1998a) Axis I comorbidity of borderline personality disorder, *American Journal of Psychiatry*, 155, 1733–1739.

Zanarini, M. C., Frankenburg, F. R., Dubo, E. D., Sickel, A. E., Trikha, A., Levin, A. and Reynolds, V. (1998b) Axis II comorbidity of borderline personality disorder, *Comprehensive Psychiatry*, 39, 296–302.

Zetzel, E. (1968) The so-called good hysteric, *International Journal of Psycho-Analysis*, 49, 250–260.

Zimmerman, M. and Coryell, W. (1989) DSM-III personality disorder diagnoses in a nonpatient sample: Demographic correlates and comorbidity, *Archives of General Psychiatry*, 46, 682–689.

Zlotnick, C., Rothschild, L. and Zimmerman, M. (2002) The role of gender in the clinical presentation of patients with borderline personality disorder, *Journal of Personality Disorders*, 16 (3), 277–282.

Chapter 13

Care and blame

The dialectic of caring

Joanna Murray

INTRODUCTION

There are 5.7 million people in England who provide regular unpaid care to a sick, disabled or elderly person (Singleton et al., 2002). Although their level of involvement varies from practical help with household tasks to intensive personal care and 24-hour vigilance, carers play a crucial role in enabling people to remain at home for as long as possible. The care they provide is also substantial in economic terms, when their hours of care-giving are subjected to economic evaluation (Schneider et al., 2003). Health and social care services could not cover the range and intensity of support that family carers provide, often for many years and at the expense of their own health and quality of life.

THE IMPACT OF CAREGIVING

A national survey has shown that the impact on the health and well-being of carers varies according to the carer's characteristics, the condition of the person they are looking after and the nature of their relationship (Singleton et al., 2002). This survey measured the prevalence of common mental disorders (such as depression, anxiety and phobias) in carers and identified factors associated with different outcomes. Female carers were more likely than males to be suffering from a common mental disorder (21% compared with 12%). This disparity between the genders was related to the caregiving role since there was no significant difference between the prevalence of mental disorders in male carers and that in non-caregiving men of the same age, whereas female carers had significantly higher rates of mental disorder than an age-matched sample of women in the general population. Although only 8% of carers said that caring had had a direct impact on their physical health, there was a strong association between carers' assessment of their physical health as only fair or poor and the extent of their mental health difficulties. Additionally, 71% of carers said their caring responsibilities caused them worry and a third said it had made them depressed.

The mental health of carers was affected by the nature of their relationship with the person they looked after, their living arrangements, the type and intensity of care they gave and the type of health problems experienced by the care recipient. Most carers in the survey were looking after elderly parents or parents-in-law (48%), their spouse or partner (16%) or another relative (15%). Only 9% were looking after their own child. The prevalence of mental health problems was highest in those looking after their spouse or child, those living with the person they cared for, those providing the greatest number of hours of care and more personal care such as washing and dressing and those who were alone in providing care. In other words, greater levels of stress were experienced by those in caregiving situations that were most demanding of time and effort and from which there was least opportunity for respite.

CARING FOR SOMEONE WITH A MENTAL HEALTH PROBLEM

Up to one and a half million people in England (26% of all carers) are involved in caring for a relative or friend with a mental disorder (Singleton et al., 2002). This group of carers has been shown to be at higher risk of emotional strain, subjective burden and poor health than those caring for someone with physical disabilities alone (Perring et al., 1990); they are much more likely to be suffering from depression and anxiety (Livingston et al., 1996). Research comparing caregivers with non-caregiving peers shows that psychological well-being is more likely to be poor in the former group (Dura et al., 1990; Kiecolt-Glaser et al., 1991) and social involvement is likely to be reduced (Haley et al., 1987). Spouses appear to fare worse than adult child caregivers (George and Gwyther, 1986), and women report more psychological difficulties than men in the role (Young and Kahana, 1989). However, most of these data derive from cross-sectional descriptive studies that do not shed light on the process that leads to poorer health in carers. Later in this chapter I shall discuss the evidence regarding adjustment to caregiving and the impact on the carer of transitions that occur during the course of mental illness.

Becoming a carer is usually an unexpected and unplanned role and not a matter of choice. Family members may be drawn into functioning as caregivers even before they define themselves as such. As with any family relationship, there is little in the way of demarcation of responsibilities and the role may come to pervade all aspects of the carer's life. Cultural and social norms and kinship patterns influence which family member assumes the role, as reflected in the higher proportion of women carers found in most studies (e.g. 60% in the ONS survey; Singleton et al., 2002). Becoming a carer seems to be a normative family role for women, with the probability increasing across the life course.

Although some carers may feel they had little choice about taking on the role, carers' motivations are shaped by their perceptions of the relationship (affection, intimacy, companionship, mutual support, reciprocity) and by their feelings for the person they are looking after (love, respect, loyalty, gratitude, indebtedness, duty). In the context of long-term relationships, there may be no recognisable change in roles, but rather a subtle shift in the level of support that people give to each other. Older couples with a shared history of mutual support may have less adjustment to make to caregiving than those with little reciprocity (Murray and Livingston, 1998). Transition to the role of carer appears to be more challenging when the onset of the illness is sudden and unexpected, as in the case of traumatic brain injury or the first episode of a severe mental illness. In this chapter, I shall consider the impact of caring for people with two contrasting mental disorders. Evidence from studies of carers for younger people with severe mental illness and older people with dementia will be used to explore the following themes: transitions and adjustment to caregiving; reciprocity and mutual exchange; and burden and rewards. Given the variation in outcome for carers, I shall consider evidence for the differential effects of gender and kinship by comparing the experiences of male, female, parent, child and spouse carers.

FAMILY RELATIONSHIPS, TRANSITIONS AND CAREGIVING

With the exception of degenerative conditions like dementia, mental disorders commonly follow an episodic course. Carers' negative experiences, such as distress, worry, stigma, shame and guilt, also seem to follow fluctuating patterns in response to their relative's mood and behaviour. Caregivers face fluctuating demands on their time, energy and tolerance. Research that addresses the experiences of carers at these different stages is essential to the development of supportive interventions.

A study of close family members of people with a first episode of psychosis (Tennakoon et al., 2000) highlighted the emotional upheaval and practical challenges of the early stages of transition to caregiving. At first, carers experienced a high degree of worry about their relative's difficult behaviours, attempts at self-harm and risk of suicide. They also worried about their relative's lost opportunities and whether they (carers) had done something to cause the illness. Concerns were expressed about the impact of the illness on other family members and the possibility of the family breaking up. Also, 60% of carers said there had been a marked change in their relationship with the relative since the onset of the illness. Women expressed more worry about the effects on the family, and stigma was more often a concern to parents than to other family members. However, at this early stage in their relative's illness, the prevalence of psychiatric illness (12%) was no greater in carers than in the general population.

However, there is evidence of high levels of subjective "burden" among carers. Schene and colleagues (1998) found a strong relationship between patient symptom severity (psychosis, agitation and apathy) and aspects of caregiver burden (tension, worry, supervision and urging). To clarify the roles of symptoms and personality traits in the patient and feelings of burden in the carer, Wolthaus and colleagues (2002) interviewed the family carers of 138 patients receiving treatment for a first or second episode of schizophrenia. As in most studies involving people with psychotic disorder, parents were most likely to be their carers and over 75% were women. Results showed that disorganisation symptoms in the patient (e.g. poor attention, disorientation) were the most burdensome to carers. These symptoms are most prevalent in early-onset schizophrenia and may explain burden in carers. Previous studies have included carers of patients with chronic psychoses, and this may explain why other symptoms have previously been linked to burden in carers.

Apart from the fluctuating demands of long-term mental illness, carers' involvement with their relative can change dramatically over time, particularly when the care recipient is suffering from a degenerative illness. The ONS survey (Singleton et al., 2002) found that after one year, 25% of respondents had ceased to regard themselves as carers: in just over a quarter of cases the person they cared for had died and in a further 10% of cases the person had moved into residential care. The most reliable method of studying the course of caregiving and the impact on carers is via prospective study.

Seltzer and Li (2000) carried out a longitudinal study of caregiving transitions in a large community sample of the wives and daughters of older people over a three-year period. They selected three key transitions in the role: entry, institutionalisation of the older relative and bereavement. To control for the effects of gender, only women were included in the sample, and to identify any kinship effects wives were compared with daughters. The researchers identified a large community sample of people aged over 60 and a sample of younger people who provided care to someone aged over 60. Telephone screening was used to identify wives and daughters currently providing care for their husband or parent. A non-caregiving sample of wives and daughters was similarly recruited. Participants were interviewed twice, with an interval of three years, using measures of social involvement, family support and psychological well-being. At three-year follow-up approximately a tenth of initially "non-carer" wives had become carers to their husbands, and one third of daughters had become carers to their parents. At three years, 68% of wives and 53% of daughters who were providing care at the outset were still providing care at home. While over 10% of daughters had placed their parent in residential care, none of the caregiving wives had done so. Ceasing to be a carer because of bereavement affected wives and daughters at the same rate (around 30%).

However, there were important differences in the impact of the transitional stages of caregiving on wives and daughters. Daughters experienced few changes in social, familial and psychological well-being after taking on and ceasing in the role of carer. In contrast, wives showed deterioration in well-being after entering the carer role and improvement after leaving it. These findings confirm the more negative impact of caregiving on wives than daughters reported in earlier studies (e.g. George and Gwyther, 1986). The explanation may lie in the greater intensity and dominance of the marital relationship compared to an adult daughter's relationship to her elderly parents. The illness and dependence of a spouse is omnipresent and may pervade all aspects of life, whereas a daughter is likely to have her own partner and family, employment, social interests and leisure interests independent of her relationship with her ill parent.

Caregiving takes place in the context of family relationships and other intimate social settings. Qualitative methods are the most appropriate for understanding phenomena from the perspective of the people involved. Interpretative analysis of narrative data provides insight into the experience of caregiving that cannot be conveyed in summary statistics. In a series of 50 extensive in-depth interviews, Karp and Tanarugsachock (2000) explored how family carers of people with depression, bipolar disorder or schizophrenia experienced and managed different emotional states over time. The focus of the interview was on explaining the kinds of emotion that arise when carers try to interpret what they "owe" to the family member at times of mental distress. Caring for a loved one with a mental illness presents quite different challenges to caring for someone with a physical condition. Social roles are disrupted, behaviour may be socially unacceptable and the carer may be treated with hostility rather than gratitude. Karp and Tanarugsachock set out to understand how carers reconcile love for a family member with emotions such as fear, bewilderment, frustration, anger and even hate. Analysis showed that carers' perceptions of their obligations to the family member changed over time. They identified four stages in the caregiving experience, each with a corresponding shift in emotional reactions: before and after diagnosis, realisation that the illness may be permanent and realisation that they (the carer) cannot control the illness. In the early stages, carers tended to doubt their own understanding of the problems exhibited by the family member and these doubts were often compounded by the patient's and health professionals' suggestions that the carer might be the cause of the problem. The self-blame that can arise prior to diagnosis is evident in this quote from a carer interview: "I

figured I just wasn't a good person because I must be a failure [as a wife]. . . .
I knew it was him, but I said [to myself], 'No maybe it isn't him. Maybe it's
me'" (Karp and Tanarugsachock, 2000: 12).

Denial was another common early response among carers, and receiving
a diagnosis represented a helpful turning point. Most carers eagerly
adopted the medical version of the problem and this enabled them to treat
the family member with the understanding and compassion due to an ill
relative. At the same time, there was a sense of obligation to provide care
and feelings of frustration at being unable to empathise with the person
with mental illness.

The realisation that the illness might never go away represented another
turning point for carers. At this stage there was great sadness that their
hopes and aspirations for their relative would no longer be realised. Parents
in particular experienced profound sadness and grief at having "lost" a
child. They also had to reduce radically their own life expectations and
talked of their relative "destroying" their (the carer's) life. They felt that
everyone's focus was so much on the ill person that their own needs and
efforts to carry on their other roles were not appreciated. Feelings of
increasing isolation led to frustration and anger. As they eventually came to
accept that they could not control or cure the illness, carers' distress began
to diminish. At this point, some felt able to begin to reduce their obligations
to care for their relative.

Being the parent of a son or daughter with severe mental illness may
bring feelings of self-blame and guilt that other carers do not have to suffer.
Until recently, the treatment of schizophrenia was based on the premise
that the family had in some way contributed to the illness. Many patients
have learned to blame their families for their condition, adding to parental
feelings of guilt and helplessness. Pejlert (2001) provides important insights
into parental feelings of guilt and shame by exploring the experiences of
parents of adults with schizophrenia who had moved to a residential care
facility in the community.

Parents' narratives focused on themes such as living with sorrow, anguish
and constant worry, living with shame, coming to terms with difficulties
and hoping for a better life for their son or daughter. Consistent with the
accounts given by families to Karp and Tanarugsachock (2000), the onset
of the illness was characterised as a "fateful event" that had transformed
the course of family life. Parents felt they had to make a life-long effort
to support their son or daughter even though they were now living in
residential care. Howard (1994) also asked mothers of adult children with
schizophrenia to take a life-span perspective in describing their experiences
of caregiving.

From an analysis of the interview data, Howard constructed a model of
stages of learning to cope with an adult child's mental illness: perceiving a
problem, searching for solutions, enduring the situation and surviving the

experiences. Similarly, Tuck et al. (1997) explored the long-term impact of schizophrenia on parenting. The diagnosis was experienced as a destructive force that transformed family life and demanded unremitting and unending parental responsibility.

In Pejlert's (2001) study, parents' experiences of contact with mental health services over the years had not been positive: they felt they had received inadequate information, blame for their child's illness and exclusion from the treatment process. When their offspring moved from more restricted treatment settings into the community care facility, parents had hoped for more involvement in their child's care. However, these hopes were not realised and a lack of co-operation between staff and parents prevailed. They were angered by what they perceived as excessive professional concern with protecting patient autonomy and confidentiality, and excluding the parents.

Some useful insights into the experience of stigma emerge from this study. Parents never mentioned their child's diagnosis by name, described feelings of shame and restricted their use of social support to parents in similar circumstances. Relationships with mental health professionals seemed to reinforce the experience of stigma by encouraging feelings of parental guilt and exclusion from the child's treatment. Pejlert (2001) emphasises the need for professional caregivers to stop regarding families as pathogenic and to give them more information and support to ease the long-term sense of burden reported by parents.

Treasure et al. (2001) found that carers of people with eating disorders experience more distress than those caring for someone with a psychotic illness. Given the typically early age of onset, the majority of care for people with eating disorders is provided by their parents. A recent exploration of the attitudes and beliefs of parents caring for someone with anorexia nervosa found similar negative impacts upon family life and parental self-blame as those reported in the studies above (Whitney et al., 2005). Mothers and fathers in this qualitative study were equally likely to blame themselves for their daughter's condition, pondering what could have been done differently to prevent the illness. Most were pessimistic about recovery and a return to normal life and believed themselves to be helpless in trying to cope with the illness.

While there was little difference between mothers and fathers in describing their daughters' behaviour as overly dependent, demanding and destructive of family cohesion, mothers were more likely to express highly emotional and anxious responses, including sleep loss, preoccupation and feelings of hopelessness. Fathers gave more detached accounts of their caregiving and expressed more affection and desire to support and protect their daughters. The authors conclude that mothers tend to exhibit higher levels of expressed emotion while fathers tend to distance themselves or use cognitive strategies to manage their anxieties.

There is consensus in the results of these studies that parents as caregivers face high levels of guilt and self-blame. The effects of long-term strain and stigma are clearly damaging to the mental health of all family members. Mental health professionals have an important role to play in supporting family caregivers, and parents in particular, by providing information and respecting their roles.

CARER BURDEN, DISTRESS AND GENDER

The long-term effects upon health, morale and quality of life among those caring for a relative with a mental disorder are often referred to as "carer burden". Although many carers derive great satisfaction from looking after a loved one, it is important to acknowledge the cumulative effects of care-giving and to use standardised measures of burden to compare outcomes for different groups of carers.

Studies of gender differences suggest that women find the role more stressful than men do (e.g. Collins and Jones, 1997). The prevalence of psychosocial difficulties in female carers is consistently higher than that found in matched community samples (Murray 1995: 47). There are problems involved in comparing the levels of stress and morbidity found in different carer studies because samples, settings and research instruments vary widely. Some studies include only carers of patients receiving specialist services, while others have drawn their samples from the membership of voluntary organisations. The most reliable prevalence data are derived from community surveys like that undertaken in the State of Victoria in Australia. This study found gender differences in the well-being of carers of people with a range of disorders (Schofield et al., 1998). While no significant differences were found between male and female carers in levels of life satisfaction or positive affect, women expressed significantly more negative affect, anger, family conflict, anxiety, depression and overload (or strain). This combination of negative feelings is often referred to as "carer burden", a self-appraisal of being overwhelmed by the role.

Schofield et al. (1998) found that daughters living with the parent they cared for were also very high in resentment of caregiving and low on measures of life satisfaction. The negative impact on both wives and co-resident daughters might be explained by Cantor's (1983) findings that emotional strain in carers is clearly linked to the closeness of the kinship bond and the availability of the carer. The study suggests that these two factors increase exposure to stressful caregiving tasks in women, especially those who perceive greater responsibility for and involvement with the family.

However, the findings of studies comparing psychiatric morbidity rather than stress in male and female carers have not found significant gender differences. Gilhooly (1984) reported lower morale in female carers but no excess levels of anxiety or depression. Similarly, O'Connor and colleagues (1990) found higher levels of strain but not of psychiatric morbidity in women, and Brodaty and Hadzi-Pavlovic (1990) also failed to find any gender differences in psychological distress. Gallichio and colleagues (2002) investigated the relationship between gender, depression and burden in a community sample of people caring for spouses, parents and other relatives. They found that female carers had almost twice the prevalence of high burden scores (27%) than male carers (14%) but there was no significant gender difference in levels of depressive symptoms. However, rates of depression were significantly higher in carers who were spouses or children and in those looking after someone with higher levels of behaviour disturbance.

Miller and Cafasso (1992) carried out a meta-analysis of the findings of 14 studies of burden in carers of people with dementia or similar impairments. The analysis revealed that, on average, females were 20% more burdened than male caregivers. However, Hinrichsen and Niederehe (1994) found no significant gender differences in either burden or psychiatric symptom scores. A recent review of the association between gender and psychiatric morbidity (Yee and Schulz, 2000) concluded that the majority of studies on depression and burden in family caregivers found higher levels of both in female compared to male carers. The review showed that both male and female carers were at elevated risk of depression when compared with non-carer peers, but that women were at higher risk of clinical depression. Some studies showed that they also had higher levels of anxiety than male carers. However, most of these studies involved older spouses; more data are needed on younger carers in a variety of different relationships with the person they look after.

What explanations have been offered for these greater stress levels in female carers? Yee and Schulz's review (2000) suggests that the caregiving provided by women is often qualitatively different from that provided by men, with women undertaking more intensive "hands-on" care. Women are more likely to take on the role in the first place and to relinquish it later than men. Men also report receiving more informal support from other family members and have more practical and less emotional coping styles. Collins and Jones (1997) reported that although both male and female carers expressed the view that women were better suited to caregiving, wives were less tolerant of dependence in their spouses, felt more obligation to care and were more likely to express the wish to give up the role. A large study of women caring for an ill or disabled parent found that women who were experiencing stress in their other roles (wife, mother, employee) were more likely to experience depression and reduced life satisfaction (Stephens and Townsend, 1997). On the other hand, experiencing rewards in their other roles (apart from employment) did not appear to buffer the negative effects of caregiving.

CARER SATISFACTION, REWARDS AND RECIPROCITY

The positive rewards of caregiving seem to be related to the amount of reciprocity or mutual exchange of support that the carer perceives in the relationship with the person they are looking after (Horwitz et al., 1996; Motenko, 1989; Murray and Livingston, 1998; Murray et al., 1999; Schwartz and Gidron, 2002).

Horwitz et al. (1996) addressed the common perception of caregiving as a one-way relationship in which a care provider gives to a dependent recipient. The researchers took the view that caregiving is a process of mutual exchange and set out to test the hypothesis that the amount of support a family member receives depends upon they amount they provide to others in the family. They also explored the factors that might influence reciprocity, such as co-residence, role relationships, patients' symptomatology and demographic characteristics. Carers were either a parent or sibling of the patient. Results showed that the amount of help given by the patient to the family strongly predicted how much support they in turn received.

Schwartz and Gidron (2002) examined the extent to which parents perceived their mentally ill son or daughter to provide practical and emotional support and whether they experienced caregiving as rewarding. All parents said they received help and support from their child, although they valued more highly the satisfaction they gained from fulfilling their parental role. Their assessment of the satisfaction they derived from caregiving was not related to their level of burden or to the severity of their child's illness.

Spouses caring for a partner with severe mental illness may experience high levels of burden at the same time as losing the support of their partner. Jungbauer and Angermeyer (2002) point out that spouses face not only the burdens of the illness but additional strains resulting from their marital and family roles. When one partner is suffering from dementia, their progressive deterioration may lead to profound feelings of loss and burden in their spouse. Reciprocity and burden are perhaps most clearly demonstrated in studies of the spouses who make up 40% of those caring for people with dementia. In old age, marriage is often the main source of companionship and support, helping to maintain independence and morale. Although dementia inevitably disrupts the relationship, spouses who find meaning and reward in looking after their partners are more likely to experience good morale (Motenko, 1989). Murray and Livingston (1998) found that spouse carers who were able to accept that the changes in their partners were the result of the illness adjusted more positively to the demands of caregiving. Although the changes were a cause for sadness, their attachment to their partners remained strong and they perceived continuity in the relationship. Those who reported a history of reciprocity in the marriage were more willing to cope with the demands of caring, while those who expressed a lack of affection for their spouse said they were caring out of a sense of duty only and wished to give up the role. This group were more often suffering from depression.

A pan-European study of spouses caring for an older person with dementia explored the difficulties associated with carer burden (Murray et al., 1999; Schneider et al., 1999). Analysis of qualitative interviews showed that most difficulties arose from the experience of loss – the feeling that the person with dementia was slipping away as their memory deteriorated. The loss of communication and intimacy resulting from passive behaviour and withdrawal formed one distinct area of distress for carers. The person with dementia was felt to be out of reach. Excessive behaviours such as aggression, restlessness, wandering, mood swings and sleep disturbance were included in a second group of symptoms or behaviours that caused distress to caregiving spouses. However, there was evidence of reward for many spouses in caring for their loved one: reciprocity, mutual affection, companionship and "job satisfaction" in providing good care were the most frequent reasons for satisfaction. Despite the burdens of care and sense of loss, most carers wished to keep their partner at home for as long as possible.

CONCLUSION

Research evidence regarding the impact of the caregiving role has shown that carers of people with different mental disorders experience strain, mental distress, rewards and burden in varying intensities. Research findings are equivocal on how these outcomes vary according to gender and relationship to the person receiving care. However, there is no doubt that unpaid family carers play an essential and irreplaceable role in mental health care. The review here shows that patients' and carers' needs for support change over time, so flexibility and access are their key requirements. In the United Kingdom, there is statutory recognition of this role (Department of Health, 1999) and carers have the right to have their needs assessed independently of the person they are looking after. Nonetheless, the knowledge base about effective support for carers of people with mental health problems is sparse (Arksey et al., 2002).

REFERENCES

Arksey, H., O'Malley, L., Baldwin, S., Harris, J., Mason, A., Newbronner, E. and Hare, P. (2002) *Overview report: Services in support of carers of people with mental health problems*, York, University of York Social Policy Research Unit and Centre for Health Economics, Acton Shapiro.

Brodaty, H. and Hadzi-Pavlovic, D. (1990) The psychological effects on carers of living with dementia, *Australian and New Zealand Journal of Psychiatry*, 24, 351–361.

Cantor, M. H. (1983) Strain among caregivers: A study of experience in the United States, *The Gerontologist*, 23, 597–604.

Collins, C. and Jones, R. (1997) Emotional distress and morbidity in dementia carers: A matched comparison of husbands and wives, *International Journal of Geriatric Psychiatry*, 12 (12), 1168–1173.

Department of Health (1999) *Caring about carers: A national strategy for carers*, London, Department of Health.

Dura, J., Stukenberg, K. W. and Kiecolt-Glaser, J. K. (1990) Chronic stress and depressive disorders in older adults, *Journal of Abnormal Psychology*, 99, 284–290.

Gallicchio, L., Siddiqi, N., Langenberg, P. and Baumgarten, M. (2002) Gender differences in burden and depression among informal caregivers of demented elders in the community, *International Journal of Geriatric Psychiatry*, 17, 154–163.

George, L. K. and Gwyther, L. P. (1986) Caregiver well-being: A multi-dimensional examination of family caregivers of demented adults, *The Gerontologist*, 26, 253–259.

Gilhooly, M. (1984) The impact of caregiving on caregivers: Factors associated with the psychological well-being of people supporting a dementing relative in the community, *British Journal of Medical Psychology*, 57, 35–44.

Haley, W. E., Levine, E. G., Brown, S. L., Berry, J. W. and Hughes, G. H. (1987) The psychological, social and health consequences of caring for a relative with senile dementia, *Journal of the American Geriatrics Society*, 35, 405–411.

Hinrichsen, G. and Niederehe, G. (1994) Dementia management strategies and adjustment of family members of older patients, *Gerontologist*, 34, 95–102.

Horwitz, A. V., Reinhard, S. C. and Howell-White, S. (1996) Caregiving as reciprocal exchange in families with seriously mentally ill members, *Journal of Health and Social Behaviour*, 37 (2), 149–162.

Howard, P. B. (1994) Lifelong maternal caregiving for children with schizophrenia, *Archives of Psychiatric Nursing*, 8 (2), 107–114.

Jungbauer, J. and Angermeyer, M. C. (2002) Living with a schizophrenic patient: a comparative study of burden as it affects parents and spouses, *Psychiatry*, 65 (2), 110–123.

Karp, D. A. and Tanarugsachock, V. (2000) Mental illness, caregiving, and emotion management, *Qualitative Health Research*, 10 (1), 6–25.

Kiecolt-Glaser, J. K., Dura, J. R., Speicher, C. E., Trask, O. and Glaser, R. (1991) Spousal caregivers of dementia victims: Longitudinal changes in immunity and health, *Psychosomatic Medicine*, 53, 345–362.

Livingston, G., Katona, C. and Manela, M. (1996) Depression and other psychiatric mordidity in carers of elderly people living at home, *British Medical Journal*, 312, 153–156.

Miller, B. and Cafasso, L. (1992) Gender differences in caregiving: Fact or artefact?, *The Gerontologist*, 32, 498–507.

Motenko, A. (1989) The frustrations, gratifications and well-being of dementia caregivers, *The Gerontologist*, 29, 166–172.

Murray, J. (1995) *Prevention of anxiety and depression in vulnerable groups*, London, Gaskell.

Murray, J. and Livingston, G. (1998) A qualitative study of adjustment to caring for an older spouse with psychiatric illness, *Ageing and Society*, 18, 659–671.

Murray, J., Schneider, J., Banerjee, S. and Mann, A. (1999) EUROCARE: A cross national study of coresident spouse carers for people with Alzheimer's dementia II: A qualitative analysis of the experience of caregiving, *International Journal of Geriatric Psychiatry*, 4, 665–661.

O'Connor, D. W., Pollitt, P. A., Brook, C. P., Roth, M. and Reiss, B. B. (1990) Problems reported by relatives in a community study of dementia, *British Journal of Psychiatry*, 156, 835–841.

Pejlert, A. (2001) Being a parent of an adult son or daughter with severe mental illness receiving professional care: Parents' narratives, *Health and Social Care in the Community*, 9 (4), 194–204.

Perring, C., Twigg, J. and Atkin, K. (1990) *Families caring for people diagnosed as mentally ill: The literature re-examined*, London, HMSO.

Schene, A. H., vav Wijngaarden, B. and Koeter, M. J. (1998) Family caregiving in schizophrenia: Domains and distress, *Schizophrenia Bulletin*, 24, 609–618.

Schneider, J., Murray, J., Banerjee, S. and Mann, A. (1999) EUROCARE: A cross national study of co-resident spouse carers for people with Alzheimer's Disease I: Factors associated with carer burden, *International Journal of Geriatric Psychiatry*, 14, 665–661.

Schneider, J., Hallam, A., Islam, M. K., Murray, J., Foley, B., Atkins, L., Banerjee, S. and Mann, A. (2003) Formal and informal care for people with dementia: Variations in costs over time, *Ageing and Society*, 23, 303–326.

Schofield, H., Bloch, S., Herrman, H., Murphy, B., Nankervis, J. and Singh, B. (1998) Family caregivers: Disability, illness and ageing, St Leornards, Australia, Allen and Unwin.

Schwartz, C. and Gidron R (2002) Parents of mentally ill adult children living at home: Rewards of caregiving, *Health and Social Work*, 27 (2), 145–154.

Seltzer, M. and Li, W. L. (2000) The dynamics of caregiving: Transitions during a three-year prospective study, *The Gerontologist*, 40 (2), 165–178.

Singleton, N., Maung, N., Cowie, A., Sparks, J., Bumpstead, R. and Meltzer, H. (2002) *Mental health of carers*, London, The Stationery Office.

Stephens, M. A. and Townsend, A. L. (1997) Stress of parent care: Positive and negative effects of women's other roles, *Psychology and Aging*, 12 (2), 376–386.

Tennakoon, L., Fannon, D., Doku, V., O'Ceallaigh, S., Soni, W., Santamaria, M., Kuipers, E. and Sharma, T. (2000) Experience of caregiving: Relatives of people experiencing a first episode of psychosis, *British Journal of Psychiatry*, 177, 529–533.

Treasure, J., Murphy, T., Todd, G., Gavan, K., Schmidt, U., Joyce, J. and Szmukler, G. (2001) The experiences of caregiving for severe mental illness: A comparison between anorexia nervosa and psychosis, *Social Psychiatry and Psychiatric Epidemiology*, 36, 343–347.

Tuck, I., du Mont, P., Evans, G. and Shupe, J. (1997) The experience of caring for an adult child with schizophrenia, *Archives of Psychiatric Nursing*, 11 (3), 118–123.

Whitney, J., Murray, J., Gavan, K., Todd, G., Whitaker, W. and Treasure, J. (2005)

The experience of caregiving for someone with anorexia nervosa: A qualitative study, *British Journal of Psychiatry*, 187, 444–449.

Wolthaus, J. E., Dingemans, P. M., Schene, A. H., Linszen, D. H., Wiersma, D., Van Den Bosch, R. J., Cahn, W. and Hijman, R. (2002) Caregiver burden in recent-onset schizophrenia and spectrum disorders: The influence of symptoms and personality traits, *Journal of Nervous and Mental Disease*, 190 (4), 241–247.

Yee, J. and Schulz, R. (2000) Gender differences in psychiatric morbidity among family caregivers: A review and analysis, *The Gerontologist*, 40 (2), 147–164.

Young, R. F. and Kahana, E. (1989) Specifying carer outcomes: Gender and relationship aspects of caregiving strain, *The Gerontologist*, 29, 660–666.

Chapter 14

Concepts of body and self in minority groups

Mervat Nasser, Dinesh Bhugra and Vanessa Chow

INTRODUCTION

In the study of self and culture, the self is discussed in terms of two paradigms: the egocentric self and the sociocentric self – in other words, in term of "individualistic" vs "collectivist" tendencies. These paradigms illustrate the complex nature of the individual's relationship to the society or culture he/she lives in (Hofstede, 1980, 1984). In group-orientated societies based on the notion of kinship, the self moves within a concentric multilayered structure in keeping with the socio-cultural orientation of the group, including its overall economic and political patterns and trends.

Hsu (1985) identified seven layers in this structure (see Figure 14.1). The deepest, most inner layers are Layers 7 and 6, which could be construed psychodynamically as representing the "unconscious" and the "precon-scious" of a person, and contain respectively repressed and semi-repressed psychic materials. Layer 5, on the other hand, is termed "unexpressible conscious" because its contents are generally kept to the individual him/ herself. These contents are usually not communicated to others because the individual may feel unable to articulate the material, believe it to engender shame or believe it to be too private to disclose to the group.

When the individual moves into Layer 4, he/she comes across the "expressible conscious", which contains communicable ideas, materials and feelings and carries with it the expectation of reciprocal feelings and feedback from the group. Some of these ideas or feelings may be very personal and represent emotions of love, hate and greed. Other material can be made public and shared with those of the same personal, socio-economic or cultural background, such as emotional expressions of patriotism.

Layer 3 is that part of the external world with which each individual has strong feelings of attachment and contains others with whom the person shares intimacy. Mutual receptivity, emotional support and verbal com-munication are all components of this level. Hsu (1985) argues that this layer contains the "significant alter", and suggests that this also contains specific cultural values, such as those connected for example with the caste

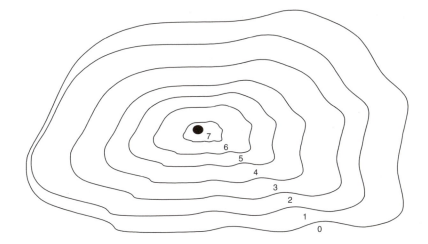

7	Unconscious
6	Pre-conscious
5	Unexpressible conscious
4	Expressible conscious
3	Intimate society and culture
2	Operative society and culture
1	Wider society and culture
0	Outer world

Figure 14.1 Man, culture and society (Hsu, 1985).

system among Hindus. Any challenges encountered within this layer could be threatening and may even have a traumatic effect on the individual; they are therefore likely to be resisted.

Level 2 is characterised by role relationships within the smaller group or subculture. Here the individual relates to the group on many different and useful levels. The cultural rules at this level are those dictated by the subculture and with which the individual deals without strong or even emotional attachments, such as courtesy rules, group customs and patterns of greeting. Layer 1, the penultimate layer, represents cultural values belonging to the larger society, with which the individual may or may not feel much connection. However, if such a relationship exists, it is not affective in nature.

Layer 0, the final layer, is where the "other" lies. It is the layer that deals with people, customs and values belonging to other, societies with which most members of a society have no contact: furthermore, preconceived ideas tend not to exist about these people, customs or values, or, if they do, they tend to be erroneous or of a distorted nature.

The relationship between the individual and these seven layers has implications for acculturation and assimilation.

Hsu (1985) argued that the traditionally conceived personality, from both psychological and anthropological angles, lies within the inner concentric layers and does not normally go beyond Layer 4. However, he was able to identify out of this structure a core that he refered to as *jen*, the Chinese word for man. The *jen* sums up the individual's transactions with all fellow human beings. The *jen* is not static or fixed but in constant motion, searching for a state of equilibrium, a desired psycho-social homostasis that revolves around the human's need for existential meaning and emotional connectedness with the world.

THE SELF IN SOCIAL CONTEXT

The dialectic between the self and the environment and collective identification strategies are dealt with in depth in Chapter 11 of this volume. "Personal identity", as proposed by Cheek (1989), is one's self-knowledge and self-evaluation, whereas "social identity" is the aspect of the self that involves interactions with others. The focus here is more on self-identification in a cultural context or, in other words, "ethnic identity", which drives the individual to behave as expected by group members, producing stereotyping, co-operation, competition, conformity and polarisation (Oaks and Turner, 1990).

Deaux (1993) suggests that personal and social identity are very closely linked and explains how people adopt identities by categorising themselves as members of various groups. Such a perspective emphasises the personal meaning individuals place on their social categories. This is behind the meaning-centred approach, which evolved through medical anthropology and is based on the relativity of both normality and abnormality, which can only be defined within the social and cultural context. Within this framework cultural differences within societies are emphasised. These differences concern variable ways of perceiving and conceptualising the world (Kleinman, 1977; Nasser, 1997).

In recent times, two powerful analyses of culture and the self have emerged. Markus and Kitayama (1991) and Triandis (1989) have traced differences in self-related thoughts and feelings to different cultural emphases on independence, individualism and collectivism. Cultures such as those in India or China are commonly considered to encourage collectivist structure of the self as opposed to individualistic cultures such as that in the USA.

Triandis (1989) made a distinction between the private self (the assessment of the self by the self) and the collective self (the assessment of the self by a referential group), and suggested that such distinction is essential for the definition of "cultural identity" and the measurement of the acculturation process. The term "acculturation" commonly refers to the identification of a small group with the values of a larger group. In contrast to Triandis' (1989) model, Markus and Kitayama (1991) focused more on how people view themselves in relation to their distance from others (see Chapter 11 in this volume).

THE SELF, BODY AND GENDER IN CULTURAL CONTEXT

What is (are) the relationship(s) between sexed bodies and gender? Is femininity synonymous with being a woman? Is it a matter of biology or a culturally and historically variable interpretation of having a female body? What assumptions are made about women of different ethnicities and social backgrounds? These are some of the questions that Chapter 1 of this volume attempts to answer.

Turner (1997) highlighted the complexity of the body in human culture by considering the language with which we describe the presence and the nature of the body in human interaction. Cultural representations of "woman" as defined in biblical terms focus on fear of women's sexuality and reproductive function (Malson and Swann, 2003).

Outside the biblical tradition, women belonging to Eastern religions have received variable definitions across the ages. In his book *Women and Power in History*, De Reincourt (1983) argues that the predominance of the female principle in the Hindu tradition stems from the worship of the divine mother (Matris). This positive attitude towards women changed somewhat following the Aryan settlement in India. Widows were discouraged from remarriage and the practice of suttee (burning of the widow on the funeral pyre of her husband) was honoured. Other sources of discomfort in relation to women's position in India have been the preservation of the caste system, the tradition of arranged marriages and the dowry needed for a prospective husband, which increased family rejection of baby girls. With the development of Buddhism, the importance given to the female principle earlier in Hinduism began to be undermined. In Buddhist tradition women are only allowed to be Sisters if they abandon women's thoughts and cultivate the thoughts of man.

However, in an extensive analysis of feminism across cultures, Nasser (1997) demonstrated that in recent times the majority of women in non-Western societies have significantly changed their social position, with increasing numbers being educated and working outside the family. A number of pressures are now placed upon women globally which convey conflicting cultural messages and impact on the forms of expression of their distress.

THE EXPRESSION OF DISTRESS IN MINORITY GROUPS

Eating disorders comprise one area of distress that has received considerable attention in recent cross-cultural research, which has aimed to explore the impact of immigration, acculturation and overall cultural change in the pathogenesis of distress and the shaping of its expression. A number of surveys have been carried out to identify whether eating pathology exists in non-Western cultures and other ethnicities, and the results indicated the emergence of these in societies, races and cultures that were, for a long time, presumed immune to this pathology (for a review of these studies refer to Gordon, 2001; Nasser, 1997). The process of acculturation commonly refered to as Westernisation was consistently offered as an explanation, although a clear distinction was not made between Westernisation and modernisation, and few studies actually attempted to measure this culture change (Katzman and Leung, 1996). The use of Westernisation as a concept fails to take into account the true societal forces that shape bodies and genders. Other research workers argued that the diagnostic methodology adopted in the field of eating disorders, with its focus on the "dread of fatness", could also lead to underestimation of the rates of these problems in some societies, such as China. These discussions highlight the need for a deeper understanding of these problems and the meaning they have, particularly self-starvation in certain societies (Lee, 2001).

This invites us to look beyond the mode of behaviour or symptomatology in search of its true meaning.

In discussing the technology of the self, Foucault (1986) speaks of an ensemble of culturally meaningful practices working on the body, which constitute and transform the self, and through which the self becomes an attitude or a way of thinking relating to contemporary society. We need, therefore, to attempt to clarify the meaning of the body and its distress in the context of social relationships and societal roles. Acculturation or Westernisation needs to be broken down to its basic elements to see the forces that lie behind the concept. These forces include urbanisation, global markets, threat to national identity, experience of discontinuity and the disappearance of traditional cultural idioms for articulating personal distress (Nasser and Katzman, 1999).

Gender-specific issues have been at the core of feminist analysis of eating disorders in connection with the position of women in the industrialised world. Thus the feminist argument has failed to address these issues in their wider cultural context and address the position of women in other societies, who were thought for a long time to be protected from such conflicts by virtue of well-defined sex roles and by adherence to traditional family structures. There was a need, therefore, to attempt to connect gender with culture and, particularly, to examine the issue of gendered imbalance at times of cultural change (Nasser, 2000).

Eating disorders and their association with self-harm behaviour and substance misuse have just begun to receive comparable attention from research workers concerned with the role played by culture in the whole phenomenon. In a study of self-harm behaviour conducted on both black and white patients with either binge eating disorder or bulimia nervosa, Dohn and colleagues (2002) found elevated rates of symptoms to be connected to a history of abuse or childhood trauma regardless of the patient's diagnostic status or ethnicity. Young populations who cut themselves seem to do it as an outlet for interpersonal conflict and mental anguish (Nasser and DiNicola, 2001).

Hunter and Harvey (2002) compared rates of self-harm behaviour among indigenous populations in Australia, New Zealand, Canada and the United Sates. They concluded that the vulnerability of young populations to self-harm behaviour was attributable to the impact of cultural breakdown. This demonstrates how young people are influenced by cultural changes and the circumstances that surround them. In line with these findings, Indian youth in Alaska have been shown to have a higher vulnerability to life-threatening behaviours than their white counterparts (Frank and Lester, 2002).

Hospital-based analyses of admissions data, as well as surveys carried out in school settings, suggest that young Asian women born in the UK are at a higher risk for attempted suicide and self-harm behaviour than white Caucasian or African-Caribbean young women (Merrill and Owens, 1986, 1988; Mumford and Whitehouse, 1988). The results of these studies have been explained as a by-product of acculturation into Western cultures (Burke, 1976; Hodes, 1990; Merrill and Owens, 1988). "Culture clash" is also thought to result from the high demands placed on young Asian women living in the UK to conform to their parental cultural and religious customs (Soni-Raleigh and Balarajan, 1992). In a more recent study, the higher rates of deliberate self-harm among young Asian women in Britain were seen as an expression of disconnection and a reaction to the sense of cultural alienation felt by this particular group (Bhugra, 2002). Thompson and Bhugra (2000) suggest that the increased rates of attempted suicide in younger Asian women are the result of a number of factors reported by younger Asians that include concepts of self, social isolation and gender roles (see Figure 14.2).

In a quote within a qualitative analysis of interviews conducted with young Asian women with self-harm behaviour in East London, a Bengali Moslem woman described her self-harm behaviour within a context of

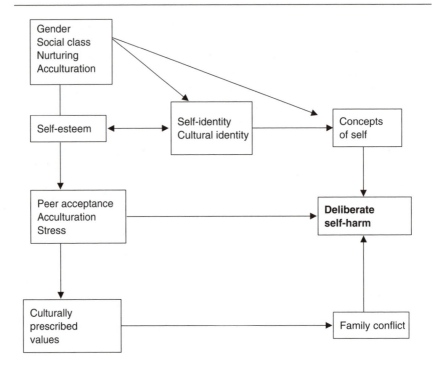

Figure 14.2 Interrelation of factors in deliberate self-harm.

distressful and emotionally painful situations; cutting was perceived as a way of communicating and releasing this distress. "When I start cutting myself . . . all my anger gets channelled into the cut and I look at the blood and I think it's a release. While I was cutting, I felt more in control, whereas before I'd cut, I sort of felt like, oh God, there is nothing I can control" (quoted in Marshall and Yazdani, 2000: 62). In this example of a young Asian woman in the United Kingdom, the body is not only a medium for expressing distress but also a means of controlling it. The patient sees the cutting behaviour as giving her an illusory sense of control (Nasser, 2004).

IMPLICATIONS FOR SERVICE DELIVERY AND CONCLUSIONS

The expression of distress – be it an eating disorder or deliberate self-harm – is symptomatic of the individual's sense of disconnection with the outside world. It is a reaction to the sense of confusion, disorganisation and disharmony felt by those who do not "fit in". This sense of rejection, which is common to ethnic minority groups, leads them to negotiate their distress through body language. With this in mind, it seems logical to deduce that the best way to help this group would be to attempt to reconnect body to voice by empowerment and placing the focus on competence rather than pathology (Nasser and Katzman, 1999).

This is in fact behind the dialectical theory of the self and dialectical behaviour therapy (DBT), which is increasingly being used with some success to manage borderline personality disorder (BPD) and deliberate self-harm. The theory incorporates some principles drawn from Zen Buddhism, with an emphasis on "mindfulness" (see Chapter 17).

However, there are still important issues to consider in the detection and management of distress among minority groups. Some have suggested separate services for black and ethnic minority individuals, in the hope that this would improve up-take of services, satisfaction with services and clinical outcomes (Bhugra and Bahl, 1999). Confidence in service delivery is likely to increase if the providers are better informed about the individual's cultural factors, language, taboos and so on. Women-only services have also been advocated. Such an approach suggests that women may feel safe and protected in such settings (Bland and Kraft, 1999; also see Chapter 20 in this volume).

However, in their analysis of young Asian women who harm themselves, Marshall and Yazdani (2000) referred to culturally linked concerns about professionals construed as belonging to the patient's cultural community (i.e. of same ethnic background). Those professionals were seen to be more likely to take up positions and values similar to those of the patient's family, in addition to being "unsafe" as they might inform the family of the consultation. They added that issues of broken confidentiality may arise from contestation regarding whether mental health problems are private/individual matters or are matters to be shared within the family. This constitutes a challenge to assumptions that cultural matching equates with culturally sensitive care. Further evidence drawn from research also suggests that ethnic matching does not improve the long-term outcome of patients, besides being not practically possible or economically viable (Marshall and Yazdani, 2000). The debate about the need for special services for minority groups or the improvement of the existing generic ones has just begun.

REFERENCES

Bhugra, D. (2002) Suicidal behaviour in South Asians in the UK, *Crisis*, 23, 108–113.

Bhugra, D. and Bahl, V. (1999) *Ethnicity: An agenda for mental health*, London, Gaskell.

Bland, I. J. and Kraft, I. (1999) The therapeutic alliance across cultures, in

S. Okapaku (ed.) *Clinical methods in transcultural psychiatry*, Washington, DC, American Psychiatric Association Press.

Burke, A. W. (1976) Attempted suicide among Asian immigrants in Birmingham, *British Journal of Psychiatry*, 128, 528–568.

Cheek, J. M. (1989) Identity orientation and self-interpretation, in D. Buss and N. Cantor (eds) *Personality psychology: Recent trends and emerging directions*, New York, Springer-Verlag.

Deaux, K. (1993) Reconstructing social identity, *Personality and Social Psychology Bulletin*, 19, 4–12.

De Reincourt, A. (1983) *Women and power in history*, London, Honeyglen Publishing.

Dohn, F. A., Striegel-Moore, R. H., Wilfley, D. E., Pike, K. M., Hook, J. and Fairburn, C. G. (2002) Self-harm and substance use in a community sample of black and white women with binge eating disorder or bulimia nervosa, *International Journal of Eating Disorders*, 32, 389–400.

Foucault, M. (1986) *The care of the self Vol. 3: The history of sexuality*, New York, Vintage Books.

Frank, M. L. and Lester, D. (2002) Self-destructive behaviours in American Indian and Alaska Native high school youth, *American Indian and Alaskan Native Mental Health Research*, 10, 24–32.

Gordon, R. (2001) Eating disorders East and West: A culture-bound syndrome unbound, in M. Nasser, M. Katzman and R. Gordon (eds) *Eating disorders and cultures in transition*, pp. 1–24, Hove, Brunner-Routledge.

Hofstede, G. (1980) *Culture's consequences*, Beverly Hills, Sage.

Hofstede, G. (1984) *Culture's consequences: Abridged*, Beverly Hills, Sage.

Hodes, M. (1990) Overdosing as communication: A cultural perspective, *British Journal of Medical Psychology*, 63, 319–333.

Hsu, F. (1985) The self in cross-cultural perspective, in A. J. Marsella, G. de Vos and F. L. Hsu (eds) *Culture and self: Asian and Western perspectives*, pp. 252–277, New York, Tavistock.

Hunter, E. and Harvey, D. (2002) Indigenous suicide in Australia, New Zealand, Canada, and the United States, *Emergency Medicine*, 14, 14–23.

Katzman, M. and Leung, F. (1996, April) *When East meets West: Does disordered eating follow?*, Paper presented at the Seventh International Conference on Eating Disorders, New York.

Kleinman, A. (1977) Depression, somatization and the "new cross-cultural psychiatry", *Social Science and Medicine*, 11, 3–10.

Lee, S. (2001) Fat phobia in anorexia nervosa: Whose obsession is it?, in M. Nasser, M. Katzman and R. Gordon (eds) *Eating disorders and cultures in transition*, pp. 40–66, Hove, Brunner-Routledge.

Malson, H. and Swann, C. (2003) Re-producing "woman's" body: Reflections on the (dis)place(ments) of "reproduction" for (post)modern women, *Journal of Gender Studies*, 12 (3), 191–201.

Markus, H. and Kitayama, S. (1991) Culture and the self: Implications for cognitive emotion and motivation, *Psychological Review*, 98, 224–253.

Marshall, H. and Yazdani, A. (2000) Young Asian women and self harm, in J. Ussher (ed.) *Women's health: Contemporary international perspectives*, pp. 56–69, London, British Psychological Society.

Merrill, J. and Owens, J. (1986) Ethnic differences in self-poisoning: A comparison of Asian and white groups, *British Journal of Psychiatry*, 148, 708–712.

Merrill, J. and Owens, J. (1988) Self-poisoning among four immigrant groups, *Acta Psychiatrica Scandinavica*, 77, 77–80.

Mumford, D. B. and Whitehouse, A. M. (1988) Increased prevalence of bulimia nervosa among Asian schoolgirls, *British Medical Journal*, 297, 718.

Nasser, M. (1997) *Culture and weight consciousness*, London, Brunner-Routledge.

Nasser, M. (2000) Gender, culture and eating disorders, in J. M. Ussher (ed.) *Women's health: Contemporary international perspectives*, pp. 379–387, Leicester, British Psychological Society.

Nasser, M. (2004) Dying to live: Eating disorders and self harm behaviour in the cultural context, in J. Levitt, R. Sasone and L. Cohn (eds) *Self-harm behaviour and eating disorders: Dynamics, assessment and treatment*, pp. 15–31, New York and Hove, Brunner-Routledge.

Nasser, M. and DiNicola, V. (2001) Changing bodies, changing cultures: An intercultural dialogue on the body as the final frontier, in M. Nasser, M. Katzman and R. Gordon (eds) *Eating disorders and cultures in transition*, pp. 171–194, London, Brunner-Routledge.

Nasser, M. and Katzman, M. (1999) Eating disorders: Transcultural perspectives inform prevention, in N. Piran, M. Levine and C. Steiner-Adair (eds) *Preventing eating disorders: A handbook of interventions and special challenges*, pp. 26–44, Philadelphia, Brunner/Mazel.

Nasser, M., Katzman, M. and Gordon, R. (2001) *Eating disorders and cultures in transition*, London, Brunner-Routledge.

Oakes, P. and Turner, J. (1990) Is limited information processing capacity the cause of social stereotyping?, in W. Stroebe and M. Hewstone (eds) *The European review of social psychology*, pp. 111–135, New York, Wiley.

Soni-Raleigh, V. and Balarajan, R. (1992) Suicide and self-burning among Indians and West Indians in England and Wales, *British Journal of Psychiatry*, 161, 365–368.

Thompson, N. and Bhugra, D. (2000) Rates of deliberate self harm in Asians: Findings and models, *International Review of Psychiatry*, 12 (3), 37–43.

Triandis, H. C. (1989) The self and social behaviour in differing cultural context, *Psychological Review*, 96, 506–520.

Turner, B. S. (1997) The body in Western society: Social theory and its perspectives, in S. Coakley (ed.) *Religion and the body*, pp. 15–41, Cambridge, Cambridge University Press.

Part V

Body-sensitive therapies

This section of the book covers some of the therapeutic techniques that are aimed at body mindfulness, including feminist/cognitive approaches and self-help manuals, and looks at issues related to gender and drug treatment. Chapter 15 deals with feminist therapeutic approaches and the social construction of illness, and aims to make women aware of the link between their own personal experience and the political context in which these experiences were constructed, including identity issues, power issues and gender politics. The increasing popularity of the "do it yourself" healing literature is the subject of Chapter 16, which focuses on the development of a number of self-help programmes, modelled on existing/structured therapeutic approaches, which take the form of written materials, audio/video tapes and computer programs. Chapter 17 describes dialectical behaviour therapy (DBT) in relation to borderline personality disorder (BPD) and highlights its emphasis on issues of wholeness and interconnectedness. The discussion in Chapter 18 is about drug treatment in women with mental illness, including the use of antipsychotic and antidepressant medication. The interface between gender and psychopharmacology is tackled, in terms of therapeutic indications, contraindications and side effects.

Chapter 15

Feminist therapies

Melanie Katzman, Mervat Nasser and Greta Noordenbos

INTRODUCTION

Feminism. Just the mention of this word evokes emotional responses from even the most dispassionate researchers and clinicians. Is there only one definition of a feminist perspective? Can a feminist perspective offer an alternative orientation to therapies to improve body image? Can a feminist approach augment or exist along with cognitive therapy? In the pages that follow we will first address the issue of definition. Then we will discuss the ways in which a feminist lens can be compatibly employed with existing cognitive and body-orientated strategies to improve body image.

Feminism, as defined by the *Webster's New Word Dictionary* (1978) is "the principle that women should have political, economic and social rights equal to those of men, as well as the movement by which women could win those rights".

The women's movement in the late 1960s prompted a reconsideration of roles for women and men in Western society. Consciousness-raising groups provided a forum for women to make the link between their personal experience and the political context in which these experiences were constructed, with its depiction of male traits as the norm and the omission of women from the knowledge base of psychology. There was increasing recognition that psychopathology may reflect "power imbalance" rather than "intrapersonal difficulty". There was also a re-evaluation by many health professionals of women's self-reported experience and a rejection of the historic tendency to attribute blame and responsibility to women for past sexual and physical violence (Worell and Remer, 1992).

These emergent views challenged the traditional structure and had an impact on the field of psychology, which began to expand in new directions. This led to the development of feminist therapists, women's therapy groups, feminist supervision and the evolution of services run by women for women. Feminist therapy embraced a multitude of perspectives that operated within the framework of evolving psychological therapies – interpersonal, psycho-analytic or cognitive-behavioural.

There was also an increasing recognition that the choice to seek care, the dialogue between the professional and the "help seeker" and the "cure" offered are all socially constructed transactions. This constituted the main tenets of feminist therapy, and although the therapy may vary in its application, at the core of it all lies the following assumptions (Worell and Remer, 1992):

1   Women's problems cannot be solved in isolation from gender politics, which often result in women's lower social status and oppression in most societies.
2   Equal status and empowerment are vital not only for women but for all oppressed groups.
3   Values enter all human enterprises: neither science nor clinical cases can be value free.
4   Women's experience and knowledge should be appreciated and studied.
5   Few individual women can achieve parity alone; individual and collective action is necessary to achieve the social and political change that underpins mental health problems.

Feminist therapy thus recognises that many of the problems women bring into therapy stem from feelings of powerlessness and low self-esteem, partly due to idealisation of masculine qualities and the general devaluation of feminine qualities. Feminist therapy helps women explore the inherent contradictions in prescribed social roles, and encourages change rather than adaptation to these roles (Sesan, 1994).

In this chapter, the various approaches to feminist therapy will be discussed under the following subheadings:

1   feminist therapy as empowerment;
2   feminist therapy as a tool for emotional/social connection;
3   feminst therapy as cognitive reconstruction of the body;
4   feminist therapy as body-orientated therapy.

FEMINIST THERAPY AS EMPOWERMENT

Definition

Empowerment – defined as authorising, delegating authority to, enabling or permitting – is often a central goal in feminist treatment. Inherent in this definition is a belief that one has the power or the free will to act on one's own behalf and to make choices. Although it is important to relinquish the idea of a unitary, modernist subject in order to explore women's differences (Hare-Mustin and Marecek, 1988), modernist concepts such as progress, self-improvement and self-determination remain essential to the theory and practice of feminist therapy. Women in therapy are helped to differentiate between cultural causes of their distress and internally imposed restrictions (Worrell and Remer, 1992). Such an analysis minimises feelings of being sick, dysfunctional or wrong, and reduces women's feelings of powerlessness and hopelessness. An empowerment model assumes that power can be reclaimed once lost and that power can be given or taught to someone. It also assumes that power to make choices, to speak for oneself and to determine one's course or direction is a positive attribute.

Empowerment models of therapy draw from several different feminist therapy perspectives (Brown, 1994; Butler, 1985; Gilbert, 1980; Travis, 1988), resulting in approximately four key principles of feminist therapy that tend to unite feminist therapists:

1　consciousness raising: clients are encouraged to explore the role of sexism and oppression and examine contradictions in prescribed sex roles;
2　egalitarian therapy: minimising the power differentials between client and therapist, which are openly examined and explored;
3　recognising women's strengths and minimising demeaning language towards women;
4　engagment with and awareness of social action to change systems which are harmful to women and others.

Put another way, a feminist analysis could be considered a power analysis. It is often too simple to confuse issues of gender with those of power (Katzman and Lee, 1997). Often, what is attributed to a female way of being could also be understood as behaviours resulting from a subordinate social position. In taking a feminist approach, issues of power are made explicit and there is an effort to respect the expertise of all involved in both treatment and training As a result a non-hierarchical approach to therapy assumes that the patient will ultimately be the expert on her own recovery.

For example, under the feminist banner clinicians began to talk about the co-existence of physical and sexual abuse in women presenting with eating problems (for a detailed discussion refer to Fallon et al., 1994). As patients and clinicians found a vocabulary and a space to discuss issues, secrets about abuse in the family as well as the treatment setting were revealed. This has prompted a more critical examination of the potential abuses of power both at home and in therapy. Although the ultimate answer is certainly not to avoid male caregivers, the questions heightened our awareness and nudged us to challenge the safety of our delivery systems.

The issue of culture

Feminist analyses in the area of eating disorders also recognise the importance of culture and cultural variables. By assessing the impact of societal expectations on behaviour, feminist approaches recognise not only the contribution of individual variables to one's social functioning but the influence of culture and society on one's individual psyche (Dolan and Gitzinger, 1994; Nasser, 1997). This is not unique to feminists and, in fact, is where feminists and trans-cultural scholars cross paths in very interesting ways (Katzman and Lee, 1997). Acknowledging social and interpersonal influences enables women to identify the impact both forces have on their choices and their sense of self. It also highlights the importance of a self-reflective stance to our culture of care and cautions against ethnocentric and andocentric views of mental health and health care delivery. Often by questioning the patriarchy we question unnamed assumptions – a level of self-consciousness that can result in growth (Katzman et al., 1994).

A feminist understanding casts eating disorders as the solution and asks, "What is the problem?" (Fallon et al., 1994). In so doing feminist approaches pave the way for theorising that recognises that food disturbances, rather than being a pathological response to sane circumstances, may in fact reflect a reasonable answer to insane conditions. The woman is not viewed in isolation but as a part of a larger system that defines illness and health.

Impact on care

The challenge for the therapist is to share the power the institution of therapy so readily confers. In training there is an effort to value personal experience and to "know what we know" – that is, to respect the textures of personal experience as well as the data that might impact on our provision of care and our attempts at prevention.

In a feminist approach, issues of power are made explicit and there is an effort to respect the expertise of all involved in both treatment and training. Hence, this approach to therapy assumes that the patient will ultimately be the expert on her recovery.

FEMINIST THERAPY AS A TOOL FOR SOCIAL/EMOTIONAL CONNECTION

Definition

Therapists/clinicians such as Steiner-Adair (1991), Fallon et al. (1994) and Kearney-Cooke (1991) have presented an alternative model which recognises women's need for social and emotional interdependence, rather than the heretofore preferred value of "independence" in which psychological maturity is defined as separation and independence. Feminist treatment environments thus enhance opportunities for connection, explore the successful navigation of competition in relationships and develop a sense of self in relation to others (Miller, 1986; Noordenbos, 1991; Sesan 1994).

Impact on care

Within the "connection model" the relationship between therapist and client is actively explored and experimented with. A feminist therapist does not use a hierarchical expert model: instead, a feminist therapist strives to reduce the power differential through psycho-education, narrowing the knowledge gap between client and therapist. This promotes an atmosphere of trust, equality and transparency.

Feminist therapy rejects the notion that the source of psychological distress is solely internal. Psychological problems are viewed within a socio-cultural and political context. Therapy challenges the notion of remaining distanced and detached in therapeutic relationships, questioning the concept of therapeutic neutrality. Interdependence, as opposed to autonomy, is set as a goal, and demands that both the therapist and client engage in a relationship in which there is mutuality and acknowledgment of the individual's sense of self and self-need for nurture, connection and care for others. Therapy thus becomes a collaborative process which includes a two-way dialogue between client and therapist, helping to demystify therapy and the therapy relationship. Such a model allows a client to rely less on the authority of others and more on her own inner authority (Steiner-Adair, 1991).

Many women we treat inhabit two worlds – the personal and the public. In their efforts to be attractive physically and relationally, many basic needs and potentially "ugly" feelings go underground, especially those that might reflect differences with a group they are trying to join. The feminist treatment, as a result, is an attempt to make explicit the unsaid and open it up for review and discussion. The ability to dialogue and connect is valued highly, as is the need to bring out from behind closed doors what we learn behind them (i.e. sexual and physical abuse). In essence, recovery becomes a movement from isolation to connection (Fallon et al., 1994) as women are encouraged to discover the value of emotional nourishment.

FEMINIST THERAPY AS COGNITIVE RECONSTRUCTION OF THE BODY

Cognitive approaches

The aim of cognitive therapy is to change maladaptive cognitions concerning body, weight and self, and to assist in the development of more positive alternative beliefs. There have been a number of extensive reviews on these techniques; the basic tenets are listed here. The first step is to explore thoughts women have about their bodies. Diaries are often employed to track the environments and emotions that may trigger negative thinking and serve as a means of capturing an alternative, healthier self-dialogue, which is the goal of cognitive interventions. The client learns to assess how realistic her thoughts and cognitions are, and then to restructure irrational thoughts and beliefs that will ultimately lead to a change in behaviour. Finally the results of this changed behaviour are evaluated, working towards the goal of developing a less critical and more realistic body image and the attainment of a more positive attitude towards one's physical being.

Based on cognitive behavioural therapy, Cash (1997) developed a self-help book for women with negative body experience with the following eight steps:

1   to understand the psychology of the physical appearance;
2   to become aware of the own personal body experience;
3   to learn to comfort the body;
4   to discuss the suppositions about the body appearance;
5   to change false and irrational thoughts about body experiences;
6   to eliminate dysfunctional thoughts and behaviours;
7   to handle the body in a correct way;
8   to keep a positive body experience and to prevent relapse.

Cognitive approaches might also challenge some of the assumptions regarding perfection and the unreal standards women set for themselves, particularly in the area of eating disorders. Programmes such as those described by Weiss and colleagues (1985, 1986) employ cognitive techniques in a feminist-orientated way for eating disorders in that women are asked to challenge assumptions they have about basic human rights, assertiveness and the ways in which one can be attractive (e.g. through behaviours) other than altering appearance (see also Chapter 6 in this volume).

FEMINIST THERAPY AS BODY-ORIENTATED THERAPY

Body-orientated therapy focuses on the use of body activities to change the body attitude in a positive way and subsequently develop positive experience of the self (Probst, 2002). It revolves around connection between women's bodily sensations and inner emotional experience across all stages of the life cycle (Kearney-Cooke and Isaacs, 2004).

A body validation exercise was developed by Weiss et al. (1985) – a technique in which first the therapist and then each woman (in a group) stands and lists the parts of her body, citing what she likes about it. In this context, a body can be celebrated because it is healthy or one could like her stomach because it feels good when tickled. No one is allowed to recite a negative quality and everyone helps anyone who has difficulty finding something positive. This affirmation of how one's body feels and what it can do is very powerful and the need to have it modelled first by the therapist is critical.

Other body-focused techniques include relaxation, sensory awareness, moving and dance therapy, bio energetic therapy, fantasy guided experiences, role playing, mirroring and video confrontation techniques. In the case of mirroring and video confrontation, the aim is to reduce avoidance and develop a more realistic perception of the body (Rekkers and Schoemaker, 2002). Through the non-verbal experience of the body, the client learns to translate bodily feelings into the verbal language of emotions and sensations (Probst, 2002). These activities have to be used with care and explained properly to the client. Women in therapy need to feel that they are in control of their body and are allowed to stop when emotions become overwhelming.

FEMINIST THERAPY: CRITIQUE AND CONCLUSION

Feminist perspectives on therapy have been criticised on the basis of being mainly "ideological" and not easily translated into clear therapeutic methodologies. In addition, it can be argued that not all psychological issues are caused by power imbalance, male dominance or oppression. Rodin et al. (1984) described women's dislike of their bodies as a "normative discontent" since it is rare for a woman to accept her physical shape unequivocally. Perhaps this is not surprising, given the historical constructions of women as the second gender and the very profitable industry created to reshape women's bodies (inside and out). Feminist approaches to women and their bodies don't stop at an analysis of dietary compliance or desires to reshape one's form, but instead encourage us to help women reclaim and reinhabit their physical being. Cognitive approaches to improved body image may take a feminist orientation or simply focus on irrational beliefs about a woman's self. Often many different therapeutic tools can be combined creatively to assist women in making the necessary changes and, as reviewed in this chapter, these include verbal as well as non-verbal techniques.

In all instances it is critical to maintain a safe and supportive environment in which the woman is in control of modulating her experiences and experimenting with new techniques. What we do as therapists as we deploy our tools says as much to our patients as any words we use. In an age in which it is common to critique one's self and one's body, therapists can serve as powerful models of comfort and as architects of a therapeutic culture that honours the women we treat. To the extent that a feminist approach prompts the exploration of new questions in our field it offers a valuable additional lens through which we can explore the impact of other theories, be they social, biological or genetic.

REFERENCES

Brown, L. S. (1994) *Subversive dialogues*, New York, Basic Books.

Butler, M. (1985) Guidelines for feminist therapy, in L. B. Rosewater and L. E. A. Walker (eds) *Handbook of feminist therapy*, pp. 24–39, New York, Springer.

Cash, T. F. (1997) *The body image work book: An 8 step program for learning to like your looks*, Oakland, New Harbinger Publications.

Dolan, B. and Gitzinger, I. (1994) *Why women? Gender issues and eating disorders*, London, Athlone Press.

Fallon, P., Katzman, M. A. and Wooley, S. (1994) *Feminist perspectives on eating disorders*, New York, Guilford Press.

Gilbert, L. A. (1980) Feminist therapy, in A. M. Brodsky and R. T. Hare-Mustin (eds) *Women and psychotherapy*, pp. 245–265, New York, Guilford Press.

Hare-Mustin, R. T. and Marecek, J. (1988) The meaning of difference: Gender theory, postmodernism and psychology, *American Psychologist*, 43, 455–464.

Katzman, M. A. and Lee, S. (1997) Beyond body image: The integration of feminist and transcultural theories in the understanding of self starvation, *International Journal of Eating Disorders*, 22 (4), 385–394.

Katzman, M. A., Wooley, S. C., Fallon, P. (1994) Eating disorders: A gendered disorder, *Eating Disorders Review*, 5 (6), 1–3.

Kearney-Cooke, A. (1991) The role of the therapist in the treatment of eating disorders: A feminist psychodynamic approach, in C. L. Johnson (ed.) *Psychodynamic treatment*, New York, Guilford Press.

Kearney-Cooke, A. and Isaacs, S. (2004) *Change your mind, change your body*, New York, Atria Books.

Miller, J. B. (1986) *Toward a new psychology of women*, Boston, Beacon Press.

Nasser, M. (1997) *Culture and weight consciousness*, London, Routledge.

Noordenbos, G. (1991) *Eating disorders: Treatment and prevention*, Utrecht, De Tijdstroom.

Probst, M. (2002) Body experience, in W. Vandereycken and G. Noordenbos (eds) *Handbook of eating disorders*, pp. 233–248, Utrecht, De Tijdstroom.

Rekkers, M. and Schoemaker, E. (eds) (2002) *Important bodies, body experience and eating disorders*, Leuven, Acco.

Rodin, J., Silberstein, L. and Striegel-Moore (1984) Women and weight: A normative discontent, in T. B. Sondergger (ed.) *Nebraska Symposium on Motivation*, Vol. 32 of *Psychology and Gender*, 267–307.

Sesan, R. (1994) Feminist inpatient treatment for eating disorders: An oxymoron?, in P. Fallon, M. A. Katzman and S. C. Wooley (eds) *Feminist perspectives on eating disorders*, pp. 251–272, New York, Guilford Press.

Steiner-Adair, C. (1991) New maps of development, new models of therapy: The psychology of women and the treatment of eating disorders, in C. Johnson (ed.) *Psychodynamic treatment of anorexia nervosa and bulimia*, pp. 225–244, New York, Guilford Press.

Travis, C. B. (1988) *Women and health psychology: Mental health issues*, Hillsdale, NJ, Lawrence Erlbaum Associates Inc.

Webster's New Word Dictionary (1978) Massachusetts, G and C Merriam Co.

Weiss, L., Katzman, M. A. and Wolchik, S. A. (1985) *Treating bulimia: A psycho-educational approach*, New York, Pergamon Press. (Translated into German by Verlag Hans Huber, 1989)

Weiss, L., Katzman, M. A. and Wolchik, S. A. (1986) *You can't have your cake and eat it too: A self-help program for controlling bulimia*, California, R and B Publishers. (Translated into Japanese by Seiwa Shoten Col, Ltd., 1991)

Worell, J. and Remer, P. (1992) *Feminist perspectives in therapy: An empowerment model for women*, New York, John Wiley and Sons.

Chapter 16

Self-help and healing narratives

Ulrike Schmidt and Varinia Sánchez-Ortiz

INTRODUCTION

Most major book shops have a section on "self-help" for emotional, physical and behavioural problems and disorders, including books and other materials such as audio or video tapes, produced for the lay public with the aim of giving information and advice. The contents, style and quality of these publications vary hugely, but the many metres of shelf space devoted to them bear witness to the growing popularity of self-help approaches. Likewise, the internet is a rich and growing source of self-help advice and materials (Williams, 2003).

Some self-help books, with particularly catchy titles or topics, top the bestseller lists for prolonged periods. Women are often seen as the prime consumers of self-help resources and this has been caricatured in the book *Bridget Jones' Diary*, where the heroine repeatedly attacks her woes with a new self-help approach, each as hopelessly ineffective as the previous one.

The aim of the present chapter is to review critically the role of self-help interventions in the treatment of common mental disorders in women. We will focus on two broad groups of disorders which are highly prevalent in women, namely depression and anxiety disorders on the one hand and eating disorders on the other, to illustrate how self-help treatments have been used in therapeutic practice. We will start with some definitional and general considerations concerning self-help.

WHAT IS SELF-HELP?

In contrast to the fairly broad lay definitions of self-help, clinicians and researchers use more specific or narrow definitions of self-help (SH, or self-management, self-care, self-instruction or bibliotherapy as it is sometimes called; e.g. see Cuijpers, 1997; Marrs, 1995). Marrs (1995) defined self-help as "the use of written materials or computer programs or the listening/viewing of audio/video tapes for the purpose of gaining understanding or solving problems relevant to a person's developmental or therapeutic needs". Thus, self-help treatment implies a more structured approach than the provision of one-off information (Cuijpers, 1997) or mere support, in that it translates a psychological treatment, based on a clear model, into a programme which people can follow over time (Lewis et al., 2003). Self-help treatments are thus programme-led, contain a longitudinal element and require the participant to follow the advice provided by the self-help material, carry out tasks and then evaluate what has been achieved. SH aims to improve clinical outcome by teaching users relevant skills to overcome and manage their health problem. It can also be defined as the "the delivery of materials that employ a media based format to treatment such as book, computer or video tape. However delivered, self-help materials aim to increase the users' knowledge about a particular problem, and also to equip them with skills to better self-manage their difficulties" (Williams, 2003).

Pure or unguided self-help (PSH) treatments are provided independently of contact with a health care practitioner or supporter, whereas in guided self-help (GSH) sessions with a practitioner/supporter are included (Williams, 2003). Guidance may focus on clarifying material, answering questions, helping the participant to remain on task or modifying the programme to fit the individual's needs. In addition, guidance allows initial assessment, ongoing risk monitoring, progress review and referral for additional or alternative treatments, as required (Gould and Clum, 1993; Wells et al., 1997). If guidance is provided the aim is for the SH material to do some of the work of treatment and thereby reduce the number and/or length of sessions patients require with a therapist. All in all, there is a continuum between pure and guided self-help and brief structured (typically cognitive-behavioural) therapies, which are therapist-led.

WHY USE SELF-HELP?

Many people with common mental health problems are unlikely to seek professional help for their problems and hold self-help strategies in higher esteem than medication or treatments delivered by health professionals (Jorm et al., 1997). Adolescents and young adults in the age group of 16–24 are least likely to seek professional help for a mental health disorder (Oliver et al., 2005). In a large community survey which investigated people's views regarding the effectiveness of interventions for common mental health problems (Jorm et al., 2004), different self-help interventions were thought to be effective by 41–84% of participants whereas only 27% of people thought that therapist-aided cognitive behavioural therapy would be effective. In another survey, one in four potential users of self-help treatment said that they would rather use the internet for help, advice and counselling than see a doctor (Graham et al., 2000). The reasons quoted for this were ease and rapidity of access, lack of stigma and embarrassment associated with self-help and not wanting a mental health record. The vast majority of potential users (91%) wanted to access self-help therapy via a computer.

In addition, there are a number of service- and resource-related reasons for recommending self-help interventions. In the UK, most psychological services have lengthy waiting lists and the demand for specialist therapies by far outstrips resources. Psychological treatment services have been criticised for offering a "one size fits all approach" with a standard length of therapy for all patients, irrespective of the complexity of their problems (Lovell and Richards, 2000). Lovell and Richards (2000) also suggest different levels of treatment intensity in psychological services with self-help interventions being the most basic level.

Thus, a number of patient- and service-related potential advantages of using self-help treatments can be identified (Williams and Whitfield, 2001):

1   They allow evidence-based specialist treatments to be accessed rapidly.
2   They are popular and acceptable to many patients.
3   They can be of low cost.
4   Such treatments respect patient's privacy and avoid the stigma or embarrassment of formal psychotherapy. This is important in view of people's reluctance to seek help for common mental disorders.
5   Self-help treatments allow patients to work in their own time and at their own pace. This is potentially important as people with mental health problems are often anxious and depressed, which may interfere with their ability to focus during a session with a therapist.
6   They empower the patient and promote collaboration.
7   They reinforce and consolidate learning.
8   They allow patients to renew or update treatment as often as they wish, and at no extra cost.

WHAT KINDS OF SELF-HELP?

Almost all self-help approaches to common mental disorders used in therapeutic settings have used a behavioural, cognitive behavioural or problem-solving approach. What these therapies have in common is that even when delivered by a therapist they all place a great deal of emphasis upon putting into practice what has been learned between the therapeutic sessions, through homework. Moreover, these therapies are all based on adult learning models and the therapist role includes that of teacher. Therefore, these therapies have been said to be essentially self-help in nature (Lewis et al., 2003).

Whilst earlier self-help programmes were mainly published as books, stand-alone therapeutic computer packages for common mental health programmes have also existed since the 1970s. Three stages of the development of computerised therapy can be identified (Cavanagh and Shapiro, 2004). These stages parallel trends in the predominant use of particular therapies. Thus, the first generation of therapy computers, most notably Eliza developed at MIT by Weizenbaum in 1966, provided a client-centred simulation of therapist–patient dialogue (for a review see Turkle, 1995). The second generation of therapy computers provided behavioural training, exposure therapy, psycho-education and simple cognitive strategies. We have now reached the third stage in this development and interactive multimedia programmes, typically based on cognitive behavioural models, have been developed for a number of common mental health problems (for a review see Proudfoot, 2004).

Whilst there are clearly "horses for courses" it could be argued that interactive computerised programmes are likely to be more effective than book-based materials for the simple reason that they are interactive, help users pace themselves and give feedback. They are therefore much more like "real therapy", and the only reason that they are dubbed "self-help" is because a health professional is not present (Richards, 2004).

SELF-HELP FOR DEPRESSION AND ANXIETY

Early studies and some recent reviews painted a promising picture of the efficacy of conventional (book-based) PSH and guided self-help (GSH) in the treatment of depression and anxiety (e.g. Den Boer et al., 2004; Gregory et al., 2004). However, other systematic reviews (Bower et al., 2001; Kaltenthaler et al., 2004; Lewis et al., 2003) introduce a considerable note of caution, pointing out that the quality of many studies of self-help is not good. Three well-designed and well-conducted recent studies assessing GSH in patients with depression and anxiety (Mead et al., 2006; Richards et al., 2003; Salkovskis et al., 2005) failed to find any advantage for guided self-help compared to either treatment as usual in primary care (Richards et al., 2003; Salkovskis et al., 2005) or waiting list in people awaiting psychological therapy (Mead et al., 2006). Salkovskis et al. (2005: 331) commented that one of the potential explanations for the lack of any between-group differences in outcome may have been "a consequence of an above-average quality of care being offered to depressed patients by the practices participating in this research". In the study by Mead et al. (2006), there was some evidence that patients in the waiting list control group sought psychological help through alternative sources more commonly than those who received GSH.

Research into computerised CBT (C-CBT) for anxiety and depression has been summarised in a number of systematic and narrative reviews (Kaltenthaler et al., 2002; National Collaborating Centre for Mental Health, 2002; Proudfoot, 2004). These reviews suggest that C-CBT is more effective than treatment as usual, is as effective and acceptable as therapist-aided CBT or bibliotherapy and requires less therapist time than conventional CBT. Moreover, a health-economic analysis suggested that C-CBT was cost effective (McCrone et al., 2004). A meta-analysis of five studies of C-CBT for depression (Cavanagh and Shapiro, 2004) found that C-CBT was better than waiting list. Two recent randomised controlled trials of internet-based self-help for depression also found it to be superior to waiting list (Andersson et al., 2005; Clarke et al., 2005). One of these studies (Clarke et al., 2005) built on an earlier randomised controlled trial of a web-based programme for overcoming depression on the internet (ODIN; Clarke et al., 2002). In the earlier trial no effect for the internet programme across the whole sample was found, probably because most intervention participants accessed the Internet site infrequently. In the second trial (ODIN 2; Clarke et al., 2005) the programme was delivered with regular telephone or postal reminders. With this added feature the intervention was superior to waiting list in terms of reduction in depression symptoms and improvement in mental and physical functioning.

A second finding from the meta-analysis by Cavanagh and Shapiro (2004) was that C-CBT did somewhat less well than therapist CBT, but the numbers included in this comparison were very low.

It is also important to consider that much of the disease burden caused by depression or anxiety in the population results from sub-clinical cases rather than cases with the full clinical disorder (Jorm and Griffiths, 2005). Guided self-help is unlikely to reduce this burden, given the large number of people with these problems and symptoms. Jorm and Griffiths (2005) advocate instead the use of what they call "informal self-help" for early intervention in sub-clinical and threshold cases of depression. They include a much broader range of self-help interventions in their definition than other authors (e.g. over the counter medication, exercise, relaxation training, bright light exposure for winter depression) and point out that the treatments with the most supporting evidence (i.e. those with several supporting randomised trials) were: the over the counter medications Kava and St John's Wort (for generalised anxiety disorder and depression respectively), exercise (for depression and generalised anxiety), relaxation training (for depression and a range of anxiety disorders), self-help books based on CBT (for depression and specific phobias) and exposure to bright light (for winter depression). Thus population-based prevention and early intervention campaigns for early identification of problems and appropriate informal self-help should complement clinically based formal self-help interventions.

SELF-HELP FOR EATING DISORDERS

Eating disorders are common and disabling conditions affecting mainly young women. Typically, these disorders develop in mid to late adolescence and are not self-limiting. Several recent systematic reviews of treatments for eating disorders include the topic of self-help (e.g. Hay et al., 2004; National Collaborating Centre for Mental Health, 2004). A recent Cochrane review (Perkins et al., 2006) focused exclusively on self-help for all eating disorders, including anorexia nervosa (AN), bulimia nervosa (BN), binge eating disorder (BED) and EDNOS (eating disorder not otherwise specified). This review aimed to evaluate the role of self-help and guided self-help treatments in the treatment of all eating disorders irrespective of the age of the sufferer. In all, 15 relevant randomised controlled trials and controlled trials were identified and included. All studies focused on BN, BED, EDNOS or combinations of these. To date no randomised controlled trials have been carried out on AN. All participants were adults. All studies used manual-based self-help with or without guidance. Studies were conducted in widely varying settings, with the majority of studies recruiting at least a proportion of their participants from the community. Compared to waiting list, pure or guided self-help produced greater improvement at the end of treatment on eating disorder symptomatology, psychiatric and mental state symptomatology and levels of interpersonal functioning. However, abstinence rates from bingeing and purging, and mean depression scores, did not differ between groups either at end of treatment or at follow-up. One small study of BED compared CBT guided self-help to a non-specific control treatment and found significantly greater improvements in terms of abstinence from bingeing and eating disorder symptomatology favouring GSH at the end of treatment (Grilo and Masheb, 2005).

Compared to other formal psychological therapies, PSH or GSH did not differ in terms of improvement on eating disorder symptomatology, abstinence from bingeing and purging (assessed separately or combined), level of interpersonal functioning or depression at end of treatment or at follow-up. There were also no differences between groups in terms of treatment dropout. However, the quality of the therapist-aided treatments was not assessed formally in the available studies (Perkins et al., 2006).

Studies comparing PSH with GSH found no differences between treatment groups on a broad range of outcome measures at the end of treatment or at follow-up (Perkins et al., 2006).

The number of studies comparing self-help with medication was too small to allow any conclusions. However, when compared to waiting list or non-specific treatments, self-help treatments for BN, BED and related disorders were effective in reducing eating disorder and some other symptoms, but these effects were not large. Future research should focus on producing large well-conducted studies of self-help treatments for eating disorders, including health-economic evaluations. Studies of different types of self-help (e.g. computerised) are needed, as are studies in different populations (e.g. AN, adolescents with eating disorders) and studies of the usefulness of self-help in particular settings (e.g. primary care or students' health care) (Perkins et al., 2006).

One ongoing controlled study (Fichter et al., 2003) focuses on self-help for AN of the binge-purge type, comparing six weeks of telephone-guided self-help with a CBT manual to waiting list prior to admission to a specialist in-patient programme for AN. Preliminary findings suggest that uptake and acceptance of the intervention are good and that GSH shows somewhat greater improvements in terms of reduction in eating disorder pathology and depression; also, the duration of admission was shorter in the GH group than in the waiting list group.

Several centres are studying computerised (CD-ROM-based) and web-based treatments for eating disorders. Williams et al. (1998) created a cognitive-behavioural CD-ROM-based multimedia SH treatment for BN. The CD-ROM treatment was evaluated in two pilot studies (Bara-Carril et al., 2004; Murray et al., 2006), in a large catchment area-based specialist eating disorder service, in patients with bulimia nervosa and EDNOS patients. In the first of these pilot studies, 60 patients were offered the package without therapist support (Bara-Carril et al., 2004). Patients accessed the treatment programme in the clinic. Patients were encouraged to complete the programme over a period of four to eight weeks. Of the 60 patients offered the intervention, 47 took it up. At follow-up there were significant reductions in bingeing and compensatory behaviours, most clearly in self-induced vomiting. The second study examined whether the addition of therapist support to the CD-ROM intervention would improve treatment uptake, adherence and outcome. It compared outcomes from the first cohort with those from a second cohort who were offered three brief focused support sessions with a therapist (Murray et al., 2006). The two cohorts were compared on treatment uptake, adherence and outcome. Patients in both groups improved significantly. There were no significant differences between the two groups in terms of treatment uptake, adherence or outcome.

A quantitative and qualitative study of the views of people who were offered the CD-ROM package was conducted by Murray and colleagues (2003). At pre-treatment, those who did not take up the package reported more frequent bingeing, but there were no other differences in demographics, eating disorder or comorbid symptoms compared to those who did take up the package. In terms of attitudes to SH, those who took up the treatment were more positive about the usefulness of SH for themselves. There were no differences between groups in the proportion with previous experience of using SH, views on previous SH or views on the usefulness of SH for others. In the qualitative analysis, those who took up the treatment seemed more willing to "give it a go" and understood that "self-help is the first step in treatment", whereas those who did not take up the treatment viewed the CD-ROM as a "cheap replacement" of a human therapist. There were no differences between those who did or did not take up the treatment in terms of confidence in using computers, knowledge about the symptoms of BN or strategies to overcome them.

An internet-based cognitive behavioural self-help guide for the treatment of bulimia (http://www2salut-ed.org/demo/) was developed within a European multicentre study, the SALUT project. Studies evaluating the efficacy and acceptability of the self-help guide were conducted in Switzerland, Sweden, Germany and Spain (Carrard et al., 2006; Fernández-Aranda, 2005; Rouget et al., 2005). Results from the full study are not available yet, but pilot results are encouraging.

An as yet unpublished randomised controlled trial compared traditional group CBT to a CD-ROM-based CBT programme and to a waiting list control among overweight adults with BED (Shapiro et al., 2005). Participants in the group therapy condition received 10 weekly sessions of CBT for BED. Individuals in the CD-ROM condition received the CD and a suggested 10-week schedule for completion, and were instructed to contact the research assistant as needed with technical questions or concerns about their clinical condition. Preliminary results at the end of the treatment phase indicated that the group CBT condition had a significantly higher dropout rate than the CD-ROM or waiting list control. At the end of treatment, compared to waiting list control, both the CD-ROM and group treatment showed somewhat decreased weight, increased daily fruit and vegetable consumption and decreased fast food consumption.

SELF-HELP AND PATIENT SELECTION FACTORS

We still know relatively little about who benefits most from self-help treatments. Many studies have simply chosen people who are keen to have self-help, recruiting them via advertisements or self-help clinics. In a study of clinically referred eating disorder patients, Murray et al. (2003) found that those people who anticipated that self-help methods of treatment would be beneficial for them were more likely to take it up than those people who were less positive about the usefulness of self-help treatments. Whilst this may seem somewhat obvious, it points towards the fact that clinicians must consider that it may be an individual's attitude towards self-help treatments that plays a key role in uptake of, compliance with and outcome from such interventions rather than symptom severity, presence of comorbidity or other illness-related factors. Indeed, a small study by Bell and Newns (2002) investigated whether bulimic patients with comorbid multi-impulsivity can benefit from guided manual-based self-help. Patients with or without multi-impulsive comorbidity significantly improved in symptoms of depression and bulimic behaviours: however, the multi-impulsive group remained moderately to severely depressed and their post-treatment eating disorder symptom scores remained at sub-clinical levels. This suggests that patients with comorbidity may benefit from self-help treatments with guidance, but may need longer or additional treatment to prevent relapse.

SELF-HELP DELIVERY

Very little is known about the optimum method of access to and delivery of self-help treatments for particular disorders. Self-help programmes have been used both as stand-alone treatments and as part of stepped care models of treatment within clinical services (Mains and Scogin, 2003). For conventional (book-based) self-help, guidance from a therapist does seem to improve uptake and outcomes. Likewise, the results of the ODIN 1 and ODIN 2 studies (see section on self-help for anxiety and depression; Clarke et al., 2002, 2005) suggest that it is hard for people to be entirely self-motivated when working with an internet-based self-help programme, and that regular reminders help to improve outcomes.

Although guidelines recommend self-help treatments, a recent large audit of care pathways for eating disorders in primary care found that few primary care practitioners suggested self-help or GSH to patients as a first step in treatment (Currin et al., 2006). One of the problems may be that practitioners are simply unsure which of the many self-help texts and other materials to recommend. In the field of self-help for depression and anxiety, Anderson et al. (2005) reviewed a range of self-help books and materials, using a number of different criteria including readability, clarity of underlying model and evidence base, to help practitioners give informed recommendations to their patients.

The attitudes of therapists to computerised and other forms of self-help have been examined. They commonly expressed a need to know more and receive training before recommending and delivering this kind of treatment. All shared the view that computerised self-help would be somewhat more effective than traditional book-based self-help, but less effective than seeing a therapist, and CBT therapists were found to have the most positive attitudes (Hitchman, 2004; Whitfield and Williams, 2004). These findings suggest that health professionals giving guidance for SH need to be familiar with the intervention they are guiding, or building on in later treatment. This may be stating the obvious, but in our experience of using self-help treatments in a clinical setting over a number of years this is an issue that constantly needs to be borne in mind. Health professionals will also need brief training in the use of SH materials in order to adapt these interventions for particular individuals.

Richardson and Richards (2006), in a thought-provoking article, discussed the need to pay attention to the so-called common factors in psychotherapy that are independent of specific techniques, such as the patient–therapist relationship and therapist empathy, and recommend they are built in to self-help programmes, to give them "personality". For example, this could be achieved through breaking material into manageable chunks and allowing flexibility of use, by including accessible language which shows respect for the client's suffering and by providing interactive negotiation of goals and the ability to review progress. These programmes would also benefit from incorporating case studies and personalising the material. It could be argued that many of the self-help materials available in the public arena do pay a lot of attention to these common therapeutic factors, and aim to give a sense of direction and instil hope.

From what has already been outlined, there are several implications that need to be taken into account in both the research and application of self-help programmes. These have been summarised in a review by Lewis et al. (2003) as follows:

1   There is still a need to investigate the relative effectiveness of pure and guided self-help, in both manual- and technology-based formats, in common mental disorders, compared to therapist-aided treatments and to medication, within large pragmatic trials in primary care and other non-specialist settings.
2   More information is needed about the type of people willing and able to follow and complete a course of SH treatment, and which model suits their needs.
3   Research should also address the question of what the "active" ingredients in SH treatments are, and whether SH based upon models, other than CBT might be effective.
4   Knowledge needs to be obtained about the acceptability of the model/ medium of different self-help programmes, different delivery settings and the extent and nature of the guidance provided.
5   Self-help materials need to be developed in collaboration with patients and their carers to meet their needs in the most appropriate fashion (Perkins and Schmidt, 2005), and fit in with the "expert patient model" recommended by the Department of Health (2001).

SUMMARY AND CONCLUSION

These are exciting times in the self-help field, in terms of the development of both informal and formal self-help strategies for common mental disorders. In the UK, clinical guidelines for the treatment of a wide range of common mental disorders (mild depression, generalised anxiety and panic disorder, eating disorders) have recommended guided self-help treatments. Part of the drive for the widespread adoption of self-help comes from health economic considerations, but another driver for this is that users of health care are becoming much more active and equal participants in health care encounters rather than passive recipients of help from an expert. New technologies such as interactive web-based multimedia programmes are likely to make specialist therapies available to many more people who traditionally would have been unable to access such help, including those who live in remote areas without easy access to specialist clinics and those whose lifestyles involve several places of abode (such as students) or very irregular hours of work (such as shift workers). However, self-help treatments are not a panacea. We need to learn much more about just how to use them, in informal and clinical settings, to achieve the best outcomes.

REFERENCES

Anderson, E., Lewis, G., Araya, R., Elgie, R., Harrison, G., Proudfoot, J., Schmidt, U., Sharp, D., Weightman, A. and Williams, C. (2005) Self-help books for depression: How can practitioners and patients make the right choice?, *British Journal of General Practice*, 55, 387–392.

Andersson, G., Bergström, J., Holländare, F., Carlbring, P., Kaldo, V. and Ekselius, L. (2005) Internet-based self-help for depression: A randomised controlled trial, *British Journal of Psychiatry*, 187, 456–461.

Bara-Carril, N., Williams, J., Pombo-Carril, M. G., Reid, Y., Murray, K., Aubin, S., Harkin, P. J. R. and Treasure, J. (2004) A preliminary investigation into the feasibility and efficacy of a CD-ROM-based cognitive-behavioral self-help intervention for bulimia nervosa, *International Journal of Eating Disorders*, 35, 538–548.

Bell, L. and Newns, K. (2002) What is multi-impulsive bulimia and can multi-impulsive patients benefit from supervised self-help?, *European Eating Disorders Review*, 10, 413–427.

Bower, P., Richards, D. and Lovell, K. (2001) The clinical and cost-effectiveness of self-help treatments for anxiety and depressive disorders in primary care: A systematic review, *British Journal of General Practice*, 51 (471), 838–845.

Carrard, I., Rouget, P., Fernández-Aranda, F., Volkart, A.-C., Damoiseau, M. and Lam, T. (2006) Evaluation and deployment of evidence based patient self-management support program for bulimia nervosa, *International Journal of Medical Informatics*, 75 (1), 101–109.

Cavanagh, K. and Shapiro, D. (2004) Computer treatment for common mental health problems, *Journal of Clinical Psychology*, 60 (3), 239–251.

Clarke, G., Reid, E., Eubanks, D., O'Connor, E., De Bar, L., Kelleher, C., Lynch, F. and Nunley, S. (2002) Overcoming depression on the internet (ODIN): A randomized controlled trial of an internet depression skills intervention program, *Journal of Medical Internet Research*, 4 (3), e14, http://www.jmir.org/2002/3/e14/

Clarke, G., Eubanks, D., Reic, E., Kelleher, C., O'Connor, E., De Bar, L. L.,

Lynch, F., Nunley, S. and Gullion, C. (2005) Overcoming depression on the internet (Odin) (2): A randomized trial of a self-help depression skills program with reminders, *Journal of Medical Internet Research*, 7 (2), e16, http://www.pubmedcentral.nih.gov/articlerender.fcgi?tool=pubmed&pubmedid=15998607

Cuijpers, P. (1997) Bibliotherapy in unipolar depression: A meta-analysis, *Journal of Behavior Therapy and Experimental Psychiatry*, 28 (2), 139–147.

Currin, L. (2006) *Primary care management of eating disorders: From diagnosis to referral*, PhD. thesis, King's College London.

Den Boer, P., Wiersma, D. and Van den Bosch, R. (2004) Why is self-help neglected in the treatment of emotional disorders? A meta-analysis, *Psychological Medicine*, 34 (6), 959–971.

Department of Health (2001) *The expert patient: A new approach towards chronic disease management for the 21st century*, London, Department of Health.

Fernández-Aranda, F. (2005, April) *Internet-based self-help: Guide for treatment of bulimia*, Paper presented at the Academy of Eating Disorders International Conference on Eating Disorders, Montreal.

Fichter, M., Cebulla, M. and Kranzlin, N. (2003) Präestationäre manualisierte Therapie und darauffolgende stationäre Behandlung bei Anorexia nervosa: Eine kontrollierte Studie, *Der Nervenarzt*, 74 (Suppl. 2), 599.

Gould, R. A. and Clum, G. A. (1993) A meta-analysis of self-help treatment approaches, *Clinical Psychology Review*, 13 (2), 169–186.

Graham, C., Franses, A., Kenwright, M. and Marks, I. (2000) Psychotherapy by computer: A postal survey of responders to a teletext article, *Psychiatric Bulletin*, 24 (9), 331–332.

Grilo, C. and Masheb, R. (2005) A randomized controlled comparison of guided self-help cognitive behavioral therapy and behavioral weight loss for binge eating disorder, *Behaviour Research and Therapy*, 43 (11), 1509–1525.

Gregory, R., Canning, S., Lee, T. and Wise, J. (2004) Cognitive bibliotherapy for depression: A meta-analysis, *Professional Psychology: Research and Practice*, 35 (3), 275–280.

Hay, P. J., Bacaltchuk, J. and Stefano, S. (2004) Psychotherapy for bulimia and bingeing, *Cochrane Database of Systematic Reviews*, 3, CD000562.

Hitchman, E. (2004) *Factors which influence the attitudes of eating disorder therapists to computer-based self-help*, Unpublished MSc thesis, University of London.

Jorm, A. F. and Griffiths, K. M. (2005) Population promotion of informal self-help strategies for early intervention against depression and anxiety, *Psychological Medicine*, 35 (1), 1–4.

Jorm, A. F., Korten, A. E., Jacomb, P. A., Rogers, B., Pollit, P., Christensen, H. and Hendersen, S. (1997) Helpfulness of interventions for mental disorders: Beliefs of health professionals compared with the general public, *British Journal of Psychiatry*, 171, 233–237.

Jorm, A. G., Griffiths, K. M., Christensen, H., Korten, A. E., Parslow, R. A. and Rodgers, B. (2004) Actions taken to cope with depression at different levels of severity: A community survey, *Psychological Medicine*, 34 (2), 293–299.

Kaltenthaler, E., Shackley, P., Stevens, K., Beverley, C., Parry, G. and Chilcott, J. (2002) A systematic review and economic evaluation of computer behaviour therapy for depression and anxiety, *Health Technology Assessment*, 6 (22), 1–89.

Kaltenthaler, E., Parry, G. and Beverley, C. (2004) Computerized cognitive behaviour therapy: A systematic review, *Behavioural and Cognitive Psychotherapy*, 32 (1), 31–55.

Lewis, G., Anderson, L., Araya, R., Elgie, R., Harrison, G., Proudfoot, J., Schmidt, U., Sharp, D., Weightman, A. and Williams, C. (2003) *Self-help interventions for mental health problems*, Leeds, National Institute for Mental Health in England.

Lovell, K. and Richards, D. (2000) Multiple access points and levels of entry (MAPLE): Ensuring, choice, accessibility and equity for CBT services, *Behavioural and Cognitive Psychotherapy*, 28 (4), 379–391.

McCrone, P., Knapp, M., Proudfoot, J., Ryden, C., Cavanagh, K., Shapiro, D. A., Ilson, S., Gray, J. A., Goldberg, D., Mann, A., Marks, I., Everitt, B. and Tylee, A. (2004) Cost-effectiveness of computerized cognitive-behavioural therapy for anxiety and depression in primary care: Randomized controlled trial, *British Journal of Psychiatry*, 185 (1), 55–62.

Mains, J. A. and Scogin, F. R. (2003) The effectiveness of self-administered treatments: A practice-friendly review of the research, *Journal of Clinical Psychology*, 59 (2), 237–246.

Marrs, R. (1995) A meta-analysis of bibliotherapy studies, *American Journal of Community Psychology*, 23 (6), 843–870.

Mead, N., Macdonald, W., Bower, P., Lovell, K., Richards, D., Roberts, C. and Bucknall, A. (2006) The clinical effectiveness of guided self-help versus waiting list control in the management of anxiety and depression: A randomized controlled trial, *Psychological Medicine*, 35 (5), 1633–1643.

Murray, K., Pombo-Carril, M. G., Bara-Carril, N., Grover, M., Reid, Y., Langham, C., Birchall, H., Williams, C., Treasure, J. and Schmidt, U. (2003) Factors determining uptake of a CD-ROM based CBT self-help treatment for bulimia: Patient characteristics and subjective appraisals of self-help treatment, *European Eating Disorders Review*, 11 (3), 243–260.

Murray, K., Schmidt, U., Pombo-Carril, M. G., Grover, M., Alenya, J., Treasure, J. and Williams, C. (in press) Does therapies guidance improve uptake, adherence and outcome from a CD-ROM based cognitive-behavioural intervention for the treatment of bulimia nervosa?, *Computers in Human Behaviour*.

National Collaborating Centre for Mental Health (2002) *Guidance on the use of computerised cognitive behavioural therapy for anxiety and depression* (technology appraisal no. 51), London, National Institute of Clinical Excellence, http://www.nice.org.uk

National Collaborating Centre for Mental Health (2004) *Eating disorders: Anorexia nervosa, bulimia nervosa and related eating disorders*, London, National Institute for Clinical Excellence.

Oliver, M. I., Pearson, N., Coe, N. and Gunnell, D. (2005) Help-seeking behaviour in men and women with common mental health problems: Cross-sectional study, *British Journal of Psychiatry*, 186 (4), 297–301.

Perkins, S. and Schmidt, U. (2005) *Self-help for eating disorders*, Oxford, Radcliffe Publishing.

Perkins, S., Murphy, R., Williams, C. and Schmidt, U. (2006) Self-help and guided self-help for eating disorders, *Cochrane Review*, 19 (3), CD004191.

Proudfoot, J. G. (2004) Computer-based treatment for anxiety and depression: Is it feasible? Is it effective?, *Neuroscience and Biobehavioral Reviews*, 28 (3), 353–363.

Richards, D. (2004) Self-help: Empowering service users or aiding cash strapped mental health services?, *Journal of Mental Health*, 13 (2), 117–123.

Richards, A., Barkham, M., Cahill, J., Richards, D., Williams, C. and Heywood, P. (2003) PHASE: A randomised, controlled trial of supervised self-help cognitive behavioural therapy in primary care, *British Journal of General Practice*, 53, 764–770.

Richardson, R. and Richards, D. A. (2006) Self-help: Towards the next generation, *Behavioural and Cognitive Psychotherapy*, 34 (1), 13–23.

Rouget, P., Carrard, I. and Archinard, M. (2005) Self-treatment for bulimia on the internet: First results in Switzerland, *Revue Medicale Suisse*, 2 (5), 359–361.

Salkovskis, P., Rimes, K., Stephenson, D., Sacks, G. and Scott, J. (2005) A randomized controlled trial of the use of self-help materials in addition to standard general practice treatment of depression compared to standard treatment alone, *Psychological Medicine*, 36 (3), 325–333.

SALUT programme, http://www.cordis.lu/itt/itt-en/04-4/prog01.htm (accessed 29 October, 2005).

Shapiro, J. R., Bulik, C. M., Reba, L. and Dymek-Valentine, M. (2005, April) *CD-ROM and web-based CBT treatment for BED and obesity*, Paper presented at the Academy of Eating Disorders International Conference on Eating Disorders, Montreal.

Turkle, S. (1995) *Life on the screen: Identity in the age of the internet*, New York, Simon and Schuster.

Wells, A. M., Garvin, V., Dohm, F. A. and Striegel-Moore, R. H. (1997) Telephone-based guided self-help for binge eating disorder: A feasibility study, *International Journal of Eating Disorders*, 21 (4), 341–346.

Whitfield, G. and Williams, C. (2004) If the evidence is so good why doesn't anyone use them? Current uses of computer-based self-help packages, *Behavioural and Cognitive Psychotherapy*, 32 (1), 57–65.

Williams, C. (2003) New technologies in self-help: Another effective way to get better? (Editorial), *European Eating Disorders Review*, 11 (3), 170–182.

Williams, C. J. and Whitfield, G. (2001) Written and computer-based self-help treatments for depression, *British Medical Bulletin*, 57, 133–144.

Williams, C. J., Aubin, S. D., Cottrell, D. and Harkin, P. J. R. (1998) *Overcoming bulimia: A self-help package*, University of Leeds/Media Innovations, available from http://www.calipso.co.uk

Chapter 17

Dialectical behaviour therapy

A treatment for borderline personality disorder

Bob Palmer and Debbie Whight

INTRODUCTION

The concepts of personality and personality disorder are open to criticism. Nevertheless, both clinicians and researchers need some term to denote those more consistent features of a person's psychology that seem to be characteristic of them over time and that would be predicted to change only rather slowly if at all. The concept of disorder is used when these characteristics are notably maladaptive for the individual. However, the downside may be that having received a diagnosis of personality disorder, a person may tend to be viewed with lowered expectations of change and general pessimism with regard to outcome. The diagnosis may be misused as a term of abuse and as an excuse for neglect or therapeutic failure. Perhaps there is now a little more optimism than before, and a recent National Health Service document has emphasised the potential for change and for successful management and treatment of people with a diagnosis of personality disorder (National Institute for Mental Health in England, 2003). The diagnosis may remain useful as a description but should not be overemphasised as a prediction and certainly not as a reason for therapeutic nihilism.

The most salient personality disorder among women presenting to psychiatric services is so-called borderline personality disorder (BPD). The disorder is typified by emotional dysregulation, unstable relationships and impulsive behaviour, often of a self damaging kind, all of which combine to leave the person feeling unsafe and desperate. Such persons lead unhappy and chaotic lives with much suffering and substantial risk. Too often those who would help them come to feel that their efforts are overwhelmed by this chaos and distress. Clinicians may feel a sense of dread and frustration. One consequence of this reaction may be that the patient is neglected, mismanaged or passed around between services. Such experiences may heighten the patient's sense of worthlessness and self hatred. Women with BPD have often experienced invalidation of their emotional responses, betrayal, rejection and abuse in their earlier lives. There may be a tragic recapitulation of such experiences when they encounter rejection by mental health services, albeit it is often rejection which has been at least in part provoked by their own behaviour. Most clinicans will have encountered situations where a potentially therapeutic relationship has been tested out to the point of destruction by a patient whose needs seem great but whose wariness or anger is greater still. Almost by definition, people – usually women – with BPD are experienced as "difficult" and demanding. However, it may be useful to think that it is our usual treatments and methods of clinical management that are difficult and demanding, and that this is especially so for women with BPD, who usually have good reason for having little trust in themselves or others (refer to Chapters 4 and 12 in this volume).

One of the reasons for some shift away from pessimism with regard to personality disorder in general and BPD in particular has been the emergence of new treatments which show some promise. Notable among these is an approach developed in the 1980s by Marsha Linehan, a clinical psychologist from Seattle. It arose from the difficulties she had experienced whilst working in a suicide prevention and crisis centre. There she saw many women attending with a diagnosis of borderline personality disorder who seemed to be experiencing unrelenting crises and who were not responding well to usual treatments. Linehan used her background in behaviour therapy and her experience in suicide prevention along with her training as a student of Zen Buddhism to develop a new approach which she called dialectical behaviour therapy (DBT). Linehan described this new treatment in a book and an accompanying skills training manual (Linehan, 1993a, 1993b). Subsequently, she tested its efficacy in two randomised controlled clinical trials. The first compared DBT against treatment as usual in women with BPD and a history of repeated self harming behaviour (Linehan et al., 1991). The second trial studied the treatment of women with BPD and comorbid substance abuse (Linehan et al., 1999). Both trials had broadly positive results. The new treatment could claim to be evidence based at a time when this could be said of no other psychological treament for BPD. Consequently, the practice of DBT grew quickly, first in the USA and then in Europe and elsewhere.

In this chapter we will describe DBT, its component parts, its structure and its stages, together with the theory that informs it.

DBT: CONCEPTUAL FRAMEWORK

DBT is essentially a pragmatic treatment. Nevertheless, it is broadly underpinned by what is called a biosocial theory of personality development. The basic premise is that the individual with BPD has a biological vulnerability to emotional dysregulation that has interacted with invalidating environments, resulting in a self perpetuating cycle of self invalidation and an inability to communicate needs effectively. The individual with a predisposition to emotional vulnerability experiences heightened sensitivity to emotional stimuli with an intense, prolonged reaction and a slow return to baseline. Such an individual has a low threshold for emotional reactivity, and tends to respond in ways which may appear to others as out of proportion to the stimulus. This does not always have to be a negative attribute. Indeed, such an individual may have a great capacity for joy or the ability to fall in love at the drop of a hat. However, these reactions are often misunderstood by those around the individual, frequently provoking invalidating and negative responses. Thus, it is proposed that individuals who go on to develop BPD experience the recurrent failure of others to validate their emotions, leading to the instability and emotional dysregulation that characterises the disorder. Consequently self invalidation arises through self mistrust in emotional experiences combined with self hatred. Thus, it is postulated that the coming together of a particular biological make-up and particular life experiences leads to the disorder.

Much of the basic thinking about DBT, however, comes from the cognitive-behavioural tradition. DBT espouses the scientific ethos. There is an emphasis on the need for open and explicit collaboration between clinician and patient, and there is substantial use of such techniques as self monitoring. However, as the name suggests, DBT also makes use of dialectical thinking. Dialectics refers to a worldview within which truth is seen as an evolving product of the opposition of different views and where "both/and" tends to be preferred to "either/or". Its relevance arises from clinical observation of the shifting and non-linear character of human emotion and experience in general, and that of the borderline patient in particular. A prime example of a dialectical stance is the emphasis on the importance of both acceptance and change. The therapist validates the patient and how she is feeling, accepting that her behaviour represents her best effort to manage life as it is, whilst at the same time advocating change in this behaviour as the only way to a life worth living. Characteristically, DBT talks of this complexity in simple, even folksy terms by suggesting that "people are, at any given point in time, doing the best they can" but that they need to do better (Linehan, 1993a: 106).

Dialectical thinking emphasises the wholeness and interconnectedness of the world. This is also true of another element of DBT, which is its use of ideas and techniques drawn from Zen Buddhism. The key concept is that of mindfulness. The person with BPD is seen as having difficulty in being at all detached from her experience and as being frequently overwhelmed by it. Developing the capacity for mindfulness and living in the moment increases the potential for feeling appropriately in charge of the self. Paradoxically, greater mastery is achieved through an increased ability to be detached. Zen is full of paradox and again there is something paradoxical in the idea that acceptance – for instance of unchangeable traumatic events in the past – may be necessary for change to be possible. The interaction between clinician and patient in DBT is sometimes compared to a dance to rapidly changing music in which each reacts to the other and the changing circumstance. The "right" step can be judged only in the context of the overall dance. But it is important to keep on the move. Humour and irreverence are invoked to this end. These too are characteristic of Zen.

In addition to these main ideas, DBT is characterised by a pragmatic – "whatever works" – attitude together with a tendency to use commonplace language and aphorisms. The treatment aims to be transparent and the principles are made explicit. The patient and the therapist should aim for an open working partnership. The overall stance of the therapist in DBT is that of being a "consultant to the patient". Although the posture is not rigid, the DBT therapist tends to work with and advise the patient but does not take over except in extreme circumstances.

DBT: COMPONENTS OF THE THERAPY

DBT is usually an outpatient treatment although it has been adapted for inpatient or day patient use (Bohus et al., 2000). Typically it runs for one year although the programme may be repeated. It has four main elements. Three of these are therapeutic activities which involve the patient: weekly sessions with an individual therapist, weekly skills training in a group and telephone contact for skills coaching between sessions. DBT is a team treatment: the fourth element is a weekly consultation group in which the team meets together to discuss the patients and the programme.

The consultation group

An important focus of the consultation group is on maintaining dialectical thinking and preventing therapist burnout, through the application to other team members of DBT techniques and principles.

The patient and therapist have to make an explicit commitment to therapy, which often has to be delicately obtained in the early stages of treatment. In fact, commitment to therapy is not uncommonly revisited many times during treatment, sometimes over and over again. Emphasis is given to the importance of the therapist/patient relationship, which becomes a powerful lever to facilitate change. Arguably, one of the strengths of DBT is the clear supportive framework that it supplies for patients and clinicians alike.

Individual therapy

Typically the patient and therapist meet once each week for around an hour. The patient fills in a diary card for the preceding week and this may be used as an initial focus of discussion. Attention is paid to topics according to a hierarchy: life threatening behaviours come top, followed by therapy inter-fering behaviours. Quality of life impairing behaviours and other issues are dealt with only if these other two topics are satisfactory. In practice, the style of the sessions may vary between therapists. However, there is an overall aim of validating the experience of the patient and encouraging her to become more skilful in the management of her feelings, her behaviours and her relationships with others. The patient is encouraged to put into practice what she is learning in the skills training group. Detailed chain analysis may be used to explore the antecedents and consequences of troublesome feelings or actions.

Skills training

The patient is taught skills in a weekly group which typically lasts for two hours or so. The style of the group is didactic. The room may be set out as a classroom, with the skills trainers – usually two – facing the patients. The training is organised around a manual that contains handouts that may be copied freely for this purpose (Linehan, 1993b). There are four modules: emotional regulation, distress tolerance, interpersonal effectiveness and mindfulness. Each module takes several weeks to teach. Often, the mind-fulness module is repeated in brief form between each of the other modules. Typically, each meeting of the group begins and ends with a mindfulness exercise. Process issues or evident emotion are dealt with only if they threaten the running of the group. Sometimes a skills trainer may also be the therapist of one or more of the patients, but this dual relationship is not dealt with in the group.

Telephone contact

Patients receiving full DBT may contact their individual therapist between sessions by telephone. The hours during which such contact is available are agreed between the therapist and the patient. What the therapist can manage is an explicit determinant of the arrangement and is usually the limiting factor. Telephone contact may occasionally be planned but is more usually in response to crises. The aim is to provide an alternative to self harm and the patient is banned from telephoning for 24 hours after such an act. The calls are typically quite brief and used to coach the patients in the use of skills to survive and weather their emotional storms.

DBT: STAGES OF THE THERAPY

DBT is divided into defined stages. The stage for which it is mainly used is Stage 1, which has as its targets the reduction or indeed the abolition of self harming behaviours and an increase in skill at managing emotion and so on. It is for behaviourally chaotic patients that DBT seems to have something special to offer. Indeed, there is rather little research illuminating the later stages of treatment. However, the further stages of DBT involve the treatment of the effects of trauma (Stage 2), the improvement of self respect and the achievement of individual goals (Stage 3), and there is even a further stage that has as its aim an increase in the person's capacity for joy. There is almost nothing written about this last stage.

Pre-treatment

Even before DBT "proper" starts, there is crucial work to be done. This involves helping the patient to commit herself to treatment. Commitment to treatment is an important and integral part of DBT. The focus of pre-treatment is a mutual and informed orientation to the treatment, with a clear understanding of the expectations of both therapist and patient. The patient identifies the changes she wants to make both in her self and in her life. The role of the therapist is to be grounded in reality, to address any unreasonable or dysfunctional beliefs the patient may have about therapy that could interfere with the process of treatment or contribute to premature termination. Characteristically, patients need to agree that they are trying to stay alive at least for the duration of the treatment. In seeking to engage the patient the therapist may well use a variety of techniques well known to people working in sales. Thus the therapist may exploit any small move toward engagement ("foot in the door") as well as using the more paradoxical technique of playing up the difficulties inherent in the treatment ("door in the face").

Such pre-treatment may well take time – it could be weeks – but work done at this pre-treatment stage is rarely wasted. The value of pre-treatment in reducing dropout rates from therapy has been highlighted by several treatment studies (Parloff et al., 1978). By its nature DBT is not a light undertaking and involves huge commitments of time, effort and availability. The therapist must ensure that the patient is fully informed about DBT. Both parties must be in agreement in feeling they can work together.

Usually a contract is made to work at DBT for a set length of time – often a year. However, the contract may lapse if the patient misses more than three sessions of one kind in a row. On the other hand the contract may be extended if the DBT seems to be helpful. Renewal of a treatment contract is contingent on the patient, with help from the therapist, achieving her targets. This is in contrast to many other approachess, where treatment tends to continue if the patient is not making progress towards "getting better". This concept is often difficult for the patient to grasp as it can dramatically alter the balance of perceived power in the therapeutic relationship.

Stage 1

The first stage of treatment (Stage 1) involves a structured hierarchy of targets, centring on behavioural change and acquisition of new skills. Target behaviours are ranked and addressed in order both within each session and in the treatment as a whole. The ordering is as follows: life threatening behaviours, then therapy interfering behaviours, then major quality of life interfering behaviours.

Learning new skills is an essential part of the therapy. In general skills are taught in the skills training group and mobilised by the patient with help from her individual therapist. This intense emphasis on skills acquisition is a characteristic of this stage of treatment that is not repeated in the later stages.

Only when the hierarchy of targets defined in the first stage has been achieved can the patient progress to the next stage – reducing post-traumatic stress. The thinking behind this is that the patient needs to have the skills to be able to cope with exposure to trauma without resorting to suicidal or life threatening behaviours. This state is often described as "quiet desperation" and is seen as progress. This can be very difficult and demanding for the patient and a frequent complaint during Stage 1 is that she doesn't feel better and can't manage life as it is without life threatening behaviours as a coping mechanism when she feels so bad. Thus the focus in DBT is not only on developing skills for life, but also on developing support structures and networks outside therapy.

Stage 2

The second stage of therapy (Stage 2) requires exposure to trauma-related cues so that the stress responses can be modified. This may necessitate therapy starting, stopping and restarting whilst the patient learns to adapt her responses and put into place learned coping strategies. Again the time-frame for this stage is negotiated and breaks in therapy are not uncommon (Linehan, 1993a).

Stage 3

The next stage of therapy (Stage 3) addresses increasing self-respect and achieving individual goals. This overlaps with the previous stages of treatment, in that it is the end towards which the patient is working. The target in this stage is ultimately to achieve independence of the therapist, by the patient learning to validate her own emotions, opinions and actions. Self respect and self reliance are skills the patient must develop to achieve this, which means starting to move away from dependence on the therapist.

Again the timescales here are flexible and are responsive to the patient's needs and life situation. It may be that the patient experiences a crisis or exposure to trauma that results in a temporary setback. The therapist reacts to these accordingly. If suicidal behaviour re-occurs, then this is targeted as per Stage 1 before returning to and renegotiating Stage 3 targets. These targets are generally generated by the patient in response to her individual needs.

COMMENTS AND CONCLUSIONS

DBT is a demanding treatment for both the patient and the therapist. However, for both it can provide a conceptual and practical frame within which therapeutic work may be accomplished. From the perspective of the service planner or manager, DBT is an expensive treatment. However, it does have some evidence of efficacy and thus it may be thought of as being likely to give better value for money than "treatment as usual". Such treatment too often involves the expenditure of substantial resources to little apparent effect. Direct costs for the service may include hospital admission for containment, the costs of dealing with self harm, referral on to other services and frequent but apparently unproductive outpatient contact. Furthermore, over and above such direct costs, there is a likelihood of substantial non-health service costs such as state benefits, time off work, effects upon friends and family and so on. Once they become involved with services, people with BPD tend to become "expensive" patients, however they are managed. So although DBT is an expensive treatment, it may be justified even on economic grounds if it is effective.

At present the evidence for effectiveness – that is the benefits of DBT when it is applied in everyday practice rather than in the research trials that have demonstrated efficacy – is limited and mainly anecdotal. Nevertheless, a mighty bandwagon has rolled and DBT has been enthusiastically embraced in the USA and more recently in Europe and elsewhere. It has been adopted and adapted for use with different client groups and in different settings (e.g. Palmer et al., 2002). Perhaps whatever the outcome of further research into its specific efficacy and effectiveness, the enthusiasm that it often seems to engender in patients and professionals alike is valuable. The person with BPD may benefit from the more positive and consistent attitude of professionals that DBT seems able to promote and sustain. Indeed, DBT is a complex treatment and there have been no adequate dismantling studies that could demonstrate which of its many elements are the most important. However, it is not impossible that the effects of DBT on the attitudes of the clinicians may be where much of its potency lies.

In an ideal world, "DBT" attitudes – acceptance, validation, openness and so on – would be widespread among mental health professionals and would be sustainable even in the face of the apparently unreasonable demands of the BPD sufferer in crisis. In an even better world they would be widespread in the population in general and there would be less stigma, less panic and less intolerance attached to the display of high emotion. Perhaps then the "career" of those on the way to developing BPD might be diverted onto more solid ground at an early stage. In principle, improvements in both informal support and early professional intervention for those children and young people who have experienced abuse or trauma might lessen the chance of the development of BPD. In practice, however, there is little evidence to support such optimism. Good practice and sensitivity should be valued as positive in themselves and should not be oversold as primary prevention of later problems such as BPD. It is likely that direct interventions for the bad aspects of BPD will remain in the domains of secondary prevention – early intervention – and tertiary prevention – amelioration of the effects and risks associated with the diagnosis. There, until better options are devised, DBT has an established place as a humane and supportive programme that may well help professionals to help sufferers to be more able to help themselves. And that is valuable.

REFERENCES

Bohus, M., Haaf, B., Stiglmayr, C., Pohl, U., Bohme, R. and Linehan, M. (2000) Evaluation of inpatient dialectical-behavioral therapy for borderline personality disorder: A prospective study, *Behaviour Research and Therapy*, 38, 875–887.

Linehan, M. M. (1993a) *Cognitive-behavioral treatment of borderline personality disorder*, New York, Guilford Press.

Linehan, M. M. (1993b) *Skills training manual for treating borderline personality disorder*, New York, Guilford Press.

Linehan, M. M., Armstrong, H. E., Suarez, A., Allman, D. and Heard, H. L. (1991) Cognitive-behavioral treatment of chronically parasuicidal borderline patients, *Archives of General Psychiatry*, 48, 1060–1064.

Linehan, M. M., Schmidt, H., Craft, J. C., Kanter, J. and Comtois, K. A. (1999) Dialectical behavior therapy for patients with borderline personality disorder and drug-dependence, *American Journal on Addictions*, 8, 279–292.

National Institute for Mental Health in England (2003) *Personality disorder: No longer a diagnosis of exclusion*, Leeds, NIMHE.

Palmer, R. L., Birchall, H., Dahmani, S., Gatward, N., McGrain, L. and Parker, A. (2002) Dialectical behaviour therapy (DBT) programme for people with eating disorder and borderline personality disorder: Description and outcome, *International Journal of Eating Disorders*, 33, 281–286.

Parloff, M. B., Waskow, I. E. and Wolfe, B. E. (1978) Research on therapist variables in relation to process and outcome, in S. L. Garfield and A. E. Bergin (eds) *Handbook of psychotherapy and behaviour change: An empirical analysis* (2nd edn), pp. 233–282, New York, Wiley.

Chapter 18

Gender and psychopharmacology

Ruth I. Ohlsen and Lyn S. Pilowsky

INTRODUCTION

That women should be treated differently to men in terms of pharmacological treatment has been recognised for some time, and for obvious reasons – women have different body composition, different rates of hormone circulation and hormonal cycles and also, in the majority of instances, will experience life events that are particular only to them, such as pregnancy, childbirth and breast feeding. Women generally also shoulder the main responsibilities involved in child care. However, research into gender-specific pharmacological treatment has not been extensively undertaken until recently, and our knowledge of how women may respond to certain treatments and dosages at different stages of their biological "career" still remains something of a mystery. The tragedies resulting from the drugs thalidomide and stilboesterol in the 1960s played a large part in the widespread reluctance to involve women of childbearing age in clinical drug trials.

Understandably, clinical and legal implications have until very recently – in fact until the advent of atypical antipsychotic medication with its lack of psychosexual and reproductive side effects – stood in the way of allowing women to become involved in medical research. However, the situation has changed, and the US Food and Drug Administration (FDA) now requires all sponsors of drug trials to include gender-specific information and outcomes, as gender differences in response to, bioavailability of and metabolism of many drugs have become apparent and are now recognised as important paradigms affecting decisions regarding prescription and dosage of a variety of medications.

Women with mental illness are exposed to a wide range of pharmacotherapy. Gender specificity needs to be taken into account when prescribing psychoactive medication for women. Although some studies have suggested otherwise (Botts et al., 2004), it is now generally accepted that women in general require lower doses of antipsychotic medication to achieve clinical efficacy (Leung and Chue, 2000; Seeman, 2004). This is partially accounted for by the fact that women generally weigh less than men, but even when body weight is controlled for, women seem to require less antipsychotic medication mg for kg, at least up until menopause. After menopause, the differential decreases significantly, probably due to the neuropsychoprotective role of oestrogen (Maric et al., 2005; Salokangas, 2004).

Cigarette smoking may be another factor (Goff et al., 1992). Male patients are more likely to smoke than female patients, and smokers are prescribed significantly higher doses of antipsychotic medication. Nicotine is a dopamine agonist, and as the principle of antipsychotic efficacy is a degree of dopamine antagonism, cigarette smoking appears to an extent, to "neutralise" the effects of dopamine blockers. However, male smokers tend to have an earlier onset of psychosis than non-smokers, so perhaps they are less well than the non-smokers, and require higher doses of medication for this reason, independent of smoking status.

This chapter will deal with gender differences in pharmacodynamics and pharmacokinetics and focus on specific aspects involved in the treatment of women with mental health problems, including issues such as menstruation, pregnancy, childbirth and lactation.

GENDER AND PHARMACOKINETIC DIFFERENCES

Women and men have different body composition, with women tending to have a higher percentage of body fat than men (Kuk et al., 2005), and men a higher muscle:fat ratio (Marshall et al., 2000). Thus, one might assume that there are gender differences in the absorption rate, clearance rate and bioavailability of some drugs. However, gender differences in body composition and fat distribution become significantly attenuated post-menopause (Kuk et al., 2005), so that dosing regimes may become more similar for men and post-menopausal women.

Psychotic and mood-related symptoms vary over the course of a female menstrual cycle, and symptom reduction is positively correlated with higher oestrogen levels. Oestrogen has been described as "a putative endogenous neuroleptic" (Hallonquist et al., 1993). It has been suggested that women should commence treatment with lower doses of antipsychotic medication to prevent interference with the neuroprotective effects of oestrogen (Hallonquist et al., 1993). Clozapine levels are significantly higher in women than men, irrespective of dose or body weight (Lane et al., 1999), and although in practice there appears to be little difference of any clinical significance in the majority of drugs so far tested (Aichhorn et al., 2005 (risperidone); Beierle et al., 1999), Miller (2001) found that women do experience more adverse effects of therapeutic drugs than men. This may be due in part to smaller body weight and differences in body composition but may also be a result of hormonal changes – for example, women are more likely to suffer from Torsades-de-Pointes syndrome as a result of lengthened QT interval brought about by some medications, including antipsychotic medications such as thioridazine, droperidol (both withdrawn in the UK because of this adverse event), quetiapine and chlorpromazine. Two-thirds of drug-induced Torsades-de-Pointes cases occur in women (Drici and Clement, 2001). Clinical practice implications of this adverse effect should include regular electrocardiograms for women taking any antipsychotic drug with a known propensity to lengthen the QT interval.

Women are thought to be at higher risk of developing tardive dyskinesia than men, and it is thought that when it occurs, it is more severe in women (Yassa and Jeste, 1992). Despite this, Mitrany and Fehr (2001) found that women were more likely to be prescribed first generation antipsychotics than men, increasing their risk further. Women therefore should be prescribed second generation antipsychotics with a low propensity for dopamine blockade wherever possible, and monitored closely for signs of extrapyramidal side effects (EPS). Elderly women are particularly vulnerable, so should be prescribed the lowest dose necessary to achieve clinical efficacy.

Drugs that block dopamine receptors – including conventional neuroleptics, risperidone and amisulpride – may cause hypersecretion of the hormone prolactin. Hyperprolactinaemia is associated with various physical manifestations such as amenorrhoea, galactorrhoea, sexual dysfunction, hypogonadism, infertility and osteopenia, which increases the risk of fractures (Meaney and O'Keane, 2003). Women appear to be particularly vulnerable to this adverse event when treated, even at low doses of risperidone and amisulpride (Kopecek et al., 2004). In view of this, the following considerations need to be borne in mind:

1   Serum prolactin levels ought to be measured at baseline and regularly when women are receiving antipsychotic medication.
2   Where possible, they should be prescribed prolactin-sparing antipsychotics, such as quetiapine, aripiprazole and olanzapine, in preference to drugs that bring about increased prolactin secretion, such as conventional neuroleptics, risperidone and amisulpride.
3   Women experiencing drug-induced amenorrhoea for a year or more should be offered regular bone density scans as they may be particularly susceptible to osteopenia.

Many other psychotropic agents cause sexual side effects in women, although they may not affect prolactin secretion. These sexual side effects are summarised in Table 18.1.

Antipsychotic-induced weight gain is troublesome, both in terms of the associated physical co-morbidity and the negative impact on psychological well-being and quality of life (Allison et al., 2003). This may result in non-

Table 18.1 Sexual side effects (partially adapted from
Jensvold et al., 1996)

Drug	Lowered libido	Orgasmic dysfunction
Amitryptiline	Yes	Yes
Imipramine	Yes	Yes
Desipramine	Yes	Yes
Clomipramine	Yes	Yes
Phenelzine	Yes	Yes
Fluoxetine	Yes	Yes
Paroxetine	No	Yes
Venlafaxine	No	Yes
Lithium	Yes	No
Sodium valproate	No	No
Semisodium valproate	No	No
Haloperidol	Yes	Yes
Risperidone	No	Yes
Chlorpromazine	Yes	Yes
Clozapine	No	No
Olanzapine	No	No
Quetiapine	No	No
Aripiprazole	No	No

adherence to medication and consequent relapse of mental illness (Weiden et al., 2004). Differential liabilities of antipsychotic medications for weight gain are now well documented (Allison et al., 1999; Goudie et al., 2005), and when prescribing antipsychotic medication for women, clinicians need to take into account not only clinical efficacy but also the manner in which side effects such as weight gain may impair quality of life and impact on physical health. This is becoming a more pressing issue since antipsychotic medication is now prescribed for bipolar affective disorder as well as schizophrenia, and patients with bipolar affective disorder are at least as badly affected by weight gain as women with schizophrenia. Additionally, many women with bipolar disorder will also be prescribed mood stabilisers such as lithium or valproate, both of which are known to cause weight gain, even without the addition of an antipsychotic agent. Women treated with lithium are significantly more vulnerable to weight gain than men (Henry, 2002), and more likely to develop hypothyroidism, which may exacerbate weight gain. Weight gain may lower self-esteem, and increase feelings of worthlessness and failure in an already vulnerable group (Haddad, 2005).

Women on psychoactive medication may be co-prescribed other drugs for physical conditions. Women seem to suffer more co-morbidity such as mood disturbance, allergies, anxiety disorders, sleep disorders and eating disorders, so are more likely to be prescribed drugs for such conditions (Seeman, 2004). These may interact – exacerbating side effects, causing metabolic abnormalities, increasing or decreasing plasma levels or clearance or rendering part of the medication regime less effective. For example, carbamazepine, oxcarbamazepine and topiramate increase the clearance rate of the oral contraceptive pill (OCP); thus women using carbamazepine should use higher doses of OCP or alternative forms of contraception (Curtis, 2005). Also, interactions between OCPs and benzodiazepines have been reported, with evidence of decreased benzodiazepine clearance during the hormone-free week of the menstrual cycle, exacerbating side effects and causing benzodiazepine toxicity.

GENDER, PHARMACOTHERAPY AND SCHIZOPHRENIA

There is a slightly higher incidence of schizophrenia in men than in women (Aleman et al., 2003). Women have a later mean onset of schizophrenia – generally by four to six years – and, largely because of this, tend to have a better prognosis and outcome, because personality integration is more developed, relationships more established and educational and/or vocational skills already in place. Premorbid global and social functioning in women diagnosed with schizophrenia is higher than in men. Women with schizophrenia also experience different symptomatology to men, exhibiting more affective symptoms, fewer negative features and fewer cognitive deficits than men (Leung and Chue, 2000).

However, schizophrenia is disabling to both sexes, and women with schizophrenia often become socially marginalised and isolated, despite their generally better prognosis, and become vulnerable in terms of financial troubles and obtaining support in areas such as housing and child care. Thus, prescribing treatment regimes that are effective, well tolerated and facilitate adherence is of vital importance.

Women are more sensitive to the adverse effects of antipsychotic medication (Miller, 2001), especially in the early stages of psychosis (Ohlsen et al., 2004). Engaging women at an early stage through a collaborative and compassionate approach to treatment is important in ensuring their continuing access to psychiatric services. Women who have a later onset of schizophrenia are more vulnerable to extrapyramidal side effects (EPS) than men, and become even more so after the menopause. This is probably due to the reduced levels of oestrogen; oestrogen supplementation has been shown to alleviate EPS (Lindamer et al., 2001).

In terms of response to medications, Goldstein et al. (2002) found that pre-menopausal women responded better than men to olanzapine and haloperidol, apart from women experiencing a first episode of psychosis: this group responded more poorly than men to haloperidol. Conversely, Ascher-Svanum and colleagues (2005) found that gender was not predictive of response to olanzapine or haloperidol, but that antipsychotic-induced weight gain was a better predictor of good response. However, as adherence to medication was not measured in this trial, it may be simply that patients who responded poorly and did not gain weight were not taking their medication in the first place.

It appears therefore that gender in general is not predictive of response to antipsychotic medication, consistent with the overall lack of predictors of response to these medications.

GENDER, PSYCHOPHARMACOLOGY AND AFFECTIVE DISORDER

Depression is far more common in women than in men (Hildebrandt et al., 2003), and two-thirds of pharmacotherapy for depression is indeed prescribed for women (Jensvold et al., 1996). Women may suffer depression as a consequence of domestic violence (Stein and Kennedy, 2001), or as a result of poor physical health. Women are more likely to attend primary care physicians than psychiatrists for depression (Rhodes et al., 2006), possibly because men often delay going for help, and as a result are more severely ill when they present, necessitating specialist intervention.

As most women with depressive symptoms present to and receive treatment from primary care physicians who may not be experienced in differential diagnosis of mood spectrum disorders, diagnostic instruments such as the Mood Disorder Questionnaire, which are valuable tools in both screening and informing management by differentiating between unipolar depression and bipolar disorder (Hirschfeld et al., 2000), should perhaps be made more available to primary care practitioners. There is a need for the development of standardised guidelines on initiating antidepressant or mood stabilising medication for female patients.

When prescribing antidepressant medication, the issue of gender requires specific consideration. Trials of antidepressant dosing in men and women showed that although women achieve greater plasma concentrations of some tricyclic antidepressants, there appears to be no relationship between dosing, side effects, and therapeutic outcome (Hildebrandt et al., 2003).

Other considerations include the patient's lifestyle, symptom profile and side effects. Features of anxiety may be exacerbated by some antidepressants such as the selective serotonin reuptake inhibitors (SSRIs); however, other types of antidepressant such as the tricyclics may cause sedation, which may be troublesome for women if they have child care responsibilities, or need to drive. Other side effects such as constipation, headache, nausea and sexual dysfunction may be troublesome enough to affect the level of compliance (Table 18.1).

Psychotherapeutic interventions such as cognitive behavioural therapy (CBT) have been shown to be useful in alleviating depressive symptoms, either as standalone treatment or as an adjunct to antidepressant pharma-cotherapy (Mohr et al., 2005; Oei and Yeoh, 1999).

Women appear to be more vulnerable to antidepressant-induced mania than men. This highlights the importance of investigating the possibility of bipolar disorder in women who present with depression. Women may ignore or fail to report hypomanic symptoms, be diagnosed as having unipolar depression and thus treated with antidepressant medication, which may in some cases induce mania.

Bipolar affective disorder occurs in both men and women, with an equal prevalence of bipolar I disorder (periods of mania, usually requiring hospitalisation, alternating with episodes of depression) among women and men, but more women than men suffer from bipolar II disorder (periods of hypomania, not usually requiring hospitalisation, alternating with periods of depression).

The onset of treatment for women diagnosed with bipolar II is sig-nificantly later than that for men (Baldessarini et al., 1999). This may be due to social factors such as the belief that women are more inherently "unstable", which is both a social construct and a biological concept, given that women tend to suffer more mood swings than men due to the fluc-tuating levels of oestrogen experienced by women during the menstrual cycle. Thus, mood swings that might clinically "qualify" women for a diagnosis of bipolar II disease may go unrecognised for long periods of time and be attributed to "neuroticism" or "instability", delaying the initiation of appropriate mood stabilising medication for many years.

Hypomanic characteristics, such as euphoric mood, are also likely to be ego-syntonic, and to go unnoticed; it is usually dysthymic and depressive symptoms that trigger treatment-seeking behaviour.

Women in the manic phase of bipolar disorder are vulnerable in many ways. They may become hypersexual, and practice unsafe sex or have indiscriminate sex with strangers or people they otherwise would not if well. This may wreak havoc within previously established relationships, and in some cases may result in divorce and loss of or reduced access to children. Overspending during the manic phase may result in debts and financial hardship, making it difficult to pay bills and rent, or buy necessities such as food, which may result in the exchange of sex for money. Mood variation during the menstrual cycle due to changing levels of oestrogen and other sex hormones may be very distressing for women suffering from bipolar I and bipolar II, necessitating careful dosing of mood stabilisers.

Women with bipolar I disorder respond as well as men to treatment with lithium (Viguera et al., 2000), but are more vulnerable to adverse effects such as weight gain and hypothyroidism. However, it appears that women experiencing rapid-cycling or mixed-state bipolar subtypes respond better to anticonvulsant mood stabilisers such as valproate, and do not do so well on lithium (Burt and Ragson, 2004).

GENDER, PSYCHOPHARMACOLOGY AND ANXIETY STATES

Anxiety disorders are the most prevalent psychiatric condition, and occur far more frequently in women than in men (Grant et al., 2005; Yonkers and Ellison, 1996). Co-morbid conditions may be both psychiatric (depression, agoraphobia, phobia, substance misuse) or physical (headaches, migraines, hypotension, allergies). Generalised anxiety disorder in women is significantly associated with alcohol abuse (Grant et al., 2005). There is a theory that women develop anxiety disorders more commonly than men not just because of biological factors, but because of socialisation: women are brought up with a sense of helplessness and increased dependence on others. They are also more likely to be confined to home for long periods of time because women are generally the primary caregivers to children and/or aging relatives.

Treatment for women with anxiety disorder may be behavioural or pharmacological or, more often, a combination of these. The most commonly used pharmacological treatment for anxiety disorders are benzodiazepines, either alone or as an adjunct to antidepressants. Benzodiazepine treatment is often initiated at key developmental milestones such as bereavement, miscarriage or pregnancy/birth/post-natally, and withdrawing treatment may be very difficult.

Gender-specific issues need to be considered when using benzodiazepines, as hormone level fluctuations alter bioavailability, and at some stages in the menstrual cycle plasma levels of benzodiazepines may fluctuate significantly (Yonkers et al., 1992). Additionally, as sedation is a by-product of benzodiazepine therapy, women need to be evaluated before prescribing to ensure appropriate dosing is instituted, so as not to cause undue risk to self or others in such activities as driving, child care etc. Dependence and abuse are also common and unwanted by-products of benzodiazepine treatment.

It is worth mentioning in this context the issue of alcohol abuse too. Although men are more likely to abuse alcohol, women who do so are more likely to suffer adverse effects and physical problems related to alcohol abuse. Women are more likely to suffer liver disease, circulatory problems and alcohol-related brain damage than men, even when drinking smaller amounts of alcohol and when body weight is accounted for. Women metabolise alcohol differently to men. There is evidence that women who drink more than two units of alcohol per day are at least 1.5 times as likely to be diagnosed with breast cancer (Marin Institute, n.d.). As alcohol abuse often occurs among women as a co-morbid condition alongside bipolar disorder, depression and anxiety disorders, prescribing appropriate treatment that can help stabilise these psychiatric conditions may prevent co-morbid alcohol abuse and its physical, psychological and social sequelae.

PSYCHOPHARMACOLOGY IN PREGNANCY AND
THE POST-PARTUM PERIOD

Prescribing psychoactive medication, or deciding not to prescribe, is a challenging task for clinicians when female psychiatric patients are pregnant and post-partum. Frequently, pregnancies in this population go unnoticed during the most vital stage of foetal development (days 17–61); by the time the mother and clinician are aware of the pregnancy, foetal exposure to psychotropic medication has already taken place. All psychotropic medications cross the placenta, causing some degree of exposure in the foetus. Risks include teratogenicity, obstetrical complications, perinatal syndromes and short- medium- and long-term post-natal behavioural problems.

Women with mental illness face problems with pregnancy, childbirth and the post-partum period as they are often on long-term medication, and the consequences of stopping treatment may pose a higher risk to both the mother and the baby than the potential hazards to the foetus in receiving antipsychotic or antidepressant medication (Baldessarini et al., 1999).

While psychosis may often remain stable during pregnancy due to the effect of raised oestrogen levels, the post-partum period – when oestrogen levels fall dramatically – is a particularly vulnerable time for both the mother and the baby. Women with bipolar disorder may relapse during pregnancy if pharmacotherapy is withdrawn, especially if this is not done gradually (Curtis, 2005). Relapse may lead to behaviour that puts both the mother and the foetus at risk. Likewise, there are risks in discontinuing medication in women who are depressed, as there may be deterioration in self-care and increased risk of substance misuse, both of which may harm the foetus (Zuckerman et al., 1989). Communication between primary care services and obstetrics and gynecology services – including visiting midwives and health visitors – and perinatal psychiatric services needs to be maintained, so that incipient psychosis may be prevented through close monitoring and knowledge of the patient's vulnerability.

So far, the "bottom line" is that there is no medication that can be regarded as totally safe to the developing foetus, but some psychotropic agents appear to carry less risk than others, and some medications, particularly older drugs, are better known and understood with respect to foetal risk. When planning management of the psychiatrically ill pregnant woman, it is necessary to conduct a risk-benefit analysis, taking into account the mother's medical and psychiatric history, social situation and level of support, potential risks to the foetus if pharmacotherapy is continued and potential risk to the mother and foetus if medication is stopped.

As women are now often prescribed second generation antipsychotics that do not affect fertility, more women have become pregnant while on medication; as a result, more evidence surrounding the relative safety of

Table 18.2 FDA guidelines for use of drugs in pregnancy

Category	Interpretation
A	Controlled studies show no risk. Adequate, well-controlled studies in pregnant women have failed to demonstrate risk to the foetus.
B	No evidence of risk in humans. Either animal findings show risk but human findings do not, or if no adequate human studies have been done, animal findings are negative.
C	Risk cannot be ruled out. Human studies are lacking, and animal studies are either positive for foetal risk or lacking as well. However, potential benefits may justify the potential risk.
D	Positive evidence of risk. Investigational or post-marketing data show risk to the foetus. Nevertheless, potential benefits may outweigh the potential risk.
X	Contraindicated in pregnancy. Studies in animals or humans, or investigational or post-marketing reports, have shown foetal risk that clearly outweighs any possible benefit to the patient.

psychoactive agents has come to light. Case reports have cited instances where antipsychotic medication was used during pregnancy to no ill effect: for example, quetiapine (Taylor et al., 2003; Tenyi et al., 2002).

McKenna and colleagues (2005) conducted a large prospective cohort study in which women were exposed to atypical antipsychotic medication during pregnancy and compared to women who were not. They concluded that there was no increased risk of major foetal malformations associated with the use of atypical antipsychotic drugs (see also Chapter 9 in this volume).

The American Academy on Pediatrics (2000) has published guidelines on which drugs may be less risky to use during pregnancy, and have devised a classification system whereby drugs are classified according to their potential risk. No psychotropic drugs are classified "A" or recommended for use in pregnancy by the US Food and Drug Administration (FDA) (see Table 18.2). Most atypical antipsychotic drugs are currently classed as "C" but psychoactive drugs with proven teratogenic effects at clinically effective doses are classed "D", and include carbamazepine (neural tube defects), lithium (Ebstein's anomaly) and valproic acid (neural tube defects).

Barbiturates, opioids and benzodiazepines may cause opiate and benzo-diazepine withdrawal in the infant when used in late pregnancy. SSRIs, especially paroxetine, may cause neonatal convulsions and neonatal with-drawal syndrome (Sanz et al., 2005).

Prescribing medication post-partum remains a dilemma for doctors. Views surrounding the safety of breast feeding whilst on psychoactive medication differ as, traditionally, women on such medications have been counselled not to breast feed, so the issue of effects on the baby of receiving psychotropic medication via breast milk is an under-researched area. There are drugs that have been shown to cause adverse reactions in the baby while breast feeding – for example clozapine, which has been cited as causing agranulocytosis and excessive sedation (Howard et al., 2004), and thus should not be used if a woman is intending to breast feed. However, some drugs may be safer, such as quetiapine (Lee et al., 2004). Olanzapine is excreted into breast milk in very small quantities, and is also thought to be safe (Gardiner et al., 2003). Carbamazepine and valproate are generally considered safe but lithium is not recommended (Burt and Ragson, 2004).

It is clear that more research is needed to determine the absolute or even relative safety of all drugs in pregnancy and lactation. It is important, however, that clinical decisions about continuing or discontinuing medication be individualised and taken carefully after a thorough and collaborative risk-benefit analysis.

CONCLUSION

Women with psychiatric diagnoses experience a different illness onset, course and outcome to men. Pre-menopausally, women require lower doses of psychoactive medication than men because of the effects of oestrogen, and while they generally respond as well as men to medication, women are more sensitive to adverse side effects. Women experience hormonal changes throughout their lives, and fluctuations of levels of sex hormones may substantially influence the metabolism of some drugs.

Psychiatrically ill women undergoing pregnancy or lactation, or who are involved in child care, need to be assessed carefully before administering pharmacotherapy, as prescribing for this group carries potentially grave risks. However, it needs to be remembered that the risks of withholding treatment could in some instances be even greater. The issues discussed in this chapter need therefore to inform all prescribing decisions for women with mental illness.

REFERENCES

Aichhorn, W., Weiss, U., Marksteiner, J., Kemmler, G., Walch, T., Zernig, G., Stelzig-Schoeler, R., Stuppaeck, C. and Geretstegger, C. (2005) Influence of age and gender on risperidone plasma concentrations, *Journal of Psychopharmacology*, 19 (4), 395–401.

Aleman, A., Kahn, R. S. and Selten, J. P. (2003) Sex differences in the risk of schizophrenia: Evidence from meta-analysis, *Archives of General Psychiatry*, 60, 565–571.

Allison, D. B., Mentore, J. L., Heo, M., Chandler, L. P., Cappelleri, J. C., Infante, M. C. and Weiden, P. J. (1999) Antipsychotic induced weight gain: A comprehensive research synthesis, *American Journal of Psychiatry*, 156 (11), 1686–1696.

Allison, D. B., Mackell, J. A. and McDonnell, D.D. (2003) The impact of weight gain on quality of life among persons with schizophrenia, *Psychiatric Services*, 54, 565–567.

American Academy of Pediatrics Drug Committee (2000) Use of psychoactive medication during pregnancy and possible effects on the fetus and newborn, *Pediatrics*, 105 (4), 880–887.

Ascher-Svanum, H., Stensland, M., Zhao, Z. and Kinon, B. J. (2005) Acute weight gain, gender and therapeutic response to antipsychotics in the treatment of patients with schizophrenia, *BioMed Central Psychiatry*, 5 (3), www.biomedcentral.com/1471-244X/5/3

Baldessarini, R. J., Tondon, L. and Hennen, J. (1999) Effects of lithium treatment and its discontinuation on suicidal behaviour in bipolar manic-depressive disorders, *Journal of Clinical Psychiatry*, 60 (Suppl. 2), 77–84.

Beierle, I., Meibohm, B. and Derendorf, H. (1999) Gender differences in pharmacokinetics and pharmacodynamics, *International Journal of Clinical Pharmacology and Therapeutics*, 37 (11), 529–547.

Botts, S., Littrell, R. and de Leon, J. (2004) Variables associated with high olanzapine dosing in a state hospital, *Journal of Clinical Psychiatry*, 65 (8), 1138–1143.

Burt, V. K. and Ragson, N. (2004) Special considerations in treating bipolar disorder in women, *Bipolar Disorders*, 6, 2–13.

Curtis, V. (2005) Women are not the same as men: Specific clinical issues for women with bipolar disorder, *Bipolar Disorders*, 7 (Suppl. 1), 16–24.

Drici, M. D. and Clement, N. (2001) Is gender a risk for adverse drug reactions? The example of drug-induced long Q-T syndrome, *Drug Safety*, 24 (8), 575–585.

Gardiner, S. J., Kristensen, J. H., Begg, E. H., Hackett, L. P., Wilson, D. A., Ilett, K. F., Kohan, R. and Rampono, J. (2003) Transfer of olanzapine into breast milk, calculation of infant drug dose, and effect on breast-fed infants, *American Journal of Psychiatry*, 160 (8), 1428–1431.

Goff, D. C., Henderson, D. C. and Amico, E. (1992) Cigarette smoking in schizophrenia: Relationship to psychopathology and medication side effects, *American Journal of Psychiatry*, 149 (9), 1189–1194.

Goldstein, J. M., Cohen, L. S., Horton, N. J., Lee, H., Anderson, S., Tohen, M., Crawford, A. K. and Tollefson, G. (2002) Sex differences in clinical response to olanzapine compared to haloperidol, *Psychiatry Research*, 110 (1), 27–37.

Goudie, A. J., Cooper, G. D. and Halford, J. C. G. (2005) Antipsychotic-induced weight gain, *Diabetes, Obesity and Metabolism*, 7 (5), 478.

Grant, B. F., Hasin, D. F., Stinson, S. F., Dawson, D. A., Ruan, W. J., Goldstein, R. B., Smith, S. M., Saha, T. D. and Huang, B. (2005) Prevalence, correlates, co-morbidity, and comparative disability of DSM IV generalized anxiety disorder in the USA: Results for the national epidemiologic survey on alcohol and related conditions, *Psychological Medicine*, 35, 1–13.

Haddad, P. (2005) Weight change with atypical antipsychotics and the treatment of schizophrenia, *Journal of Psychopharmacology*, 9 (Suppl. 6), 16–27.

Hallonquist, J. D., Seeman, M. V., Lang, M. and Rector, N. A. (1993) Variation in symptom severity over the menstrual cycle of schizophrenics, *Biological Psychiatry*, 33, 207–209.

Henry, C. (2002) Lithium side effects and predictors of hypothyroidism in patients with bipolar disorder: Sex differences, *Journal of Psychiatry and Neuroscience*, 27 (20), 104–107.

Hildebrandt, M. G., Steyerberg, E. W., Stage, K. B., Passchier, J., Kragh-Soerensen, P. and the Danish University Antidepressant Group (2003) Are gender differences important for the clinical effects of antidepressants?, *American Journal of Psychiatry*, 160, 1643–1650.

Hirschfeld, R. M., Williams, J. B., Spitzer, R. L., Calabrese, J. R., Flynn, L., Keck, P. E. Jr, Lewis, L., McElroy, S. L., Post, R. M., Rapport, D. J., Russell, J. M., Sachs, G. M. and Zajecka, J. (2000) Development and validation of a screening instrument for bipolar spectrum disorder: The Mood Disorder Questionnaire, *American Journal of Psychiatry*, 157 (11), 1873–1875.

Howard, L., Webb, R. and Abel, K. (2004) Safety of antipsychotic drugs for pregnant and breastfeeding women with non-affective psychosis, *British Medical Journal*, 329, 933–934.

Jensvold, M. F., Halbreich, U. and Hamilton, J. A. (1996) Gender-sensitive psychopharmacology: An overview, in M. F. Jensvold, U. Halbreich and J. A. Hamilton (eds) *Psychopharmacology and women: Sex, gender and hormones*, pp. 3–10, Washington, DC, American Psychiatric Press Inc.

Kopecek, M., Bares, M., Svarc, J., Dockery, C. and Horacek, J. (2004) Hyper-prolactinaemia after low dose of amisulpride, *Neuroendocrinology Letters*, 25 (6), 419–422.

Kuk, J. L., Lee, S., Heymsfield, S. B. and Ross, R. (2005) Waist circumference and abdominal adipose tissue distribution: Influence of age and sex, *American Journal of Clininical Nutrition*, 81 (6), 1330–1334.

Lane, H. Y., Chang, Y. C., Chang, W. H., Lin, S. K., Tseng, Y. T. and Jann, M. W. (1999) Effects of gender and age on plasma levels of clozapine and its metabolites: Analysed by critical statistics, *Journal of Clinical Psychiatry*, 60 (1), 36–40.

Lee, A., Giesbrecht, E., Dunn, E. and Ito, S. (2004) Excretion of quetiapine in breast milk, *American Journal of Psychiatry*, 161, 1715–1716.

Leung, A. and Chue, P. (2000) Sex differences in schizophrenia: A review of the literature, *Acta Psychiatrica Scandinavica*, 101 (Suppl. 401), 3–38.

Lindamer, L., Lohr, J. B., Caligiuri, M. P. and Jeste, D. V. (2001) Relationship of gender and age at onset of schizophrenia to severity of dyskinesia, *Journal of Neuropsychiatry and Clinical Neuroscience*, 13, 399–402.

McKenna, K., Koren, G., Tetelbaum, M., Wilton, L., Shakir, S., Diav-Citrin, O., Levinson, A., Zipursky, R. B. and Einarson, A. (2005) Pregnancy outcome of women using atypical antipsychotic drugs: A prospective comparison study, *Journal of Clinical Psychiatry*, 66 (4), 444–449.

Maric, N., Popovic, V., Jasovic-Gasic, M., Pilipovic, N. and Van Os, J. (2005) Cumulative exposure to estrogen and psychosis: A peak bone-mass case-controlled study in first episode psychosis, *Schizophrenia Research*, 73 (2–3), 351–355.

Marin Institute (n.d.) *Breast cancer and alcohol in Marin*, http://www.marininstitute.org/marin/breast_cancer.htm (accessed November 2005).

Marshall, J. A., Grunwald, G. K., Donahoo, W. T., Scarbro, S. and Shetterly, S. M. (2000) Percent body fat and lean mass explain the gender difference in leptin: Analysis and interpretation of leptin in Hispanic and non-Hispanic white adults, *Obesity Research*, 8, 543–522.

Meaney, A. M. and O'Keane, V. (2003) Reduced bone mineral density in patients with schizophrenia receiving prolactin raising antipsychotic medication, *Journal of Psychopharmacology*, 17 (4), 455–458.

Miller, M. A. (2001) Gender based differences in the toxicity of pharmaceuticals: The Food and Drug Administration's perspective, *International Journal of Toxicology*, 20 (3), 149–152.

Mitrany, D. and Fehr, A. M. (2001) Examining the factors that influence antipsychotic prescribing decisions, *Psychiatric Times*, 18 (5).

Mohr, D. C., Hart, S. L., Julian, L., Catledge, C., Honos-Webb, L., Vella, L. and Tasch, E. T. (2005) Telephone administered psychotherapy for depression, *Archives of General Psychiatry*, 62 (9), 1007–1014.

Oei, T. P. and Yeoh, A. E. (1999) Pre-existing antidepressant medication and the outcome of group cognitive-behavioural therapy, *Australian and New Zealand Journal of Psychiatry*, 33 (1), 70–76.

Ohlsen, R. I., O'Toole, M. S., Purvis, R. G., Walters, J. T. R., Taylor, T. M., Jones, H. M. and Pilowsky, L. S. (2004) Clinical effectiveness in first-episode patients, *European Neuropsychopharmacology*, 14, S445–S451.

Physicians' Desk Reference (2003) Montvale, NJ, Medical Economics Co.

Rhodes, A., Jaakkimainen, L., Bondy, S. and Fung, K. (2006) Depression and mental health visits to physicians: A prospective records-based study, *Social Science and Medicine*, 62 (4), 828–834.

Salokangas, R. K. (2004) Gender and the use of neuroleptics in schizophrenia, *Schizophrenia Research*, 66 (1), 41–49.

Sanz, E. J., De Las Cuevas, C., Kiuru, A., Bate, A. and Edwards, R. (2005) Selective serotonin reuptake inhibitors in pregnant women and neonatal withdrawal syndrome: A database analysis, *Lancet*, 365 (9458), 482–487.

Seeman, M. V. (2004) Gender differences in the prescribing of antipsychotic drugs, *American Journal of Psychiatry*, 161 (8), 1324–1333.

Stein, M. B. and Kennedy, C. (2001) Major depressive and post-traumatic stress disorder comorbidity in female victims of intimate partner violence, *Journal of Affective Disorders*, 66 (2–3), 133–138.

Taylor, T. M., O'Toole, M. S., Ohlsen, R. I., Walters, J. and Pilowsky, L. S. (2003) Safety of quetiapine during pregnancy, *American Journal of Psychiatry*, 160 (3), 588–589.

Tenyi, T., Trixler, M. and Keresztes, Z. (2000) Quetiapine and pregnancy, *American Journal of Psychiatry*, 159 (4), 674.

Viguera, A. C., Tondo, L. and Baldessarini, R. J. (2000) Sex differences in response to lithium treatment, *American Journal of Psychiatry*, 157 (9), 1509–1511.

Weiden, P. J., Mackell, J. A. and McDonnell, D. D. (2004) Obesity as a risk factor for antipsychotic non-compliance, *Schizophrenia Research*, 66 (1), 51–57.

Yassa, R. and Jeste, D. V. (1992) Gender difference in tardive dyskinesia: A critical review of the literature, *Schizophrenia Bulletin*, 18 (4), 701–715.

Yonkers, K. A. and Ellison, J. M. (1996) Anxiety disorders in women and their pharmacological treatment, in M. F. Jensvold, U. Halbreich and J. A. Hamilton (eds) *Psychopharmacology and women: Sex, gender and hormones*, pp. 261–285, Washington, DC, American Psychiatric Press Inc.

Yonkers, K. A., Kando, J. C., Cole, J. O. and Blumenthal, S. (1992) Gender differences in pharmacokinetics and pharmacodynamics of psychotropic medication, *American Journal of Psychiatry*, 149 (5), 587–595.

Zuckerman, B., Amaro, H., Bauchner, H. and Cabral, H. (1989) Depressive symptoms during pregnancy: Relationship to poor health behaviours, *American Journal of Obstetrics and Gynecology*, 160 (5 Pt 1), 1107–1111.

Part VI

The body on my mind

This section deals with women's services, including new ideas and innovations in setting up such services and how to deal with issues of gender sensitivity and competence in education and training programmes Chapter 19 asks whether women need specific services, and if so, what form they should take and how to go about it. The final chapter of this volume, Chapter 20, focuses on issues of research and training, drawing attention to the work of the Royal College of Psychiatrists in London.

Do women need specific services?

Janet Davies and Sue Waterhouse

INTRODUCTION

Mental health care services today are building on the standards and guidance set out in the *National Service Framework* (NSF) for mental health (DoH, 1999). The NSF provided an evidence-based foundation for more patient-focused mental health services. The Framework's stated aim was to "raise standards, tackle inequalities and meet the special needs of women, men and different ethnic groups". It set the foundations for increased impetus towards promoting single-sex accommodation, better responses to violence and abuse, better crisis housing and tackling inequalities in secure provision for women.

More recent policy publications have aimed to provide a clearer understanding of, and the development of services that respond better to, the context of individuals' needs and life experiences – not least the national mental health strategies around women and gender (DoH, 2002) and race and ethnicity (DoH, 2004).

The government's consultation document *Women's Mental Health: Into the Mainstream* (DoH, 2002) and the implementation guidance *Mainstreaming Gender and Women's Mental Health* (DoH, 2003) set out a clear and comprehensive exposition of the major differences in the occurrence of mental ill health between women and men; the factors important to the causation of mental ill health and those that may be protective; and groups of women who may be particularly vulnerable to mental ill health.

These gender issues have consequences for the planning and delivery of mental health services, which should respond positively to these differences and ensure that they are sensitive to the needs of women. This means, at times, that specialist and specific services, in particular single-sex services, will be required – but also that mainstream services should be working towards being more sensitive to gender and health, for women and for men.

In this chapter we aim to explore how organisations have risen to these policy challenges and developed services to meet women's needs in a gendered context. Although we highlight some critical successes, we wish to be clear that there are still serious criticisms of some aspects of mixed-gender care, particularly in acute in-patient, community residential and secure care settings. Many women continue to voice fears of being admitted to mixed-sex hospitals, yet many organisations and staff still resist the move towards single-sex services. We aim to set out here the case for these services, within a gendered general provision, and also give some examples of innovation and success.

WHY SPECIALIST AND SINGLE-SEX SERVICES?

There is a substantial literature and has been substantial discussion about women's mental health. Many authors provide an argument for gender-specific services, yet this has had little impact on the development and provision of statutory mental health services. It has become more widely recognised that mental health services are not always sensitive to the needs of women (DoH, 1998, 1999, 2000).

Women are not necessarily considered a priority – this is seen in the evidence that some of the problems that are especially prevalent among women are not given the high priority they warrant (Abel et al., 1996). Emotional disorders following rape, domestic violence and childhood sexual abuse are widespread among women, but have only recently become significant targets for service provision.

A major element which helps to shape psychiatric treatment for men and women is the attitude of doctors. Feminists have long argued that the medical profession holds stereotypical views of women (Fee, 1975; Oakley and Mitchell, 1976), and that this is particularly evident in psychiatry (Busfield, 1989, 1996; Chesler, 1974). One well-known study (Broverman et al., 1970) found that clinicians held different models of mental health for women and for men, and that women were trapped within a "double bind". On the one hand, those who were independent, objective and confident were viewed as abnormal and unhealthy, because they did not fit the feminine stereotype. On the other hand, women who did conform were also viewed as unhealthy, because the model of good mental health was a male one: "Either way, the woman loses" (Johnstone, 1989).

Evidence suggests that a higher number of men are referred from primary care to secondary care. Despite this apparent bias, women occupy more psychiatric in-patient beds than men, and this has been the case for the past 150 years (Abel et al., 1996). There are some women who want in-patient treatment as a respite from a difficult situation, as "asylum" when they feel unsafe in the world outside (Chesler, 1974; Perkins et al., 1996; Ussher, 1991). Such an option is no longer available in many areas, particularly in the inner city where there is the greatest demand for in-patient treatment (House of Commons Health Committee, 1994). In addition, the severity of illness among those who are admitted to hospital is now such that the experience of in-patient treatment may be harmful in new ways. Community psychiatric workers describe hospital services as "an exercise in containment" (Payne, 1995). In such circumstances the hospital is unlikely to be able to offer "asylum", let alone a therapeutic environment.

In current debates around choice and mental health the different needs of women and men are little discussed. A recent Department of Health publication (2006) on choice in mental health care refers to the need to provide the choice of single-sex services but does not develop discussions of gender and choice further. Policy thinking at both the local and the national level must be developed further, as the choice agenda is soon to form an integral part of the emerging standards framework for mental health. However, this is not a simple issue. Some women service users, when faced with decisions around using mixed-sex or single-sex services (where these exist), do sometimes choose the former. This can be an informed decision based on where they are on their recovery path, but can also be the result of pressures to conform to "normal" societal settings in their progress to recovery – at times before they are ready for this. A full exploration of a woman's history, particularly around abuse, needs to be carefully explored with her when helping her make these decisions.

There is a substantial body of knowledge about the nature, extent and effects of child sexual and physical abuse, domestic violence, rape and sexual assault, and their impact on women's mental health (DoH, 2005). Many voluntary sector organisations provide counselling and other therapeutic interventions for victims of domestic violence, rape, sexual assault and child sexual abuse. Such specialist services are less well developed in the statutory sector.

Many critics of the NHS have drawn attention to women's lack of influence in a system in which they make up about 75% of workers as well as the majority of users. Most of the power remains with the medical profession and with senior managers, the majority of whom are male. Although the last few years have seen a marked curtailment of their "clinical freedom", doctors still exercise a significant degree of control. In the UK mental health is one of the few areas of healthcare where women have been actively creating alternatives outside the state sector, and this is largely the result of the failure of the public sector to meet women's needs. At every level – from hospital in-patient treatment through to the primary healthcare sector – women users have expressed concern over the way services are delivered.

Most noticeable has been the increased attention directed to those women whose behaviour and needs provoke responses of control and containment. These include women currently within secure mental health services and those in other hospital and community settings. This group of women has come into focus because they are considered to be particularly poorly served by mental health services, and also because they are con-sidered to pose serious challenges for mental health service providers.

The quality and safety of secure mental health provision has been the focus of many debates and campaigns (Allen, 1987; Potier, 1993; Women in Special Hospitals, 1998). It has been repeatedly noted that women within these services are disadvantaged by their minority status. Women make up approximately 15% of the secure psychiatric population. Therefore, women in these contexts receive services that have been primarily developed with men in mind. Increased awareness of the risk to women of harassment and assault in mixed-sex facilities (Warner and Ford, 1999) has led to local secure units frequently being deemed unsuitable for "difficult" women. Women-only wards and units have been pioneered by medium secure services in the private sector, and despite the costs and the implications of out-of-area placement this involves, it has become the emergent solution for many commissioners and service providers. The annual costs of such placements are rising dramatically. This has an implication for budgets that might otherwise have been spent on community-based services that could offer early intervention and prevention. "Psychiatry has been vociferously criticised for lack of attention to the social basis of women's mental health problems and for failure to meet their needs" (Abel et al., 1996). "There is a lack of specialist services for women patients with the NHS, resulting in the inappropriate placement of many women both within existing services and in prison" (Jeffcote and Watson, 2004). Hence there appears to be a strong link between the deficiencies in service provision and the escalating extra-contractual referral costs in mental health trusts.

Specialist and specific services are needed – women require:

1   single-sex services (particularly in in-patient settings) when mental distress has resulted from male-perpetrated violence and abuse, and they will be vulnerable in mixed-sex settings;
2   single-sex services for reasons of race or religion and gender (see Chapter 20 in this volume);
3   staff skilled in understanding and supporting women who self-harm;
4   staff skilled in enabling women to disclose histories of trauma and abuse;
5   specialist services which can deal therapeutically with the often long-neglected impact of child sexual and other abuse and trauma on mental health.

When asked, women generally "experience women-only services as safe and more attuned and responsive to their needs" (DoH, 2002). *Mainstreaming Gender and Women's Mental Health: Implementation Guidance* (DoH, 2003) highlights areas of specialist mental health services that require addition or reconfiguration to provide women-only provision. The document states that the key areas for establishment of women-only provision are in acute and secure settings.

WHAT FORM SHOULD THESE SERVICES TAKE?

For the development of *Women's Mental Health: Into the Mainstream* (DoH, 2002) the Department of Health carried out a number of listening events with women service users. They found that women wanted, in addition to their fundamental right to be kept safe, services that:

1   promote empowerment, choice and self-determination;
2   place importance on the underlying causes and context of women's distress in addition to their symptoms;
3   address important issues relating to women's role as mothers, and the need for accommodation and work;
4   value women's strengths and abilities and potential for recovery.

Some examples of services which are aiming to meet the needs of women in innovative ways are described below.

East Sussex

Women's mental health services were developed in East Sussex following a one-year research project (the Women's Service Development Project) which investigated the needs of women with mental health issues. The services in East Sussex have been developed on the basis of the recommendations made by the research project, and are very much needs-led and person-centred. The main feature of this service, which consists of a six-bed medium secure unit and a six-bed residential community facility, can be found in the philosophy of the service.

The philosophical approach/working ethos of this development is integral to the success of the service. The Women's Service Development Project consulted extensively with service users, both current and past, and with staff at all levels. The final report states that both staff and service users identified the same main factors as being crucial to effective service provision for this client group. The vast majority of the women interviewed stated that they felt their needs would be better met within a women-only environment; this was substantiated by numerous personal accounts of abusive incidents within mixed-sex settings. The women interviewed also stated that the most important features for enabling recovery were:

1   staff attitude;
2   safe environment;

3   being listened to;
4   having their experiences validated;
5   high levels of support (both practical and emotional).

The basic assumption is that with the right support and input, recovery (of varying degrees) is possible. This can be promoted by developing real, ongoing relationships with clients and working alongside them in a respectful and empowering way with an emphasis on self-responsibility. The focus on self-responsibility enables staff to take a positive approach to risk management. It is crucial that control is not taken away from the woman, as this is likely to be reminiscent of early abusive experiences. The response to self-harm is an example of where women can be empowered. An approach that focuses more on harm minimisation than containment allows the individual to remain in control whilst learning to maintain her own safety.

Ella Villa

Ella Villa is a recently developed, voluntary sector, high support home in west London that gives women with complex mental health needs the chance to live in the community. Most of the women are from secure/forensic services or have histories of numerous hospital admission and failed community placements. This multi-disciplinary hybrid service, which has drawn on concepts from other service models (including assertive engagement), aims to provide a "wraparound" service to up to eight women, some of whom have been in hospital for 10–15 years. One particularly innovative and surprising development has been meeting the need of some of the women to maintain links to the hospitals that had been their "homes" for some years, with planned re-admittances to hospital rather than crisis responses. Director Tracey Dann lists some of the early learning points as:

1   some cross-authority protocols being difficult to implement on the ground (some consultants want to discharge their duty sooner than agreed);
2   difficulty in recruiting occupational therapists and a psychologist to the multi-disciplinary team;
3   convincing statutory sector placing authorities that it is possible to work with such a complex group and to understand Ella Villa's approach.

South London and Maudsley Mental Health Trust

In 2002 South London and Maudsley Mental Health Trust produced an acute in-patient strategy to reorganise and redesign Southwark in-patient services into single-sex wards. The drivers for this were reports from service users about repeated incidents of sexual harassment, the unacceptable frequency of sexual assaults against female service users, the risk of unsubstantiated accusations made against male service users and the amount of violence and aggression in general on the wards. This initiative, despite awaiting evaluation, has been innovative in that it has placed emphasis on the positive aspects of male-only wards as well as meeting the needs of women.

Values underpinning these services

The notion of recovery of mental health service users is a popular concept, which should underpin services for women. It can be achieved by facilitating a range of opportunities and activities, and by fully involving clients in the management of their environment and the planning/running of the service. In East Sussex there is an obvious mutual respect between clients and staff, further enhancing the sense of both cohesion within the service and responsiveness to individual need. Deegan (1996) states: "The concept of recovery is rooted in the simple yet profound realisation that people who have been diagnosed with mental illness are human beings."

If we are going to achieve a different approach and create new distinctive services there is a need to ensure that the skill mix of the staff establishment is right. Working with women who have complex needs and presentations can pose many challenges for staff. It is necessary to provide a high level of training and ensure that there are robust supervision structures, to prevent negative cultures developing and to ensure reflective practice.

The physical environment of any service can make a valuable contribution to the whole system effect of that service. It is crucial that women have safe opportunities to maintain contact with their families and friends, as this recognises the importance of their role within the family. It is also essential that there are opportunities to maintain or develop self-care skills. Women often feel de-skilled even after relatively short stays in hospital or residential care.

DEVELOPING SPECIFIC SERVICES FOR WOMEN

The Department of Health's implementation guidance (2003) offers clear direction on developing services for women and improving gender sensitivity in existing services. It recognises that organisations have competing priorities. The implementation guide suggests an approach, setting out a series of steps in the planning process. The planning process is of course the most obvious place to start for organisations that have not yet given this issue a great deal of consideration.

Each mental health trust and primary care trust is required to appoint a lead person to "steer" the development of the local planning process. The most effective leads are those who have previous knowledge and interest in this field. They also need to be at a senior enough level to be able to make real changes and progress. Experience to date shows that the most effective leads are those who have been afforded work time to carry out this role and who have the support of their board. Ideally the lead should report directly to the board of the organisation.

A whole system perspective offers many opportunities. East Sussex's model of bringing back women who were placed in high-cost out-of-area placements provided an opportunity to develop better services, more locally, whilst making significant savings to the local health economy. This is a model that could be replicated elsewhere.

Opportunities that lie within existing services should not be overlooked. In-patient and residential services can be reconfigured to provide adequate women-only provision. Those choosing this route need to be mindful of the fact that it is not just structural changes that are required. Many of the criticisms levelled against mental health services seem valid, and they need to be taken into account if we are to develop appropriate services (Abel et al., 1996). Changes to the culture of staff teams are necessary, and are only possible with a greater understanding of the causes of women's mental health issues. The same is required in all existing services. Staff of all levels and disciplines do not currently have an adequate understanding of the causes of women's distress. It is essential that their understanding is enhanced through service user and carer consultation if the mental health services they provide are truly to be responsive to individual need. A positively gendered mental health policy would recognise both female and male users of the mental health system in ways which identify and support differences – both between men and women and between women them- selves (Abel et al., 1996).

It is necessary for senior management to validate this work. It is well recognised (Chesler, 1994) that in the context of wider gender inequality in society, efforts to develop better mental health services for women can be undermined by a culture that does not authorise or accord value to these activities. It is important, therefore, that action is taken to prevent this happening. Health authorities, NHS trusts and social services need to find ways of giving structural authority and legitimacy to these efforts. One possibility for consideration is the creation of a budget-holding service development unit for women (two or three dedicated posts) to facilitate development and change in service provision for women (Williams and Waterhouse, 2000). This is illustrated in Figure 19.1.

This is an area of development where it is important to think creatively and beyond the boundaries of statutory services. Progress in this area is not easy (Kohen, 2000). Some resistance to change can be expected because

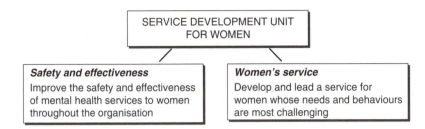

Figure 19.1 Key functions and responsibilities.

staff may feel overburdened, ambivalent about women-centred initiatives, or don't want to acknowledge or work with some of the social causes of women's distress. However, many staff recognise the need for change, and want to be in a position to offer more constructive help to women whose mental health needs are complex and challenging. The case for change is very clear, and it is timely to begin to take action now.

CONCLUSION

Women need specialist and specific services, but they also need mainstream services and staff that are better equipped and trained to identify and meet their needs – and that involves understanding and tackling issues of gender, race and social inequalities. Government policies are clear in this respect.

New and redesigned services, including more single-sex services, are being developed but women's experiences of mental health services are still mostly in non-gendered and mixed-sex settings. Some mental health trusts have developed strategies around women's mental health that have led to positive developments. But in the main, women's needs are still often not adequately addressed.

There is still no "mainstreamed" approach to issues of gender, despite government guidance in this area. Organisations need to adopt the rigour of a gender equality impact assessment to develop an understanding of the effects that policies, practice, service commissioning, planning, provision and staff training and support (or lack of it) differentially have on women and men.

Department of Trade and Industry (DTI) proposals for a public duty to promote gender equality, which will aim to encourage public bodies (as employers and/or service providers) to take a proactive approach to the differing needs of women and men, may help to tackle this lack of progress. This new public duty requirement will complement other legislation that places a positive obligation on public authorities to reduce discrimination (such as the Race Relations (Amendment) Act 2000). The DTI consultation document points out that "systemic change is required . . . if the needs of staff and customers are to be adequately met." Mental health services have made a significant contribution in this respect. We hope that this new legislation can lend added impetus.

REFERENCES

Abel, K., Buszewicz, M., Davison, S., Johnson, S. and Staples, E. (eds) (1996) *Planning community mental health services for women*, London, Routledge.

Allen, H. (1987) *Justice unbalanced: Gender, psychiatry and judicial decision*, Milton Keynes, Open University Press.

Broverman, I. et al. (1970) Sex role stereotypes and clinical judgements of mental health, *Journal of Counselling and Clinical Psychology*, 34, 1–7.

Busfield, J. (1989) Sexism and psychiatry, *Sociology*, 23 (3), 343–364.

Busfield, J. (1996) *Men, women and madness: Understanding gender and mental disorder*, London, Macmillan.

Chesler, P. (1974) *Women and madness*, London, Routledge.

Deegan, P. (1996) Recovery as a journey of the heart, *Psychiatric Rehabilitation Journal*, 19 (3), 91–97.

Department of Health (1998) *Modernising mental health services: Safe, sound and supportive*, London, HMSO.

Department of Health (1999) *National service framework*, London, HMSO.

Department of Health (2000) *The NHS plan* (Cm 4818-1), Norwich, HMSO.

Department of Health (2002) *Women's mental health: Into the mainstream. Strategic development of mental health care for women*, London, Department of Health.

Department of Health (2003) *Mainstreaming gender and women's mental health: Implementation guidance*, London, Department of Health.

Department of Health (2004) *Delivering race equality in mental health*, London, Department of Health.

Department of Health (2005) *Tackling the health and mental health effects of domestic violence and sexual violence and abuse*, London, Department of Health.

Department of Health (2006) *Our choices in mental health: A framework for improving choice for people who use mental health services and their carers*, London, Department of Health.

Fee, E. (1975) Women and health care: A comparison of theories, *International Journal of Health Services*, 5 (3), 397–415.

House of Commons Health Committee (1994) *Better off in the community? The care of people who are seriously mentally ill: First report*, London, HMSO.

Jeffcote, N. and Watson, T. (2004) *Working therapeutically with women in secure mental health settings*, London, Jessica Kingsley Publishers.

Johnstone, L. (1989) *Users and abusers of psychiatry: A critical look at psychiatric practice*, London, Routledge.

Kohen, D. (2000) *Women and mental health*, London, Routledge.

Oakley, A. and Mitchell, J. (1976) Wise women and medicine men, in J. Mitchell and A. Oakley (eds) *The rights and wrongs of women*, Harmondsworth, Penguin.

Payne, S. (1995) The rationing of psychiatric beds: Changing trends in sex ratios in admission to psychiatric hospital, *Health and Social Care in the Community*, 3 (5), 289–300.

Perkins, R. et al. (1996) *Women in context: Good practice in mental health services for women*, London, Good Practices in Mental Health.

Potier, M. (1993) Giving evidence: Women's lives in Ashworth Maximum Security Psychiatric Hospital, *Feminism and Psychology*, 3 (3), 335–347.

Ussher, J. (1991) *Women's madness: Misogyny or mental illness?*, Amherst, MA, University of Massachusetts Press.

Warner, L. and Ford, R. (1999) Conditions for women in in-patient psychiatric units: The Mental Health Act Commission 1996 national visit, *Mental Health Care*, 11 (7), 225–228.

Williams, J. and Waterhouse, S. (2000) *Women whose needs and behaviours challenge mental health services in East Sussex*, Eastbourne and County NHS Trust, unpublished.

Women in Special Hospitals (1998) *Annual report 1997–1998*, London, WISH.

Chapter 20

Gender-sensitive education and gender competence training

The perspective of the Royal College of Psychiatrists and beyond

Rosalind Ramsay and Nisha Dogra

WOMEN'S MENTAL HEALTH NEEDS

About half of the patients in mental health services are women, and women like men suffer from a range of mental disorders. However, as already outlined through this volume, there are some differences in the prevalence of different disorders and in their presentation and management. Some disorders occur exclusively in women.

A survey of 10,000 adults living in private households in the UK (by the Office of Population Censuses and Surveys) found that women were more likely than men to suffer from a neurotic health problem, such as depression or anxiety, but men were four times more likely than women to suffer from alcohol dependence and over twice as likely to suffer from drug dependence (Singleton et al., 2001). For anorexia nervosa, the gender difference in prevalence is particularly striking, with fewer than one in 10 patients being male. On the other hand, the prevalence of psychotic disorder in men and women is similar (see Chapter 1 in this volume).

Suicide rates among women are significantly lower than among men (National Statistics, 2002). Unlike in young men, in whom there was a noticeable increase in suicide rate in the last quarter of the twentieth century, the rate in women aged 15–24 has remained relatively stable at around four per 100,000. Among women over the age of 45, rates more than halved in the same period.

In younger age groups, conduct disorders, autism and attention deficit disorder are all more common in boys (Dogra et al., 2001; Earls and Mezzacappa, 2002). For depression the prevalence across gender changes with age, shifting from a similar distribution or slight excess in boys before puberty to significantly more girls than boys affected by late adolescence (Harrington, 2002). Suicidal ideation and self-harm are more common in girls, but completed suicide more common in boys (Shaffer and Gutstein, 2002; see Chapter 3 in this volume). Patterns of substance misuse differ; alcohol abuse in particular is much more common in boys than in girls (Weinberg et al., 2002).

In older adults, Alzheimer's disease appears to be more prevalent in women than men, even taking into account the greater longevity of women, while multi-infarct dementia is less common in women, a reflection of gender differences in cardiovascular disease. Female carers may experience more stress and receive less support, and older women may also be at increased risk of abuse (see Chapter 13 in this volume).

Other mental disorders, such as puerperal psychosis, postnatal depression and premenstrual dysphoric disorder, are specific to women and occur in relation to childbearing and women's reproductive functioning. Of note is the very high incidence of psychosis after childbirth: in primiparous women there is a 35-fold increased risk of developing a psychotic illness and needing hospital admission in the first month after delivery (Kendell et al., 1987; also Chapter 9 in this volume).

Within specific illnesses there may be significant gender differences in terms of presentation and outcome. For example, in schizophrenia men appear to have a more severe form of the illness with an early age of onset, poor premorbid adjustment, negative symptoms and a poor outcome, while in women the onset tends to be later and a more affective component is apparent (Castle and Murray, 1991). Such differences may in part be attributed to biological differences: for example, men may be more likely to have a neurodevelopmental form of the illness and women a stronger genetic component. There are also gender differences in response to drug treatment that may be attributed to hormonal differences. Oestrogen can potentiate the neuroleptic effects of antipsychotic medication, so women may require a lower dose than men in both the acute and the maintenance phases of treatment (Gold, 1998; see also Chapter 18 in this volume).

WOMEN'S SOCIAL CONTEXT

There is increasing awareness of the impact of violence against women, including the effects of childhood sexual abuse, domestic violence and sexual violence and rape. Childhood abuse correlates with increased risk for a range of mental health problems (Mullen et al., 1994), while victims of completed rape experience high levels of psychological distress including rape-related PTSD (Royal College of Psychiatrists, 1996; see also Chapter 4 in this volume).

Within a social context women may have a number of different roles as carers, not only to their children but also to other family members, for example their own parents. We can consider the situation of women in terms of their social support, training and employment opportunities. Women who display self neglect and self harming behaviours face additional problems when they try to secure accommodation or work (Ramsay et al., 2001), and those who look after young children and are socially isolated without a confiding relationship are at an increased risk of developing depression (Brown and Harris, 1978; see also Chapter 11 in this volume).

SERVICES FOR WOMEN PATIENTS

Women are represented in different proportions at different levels of service from primary care to specialist care. Although women present more to their GP with psychological complaints, GPs refer a higher proportion of men to secondary care services (Johnson and Buszewicz, 1996). There are also gender differences in the use of inpatient care. Looking at use of the Mental Health Act (1983) in England, over the past 15 years there has been a smaller increase in the number of formal admissions of women than of men. Differences are most striking in high security care, where approximately 10 times more men than women are detained (Hatloy, 2005).

There has been criticism of mixed-sex inpatient care, community residential care and secure care in relation to women's safety, with concerns about the vulnerability of women patients to harassment, intimidation, violence and abuse by other patients, visitors, intruders or staff (Department of Health, 2002). *Into the Mainstream* reported women wanting services that would keep them safe, promote empowerment and choice, place importance on understanding the causes of their symptoms, address issues relating to their roles as mothers, and provide safe accommodation and access to education and work opportunities, with a focus on recovery (Department of Health, 2002).

Gender-sensitive services take account of the specific needs of women patients. There is also a place for gender-specific services for women only, for example for women with experience of violence and abuse, women with sexually disinhibited behaviour or lesbian women. Forensic mental health has seen the development of gender-specific services, particularly in low security, a recognition of the distinct social and offending profiles of men and women patients. Some specialist services for trauma, eating disorders and perinatal illness deal mainly or entirely with women patients, but these are not uniformly available throughout the UK (Ramsay, 2004; see also Chapter 19 in this volume).

WOMEN IN PSYCHIATRY SPECIAL INTEREST GROUP

Within the Royal College of Psychiatrists there is evidence of an increasing number of women working in psychiatry. Currently 45% of basic specialist trainees, 48% of higher specialist trainees, 53% of non-consultant career grade psychiatrists and 36% of consultants are women (Royal College of

Psychiatrists Membership Manager, personnal communication, July 2005). Additionally, 23% of the Fellows (senior members) of the College are women, and the UK has 21 female professors of psychiatry. One in five specialist registrars in psychiatry trains flexibly (Ramsay, 2004).

In 1995 the Women in Psychiatry Special Interest Group was formed within the College. It has two aims: to improve the working lives of women psychiatrists and to provide holistic care to women using mental health services. Initially the group concentrated on the needs of women psychiatrists. The increasing awareness of women service users and their needs, and the new interest in services for women with the publication of *Into the Mainstream* by the Department of Health in 2002, has encouraged the group to look more at this issue.

Within the Royal College of Psychiatrists, the Ethnic Issues Project Group has recommended that "the College should undertake a systematic review of its structures to determine whether or not there is evidence of institutional racism. This review should be carried out by an external monitoring agency and any report presented to Council for action and further review" (Royal College of Psychiatrists, 2001: 4). The College commissioned the Centre for Ethnicity and Health at the University of Central Lancashire to undertake an independent review of College structures, policies and procedures to identify and address any institutional racism. In its report *Moving Forward* (2002), the Centre for Ethnicity and Health referred to several comments about gender equality issues which respondents had made. For example, "In terms of policies and procedures over the last 10 or 15 years [I] have observed it to be an old boys' network . . . sexist, racist, white, middle class and it is difficult to say that these attitudes don't exist." Later, in relation to member to staff discrimination, there is a comment about sexual harassment being "a much bigger problem".

The College president at that time responded by inviting Professor Sheila Hollins to set up a project group to address wider equality issues in the College. The group has focused on gender equality and invited interested College members to participate in its work of addressing equality issues in the life of the College and in members' day to day professional work. It has developed a gender equality statement, which the College formally accepted in 2004, and based on this statement the group has put together an action plan.

GENDER EQUALITY STATEMENT OF INTENT

The Royal College of Psychiatrists is committed to gender equality in the promotion and practice of psychiatry by the eradication of unlawful discrimination, and the promotion of equal opportunities with respect to its role as an employer, in the development and implementation of the standards and practice for psychiatrists and in the development and implementation of College policies and procedures.

As part of this commitment the College will not tolerate any gender discriminatory behaviour through the application of its policies, procedures and standards or in the behaviour of its staff, members, associates or trainees. Contractors will also be expected to follow the commitment of the College to gender equality. . . . Priority will be given to the following areas:

- Having a written policy of zero tolerance regarding gender harassment, intimidation, bullying, victimisation or unjustified discrimination by or between members, associates, trainees and staff
- Ensuring that core training and education of members, associates and trainees includes capability in gender issues
- Ensuring that all members, associates and trainees have access to and are able to fully benefit from all functions of the College regardless of gender
- Taking action to support members in ensuring that service users and carers have access to gender sensitive mental health services
- Promoting awareness of the potential for discrimination in the use of mental health legislation
- Ensuring that all research directed or influenced by the College takes appropriate account of gender
- Ensuring gender equality is an integral part of College monitoring and quality assurance policies, procedures and standards.

All staff, members, associates and trainees are expected to actively support these recommendations. The College Council will ensure that this statement and the work plans and framework referred to within it are developed, implemented and monitored on an annual basis.

(Endorsed by Council, 2004)

This is in line with *Good Psychiatric Practice* (Royal College of Psychiatrists, 2004), which states that the core attributes required for good psychiatric practice include being fully sensitive to gender, ethnicity and culture, and a commitment to equality, anti-discriminatory practice and working with diversity.

TRAINING IN DIVERSITY ISSUES

It is in the context of different project groups for different aspects of diversity that we discuss training in gender issues for psychiatrists. Ethnicity and gender issues have had prominence in the College but increasingly other minority groups may justifiably demand the same recognition – for example, around sexual orientation, disability and so on. To date there have been a few programmes in medical education and healthcare which specifically focus on gender issues with, for example, five degree courses available at the Gender Institute of the London School of Economics. The rest generally include gender within the broader diversity agenda.

In this section, we present a brief overview of training in diversity and related issues. We then consider the advantages and disadvantages of training in gender issues as a separate entity. We explore the question of how to decide on the contents of gender training and suggest how to incorporate gender issues into wider diversity training, and discuss the relative merits of this approach.

Dogra and Karim (2005) have addressed training in diversity for psychiatrists. They argue that there are several issues that need consideration if we want to know whether this training influences healthcare and how psychiatrists can be trained to provide care appropriate to an individual patient. The following are relevant:

1   educational models to teach about diversity;
2   how patients are viewed;
3   developing clarity about service models;
4   policies regarding diversity training;
5   how practitioners can make a difference.

There are philosophical and practical reasons to consider training in gender issues within the context of diversity training rather than as a separate agenda. One can review the advantages and disadvantages of addressing gender issues separately or as part of the broader range of diversity training. Either approach, however, is only possible when there is a coherent approach to training (Dogra, 2003).

Using Weber's construct of ideal types, Dogra (2003) compared the educational concepts of "cultural expertise" and "cultural sensibility" with regard to several characteristics of course development. These were grouped into four major areas: educational philosophy and policy; educational process; educational contents; and educational and clinical outcomes.

Cultural expertise

A dictionary definition of expertise (Thompson, 1995) is expert skill, knowledge or judgement, with expert being defined as having special skill at a task or knowledge in a subject. There is a view that through gaining knowledge about other cultures, one can develop cultural expertise. This model encompasses programmes trying to achieve "cultural competence".

Cultural sensibility

Cultural sensibility is proposed as a way to broaden the concept of cultural sensitivity which, in general, has been a tentative alternative to the idea of cultural expertise. A dictionary definition of sensibility (Thompson, 1995) is an openness to emotional impressions, susceptibility and sensitiveness. It relates to a person's moral, emotional or aesthetic ideas or standards. Cultural sensitivity is not the same as cultural sensibility. (Refer to chapter 14 in this volume.)

Dogra (2003) argued that as each of these two concepts has a different philosophical ideology, the educational philosophy, educational process, contents and outcomes of using the two approaches will be different. Cultural expertise and cultural sensibility view the context of identity differently. Cultural expertise points to a more externally ascribed identity based on a group characteristic, for example ethnicity or gender.

Using the educational model proposed by Dogra (2003), it would make sense for gender to be taught within a broader contex.

HOW WE VIEW PATIENTS

Frosh (1999: 413) described the view that identity draws from culture but is not simply formed by it, in the following way:

> Recent sociological and psychological theory has stressed that a person's identity is in fact something multiple and potentially fluid, constructed through experience and linguistically coded. In developing their identities (and their sense of cultural belonging) people draw upon culturally available resources in their immediate social networks in society as a whole.

It is helpful to have a definition of culture which extends beyond ethnicity and includes gender (see also Chapter 2 in this volume). The Association of American Medical Colleges (AAMC) (1999: 25) has provided the following definition:

> Culture is defined by each person in relationship to the group or groups with whom he or she identifies. An individual's cultural identity may be based on heritage as well as individual circumstances and personal choice. Cultural identity may be affected by such factors as race, ethnicity, age, language, country of origin, acculturation, sexual orientation, gender, socioeconomic status, religious/spiritual beliefs, physical

abilities, [and] occupation, among others. These factors may impact on behaviours such as communication styles, diet preferences, health beliefs, family roles, lifestyle, rituals, and decision-making processes. All of these beliefs and practices, in turn, can influence how patients and heath care professionals perceive health and illness and how they interact with one another.

This is a patient-centred definition and can be applied to clinical situations. The AAMC definition is an application in practice of Frosh's definition – that is, that individuals draw upon a range of resources for themselves, and through the interplay of external and internal meanings construct a sense of identity and unique culture. Patients will themselves define which aspect of their cultural belonging is relevant at any particular point. This may change in different clinical contexts and at different stages of an individual's life and may also depend on the clinical presentation itself. For example, the issue of gender may be more relevant to a woman who faces the possibility of a mastectomy because of breast cancer than to a woman who requires abdominal surgery (see Chapter 6 in this volume). This is not to underplay the complexity of the term culture, but to use it in a way that is suitable for the context and to be transparent about how it is being used.

There is a vast sociological literature relating to culture. We do not discuss it further here because academic debates about the meaning of culture are less relevant for us than the interplay between culture and identity, which involves an individual's perception, and is more relevant in medical education and clinical contexts.

There is also the issue of how patients view themselves. Women with non-UK backgrounds may have different perspectives on the role and position of women in society. How can service providers take these values into account without losing their own values? Do women from all cultures have equal access to healthcare, and do they have opportunities to make choices about their own healthcare or are decisions made on their behalf? For example, Maitra (2004) has argued that research from many parts of Africa and South Asia repeatedly shows that women decide to have larger numbers of children than women in Europe and North America for a variety of reasons. However, the degree of choice that women in Africa and South Asia have about their own lives is debatable. It may be too simplistic to see gender as an isolated issue that warrants training.

SERVICE MODELS

While public healthcare may be about services to groups of the population, clinical care is about service provision to individuals. We must consider how to tailor public services to meet the needs of individuals. If we consider diversity among patients and use the AAMC (1999) definition, the focus is on individuals, not groups. Gender is one component making up an individual. Simplistic notions about staff from "similar cultural backgrounds" rest on the assumption that people who originate from similar geographical regions, or have similar skin colours, are likely to share views or understand one another on a complex range of elements that comprise culture and race.

Service models need to take into account the following legislation as it applies to gender:

1   Sex Discrimination Act 1975 (amended 1986): this Act makes it unlawful to discriminate directly or indirectly on the grounds of sex or marital status, or to apply requirements or conditions which have a disproportionately disadvantageous effect on people of a particular sex or marital status if these cannot be justified.
2   Sex Discrimination (Gender Reassignment) Regulations 1999: this extends the Sex Discrimination Act 1975 to cover discrimination on the grounds of gender reassignment in cases in which an individual is treated less favourably by another person on the grounds that the individual intends to undergo, is undergoing or has undergone gender reassignment.

There are provisions under the above legislation and that of the Race Discrimination Act (1976) for gender-specific service provision through the use of genuine occupational qualifications (GOQs). There are a few situations in which it is lawful to recruit only women, men or specific ethnic groups on the grounds that such discrimination satisfies a GOQ. Examples include recruiting specifically a man or a woman:

1   if authenticity is required, for example in acting or modelling;
2   for reasons of decency or privacy, for example changing room attendants;
3   for work taking place in a single-sex prison or hospital;
4   if the job involves working outside the UK in a country whose laws and customs are such that duties could not be performed by a person of the opposite sex;
5   the law requires the person to be of a particular sex, for example women are not legally permitted to work down mines.

From a legal perspective, doctors are gender-neutral. When gender-specific services are offered (for example, in rape counselling), it is perhaps not so much in the expectation that another woman will – on the basis of gender – understand the victim's perspective, but more that the victim should feel safe and not face potential further trauma as a result of discussing her experiences with a man. In child and adolescent mental health, while there has been a tendency to comply with requests for therapists of a specific gender (usually women), there has also been an attempt to question whether at some point in the therapeutic process gender issues need to be raised, and what the expectations are of having a therapist of a particular gender.

TRAINING IN GENDER ISSUES: SEPARATELY OR AS PART OF A BROADER CONTEXT?

In discussing how we view patients and service models, it becomes evident that issues of gender do not exist within a vacuum but rather that they overlap with other aspects of diversity. The major advantage to training in gender issues separately is that this would leave no doubt that the subject had been addressed, although there is often no consideration of the effectiveness of the training. It could be argued that gender issues affect us all, but this might imply that gender has equal significance for everyone. Whether gender is more important to someone's sense of self than his or her sexual orientation or social class will depend on the individual's own context and experiences.

The major disadvantage is that gender is only one component of many (albeit a fairly major one) that make up someone's identify. As Dogra and Karim (2005) argue, there has to be consideration of whether or not information about specific groups is helpful or not. As discussed at the start of the chapter, there are gender differences in the prevalence and management of mental illness. We do not have evidence to show whether having such information influences healthcare outcomes for better or worse. However, such information may do more to reinforce stereotypes than to challenge practitioners to question their own biases in decision-making processes. Although public healthcare is about the provision of services to groups in the population, clinical care is about service provision to individuals. We must consider how we tailor public services designed for population groups to meet individual needs. This seems to be a fundamental and as yet unresolved issue (Dogra and Karim, 2005).

Practical issues are also important for both employers and employees. If training about each "minority" group is given even an hour's time slot (probably the minimum time to take a sensible approach), the time required for training would be significant. It can be argued that if training is actually just about providing information, there are more effective ways of doing this than by lecturing, for example by providing access to information in the form of websites or brochures. It is also arguable that training in diversity should take into account the principles of sound educational practice. These include:

1   employing active rather than passive learning techniques;
2   producing clear and achievable learning objectives with measurable outcomes;
3   providing a training session that is relevant and useful to the group receiving it;
4   using a variety of teaching methods that enable the learning objectives to be met effectively;
5   encouraging and facilitating learners to arrive at appropriate solutions rather than just providing information;
6   building on the experience and skills learners already possess;
7   ensuring that training aims to be enjoyable;
8   being aware of practical limitations such as the time and facilities available (Reece and Walker, 1997).

There are good philosophical and educational reasons for teaching gender as part of diversity rather than separately, although to date there has been little convincing evidence that training in any of these issues changes healthcare outcomes (Dogra and Carter-Pokras, 2005). The US Task Force for Preventive Services conducted a systematic review of five interventions to improve cultural competence in healthcare systems, including cultural competence training for healthcare providers (Anderson et al., 2003). The Task Force identified only one well-conducted study and therefore concluded that the evidence was insufficient to determine the effectiveness of cultural diversity training for healthcare providers. A more extensive review by the Agency for Healthcare Research and Quality (Beach et al., 2005) found excellent evidence for improvement in provider knowledge, and good evidence for improvement in provider attitudes and skills and in patient satisfaction (which is not necessarily linked to improved healthcare outcomes; Garland et al., 2003). Both reviews found a lack of consistency in intervention methods and measured outcomes.

It may be helpful to offer gender training using different models and contexts and to try and identify through evaluation which, if any, most influences clinical outcome.

POLICIES REGARDING TRAINING IN CULTURAL DIVERSITY

There is little evidence to suggest that policies for training in diversity issues including gender are related to research data. Dogra and Karim (2005) argued that:

1   Training needs to be educationally led, using an evidence base if possible.

2 Policies should be transparent and clear regarding their philosophical stance.
3 Policy needs to be implemented in a meaningful way that affects outcomes.
4 There is an urgent need to develop outcome measures that can demonstrate whether diversity training affects outcomes in mental health.

WHAT SHOULD WE TEACH IF WE OFFER GENDER TRAINING?

What services and individual clinicians can do to make a difference will, to some extent, depend on local policies and the training that is available to staff. If we are serious about providing effective training, we need to be aware of the gender differences in mental health, as discussed above. This information raises the question of whether in offering gender training, we should be suggesting, for example, which types of intervention may be more beneficial to women or men. However, it could be argued that this is stereotypical and that such an approach suggests that clinicians can plan the management of an individual on data which comment on trends rather than specifics.

The evidence to support any particular model is also limited. However, in line with professional expectations of continued professional development (General Medical Council, 2001) and the principles of the reflective practitioner (Schon, 1983), it may be more useful to offer training that challenges the views held by those attending. Having their views challenged in training can make students aware of the subtle and not-so-subtle ways in which their own outlook and values shape the care they deliver.

In summary, the evidence for gender training is limited – but rather than allowing this to prevent the development of training to address this issue, we should view it as an opportunity to develop training which is educationally sound and can be properly evaluated to demonstrate effectiveness.

ACKNOWLEDGEMENTS

With thanks to Paul Harrington, librarian at Lambeth Hospital, for information, and Dr Elaine Arnold for comments.

REFERENCES

Anderson, L. M., Scrimshaw, S. C., Fullilove, M. T., Fielding, J. E., Normand, J. and the Task Force on Community Preventive Services (2003) Culturally competent healthcare systems: A systematic review, 24 (3S), 68–79. Available at http://www.thecommunityguide.org/social/soc-ajpm-evrev-healthcare-systems.pdf

Association of American Medical Colleges (1999) *Report III contemporary issues in medicine. Communication in medicine: Spirituality, cultural issues and end of life care*, Washington, DC, Medical School Objectives Project, Association of American Medical Colleges.

Beach, M. C., Price, E. G., Gary, T. L. Robinson, K. A., Gozu, A. and Palacio, A. (2005) Cultural competence: A systematic review of health care provider educational interventions, *Medical Care*, 43 (4), 356–373.

Brown, G. W. and Harris, T. O. (1978) *Social origins of depression*, London, Tavistock.

Castle, D. J. and Murray, R. M. (1991) The neurodevelopmental basis of sex differences in schizophrenia, *Psychological Medicine*, 21, 565–575.

Department of Health (2002) *Women's mental health: Into the mainstream*, London, Department of Health.

Dogra, N. (2003) Cultural competence or cultural sensibility? A comparison of two ideal type models to teach cultural diversity to medical students, *International Journal of Medicine*, 5 (4), 223–231.

Dogra, N. and Carter-Pokras, O. (2005) Stakeholder views regarding cultural diversity teaching outcomes: A qualitative study, *BMC Medical Education*, 5, 37.

Dogra, N. and Karim, K. (2005) Training in diversity for psychiatrists, *Advances in Psychiatric Treatment*, 11, 159–167.

Dogra, N., Parkin, A., Gale, F. and Frake, C. (2001) *A multidisciplinary handbook of child and adolescent mental health for front-line professionals*, London, Jessica Kingsley.

Earls, F. and Mezzacappa, E. (2002) Conduct and oppositional disorders, in M. Rutter and E. Taylor (eds) *Child and adolescent psychiatry*, pp. 419–436, Oxford, Blackwell Science.

Frosh, S. (1999) Identity, in A. Bullock and S. Trombley (eds) *The new Fontana dictionary of modern thought* (3rd edn), p. 413, London, Harper Collins.

Garland, A. F., Aarons, G. A., Hawley, K. M. and Hough, R. L. (2003) Relationship of youth satisfaction with mental health services and changes in symptoms and functioning, *Psychiatric Services*, 54, 1544–1546.

General Medical Council (2001) *Good medical practice*, London, GMC.

Gold, J. H. (1998) Gender differences in psychiatric illness and treatments, *Journal of Nervous and Mental Disease*, 186, 769–775.

Harrington, R. (2002) Affective disorders, in M. Rutter and E. Taylor (eds) *Child and adolescent psychiatry*, pp. 463–485, Oxford, Blackwell Science.

Hatloy, I. (2005) *Statistics 4: The Mental Health Act 1983*, http://www.mind.org.uk/information/factsheets/statistics/statistics+4.htm (accessed on August 11, 2005).

Johnson, S. and Buszewicz, M. (1996) Women's mental illness, in K. Abel, M. Buuszewicz, S. Davison et al. (eds) *Planning community mental health services for women: A multiprofessional handbook*, pp. 6–19, London, Routledge.

Kendell, R. E., Chalmers, J. C. and Platz, C. (1987) Epidemiology of puerperal psychoses, *British Journal of Psychiatry*, 150, 662–673.

Maitra, B. (2004) The cultural relevance of the mental health disciplines, in M. Malek and C. Joughin (eds) *Mental health services for minority ethnic children and adolescents*, pp. 49–65, London, Jessica Kingsley Publishers.

Mullen, P. E., Martin, J. L., Anderson, J. C., Romans, S. E. and Herbison, G. P.

(1994) The effect of child sexual abuse on social, interpersonal and sexual function in adult life, *British Journal of Psychiatry*, 165, 35–47.

National Statistics (2002) *Death rates from suicide: By gender and age, 1974–2000* (Social Trends 32), http://www.statistics.gov.uk/statbase/ssdataset.asp?vlnk=5228 &more=y (accessed 4 August 2005).

Ramsay, R. (2004) Women in Psychiatry Special Interest Group, *BMJ Careers*, 20 March, 116.

Ramsay, R., Welch, S. and Youard, E. (2001) Needs of women patients with mental illness, *Advances in Psychiatric Treatment*, 7, 85–92.

Reece, I. and Walker, S. (1997) *Teaching, training and learning: A practical guide* (3rd edn), Sunderland, Business Education Publishers.

Royal College of Psychiatrists (1996) *Rape* (Council Report 47), London, Royal College of Psychiatrists.

Royal College of Psychiatrists (2001) *Report of the Ethnic Issues Project Group* (Council Report 92), London, Royal College of Psychiatrists.

Royal College of Psychiatrists (2004) *Good psychiatric practice* (Council Report 125, 2nd edn), London, Royal College of Psychiatrists.

Schon, D. A. (1983) *The reflective practitioner*, New York, Basic Books.

Sex Discrimination Act (1975) London, HMSO.

Sex Discrimination (Gender Reassignment) Regulations (1999) London, HMSO.

Shaffer, D. and Gutstein, J. (2002) Suicide and attempted suicide, in M. Rutter and E. Taylor (eds) *Child and adolescent psychiatry* (4th edn), pp. 529–554, Oxford, Blackwell Science.

Singleton, N., Meltzer, H., Gill, B., Petticrew, M. and Hinds, K. (2001) *Psychiatric morbidity among adults living in private households*, London, HMSO.

Thompson, D. (ed.) (1995) *The concise Oxford dictionary of current English*, Oxford, Clarendon Press.

Weinberg, W. A., Harper, C. and Brumback, R. A. (2002) Substance use and abuse: Epidemiology, pharmacological considerations, identification and suggestions towards management, in M. Rutter and E. Taylor (eds) *Child and adolescent psychiatry* (4th edn), pp. 437–454, Oxford, Blackwell Science.

Index

Page entries for headings with subheadings refer only to general aspects of that topic
Page entries for figures/tables are shown in **bold** type